THE NEW
WESTERN
TYPE BOOK

The New Western Type Book

ANALYSED PAGE SPECIMENS OF
MONOTYPE, LINOTYPE AND INTERTYPE FACES
AND VIP PHOTOSET TYPEFACES
AVAILABLE AT WESTERN PRINTING SERVICES

WITH A FOREWORD BY JOHN RYDER

PUBLISHED BY HAMISH HAMILTON LTD · LONDON
FOR WESTERN PRINTING SERVICES LTD · BRISTOL

Printed in Great Britain

Hot-metal typefaces set and printed letterpress by
Western Printing Services Ltd, Bristol

VIP *typefaces photoset by Western Printing Services*
and printed litho by the Pitman Press Ltd, Bath

Bound at the Pitman Press, Bath

Designed by Peter Bate MSIAD

First edition 1960
Second edition 1962 *Third edition* 1970
New revised edition 1980

ISBN 0 241 89984 2

CONTENTS

ACKNOWLEDGEMENTS

We must thank the production departments of the publishers for whom we work.
Their suggestions are largely responsible for any improvements in this new edition.

FOREWORD

by John Ryder FSIAD, FSTD

'Among the illustrations common to books on typography there is a familiar plate which is an admirable lesson to the modern printer –' wrote Updike in 1924, 'that showing the 1486 specimen sheet of Erhard Ratdolt. . . .' The whole sheet measured something like 40 × 25 centimetres and displayed ten sizes of blackletter, three sizes of roman and one of Greek. Updike continued, 'The books printed from this limited collection of types were beautiful because the types were so in themselves and because the very limitations of his material produced a restraint and harmony that gave the work style.' Updike ended his paragraph, 'Today, no printing house would dare to confine itself to such a small equipment.'

Such 'style' as Updike would encourage us to believe in and practise derives from the typographic standards set by Ratdolt and Gutenberg before him and his immediate successors at Venice and later in Paris, Lyons, Antwerp, right down to Mardersteig of our own times at Verona. These standards are based on relief printing from separately cast metal letters. No matter how sophisticated modern 'printing' technology becomes, it is the established fifteenth- and sixteenth-century standards which the reader expects—always assuming printing is yet designed to be read.

'To design,' said Sir Hugh Casson in his Romanes lecture at Oxford in 1979, 'is to decide.' He was introducing a theme in which the designer is at the centre of decision making rather than the decision-maker. He said that not even designers believe all decisions should be made by themselves. The design of a book may involve editorial, financial, technical, political and even circumstantial decisions. 'Usually the task of the designer,' continued Sir Hugh, 'like that of the politician, is to reconcile conflicts and imbalance.'

Now is the exact moment—now that computer-aided photosetting is doing its worst and its best, simultaneously, for the appearance of the printed word—to introduce a new edition of the present work and to offer continuation of this traditional service to publishers of books. Tradition, for the reader, plus a better understanding of the designer's position, also for the reader, may join to promote legibility and through legibility the continuation of literacy. What higher value could *The New Western Type Book* hope to claim?

But this book must be used with critical faculties and experience. It will be immediately obvious that not all the examples of page settings are commendable. Many of them simply demonstrate what happens when a certain typeface is set to a given size, measure, leading and depth. The experienced typographer, with a little insight and with a careful reading of the tables set at the foot of each specimen, will quickly make mental adjustments to suit his projected setting.

New material in this 1980 edition of *The New Western Type Book* includes a 10 point synopsis of every typeface used and, extra to the 19 Monotype designs and the 5 slug-set designs, there are various settings of 11 VIP photoset faces. Comparative alphabet widths in 12 point are given for every typeface included in the book. These details plus the fact that all hot metal setting is printed by letterpress and all filmset material by offset on the same paper make this present edition of considerable value to designers and no less to serious readers of the printed word.

January 1980

EXPLANATION OF CONTENTS

I. ANALYSIS OF SPECIMENS. The panel at the foot of each specimen gives the designer most of the information needed for the preparation of a MS for the face concerned in a Royal 8vo, Demy 8vo, Large Crown 8vo or Crown 8vo format. The information appears thus:

MONOTYPE TIMES 327 L.D. 9 point, 1 point leaded

FORMAT	PICAS	LINES	WPL	CPL	WPP	CPP
Royal 8vo	26×43	51	14.0	76	714	3876
Demy 8vo	24×40	48	13.0	70	623	3360
Large Crown 8vo	23×36	43	12.5	67	539	2881
Crown 8vo	21×34	41	11.3	61	463	2501

- 327 denotes Monotype series number.
- LD denotes long descenders.
- The following trimmed page sizes have been assumed:

Royal 8vo	234×156 mm
Demy 8vo	216×138 mm
Large Crown 8vo	198×129 mm
Crown 8vo	186×123 mm

- The type area in picas excludes the headline and folio.
- WPL is a calculation of the average number of Words Per Line obtained by dividing the total Words Per Page by the number of lines on that page.
- CPL shows the average number of lower-case Characters Per Line, including punctuation and spaces. The figures for hot-metal typefaces have been calculated from Monotype, Linotype and Intertype copy-fitting tables. The VIP figures have been calculated by dividing the total number of characters on each specimen page by the number of lines on that page.
- WPP shows an actual count of the number of Words Per Page making no allowance for white spaces at the end of paragraphs.
- CPP is a multiplication of CPL by the number of lines.
- D denotes Didot. A face cut for continental size type. For Anglo-American size type these should be cast on a one point larger body.

Information about the number of words per page has thus been obtained from a count of the passage used for the specimens, but does not necessarily apply accurately to all copy received for setting. Although the information about VIP characters per line has also been calculated from counts of the specimen pages, the figures for hot-metal typefaces are more theoretical in origin and, suitably interpreted, have more universal application.

2. THE PASSAGE used is taken from Chapter One of Anthony Trollope's *The Small House at Allington* and the average number of characters per word throughout (including punctuation and spaces) is 5.5. Repetition of the same text in the same area in so many different faces and sizes perhaps needs an apology: but it has two merits. First, it makes each page directly comparable with all other pages. Second, it limits distraction of the designer's attention from the visual and other qualities in which he is primarily interested.

3. THE HEADLINES are varied as far as possible. With 11 point and smaller faces they are either small capitals, italic upper and lower case, or roman caps, all of text size. With 12 point and larger faces they are usually small caps of text size, but there are the following exceptions: 14 pt Garamond and 16 pt Bembo and Poliphilus have 10 pt caps. 18 pt Garamond and Imprint have 12 pt caps.

4. EACH TYPEFACE is preceded by a synopsis showing 10 point alphabets, punctuation and figures. It also shows the point sizes available and the classes of accents held at Western Printing Services.

LIST OF TYPE SPECIMENS

MONOTYPE FACES

LINOTYPE AND INTERTYPE FACES

VIP PHOTOSET FACES

1

SPECIMEN PAGES
OF
MONOTYPE FACES

MONOTYPE BASKERVILLE 169

Synopsis in 10 point

ABCDEFGHIJKLMNOPQRSTUVWXYZ&ÆŒ

ABCDEFGHIJKLMNOPQRSTUVWXYZÆŒ

abcdefghijklmnopqrstuvwxyzæœfiffflffiffl

ABCDEFGHIJKLMNOPQRSTUVWXYZ&ÆŒ

abcdefghijklmnopqrstuvwxyzæœfiffflffiffl

.,:;!?‘’-()[]£ *:;!?*

1234567890 *1234567890* 1234567890 *1234567890*

Related bold · Series 312

ABCDEFGHIJKLMNOPQRSTUVWXYZ&ÆŒ

abcdefghijklmnopqrstuvwxyzæœfiffflffiffl

.,:;!?‘’-()£ 1234567890

Related semi-bold · Series 313

ABCDEFGHIJKLMNOPQRSTUVWXYZ&ÆŒ

abcdefghijklmnopqrstuvwxyzæœfiffflffiffl

.,:;!?‘’-()£ 1234567890 1234567890

All normal European accents available

Series 169 *and* 312 *available in composition sizes* 6, 8, 9, 10, 11, 12 *point*

Series 313 *available in composition sizes* 8, 9, 10, 11, 12 *point*

father to son, and from uncle to nephew, and, in one instance, from second cousin to second cousin, the sceptre had descended in the family of the Dales; and the acres had remained intact, growing in value and not decreasing in number, though guarded by no entail and protected by no wonderful amount of prudence or wisdom. The estate of Dale of Allington had been coterminous with the parish of Allington for some hundreds of years; and though, as I have said, the race of squires had possessed nothing of superhuman discretion, and had perhaps been guided in their walks through life by no very distinct principles, still there had been with them so much of adherence to a sacred law, that no acre of the property had ever been parted from the hands of the existing squire. Some futile attempts had been made to increase the territory, as indeed had been done by Kit Dale, the father of Christopher Dale, who will appear as our squire of Allington when the persons of our drama are introduced. Old Kit Dale, who had married money, had bought outlying farms—a bit of ground here and a bit there—talking, as he did so, much of political influence and of the good old Tory cause. But these farms and bits of ground had gone again before our time. To them had been attached no religion. When old Kit had found himself pressed in that matter of the majority of the Nineteenth Dragoons, in which crack regiment his second son made for himself quite a career, he found it easier to sell than to save—seeing that that which he sold was his own and not the patrimony of the Dales. At his death the remainder of these purchases had gone. Family arrangements required completion, and Christopher Dale required ready money. The outlying farms flew away, as such new purchases had flown before; but the old patrimony of the Dales remained untouched, as it had ever remained.

It had been a religion among them; and seeing that the worship had been carried on without fail, that the vestal fire had never gone down upon the hearth, I should not have said that the Dales had walked their ways without high principle. To this religion they had adhered, and the new heir had ever entered in upon his domain without other encumbrances than those with which he himself was then already burdened. And yet there had been no entail. The idea of an entail was not in accordance with the peculiarities of the Dale mind. It was necessary to the Dale religion that each squire should have the power of wasting them. I remember to have dined at a house, the whole glory and fortune of which depended on the safety of a glass goblet. We all know the story. If the luck of Edenhall should be shattered, the doom of the family would be sealed. Nevertheless I was bidden to drink out of the fatal glass, as were all guests in that house. It would not have contented the chivalrous mind of the master to protect his doom by lock and key and padded chest. And so it was with the Dales of Allington. To them an entail would have been a lock and key and a padded chest; but the old chivalry of their house denied to them the use of such protection.

I have spoken something slightingly of the acquirements and doings of the family; and indeed their acquirements had been few and their doings little. *At Allington, Dale of Allington had always been known as a king. At Guestwick, the neighbouring market town, he was a great man—to be seen frequently on Saturdays, standing in the market-place, and laying down the law as to barley and oxen among*

MONOTYPE BASKERVILLE 169

9 point, 1 point leaded

FORMAT	PICAS	LINES	WPL	CPL	WPP	CPP
Royal 8vo	26×43	52	14.4	77	749	4004
Demy 8vo	24×40	48	13.3	71	641	3408
Large Crown 8vo	23×36	43	12.4	68	536	2924
Crown 8vo	21×34	41	11.5	62	471	2542

father to son, and from uncle to nephew, and, in one instance, from second cousin to second cousin, the sceptre had descended in the family of the Dales; and the acres had remained intact, growing in value and not decreasing in number, though guarded by no entail and protected by no wonderful amount of prudence or wisdom. The estate of Dale of Allington had been coterminous with the parish of Allington for some hundreds of years; and though, as I have said, the race of squires had possessed nothing of superhuman discretion, and had perhaps been guided in their walks through life by no very distinct principles, still there had been with them so much of adherence to a sacred law, that no acre of the property had ever been parted from the hands of the existing squire. Some futile attempts had been made to increase the territory, as indeed had been done by Kit Dale, the father of Christopher Dale, who will appear as our squire of Allington when the persons of our drama are introduced. Old Kit Dale, who had married money, had bought outlying farms—a bit of ground here and a bit there—talking, as he did so, much of political influence and of the good old Tory cause. But these farms and bits of ground had gone again before our time. To them had been attached no religion. When old Kit had found himself pressed in that matter of the majority of the Nineteenth Dragoons, in which crack regiment his second son made for himself quite a career, he found it easier to sell than to save—seeing that that which he sold was his own and not the patrimony of the Dales. At his death the remainder of these purchases had gone. Family arrangements required completion, and Christopher Dale required ready money. The outlying farms flew away, as such new purchases had flown before; but the old patrimony of the Dales remained untouched, as it had ever remained.

It had been a religion among them; and seeing that the worship had been carried on without fail, that the vestal fire had never gone down upon the hearth, I should not have said that the Dales had walked their ways without high principle. To this religion they had all adhered, and the new heir had ever entered in upon his domain without other encumbrances than those with which he himself was then already burdened. And yet there had been no entail. The idea of an entail was not in accordance with the peculiarities of the Dale mind. It was necessary to the Dale religion that each squire should have the power of wasting them. I remember to have dined at a house, the whole glory and fortune of which depended on the safety of a glass goblet. We all know the story. If the luck of Edenhall should be shattered, the doom of the family would be sealed. Nevertheless I was bidden to drink out of the fatal glass, as were all guests in that house. It would not have contented the chivalrous mind of the master to protect his doom by lock and key and padded chest. And so it was with the Dales of Allington. To them an entail would *have been a lock and key and a padded chest; but the old chivalry of their house denied to them the use of such protection.*

I have spoken something slightingly of the acquirements and doings of the

MONOTYPE BASKERVILLE 169

10 point solid

FORMAT	PICAS	LINES	WPL	CPL	WPP	CPP
Royal 8vo	26×43	52	13.2	69	686	3588
Demy 8vo	24×40	48	12.2	64	584	3072
Large Crown 8vo	23×36	43	11.3	61	487	2623
Crown 8vo	21×34	41	10.4	56	427	2296

father to son, and from uncle to nephew, and, in one instance, from second cousin to second cousin, the sceptre had descended in the family of the Dales; and the acres had remained intact, growing in value and not decreasing in number, though guarded by no entail and protected by no wonderful amount of prudence or wisdom. The estate of Dale of Allington had been coterminous with the parish of Allington for some hundreds of years; and though, as I have said, the race of squires had possessed nothing of superhuman discretion, and had perhaps been guided in their walks through life by no very distinct principles, still there had been with them so much of adherence to a sacred law, that no acre of the property had ever been parted from the hands of the existing squire. Some futile attempts had been made to increase the territory, as indeed had been done by Kit Dale, the father of Christopher Dale, who will appear as our squire of Allington when the persons of our drama are introduced. Old Kit Dale, who had married money, had bought outlying farms—a bit of ground here and a bit there—talking, as he did so, much of political influence and of the good old Tory cause. But these farms and bits of ground had gone again before our time. To them had been attached no religion. When old Kit had found himself pressed in that matter of the majority of the Nineteenth Dragoons, in which crack regiment his second son made for himself quite a career, he found it easier to sell than to save—seeing that that which he sold was his own and not the patrimony of the Dales. At his death the remainder of these purchases had gone. Family arrangements required completion, and Christopher Dale required ready money. The outlying farms flew away, as such new purchases had flown before; but the old patrimony of the Dales remained untouched, as it had ever remained.

It had been a religion among them; and seeing that the worship had been carried on without fail, that the vestal fire had never gone down upon the hearth, I should not have said that the Dales had walked their ways without high principle. To this religion they had all adhered, and the new heir had ever entered in upon his domain without other encumbrances than those with which he himself was then already burdened. And yet there had been no entail. The idea of an entail was not in accordance with the peculiarities of the Dale mind. It was necessary to the Dale religion that each squire should have the power of wasting them. I remember to have dined at a house, the whole glory and fortune of which depended on the safety of a glass goblet. We all know the story. If the luck of Edenhall should be shattered, the doom of the family would be sealed. Never*theless I was bidden to drink out of the fatal glass, as were all guests in that house. It would not have contented the chivalrous mind of the master to protect his doom by lock and key and padded chest. And so it was with the*

MONOTYPE BASKERVILLE 169

10 point, 1 point leaded

FORMAT	PICAS	LINES	WPL	CPL	WPP	CPP
Royal 8vo	26×43	47	13.2	69	620	3243
Demy 8vo	24×40	44	12.2	64	539	2816
Large Crown 8vo	23×36	39	11.3	61	439	2379
Crown 8vo	21×34	37	10.4	56	383	2072

father to son, and from uncle to nephew, and, in one instance, from second cousin to second cousin, the sceptre had descended in the family of the Dales; and the acres had remained intact, growing in value and not decreasing in number, though guarded by no entail and protected by no wonderful amount of prudence or wisdom. The estate of Dale of Allington had been coterminous with the parish of Allington for some hundreds of years; and though, as I have said, the race of squires had possessed nothing of superhuman discretion, and had perhaps been guided in their walks through life by no very distinct principles, still there had been with them so much of adherence to a sacred law, that no acre of the property had ever been parted from the hands of the existing squire. Some futile attempts had been made to increase the territory, as indeed had been done by Kit Dale, the father of Christopher Dale, who will appear as our squire of Allington when the persons of our drama are introduced. Old Kit Dale, who had married money, had bought outlying farms—a bit of ground here and a bit there—talking, as he did so, much of political influence and of the good old Tory cause. But these farms and bits of ground had gone again before our time. To them had been attached no religion. When old Kit had found himself pressed in that matter of the majority of the Nineteenth Dragoons, in which crack regiment his second son made for himself quite a career, he found it easier to sell than to save—seeing that that which he sold was his own and not the patrimony of the Dales. At his death the remainder of these purchases had gone. Family arrangements required completion, and Christopher Dale required ready money. The outlying farms flew away, as such new purchases had flown before; but the old patrimony of the Dales remained untouched, as it had ever remained.

It had been a religion among them; and seeing that the worship had been carried on without fail, that the vestal fire had never gone down upon the hearth, I should not have said that the Dales had walked their ways without high principle. To this religion they had all adhered, and the new heir had ever entered in upon his domain without other encumbrances than those with which he himself was then already burdened. And yet there had been no entail. The idea of an entail was not in accordance with the peculiarities of the Dale mind. It was necessary to the Dale religion that each squire should *have the power of wasting them. I remember to have dined at a house, the whole glory and fortune of which depended on the safety of a glass goblet. We all know the story. If the luck of Edenhall should be shattered, the doom of*

MONOTYPE BASKERVILLE 169

10 point, 2 point leaded

FORMAT	PICAS	LINES	WPL	CPL	WPP	CPP
Royal 8vo	26×43	43	13.2	69	567	2967
Demy 8vo	24×40	40	12.2	64	488	2560
Large Crown 8vo	23×36	36	11.3	61	407	2196
Crown 8vo	21×34	34	10.4	56	354	1904

father to son, and from uncle to nephew, and, in one instance, from second cousin to second cousin, the sceptre had descended in the family of the Dales; and the acres had remained intact, growing in value and not decreasing in number, though guarded by no entail and protected by no wonderful amount of prudence or wisdom. The estate of Dale of Allington had been coterminous with the parish of Allington for some hundreds of years; and though, as I have said, the race of squires had possessed nothing of superhuman discretion, and had perhaps been guided in their walks through life by no very distinct principles, still there had been with them so much of adherence to a sacred law, that no acre of the property had ever been parted from the hands of the existing squire. Some futile attempts had been made to increase the territory, as indeed had been done by Kit Dale, the father of Christopher Dale, who will appear as our squire of Allington when the persons of our drama are introduced. Old Kit Dale, who had married money, had bought outlying farms—a bit of ground here and a bit there—talking, as he did so, much of political influence and of the good old Tory cause. But these farms and bits of ground had gone again before our time. To them had been attached no religion. When old Kit had found himself pressed in that matter of the majority of the Nineteenth Dragoons, in which crack regiment his second son made for himself quite a career, he found it easier to sell than to save—seeing that that which he sold was his own and not the patrimony of the Dales. At his death the remainder of these purchases had gone. Family arrangements required completion, and Christopher Dale required ready money. The outlying farms flew away, as such new purchases had flown before; but the old patrimony of the Dales remained untouched, as it had ever remained.

It had been a religion among them; and seeing that the worship had been carried on without fail, that the vestal fire had never gone down upon the hearth, I should not have said that the Dales had walked their ways without high principle. To this religion they had all adhered, and the new heir had ever entered in upon his domain without other encumbrances than those with which he himself was then already burdened. And yet there had been no entail. The idea of an entail was not in accordance with the peculiarities of the Dale mind. It was necessary to the Dale religion that each squire should have the *power of wasting them. I remember to have dined at a house, the whole glory and fortune of which depended on the safety of a glass goblet. We all know the story. If the luck of Edenhall should be shattered, the doom*

MONOTYPE BASKERVILLE 169

11 point solid

FORMAT	PICAS	LINES	WPL	CPL	WPP	CPP
Royal 8vo	26×43	47	12.0	64	564	3008
Demy 8vo	24×40	44	11.1	59	487	2596
Large Crown 8vo	23×36	39	10.2	57	395	2223
Crown 8vo	21×34	37	9.5	54	349	1998

father to son, and from uncle to nephew, and, in one instance, from second cousin to second cousin, the sceptre had descended in the family of the Dales; and the acres had remained intact, growing in value and not decreasing in number, though guarded by no entail and protected by no wonderful amount of prudence or wisdom. The estate of Dale of Allington had been coterminous with the parish of Allington for some hundreds of years; and though, as I have said, the race of squires had possessed nothing of superhuman discretion, and had perhaps been guided in their walks through life by no very distinct principles, still there had been with them so much of adherence to a sacred law, that no acre of the property had ever been parted from the hands of the existing squire. Some futile attempts had been made to increase the territory, as indeed had been done by Kit Dale, the father of Christopher Dale, who will appear as our squire of Allington when the persons of our drama are introduced. Old Kit Dale, who had married money, had bought outlying farms—a bit of ground here and a bit there—talking, as he did so, much of political influence and of the good old Tory cause. But these farms and bits of ground had gone again before our time. To them had been attached no religion. When old Kit had found himself pressed in that matter of the majority of the Nineteenth Dragoons, in which crack regiment his second son made for himself quite a career, he found it easier to sell than to save—seeing that that which he sold was his own and not the patrimony of the Dales. At his death the remainder of these purchases had gone. Family arrangements required completion, and Christopher Dale required ready money. The outlying farms flew away, as such new purchases had flown before; but the old patrimony of the Dales remained untouched, as it had ever remained.

It had been a religion among them; and seeing that the worship had been carried on without fail, that the vestal fire had never gone down upon the hearth, I should not have said that the Dales had walked their ways without high principle. To this religion they had all adhered, and the new heir had ever entered in upon his domain without other encumbrances than *those with which he himself was then already burdened. And yet there had been no entail. The idea of an entail was not in accordance with the peculiarities of the Dale mind. It was necessary to the Dale religion*

MONOTYPE BASKERVILLE 169

11 point, 1 point leaded

FORMAT	PICAS	LINES	WPL	CPL	WPP	CPP
Royal 8vo	26×43	43	11.9	64	511	2752
Demy 8vo	24×40	40	11.0	59	439	2360
Large Crown 8vo	23×36	36	10.2	57	368	2052
Crown 8vo	21×34	34	9.5	52	323	1768

father to son, and from uncle to nephew, and, in one instance, from second cousin to second cousin, the sceptre had descended in the family of the Dales; and the acres had remained intact, growing in value and not decreasing in number, though guarded by no entail and protected by no wonderful amount of prudence or wisdom. The estate of Dale of Allington had been coterminous with the parish of Allington for some hundreds of years; and though, as I have said, the race of squires had possessed nothing of superhuman discretion, and had perhaps been guided in their walks through life by no very distinct principles, still there had been with them so much of adherence to a sacred law, that no acre of the property had ever been parted from the hands of the existing squire. Some futile attempts had been made to increase the territory, as indeed had been done by Kit Dale, the father of Christopher Dale, who will appear as our squire of Allington when the persons of our drama are introduced. Old Kit Dale, who had married money, had bought outlying farms—a bit of ground here and a bit there—talking, as he did so, much of political influence and of the good old Tory cause. But these farms and bits of ground had gone again before our time. To them had been attached no religion. When old Kit had found himself pressed in that matter of the majority of the Nineteenth Dragoons, in which crack regiment his second son made for himself quite a career, he found it easier to sell than to save—seeing that that which he sold was his own and not the patrimony of the Dales. At his death the remainder of these purchases had gone. Family arrangements required completion, and Christopher Dale required ready money. The outlying farms flew away, as such new purchases had flown before; but the old patrimony of the Dales remained untouched, as it had ever remained.

It had been a religion among them; and seeing that the worship had been carried on without fail, that the vestal fire had never gone down upon the hearth, I should not have said that *the Dales had walked their ways without high principle. To this religion they had all adhered, and the new heir had ever entered in upon his domain without other encumbrances than those with which he himself*

MONOTYPE BASKERVILLE 169

11 point, 2 point leaded

FORMAT	PICAS	LINES	WPL	CPL	WPP	CPP
Royal 8vo	26×43	40	11.9	64	476	2560
Demy 8vo	24×40	37	11.0	59	407	2183
Large Crown 8vo	23×36	33	10.2	57	337	1881
Crown 8vo	21×34	31	9.5	52	295	1612

father to son, and from uncle to nephew, and, in one instance, from second cousin to second cousin, the sceptre had descended in the family of the Dales; and the acres had remained intact, growing in value and not decreasing in number, though guarded by no entail and protected by no wonderful amount of prudence or wisdom. The estate of Dale of Allington had been coterminous with the parish of Allington for some hundreds of years; and though, as I have said, the race of squires had possessed nothing of superhuman discretion, and had perhaps been guided in their walks through life by no very distinct principles, still there had been with them so much adherence to a sacred law, that no acre of the property had ever been parted from the hands of the existing squire. Some futile attempts had been made to increase the territory, as indeed had been done by Kit Dale, the father of Christopher Dale, who will appear as our squire of Allington when the persons of our drama are introduced. Old Kit Dale, who had married money, had bought outlying farms—a bit of ground here and a bit there—talking, as he did so, much of political influence and of the good old Tory cause. But these farms and bits of ground had gone again before our time. To them had been attached no religion. When old Kit had found himself pressed in that matter of the majority of the Nineteenth Dragoons, in which crack regiment his second son made for himself quite a career, he found it easier to sell than to save—seeing that that which he sold was his own and not the patrimony of the Dales. At his death the remainder of these purchases had gone. Family arrangements required completion, and Christopher Dale required ready money. The outlying farms flew away, as such new purchases had flown before; but the old patrimony of the Dales remained untouched, as it *had ever remained.*

It had been a religion among them; and seeing that the worship had been carried on without fail, that the vestal fire had never

MONOTYPE BASKERVILLE 169

12 point, 1 point leaded

FORMAT	PICAS	LINES	WPL	CPL	WPP	CPP
Royal 8vo	26×43	40	10.6	57	424	2280
Demy 8vo	24×40	37	9.8	53	358	1961
Large Crown 8vo	23×36	33	8.8	51	291	1683
Crown 8vo	21×34	31	8.3	47	258	1457

father to son, and from uncle to nephew, and, in one instance, from second cousin to second cousin, the sceptre had descended in the family of the Dales; and the acres had remained intact, growing in value and not decreasing in number, though guarded by no entail and protected by no wonderful amount of prudence or wisdom. The estate of Dale of Allington had been coterminous with the parish of Allington for some hundreds of years; and though, as I have said, the race of squires had possessed nothing of superhuman discretion, and had perhaps been guided in their walks through life by no very distinct principles, still there had been with them so much adherence to a sacred law, that no acre of the property had ever been parted from the hands of the existing squire. Some futile attempts had been made to increase the territory, as indeed had been done by Kit Dale, father of Christopher Dale, who will appear as our squire of Allington when the persons of our drama are introduced. Old Kit Dale, who had married money, had bought outlying farms—a bit of ground here and a bit there—talking, as he did so, much of political influence and of the good old Tory cause. But these farms and bits of ground had gone again before our time. To them had been attached no religion. When old Kit had found himself pressed in that matter of the majority of the Nineteenth Dragoons, in which crack regiment his second son made for himself quite a career, he found it easier to sell than to save—seeing that that which he sold was his own and not the patrimony of the Dales. At his death the remainder of these purchases had gone. Family arrangements required completion, and Christopher *Dale required ready money. The outlying farms flew away, as such new purchases had flown before; but the old patrimony of the Dales remained untouched, as it had ever remained.*

MONOTYPE BASKERVILLE 169

12 point, 2 point leaded

FORMAT	PICAS	LINES	WPL	CPL	WPP	CPP
Royal 8vo	26×43	37	10.6	57	392	2109
Demy 8vo	24×40	34	9.8	53	334	1802
Large Crown 8vo	23×36	31	8.8	51	273	1581
Crown 8vo	21×34	29	8.3	47	241	1363

MONOTYPE BELL 341

Synopsis in 10 *point*

ABCDEFGHIJKLMNOPQRSTUVWXYZ&ÆŒ

ABCDEFGHIJKLMNOPQRSTUVWXYZÆŒ

abcdefghijklmnopqrstuvwxyzæœfiffflffiffl

ABCDEFGHIJKLMNOPQRSTUVWXYZ&ÆŒ

abcdefghijklmnopqrstuvwxyzæœfiffflffiffl

.,:;!?‘’-()[]£ *:;!?*

1234567890 *1234567890*

All normal European accents available

Available in composition sizes 8, 10, 11, 12, 14 *point*

father to son, and from uncle to nephew, and, in one instance, from second cousin to second cousin, the sceptre had descended in the family of the Dales; and the acres had remained intact, growing in value and not decreasing in number, though guarded by no entail and protected by no wonderful amount of prudence or wisdom. The estate of Dale of Allington had been coterminous with the parish of Allington for some hundreds of years; and though, as I have said, the race of squires had possessed nothing of superhuman discretion, and had perhaps been guided in their walks through life by no very distinct principles, still there had been with them so much of adherence to a sacred law, that no acre of the property had ever been parted from the hands of the existing squire. Some futile attempts had been made to increase the territory, as indeed had been done by Kit Dale, the father of Christopher Dale, who will appear as our squire of Allington when the persons of our drama are introduced. Old Kit Dale, who had married money, had bought outlying farms—a bit of ground here and a bit there—talking, as he did so, much of political influence and of the good old Tory cause. But these farms and bits of ground had gone again before our time. To them had been attached no religion. When old Kit had found himself pressed in that matter of the majority of the Nineteenth Dragoons, in which crack regiment his second son made for himself quite a career, he found it easier to sell than to save—seeing that that which he sold was his own and not the patrimony of the Dales. At his death the remainder of these purchases had gone. Family arrangements required completion, and Christopher Dale required ready money. The outlying farms flew away, as such new purchases had flown before; but the old patrimony of the Dales remained untouched, as it had ever remained.

It had been a religion among them; and seeing that the worship had been carried on without fail, that the vestal fire had never gone down upon the hearth, I should not have said that the Dales had walked their ways without high principle. To this religion they had all adhered, and the new heir had ever entered in upon his domain without other encumbrances than those with which he himself was then already burdened. And yet there had been no entail. The idea of an entail was not in accordance with the peculiarities of the Dale mind. It was necessary to the Dale religion that each squire should have the power of wasting them. I remember to have dined at a house, the whole glory and fortune of which depended on the safety of a glass goblet. We all know the story. If the luck of Edenhall should be shattered, the doom of the family would be sealed. Nevertheless I was bidden to drink out of the fatal glass, as were all guests in that house. It would not have contented the chivalrous mind of the master to protect his doom by lock and key and padded chest. And so it was with the Dales of Allington. To them an entail would have been a lock and key and a padded chest; *but the old chivalry of their house denied to them the use of such protection.*

I have spoken something slightingly of the acquirements and doings of the family; and indeed their acquirements had been few and their doings little.

MONOTYPE BELL 341

10 point solid

FORMAT	PICAS	LINES	WPL	CPL	WPP	CPP
Royal 8vo	26×43	52	13.4	71	697	3692
Demy 8vo	24×40	48	12.4	66	596	3168
Large Crown 8vo	23×36	43	11.5	63	493	2709
Crown 8vo	21×34	41	10.6	58	436	2378

father to son, and from uncle to nephew, and, in one instance, from second cousin to second cousin, the sceptre had descended in the family of the Dales; and the acres had remained intact, growing in value and not decreasing in number, though guarded by no entail and protected by no wonderful amount of prudence or wisdom. The estate of Dale of Allington had been coterminous with the parish of Allington for some hundreds of years; and though, as I have said, the race of squires had possessed nothing of superhuman discretion, and had perhaps been guided in their walks through life by no very distinct principles, still there had been with them so much of adherence to a sacred law, that no acre of the property had ever been parted from the hands of the existing squire. Some futile attempts had been made to increase the territory, as indeed had been done by Kit Dale, the father of Christopher Dale, who will appear as our squire of Allington when the persons of our drama are introduced. Old Kit Dale, who had married money, had bought outlying farms—a bit of ground here and a bit there—talking, as he did so, much of political influence and of the good old Tory cause. But these farms and bits of ground had gone again before our time. To them had been attached no religion. When old Kit had found himself pressed in that matter of the majority of the Nineteenth Dragoons, in which crack regiment his second son made for himself quite a career, he found it easier to sell than to save—seeing that that which he sold was his own and not the patrimony of the Dales. At his death the remainder of these purchases had gone. Family arrangements required completion, and Christopher Dale required ready money. The outlying farms flew away, as such new purchases had flown before; but the old patrimony of the Dales remained untouched, as it had ever remained.

It had been a religion among them; and seeing that the worship had been carried on without fail, that the vestal fire had never gone down upon the hearth, I should not have said that the Dales had walked their ways without high principle. To this religion they had all adhered, and the new heir had ever entered in upon his domain without other encumbrances than those with which he himself was then already burdened. And yet there had been no entail. The idea of an entail was not in accordance with the peculiarities of the Dale mind. It was necessary to the Dale religion that each squire should have the power of wasting them. I remember to have dined at a house, the whole glory and fortune of which depended on the safety of a glass goblet. We all know the story. If the luck of Edenhall should be shattered, the doom of the family would be sealed. Nevertheless I was bidden to drink out of the *fatal glass, as were all guests in that house. It would not have contented the chivalrous mind of the master to protect his doom by lock and key and padded chest. And so it was with the Dales of Allington. To them an entail*

MONOTYPE BELL 341

10 point, 1 point leaded

FORMAT	PICAS	LINES	WPL	CPL	WPP	CPP
Royal 8vo	26×43	47	13.4	71	629	3337
Demy 8vo	24×40	44	12.4	66	546	2904
Large Crown 8vo	23×36	39	11.5	63	445	2457
Crown 8vo	21×34	37	10.6	58	393	2146

father to son, and from uncle to nephew, and, in one instance, from second cousin to second cousin, the sceptre had descended in the family of the Dales; and the acres had remained intact, growing in value and not decreasing in number, though guarded by no entail and protected by no wonderful amount of prudence or wisdom. The estate of Dale of Allington had been coterminous with the parish of Allington for some hundreds of years; and though, as I have said, the race of squires had possessed nothing of superhuman discretion, and had perhaps been guided in their walks through life by no very distinct principles, still there had been with them so much of adherence to a sacred law, that no acre of the property had ever been parted from the hands of the existing squire. Some futile attempts had been made to increase the territory, as indeed had been done by Kit Dale, the father of Christopher Dale, who will appear as our squire of Allington when the persons of our drama are introduced. Old Kit Dale, who had married money, had bought outlying farms—a bit of ground here and a bit there—talking, as he did so, much of political influence and of the good old Tory cause. But these farms and bits of ground had gone again before our time. To them had been attached no religion. When old Kit had found himself pressed in that matter of the majority of the Nineteenth Dragoons, in which crack regiment his second son made for himself quite a career, he found it easier to sell than to save—seeing that that which he sold was his own and not the patrimony of the Dales. At his death the remainder of these purchases had gone. Family arrangements required completion, and Christopher Dale required ready money. The outlying farms flew away, as such new purchases had flown before; but the old patrimony of the Dales remained untouched, as it had ever remained.

It had been a religion among them; and seeing that the worship had been carried on without fail, that the vestal fire had never gone down upon the hearth, I should not have said that the Dales had walked their ways without high principle. To this religion they had all adhered, and the new heir had ever entered in upon his domain without other encumbrances than those with which he himself was then already burdened. And yet there had been no entail. The idea of an entail was not in accordance with the peculiarities of the Dale mind. It was necessary to the Dale religion that each squire should have the power of wasting *them. I remember to have dined at a house, the whole glory and fortune of which depended on the safety of a glass goblet. We all know the story. If the luck of Edenhall should be shattered, the doom of the*

MONOTYPE BELL 341

11 point solid

FORMAT	PICAS	LINES	WPL	CPL	WPP	CPP
Royal 8vo	26×43	47	12.0	65	564	3055
Demy 8vo	24×40	44	11.1	60	489	2640
Large Crown 8vo	23×36	39	10.1	58	396	2262
Crown 8vo	21×34	37	9.4	53	346	1881

father to son, and from uncle to nephew, and, in one instance, from second cousin to second cousin, the sceptre had descended in the family of the Dales; and the acres had remained intact, growing in value and not decreasing in number, though guarded by no entail and protected by no wonderful amount of prudence or wisdom. The estate of Dale of Allington had been coterminous with the parish of Allington for some hundreds of years; and though, as I have said, the race of squires had possessed nothing of superhuman discretion, and had perhaps been guided in their walks through life by no very distinct principles, still there had been with them so much of adherence to a sacred law, that no acre of the property had ever been parted from the hands of the existing squire. Some futile attempts had been made to increase the territory, as indeed had been done by Kit Dale, the father of Christopher Dale, who will appear as our squire of Allington when the persons of our drama are introduced. Old Kit Dale, who had married money, had bought outlying farms—a bit of ground here and a bit there—talking, as he did so, much of political influence and of the good old Tory cause. But these farms and bits of ground had gone again before our time. To them had been attached no religion. When old Kit had found himself pressed in that matter of the majority of the Nineteenth Dragoons, in which crack regiment his second son made for himself quite a career, he found it easier to sell than to save—seeing that that which he sold was his own and not the patrimony of the Dales. At his death the remainder of these purchases had gone. Family arrangements required completion, and Christopher Dale required ready money. The outlying farms flew away, as such new purchases had flown before; but the old patrimony of the Dales remained untouched, as it had ever remained.

It had been a religion among them; and seeing that the worship had been carried on without fail, that the vestal fire had never gone down upon the hearth, I should not have said that the Dales had walked their ways without high principle. To this religion they had all adhered, and the new heir had ever entered in upon his domain without other encumbrances than those with *which he himself was then already burdened. And yet there had been no entail. The idea of an entail was not in accordance with the peculiarities of the Dale mind. It was necessary to the Dale religion*

MONOTYPE BELL 341

11 point, 1 point leaded

FORMAT	PICAS	LINES	WPL	CPL	WPP	CPP
Royal 8vo	26×43	43	11.9	65	511	2795
Demy 8vo	24×40	40	11.0	60	439	2400
Large Crown 8vo	23×36	36	10.1	58	365	2088
Crown 8vo	21×34	34	9.4	53	319	1802

father to son, and from uncle to nephew, and, in one instance, from second cousin to second cousin, the sceptre had descended in the family of the Dales; and the acres had remained intact, growing in value and not decreasing in number, though guarded by no entail and protected by no wonderful amount of prudence or wisdom. The estate of Dale of Allington had been coterminous with the parish of Allington for some hundreds of years; and though, as I have said, the race of squires had possessed nothing of superhuman discretion, and had perhaps been guided in their walks through life by no very distinct principles, still there had been with them so much of adherence to a sacred law, that no acre of the property had ever been parted from the hands of the existing squire. Some futile attempts had been made to increase the territory, as indeed had been done by Kit Dale, the father of Christopher Dale, who will appear as our squire of Allington when the persons of our drama are introduced. Old Kit Dale, who had married money, had bought outlying farms—a bit of ground here and a bit there—talking, as he did so, much of political influence and of the good old Tory cause. But these farms and bits of ground had gone again before our time. To them had been attached no religion. When old Kit had found himself pressed in that matter of the majority of the Nineteenth Dragoons, in which crack regiment his second son made for himself quite a career, he found it easier to sell than to save—seeing that that which he sold was his own and not the patrimony of the Dales. At his death the remainder of these purchases had gone. Family arrangements required completion, and Christopher Dale required ready money. The outlying farms flew away, as such new purchases had flown before; but the old patrimony of the Dales remained untouched, as it had ever remained.

It had been a religion among them; and seeing that the worship had been carried on without fail, that the vestal fire had never gone down upon the hearth, I should not have said that the Dales had walked their ways without *high principle. To this religion they had all adhered, and the new heir had ever entered in upon his domain without other encumbrances than those with which he himself was then already*

MONOTYPE BELL 341

12 point solid

FORMAT	PICAS	LINES	WPL	CPL	WPP	CPP
Royal 8vo	26×43	43	11.0	59	473	2537
Demy 8vo	24×40	40	10.2	55	408	2200
Large Crown 8vo	23×36	36	9.3	52	335	1872
Crown 8vo	21×34	34	8.7	48	294	1632

father to son, and from uncle to nephew, and, in one instance, from second cousin to second cousin, the sceptre had descended in the family of the Dales; and the acres had remained intact, growing in value and not decreasing in number, though guarded by no entail and protected by no wonderful amount of prudence or wisdom. The estate of Dale of Allington had been coterminous with the parish of Allington for some hundreds of years; and though, as I have said, the race of squires had possessed nothing of superhuman discretion, and had perhaps been guided in their walks through life by no very distinct principles, still there had been with them so much of adherence to a sacred law, that no acre of the property had ever been parted from the hands of the existing squire. Some futile attempts had been made to increase the territory, as indeed had been done by Kit Dale, the father of Christopher Dale, who will appear as our squire of Allington when the persons of our drama are introduced. Old Kit Dale, who had married money, had bought outlying farms—a bit of ground here and a bit there—talking, as he did so, much of political influence and of the good old Tory cause. But these farms and bits of ground had gone again before our time. To them had been attached no religion. When old Kit had found himself pressed in that matter of the majority of the Nineteenth Dragoons, in which crack regiment his second son made for himself quite a career, he found it easier to sell than to save—seeing that that which he sold was his own and not the patrimony of the Dales. At his death the remainder of these purchases had gone. Family arrangements required completion, and Christopher Dale required ready money. The outlying farms flew away, as such new purchases had flown before; but the old patrimony of the Dales remained untouched, as it had ever remained.

It had been a religion among them; and seeing that the *worship had been carried on without fail, that the vestal fire had never gone down upon the hearth, I should not have said that the Dales had walked their ways without high principle.*

MONOTYPE BELL 341

12 point, 1 point leaded

FORMAT	PICAS	LINES	WPL	CPL	WPP	CPP
Royal 8vo	26×43	40	11.0	59	440	2360
Demy 8vo	24×40	37	10.2	55	378	2035
Large Crown 8vo	23×36	33	9.3	52	304	1716
Crown 8vo	21×34	31	8.7	48	268	1488

father to son, and from uncle to nephew, and, in one instance, from second cousin to second cousin, the sceptre had descended in the family of the Dales; and the acres had remained intact, growing in value and not decreasing in number, though guarded by no entail and protected by no wonderful amount of prudence or wisdom. The estate of Dale of Allington had been coterminous with the parish of Allington for some hundreds of years; and though, as I have said, the race of squires had possessed nothing of superhuman discretion and had perhaps been guided in their walks through life by no very distinct principles, still there had been with them so much of adherence to a sacred law, that no acre of the property had ever been parted from the hands of the existing squire. Some futile attempts had been made to increase the territory, as indeed had been done by Kit Dale, the father of Christopher Dale, who will appear as our squire of Allington when the persons of our drama are introduced. Old Kit Dale, who had married money, had bought outlying farms—a bit of ground here and a bit there—talking, as he did so, much of political influence and of the good old Tory cause. But these farms and bits of ground had gone again before our time. To them had been attached no religion. When old Kit had found himself pressed in that matter of the majority of the Nineteenth Dragoons, in which crack regiment his second son made for himself quite a career, he found it easier to sell than to save—seeing that that which he sold was his own and not the patrimony of the Dales. At his *death the remainder of these purchases had gone. Family arrangements required completion, and Christopher Dale required ready money. The outlying farms flew away, as*

MONOTYPE BELL 341

14 point solid

FORMAT	PICAS	LINES	WPL	CPL	WPP	CPP
Royal 8vo	26×43	37	9.9	53	366	1961
Demy 8vo	24×30	34	9.2	49	314	1666
Large Crown 8vo	23×36	31	8.6	47	267	1457
Crown 8vo	21×34	29	7.9	43	229	1247

MONOTYPE BEMBO 270

Synopsis in 10 point

ABCDEFGHIJKLMNOPQRSTUVWXYZ &ÆŒ

ABCDEFGHIJKLMNOPQRSTUVWXYZÆŒ

abcdefghijklmnopqrstuvwxyzæœfiffflffiffl

ABCDEFGHIJKLMNOPQRSTUVWXYZ &ÆŒ

abcdefghijklmnopqrstuvwxyzæœfiffflffiffl

.,:;!?‘’-()[]£ *:;!?*

1234567890 **1234567890** 1234567890 *1234567890*

Related bold · Series 428

ABCDEFGHIJKLMNOPQRSTUVWXYZ &ÆŒ

abcdefghijklmnopqrstuvwxyzæœfiffflffiffl

.,:;?‘’-()[]£ 1234567890

All normal European accents available

Series 270 *available in composition sizes* 6, 8, 9, 10, 11, 12, 13, 16 *point*

Series 428 *available in composition sizes* 6, 8, 9, 10, 11, 12 *point*

father to son, and from uncle to nephew, and, in one instance, from second cousin to second cousin, the sceptre had descended in the family of the Dales; and the acres had remained intact, growing in value and not decreasing in number, though guarded by no entail and protected by no wonderful amount of prudence or wisdom. The estate of Dale of Allington had been coterminous with the parish of Allington for some hundreds of years; and though, as I have said, the race of squires had possessed nothing of superhuman discretion and had perhaps been guided in their walks through life by no very distinct principles, still there had been with them so much of adherence to a sacred law, that no acre of the property had ever been parted from the hands of the existing squire. Some futile attempts had been made to increase the territory, as indeed had been done by Kit Dale, the father of Christopher Dale, who will appear as our squire of Allington when the persons of our drama are introduced. Old Kit Dale, who had married money, had bought outlying farms—a bit of ground here and a bit there—talking, as he did so, much of political influence and of the good old Tory cause. But these farms and bits of ground had gone again before our time. To them had been attached no religion. When old Kit had found himself pressed in that matter of the majority of the Nineteenth Dragoons, in which crack regiment his second son made for himself quite a career, he found it easier to sell than to save—seeing that that which he sold was his own and not the patrimony of the Dales. At his death the remainder of these purchases had gone. Family arrangements required completion, and Christopher Dale required ready money. The outlying farms flew away, as such new purchases had flown before; but the old patrimony of the Dales remained untouched, as it had ever remained.

It had been a religion among them; and seeing that the worship had been carried on without fail, that the vestal fire had never gone down upon the hearth, I should not have said that the Dales had walked their ways without high principle. To this religion they had all adhered, and the new heir had ever entered in upon his domain without other encumbrances that those with which he himself was then already burdened. And yet there had been no entail. The idea of an entail was not in accordance with the peculiarities of the Dale mind. It was necessary to the Dale religion that each squire should have the power of wasting them. I remember to have dined at a house, the whole glory and fortune of which depended on the safety of a glass goblet. We all know the story. If the luck of Edenhall should be shattered, the doom of the family would be sealed. Nevertheless I was bidden to drink out of the fatal glass, as were all guests in that house. It would not have contented the chivalrous mind of the master to protect his doom by lock and key and padded chest. And so it was with the Dales of Allington. To them an entail would have been a lock and a key and a padded chest; but the old chivalry of their house denied to them the use of such protection.

I have spoken something slightingly of the acquirements and doings of the family; and indeed their acquirements had been few and their doings little. At Allington, Dale of Allington had always been known as a king. At Guestwick, the neighbouring market town, he was a great man—to be seen frequently on *Saturdays, standing in the market-place, and laying down the law as to barley and oxen among men who knew usually more about barley and oxen than he did. At Hamersham, the assize town, he was generally in some repute, being a constant grand juror for the*

MONOTYPE BEMBO 270

9 point, 1 point leaded

FORMAT	PICAS	LINES	WPL	CPL	WPP	CPP
Royal 8vo	26×43	52	15.1	82	785	4264
Demy 8vo	24×40	48	14.0	76	671	3648
Large Crown 8vo	23×36	43	12.8	73	550	3139
Crown 8vo	21×34	41	11.9	67	488	2747

father to son, and from uncle to nephew, and, in one instance, from second cousin to second cousin, the sceptre had descended in the family of the Dales; and the acres had remained intact, growing in value and not decreasing in number, though guarded by no entail and protected by no wonderful amount of prudence or wisdom. The estate of Dale of Allington had been coterminous with the parish of Allington for some hundreds of years; and though, as I have said, the race of squires had possessed nothing of superhuman discretion and had perhaps been guided in their walks through life by no very distinct principles, still there had been with them so much of adherence to a sacred law, that no acre of the property had ever been parted from the hands of the existing squire. Some futile attempts had been made to increase the territory, as indeed had been done by Kit Dale, the father of Christopher Dale, who will appear as our squire of Allington when the persons of our drama are introduced. Old Kit Dale, who had married money, had bought outlying farms—a bit of ground here and a bit there—talking, as he did so, much of political influence and of the good old Tory cause. But these farms and bits of ground had gone again before our time. To them had been attached no religion. When old Kit had found himself pressed in that matter of the majority of the Nineteenth Dragoons, in which crack regiment his second son made for himself quite a career, he found it easier to sell than to save—seeing that that which he sold was his own and not the patrimony of the Dales. At his death the remainder of these purchases had gone. Family arrangements required completion, and Christopher Dale required ready money. The outlying farms flew away, as such new purchases had flown before; but the old patrimony of the Dales remained untouched, as it had ever remained.

It had been a religion among them; and seeing that the worship had been carried on without fail, that the vestal fire had never gone down upon the hearth, I should not have said that the Dales had walked their ways without high principle. To this religion they had all adhered, and the new heir had ever entered in upon his domain without other encumbrances than those with which he himself was then already burdened. And yet there had been no entail. The idea of an entail was not in accordance with the peculiarities of the Dale mind. It was necessary to the Dale religion that each squire should have the power of wasting them. I remember to have dined at a house, the whole glory and fortune of which depended on the safety of a glass goblet. We all know the story. If the luck of Edenhall should be shattered, the doom of the family would be sealed. Nevertheless I was bidden to drink out of the fatal glass, as were all guests in that house. It would not have contented the chivalrous mind of the master to protect his doom by lock and key and padded chest. And so it was with the Dales of Allington. To them an entail would have been a lock and key and a padded chest; but the old chivalry of their house denied to them the use of such protection.

I have spoken something slightingly of the acquirements and doings of the family; and indeed their acquirements had been few and their doings little. At Allington, Dale of Allington had always been known as a king. At Guestwick, *the neighbouring market town, he was a great man—to be seen frequently on Saturdays, standing in the market-place, and laying down the law as to barley and oxen among men who knew usually more about barley and oxen than he did. At Hamersham,*

MONOTYPE BEMBO 270

10 point solid

FORMAT	PICAS	LINES	WPL	CPL	WPP	CPP
Royal 8vo	26×43	52	14.7	80	764	4160
Demy 8vo	24×40	48	13.6	74	655	3552
Large Crown 8vo	23×36	43	12.6	71	541	3053
Crown 8vo	21×34	41	12.0	64	493	2624

father to son, and from uncle to nephew, and, in one instance, from second cousin to second cousin, the sceptre had descended in the family of the Dales; and the acres had remained intact, growing in value and not decreasing in number, though guarded by no entail and protected by no wonderful amount of prudence or wisdom. The estate of Dale of Allington had been coterminous with the parish of Allington for some hundreds of years; and though, as I have said, the race of squires had possessed nothing of superhuman discretion and had perhaps been guided in their walks through life by no very distinct principles, still there had been with them so much of adherence to a sacred law, that no acre of the property had ever been parted from the hands of the existing squire. Some futile attempts had been made to increase the territory, as indeed had been done by Kit Dale, the father of Christopher Dale, who will appear as our squire of Allington when the persons of our drama are introduced. Old Kit Dale, who had married money, had bought outlying farms—a bit of ground here and a bit there—talking, as he did so, much of political influence and of the good old Tory cause. But these farms and bits of ground had gone again before our time. To them had been attached no religion. When old Kit had found himself pressed in that matter of the majority of the Nineteenth Dragoons, in which crack regiment his second son made for himself quite a career, he found it easier to sell than to save—seeing that that which he sold was his own and not the patrimony of the Dales. At his death the remainder of these purchases had gone. Family arrangements required completion, and Christopher Dale required ready money. The outlying farms flew away, as such new purchases had flown before; but the old patrimony of the Dales remained untouched, as it had ever remained.

It had been a religion among them; and seeing that the worship had been carried on without fail, that the vestal fire had never gone down upon the hearth, I should not have said that the Dales had walked their ways without high principle. To this religion they had all adhered, and the new heir had ever entered in upon his domain without other encumbrances than those with which he himself was then already burdened. And yet there had been no entail. The idea of an entail was not in accordance with the peculiarities of the Dale mind. It was necessary to the Dale religion that each squire should have the power of wasting them. I remember to have dined at a house, the whole glory and fortune of which depended on the safety of a glass goblet. We all know the story. If the luck of Edenhall should be shattered, the doom of the family would be sealed. Nevertheless I was bidden to drink out of the fatal glass, as were all guests in that house. It would not have contented the chivalrous mind of the master to protect his doom by lock and key and padded chest. And so it was with the Dales of Allington. To them an entail would have been a lock and key and a padded chest; but the old chivalry of their house denied to them *the use of such protection.*

I have spoken something slightingly of the acquirements and doings of the family; and indeed their acquirements had been few and their doings little. At Allington, Dale

MONOTYPE BEMBO 270

10 point, 1 point leaded

FORMAT	PICAS	LINES	WPL	CPL	WPP	CPP
Royal 8vo	26×43	47	14.7	80	690	3760
Demy 8vo	24×40	44	13.6	74	599	3256
Large Crown 8vo	23×36	39	12.6	71	494	2796
Crown 8vo	21×34	37	12.0	64	440	2368

father to son, and from uncle to nephew, and, in one instance, from second cousin to second cousin, the sceptre had descended in the family of the Dales; and the acres had remained intact, growing in value and not decreasing in number, though guarded by no entail and protected by no wonderful amount of prudence or wisdom. The estate of Dale of Allington had been coterminous with the parish of Allington for some hundreds of years; and though, as I have said, the race of squires had possessed nothing of superhuman discretion and had perhaps been guided in their walks through life by no very distinct principles, still there had been with them so much of adherence to a sacred law, that no acre of the property had ever been parted from the hands of the existing squire. Some futile attempts had been made to increase the territory, as indeed had been done by Kit Dale, the father of Christopher Dale, who will appear as our squire of Allington when the persons of our drama are introduced. Old Kit Dale, who had married money, had bought outlying farms—a bit of ground here and a bit there—talking, as he did so, much of political influence and of the good old Tory cause. But these farms and bits of ground had gone again before our time. To them had been attached no religion. When old Kit had found himself pressed in that matter of the majority of the Nineteenth Dragoons, in which crack regiment his second son made for himself quite a career, he found it easier to sell than to save—seeing that that which he sold was his own and not the patrimony of the Dales. At his death the remainder of these purchases had gone. Family arrangements required completion, and Christopher Dale required ready money. The outlying farms flew away, as such new purchases had flown before; but the old patrimony of the Dales remained untouched, as it had ever remained.

It had been a religion among them; and seeing that the worship had been carried on without fail, that the vestal fire had never gone down upon the hearth, I should not have said that the Dales had walked their ways without high principle. To this religion they had all adhered, and the new heir had ever entered in upon his domain without other encumbrances than those with which he himself was then already burdened. And yet there had been no entail. The idea of an entail was not in accordance with the peculiarities of the Dale mind. It was necessary to the Dale religion that each squire should have the power of wasting them. I remember to have dined at a house, the whole glory and fortune of which depended on the safety of a glass goblet. We all know the story. If the luck of Edenhall should be shattered, the doom of the family would be sealed. Nevertheless I was bidden to drink out of *the fatal glass, as were all guests in that house. It would not have contented the chivalrous mind of the master to protect his doom by lock and key and padded chest. And so it was with the Dales of Allington. To them an entail would*

MONOTYPE BEMBO 270

11 point solid

FORMAT	PICAS	LINES	WPL	CPL	WPP	CPP
Royal 8vo	26×43	47	13.4	71	629	3373
Demy 8vo	24×40	44	12.4	66	547	2904
Large Crown 8vo	23×36	39	11.3	63	442	2457
Crown 8vo	21×34	37	10.4	58	383	2146

father to son, and from uncle to nephew, and, in one instance, from second cousin to second cousin, the sceptre had descended in the family of the Dales; and the acres had remained intact, growing in value and not decreasing in number, though guarded by no entail and protected by no wonderful amount of prudence or wisdom. The estate of Dale of Allington had been coterminous with the parish of Allington for some hundreds of years; and though, as I have said, the race of squires had possessed nothing of superhuman discretion and had perhaps been guided in their walks through life by no very distinct principles, still there had been with them so much of adherence to a sacred law, that no acre of the property had ever been parted from the hands of the existing squire. Some futile attempts had been made to increase the territory, as indeed had been done by Kit Dale, the father of Christopher Dale, who will appear as our squire of Allington when the persons of our drama are introduced. Old Kit Dale, who had married money, had bought outlying farms—a bit of ground here and a bit there—talking, as he did so, much of political influence and of the good old Tory cause. But these farms and bits of ground had gone again before our time. To them had been attached no religion. When old Kit had found himself pressed in that matter of the majority of the Nineteenth Dragoons, in which crack regiment his second son made for himself quite a career, he found it easier to sell than to save—seeing that that which he sold was his own and not the patrimony of the Dales. At his death the remainder of these purchases had gone. Family arrangements required completion, and Christopher Dale required ready money. The outlying farms flew away, as such new purchases had flown before; but the old patrimony of the Dales remained untouched, as it had ever remained.

It had been a religion among them; and seeing that the worship had been carried on without fail, that the vestal fire had never gone down upon the hearth, I should not have said that the Dales had walked their ways without high principle. To this religion they had all adhered, and the new heir had ever entered in upon his domain without other encumbrances than those with which he himself was then already burdened. And yet there had been no entail. The idea of an entail was not in accordance with the peculiarities of the Dale mind. It was necessary to the Dale religion that each squire should have the power of wasting *them. I remember to have dined at a house, the whole glory and fortune of which depended on the safety of a glass goblet. We all know the story. If the luck of Edenhall should be shattered, the doom of the family would be sealed.*

MONOTYPE BEMBO 270

11 point, 1 point leaded

FORMAT	PICAS	LINES	WPL	CPL	WPP	CPP
Royal 8vo	26×43	43	13.4	71	576	3053
Demy 8vo	24×40	40	12.4	66	493	2640
Large Crown 8vo	23×36	36	11.3	63	405	2268
Crown 8vo	21×34	34	10.4	58	353	1972

father to son, and from uncle to nephew, and, in one instance, from second cousin to second cousin, the sceptre had descended in the family of the Dales; and the acres had remained intact, growing in value and not decreasing in number, though guarded by no entail and protected by no wonderful amount of prudence or wisdom. The estate of Dale of Allington had been coterminous with the parish of Allington for some hundred of years; and though, as I have said, the race of squires had possessed nothing of superhuman discretion and had perhaps been guided in their walks through life by no very distinct principles, still there had been with them so much of adherence to a sacred law, that no acre of the property had ever been parted from the hands of the existing squire. Some futile attempts had been made to increase the territory, as indeed had been done by Kit Dale, the father of Christopher Dale, who will appear as our squire of Allington when the persons of our drama are introduced. Old Kit Dale, who had married money, had bought outlying farms—a bit of ground here and a bit there—talking, as he did so, much of political influence and of the good old Tory cause. But these farms and bits of ground had gone again before our time. To them had been attached no religion. When old Kit had found himself pressed in that matter of the majority of the Nineteenth Dragoons, in which crack regiment his second son made for himself quite a career, he found it easier to sell than to save—seeing that that which he sold was his own and not the patrimony of the Dales. At his death the remainder of these purchases had gone. Family arrangements required completion, and Christopher Dale required ready money. The outlying farms flew away, as such new purchases had flown before; but the old patrimony of the Dales remained untouched, as it had ever remained.

It had been a religion among them; and seeing that the worship had been carried on without fail, that the vestal fire had never gone down upon the hearth, I should not have said that the Dales had walked their ways without high principle. To this religion they had all adhered, and the new heir had ever entered in upon his domain without other encumbrances than those with which he himself was then already burdened. And yet there had been no *entail. The idea of an entail was not in accordance with the peculiarities of the Dale mind. It was necessary to the Dale religion that each squire should have the power of wasting them. I remember to have dined at a*

MONOTYPE BEMBO 270

12 point solid

FORMAT	PICAS	LINES	WPL	CPL	WPP	CPP
Royal 8vo	26×43	43	12.3	67	528	2881
Demy 8vo	24×40	40	11.4	62	456	2480
Large Crown 8vo	23×36	36	10.6	59	380	2124
Crown 8vo	21×34	34	9.3	53	316	1802

father to son, and from uncle to nephew, and, in one instance, from second cousin to second cousin, the sceptre had descended in the family of the Dales; and the acres had remained intact, growing in value and not decreasing in number, though guarded by no entail and protected by no wonderful amount of prudence or wisdom. The estate of Dale of Allington had been coterminous with the parish of Allington for some hundreds of years; and though, as I have said, the race of squires had possessed nothing of superhuman discretion and had perhaps been guided in their walks through life by no very distinct principles, still there had been with them so much of adherence to a sacred law, that no acre of the property had ever been parted from the hands of the existing squire. Some futile attempts had been made to increase the territory, as indeed had been done by Kit Dale, the father of Christopher Dale, who will appear as our squire of Allington when the persons of our drama are introduced. Old Kit Dale, who had married money, had bought outlying farms—a bit of ground here and a bit there—talking, as he did so, much of political influence and of the good old Tory cause. But these farms and bits of ground had gone again before our time. To them had been attached no religion. When old Kit had found himself pressed in that matter of the majority of the Nineteenth Dragoons, in which crack regiment his second son made for himself quite a career, he found it easier to sell than to save—seeing that that which he sold was his own and not the patrimony of the Dales. At his death the remainder of these purchases had gone. Family arrangements required completion, and Christopher Dale required ready money. The outlying farms flew away, as such new purchases had flown before; but the old patrimony of the Dales remained untouched, as it had ever remained.

It had been a religion among them; and seeing that the worship had been carried on without fail, that the vestal fire had never gone down upon the hearth, I should not have said that the Dales had walked their ways without high principle. To this religion *they had all adhered, and the new heir had ever entered in upon his domain without other encumbrances than those with which he himself was then already burdened. And yet there had been no entail. The*

MONOTYPE BEMBO 270

12 point, 1 point leaded

FORMAT	PICAS	LINES	WPL	CPL	WPP	CPP
Royal 8vo	26×43	40	12.2	67	488	2680
Demy 8vo	24×40	37	11.3	62	417	2294
Large Crown 8vo	23×36	33	10.6	59	349	1947
Crown 8vo	21×34	31	9.3	53	291	1643

father to son, and from uncle to nephew, and, in one instance, from the second cousin to the second cousin, the sceptre had descended in the family of the Dales; and the acres had remained intact, growing in value and not decreasing in number, though guarded by no entail and protected by no wonderful amount of prudence or wisdom. The estate of Dale of Allington had been coterminous with the parish of Allington for some hundreds of years; and though, as I have said, the race of squires had possessed nothing of superhuman discretion and had perhaps been guided in their walks through life by no very distinct principles, still there had been with them so much of adherence to a sacred law, that no acre of the property had ever been parted from the hands of the existing squire. Some futile attempts had been made to increase the territory, as indeed had been done by Kit Dale, the father of Christopher Dale, who will appear as our squire of Allington when the persons of our drama are introduced. Old Kit Dale, who had married money, had bought outlying farms—a bit of ground here and a bit there—talking, as he did so, much of political influence and of the good old Tory cause. But these farms and bits of ground had gone again before our time. To them had been attached no religion. When old Kit had found himself pressed in that matter of the majority of the Nineteenth Dragoons, in which crack regiment his second son made for himself quite a career, he found it easier to sell than to save—seeing that that which he sold was his own and not the patrimony of the Dales. At his death the remainder of these purchases had gone. Family arrangements required completion, and Christopher Dale required ready money. The outlying farms flew away, as such new purchases had flown before; but the old patrimony of the *Dales remained untouched, as it had ever remained.*

It had been a religion among them; and seeing that the worship had been carried on without fail, that the vestal fire had never gone

MONOTYPE BEMBO 270

13 point, 1 point leaded

FORMAT	PICAS	LINES	WPL	CPL	WPP	CPP
Royal 8vo	26×43	37	11.4	62	422	2294
Demy 8vo	34×40	34	10.6	57	359	1938
Large Crown 8vo	23×36	31	10.0	55	310	1705
Crown 8vo	21×34	29	9.1	50	266	1450

father to son, and from uncle to nephew, and, in one instance, from second cousin to second cousin, the sceptre had descended in the family of the Dales; and the acres had remained intact, growing in value and not decreasing in number, though guarded by no entail and protected by no wonderful amount of prudence or wisdom. The estate of Dale of Allington had been coterminous with the parish of Allington for some hundreds of years; and though, as I have said, the race of squires had possessed nothing of superhuman discretion and had perhaps been guided in their walks through life by no very distinct principles, still there had been with them so much of adherence to a sacred law, that no acre of the property had ever been parted from the hands of the existing squire. Some futile attempts had been made to increase the territory, as indeed had been done by Kit Dale, the father of Christopher Dale, who will appear as our squire of Allington when the persons of our drama are introduced. Old Kit Dale, who had married money, had bought outlying farms—a bit of ground here and a bit there—talking, as he did so, much of political influence and of the good old Tory cause. But these farms and bits of ground had gone again before our time. To them had been attached no religion. When old Kit *had found himself pressed in that matter of the majority of the Nineteenth Dragoons, in which crack regiment his second son made for himself quite a career, he found*

MONOTYPE BEMBO 270

16 point solid

FORMAT	PICAS	LINES	WPL	CPL	WPP	CPP
Royal 8vo	26×43	32	9.5	51	304	1632
Demy 8vo	24×40	30	8.8	47	265	1410
Large Crown 8vo	23×36	27	8.1	45	218	1215
Crown 8vo	21×34	25	7.6	41	189	1025

MONOTYPE BODONI 135

Synopsis in 10 *point*

ABCDEFGHIJKLMNOPQRSTUVWXYZ&ÆŒ

ABCDEFGHIJKLMNOPQRSTUVWXYZÆŒ

abcdefghijklmnopqrstuvwxyzæœfiffflffiffl

ABCDEFGHIJKLMNOPQRSTUVWXYZ&ÆŒ

abcdefghijklmnopqrstuvwxyzæœfiffflffiffl

.,:;!?"-()[]£ *:;!?* 1234567890

Related bold · *Series* 260

ABCDEFGHIJKLMNOPQRSTUVWXYZ &ÆŒ

abcdefghijklmnopqrstuvwxyzæœfiffflffiffl

.,:;!?"-()[]£ 1234567890

ABCDEFGHIJKLMNOPQRSTUVWXYZ&ÆŒ

abcdefghijklmnopqrstuvwxyzæœfiffflffiffl

.,:;!?"()£ 1234567890

All normal European accents available

Roman and italic available in composition sizes 8, 10, 11 (*small face*), 11 (*large face*), 12 *point*

Series 260 *available in composition sizes* 8, 10, 12 *point*

father to son, and from uncle to nephew, and, in one instance, from second cousin to second cousin, the sceptre had descended in the family of the Dales; and the acres had remained intact, growing in value and not decreasing in number, though guarded by no entail and protected by no wonderful amount of prudence or wisdom. The estate of Dale of Allington had been coterminous with the parish of Allington for some hundreds of years; and though, as I have said, the race of squires had possessed nothing of superhuman discretion and had perhaps been guided in their walks through life by no very distinct principles, still there had been with them so much of adherence to a sacred law, that no acre of the property had ever been parted from the hands of the existing squire. Some futile attempts had been made to increase the territory, as indeed had been done by Kit Dale, the father of Christopher Dale, who will appear as our squire of Allington when the persons of our drama are introduced. Old Kit Dale, who had married money, had bought outlying farms—a bit of ground here and a bit there—talking, as he did so, much of political influence and of the good old Tory cause. But these farms and bits of ground had gone again before our time. To them had been attached no religion. When old Kit had found himself pressed in that matter of the majority of the Nineteenth Dragoons, in which crack regiment his second son made for himself quite a career, he found it easier to sell than to save—seeing that that which he sold was his own and not the patrimony of the Dales. At his death the remainder of these purchases had gone. Family arrangements required completion, and Christopher Dale required ready money. The outlying farms flew away, as such new purchases had flown before; but the old patrimony of the Dales remained untouched, as it had ever remained.

It had been a religion among them; and seeing that the worship had been carried on without fail, that the vestal fire had never gone down upon the hearth, I should not have said that the Dales had walked their ways without high principle. To this religion they had all adhered, and the new heir had ever entered in upon his domain without other encumbrances than those with which he himself was then already burdened. And yet there had been no entail. The idea of an entail was not in accordance with the peculiarities of the Dale mind. It was necessary to the Dale religion that each squire should have the power of wasting them. I remember to have dined at a house, the whole glory and fortune of which depended on the safety of a glass goblet. We all know the story. If the luck of Edenhall should be shattered, the doom of the family would be sealed. Nevertheless I was bidden to drink out of the fatal glass, as were all guests in that house. It would not have contented the chivalrous mind of the master to protect his doom by lock and key and padded chest. And so it was with the Dales of Allington. To them an entail would have been a lock and key and a *padded chest; but the old chivalry of their house denied to them the use of such protection.*

I have spoken something slightingly of the acquirements and doings of

MONOTYPE BODONI 135

10 point solid

FORMAT	PICAS	LINES	WPL	CPL	WPP	CPP
Royal 8vo	26×43	52	13.6	71	707	3692
Demy 8vo	24×40	48	12.1	66	583	9817
Large Crown 8vo	23×36	43	11.4	63	492	2036
Crown 8vo	21×34	41	10.4	58	425	2378

father to son, and from uncle to nephew, and, in one instance, from second cousin to second cousin, the sceptre had descended in the family of the Dales; and the acres had remained intact, growing in value and not decreasing in number, though guarded by no entail and protected by no wonderful amount of prudence or wisdom. The estate of Dale of Allington had been coterminous with the parish of Allington for some hundreds of years; and though, as I have said, the race of squires had possessed nothing of superhuman discretion and had perhaps been guided in their walks through life by no very distinct principles, still there had been with them so much of adherence to a sacred law, that no acre of the property had ever been parted from the hands of the existing squire. Some futile attempts had been made to increase the territory, as indeed had been done by Kit Dale, the father of Christopher Dale, who will appear as our squire of Allington when the persons of our drama are introduced. Old Kit Dale, who had married money, had bought outlying farms—a bit of ground here and a bit there—talking, as he did so, much of political influence and of the good old Tory cause. But these farms and bits of ground had gone again before our time. To them had been attached no religion. When old Kit had found himself pressed in that matter of the majority of the Nineteenth Dragoons, in which crack regiment his second son made for himself quite a career, he found it easier to sell than to save —seeing that that which he sold was his own and not the patrimony of the Dales. At his death the remainder of these purchases had gone. Family arrangements required completion, and Christopher Dale required ready money. The outlying farms flew away, as such new purchases had flown before; but the old patrimony of the Dales remained untouched, as it had ever remained.

It had been a religion among them; and seeing that the worship had been carried on without fail, that the vestal fire had never gone down upon the hearth, I should not have said that the Dales had walked their ways without high principle. To this religion they had all adhered, and the new heir had ever entered in upon his domain without other encumbrances than those with which he himself was then already burdened. And yet there had been no entail. The idea of an entail was not in accordance with the peculiarities of the Dale mind. It was necessary to the Dale religion that each squire should have the power of wasting them. I remember to have dined at a house, the whole glory and fortune of which depended on the safety of a glass goblet. We all know the story. If the luck of Edenhall should be shattered, the doom of the family would be sealed. Nevertheless I was bidden to *drink out of the fatal glass, as were all guests in that house. It would not have contented the chivalrous mind of the master to protect his doom by lock and key and padded chest. And so it was with the Dales of Allington.*

MONOTYPE BODONI 135

10 point, 1 point leaded

FORMAT	PICAS	LINES	WPL	CPL	WPP	CPP
Royal 8vo	26×43	47	13.3	71	625	3337
Demy 8vo	24×40	44	12.3	66	542	2904
Large Crown 8vo	23×36	39	11.4	63	444	2457
Crown 8vo	21×34	37	10.3	58	381	2146

father to son, and from uncle to nephew, and, in one instance, from second cousin to second cousin, the sceptre had descended in the family of the Dales; and the acres had remained intact, growing in value and not decreasing in number, though guarded by no entail and protected by no wonderful amount of prudence or wisdom. The estate of Dale of Allington had been coterminous with the parish of Allington for some hundreds of years; and though, as I have said, the race of squires had possessed nothing of superhuman discretion and had perhaps been guided in their walks through life by no very distinct principles, still there had been with them so much of adherence to a sacred law, that no acre of property had ever been parted from the hands of the existing squire. Some futile attempts had been made to increase the territory, as indeed had been done by Kit Dale, the father of Christopher Dale, who will appear as our squire of Allington when the persons of our drama are introduced. Old Kit Dale, who had married money, had bought outlying farms—a bit of ground here and a bit there—talking, as he did so, much of political influence and of the good old Tory cause. But these farms and bits of ground had gone again before our time. To them had been attached no religion. When old Kit had found himself pressed in that matter of the Nineteenth Dragoons, in which crack regiment his second son made for himself quite a career, he found it easier to sell than to save—seeing that that which he sold was his own and not the patrimony of the Dales. At his death the remainder of these purchases had gone. Family arrangements required completion, and Christopher Dale required ready money. The outlying farms flew away, as such new purchases had flown before; but the old patrimony of the Dales remained untouched, as it had ever remained.

It had been a religion among them; and seeing that the worship had been carried on without fail, that the vestal fire had never gone down upon the hearth, I should not have said that the Dales had walked their ways without high principle. To this religion they had all adhered, and the new heir had ever entered in upon his domain without other encumbrances than those with which he himself was then already burdened. And yet there had been no entail. The idea of an entail was not in accordance with the peculiarities of the Dale mind. It was necessary to the Dale religion that each squire should have the power of wasting them. I remember to have dined at a house, the whole glory and fortune *of which depended on the safety of a glass goblet. We all know the story. If the luck of Edenhall should be shattered, the doom of the family would be sealed. Nevertheless I was bidden to drink out of the*

MONOTYPE BODONI 135

11 point (small face) solid

FORMAT	PICAS	LINES	WPL	CPL	WPP	CPP
Royal 8vo	26×43	47	12.3	66	578	3102
Demy 8vo	24×40	44	11.4	61	502	2684
Large Crown 8vo	23×36	39	10.4	58	406	2262
Crown 8vo	21×34	37	9.5	53	353	1961

father to son, and from uncle to nephew, and, in one instance, from second cousin to second cousin, the sceptre had descended in the family of the Dales; and the acres had remained intact, growing in value and not decreasing in number, though guarded by no entail and protected by no wonderful amount of prudence or wisdom. The estate of Dale of Allington had been coterminous with the parish of Allington for some hundreds of years; and though, as I have said, the race of squires had possessed nothing of superhuman discretion and had perhaps been guided in their walks through life by no very distinct principles, still there had been with them so much of adherence to a sacred law, that no acre of property had ever been parted from the hands of the existing squire. Some futile attempts had been made to increase the territory, as indeed had been done by Kit Dale, the father of Christopher Dale, who will appear as our squire of Allington when the persons of our drama are introduced. Old Kit Dale, who had married money, had bought outlying farms—a bit of ground here and a bit there—talking, as he did so, much of political influence and of the good old Tory cause. But these farms and bits of ground had gone again before our time. To them had been attached no religion. When old Kit had found himself pressed in that matter of the Nineteenth Dragoons, in which crack regiment his second son made for himself quite a career, he found it easier to sell than to save—seeing that that which he sold was his own and not the patrimony of the Dales. At his death the remainder of these purchases had gone. Family arrangements required completion, and Christopher Dale required ready money. The outlying farms flew away, as such new purchases had flown before; but the old patrimony of the Dales remained untouched, as it had ever remained.

It had been a religion among them; and seeing that the worship had been carried on without fail, that the vestal fire had never gone down upon the hearth, I should not have said that the Dales had walked their ways without high principle. To this religion they had all adhered, and the new heir had ever entered in upon his domain without other encumbrances than those with which he himself was then already burdened. And yet there had *been no entail. The idea of an entail was not in accordance with the peculiarities of the Dale mind. It was necessary to the Dale religion that each squire should have the power of wasting them. I remember*

MONOTYPE BODONI 135

11 point (small face), 1 point leaded

FORMAT	PICAS	LINES	WPL	CPL	WPP	CPP
Royal 8vo	26×43	43	12.2	66	524	2836
Demy 8vo	24×40	40	11.3	61	451	2440
Large Crown 8vo	23×36	36	10.3	58	372	2088
Crown 8vo	21×34	34	9.5	53	325	1802

father to son, and from uncle to nephew, and, in one instance, from second cousin to second cousin, the sceptre had descended in the family of the Dales; and the acres had remained intact, growing in value and not decreasing in number, though guarded by no entail and protected by no wonderful amount of prudence or wisdom. The estate of Dale of Allington had been coterminous with the parish of Allington for some hundreds of years; and though, as I have said, the race of squires had possessed nothing of superhuman discretion and had perhaps been guided in their walks through life by no very distinct principles, still there had been with them so much of adherence to a sacred law, that no acre of the property had ever been parted from the hands of the existing squire. Some futile attempts had been made to increase the territory, as indeed had been done by Kit Dale, the father of Christopher Dale, who will appear as our squire of Allington when the persons of our drama are introduced. Old Kit Dale, who had married money, had bought outlying farms—a bit of ground here and a bit there—talking, as he did so, much of political influence and of the good old Tory cause. But these farms and bits of ground had gone again before our time. To them had been attached no religion. When old Kit had found himself pressed in that matter of the majority of the Nineteenth Dragoons, in which crack regiment his second son made for himself quite a career, he found it easier to sell than to save —seeing that that which he sold was his own and not the patrimony of the Dales. At his death the remainder of these purchases had gone. Family arrangements required completion, and Christopher Dale required ready money. The outlying farms flew away, as such new purchases had flown before; but the old patrimony of the Dales remained untouched, as it had ever remained.

It had been a religion among them; and seeing that the worship had been carried on without fail, that the vestal fire had never gone down upon the hearth, I should not have said that the Dales had walked their ways without high principle. To this religion they had all adhered, and the new heir had ever entered in upon his domain without other encumbrances than those with which he himself was then already burdened. And yet there had been no entail. The *idea of an entail was not in accordance with the peculiarities of the Dale mind. It was necessary to the Dale religion that each squire should have the power of wasting them. I remember*

MONOTYPE BODONI 135

11 point (large face) solid

FORMAT	PICAS	LINES	WPL	CPL	WPP	CPP
Royal 8vo	26×43	47	11.1	61	521	2867
Demy 8vo	24×40	44	10.3	56	451	2464
Large Crown 8vo	23×36	39	9.4	54	367	2106
Crown 8vo	21×34	37	8.7	49	324	1813

father to son, and from uncle to nephew, and, in one instance, from second cousin to second cousin, the sceptre had descended in the family of the Dales; and the acres had remained intact, growing in value and not decreasing in number, though guarded by no entail and protected by no wonderful amount of prudence or wisdom. The estate of Dale of Allington had been coterminous with the parish of Allington for some hundreds of years; and though, as I have said, the race of squires had possessed nothing of superhuman discretion and had perhaps been guided in their walks through life by no very distinct principles, still there had been with them so much of adherence to a sacred law, that no acre of the property had ever been parted from the hands of the existing squire. Some futile attempts had been made to increase the territory, as indeed had been done by Kit Dale, the father of Christopher Dale, who will appear as our squire of Allington when the persons of our drama are introduced. Old Kit Dale, who had married money, had bought outlying farms—a bit of ground here and a bit there—talking, as he did so, much of political influence and of the good old Tory cause. But these farms and bits of ground had gone again before our time. To them had been attached no religion. When old Kit had found himself pressed in that matter of the majority of the Nineteenth Dragoons, in which crack regiment his second son made for himself quite a career, he found it easier to sell than to save—seeing that that which he sold was his own and not the patrimony of the Dales. At his death the remainder of these purchases had gone. Family arrangements required completion, and Christopher Dale required ready money. The outlying farms flew away, as such new purchases had flown before; but the old patrimony of the Dales remained untouched, as it had ever remained.

It had been a religion among them; and seeing that the worship had been carried on without fail, that the vestal fire had never gone down upon the hearth, I should not have said that the Dales had walked their ways without high *principle. To this religion they had all adhered, and the new heir had ever entered in upon his domain without other encumbrances than those with which he himself was then already*

MONOTYPE BODONI 135

11 point (large face), 1 point leaded

FORMAT	PICAS	LINES	WPL	CPL	WPP	CPP
Royal 8vo	26×43	43	11.1	61	477	2623
Demy 8vo	24×40	40	10.3	56	408	2240
Large Crown 8vo	23×36	36	9.4	54	338	1944
Crown 8vo	21×34	34	8.7	49	295	1666

father to son, and from uncle to nephew, and, in one instance, from the second cousin to the second cousin, the sceptre had descended in the family of the Dales; and the acres had remained intact, growing in value and not decreasing in number, though guarded by no entail and protected by no wonderful amount of prudence or wisdom. The estate of Dale of Allington had been coterminous with the parish of Allington for some hundreds of years; and though, as I have said, the race of squires had possessed nothing of superhuman discretion and had perhaps been guided in their walks through life by no very distinct principles, still there had been with them so much of adherence to a sacred law, that no acre of the property had ever been parted from the hands of the existing squire. Some futile attempts had been made to increase the territory, as indeed had been done by Kit Dale, the father of Christopher Dale, who will appear as our squire of Allington when the persons of our drama are introduced. Old Kit Dale, who had married money, had bought outlying farms—a bit of ground here and a bit there—talking, as he did so, much of political influence and of the good old Tory cause. But these farms and bits of ground had gone again before our time. To them had been attached no religion. When old Kit had found himself pressed in that matter of the majority of the Nineteenth Dragoons, in which crack regiment his second son made for himself quite a career, he found it easier to sell than to save—seeing that that which he sold was his own and not the patrimony of the Dales. At his death the remainder of these purchases had gone. Family arrangements required completion, and Christopher Dale required ready money. The outlying farms flew away, as such new purchases had flown before; but the old patrimony of the Dales *remained untouched, as it had ever remained.*

It had been a religion among them; and seeing that the worship had been carried on without fail, that the vestal

MONOTYPE BODONI 135

12 point, 1 point leaded

FORMAT	PICAS	LINES	WPL	CPL	WPP	CPP
Royal 8vo	26×43	40	10.5	57	420	2280
Demy 8vo	24×40	37	9.7	53	355	1961
Large Crown 8vo	23×36	33	9.0	51	297	1683
Crown 8vo	21×34	31	8.3	46	260	1426

MONOTYPE CASLON 128

Synopsis in 10 *point*

ABCDEFGHIJKLMNOPQRSTUVWXYZ&ÆŒ

ABCDEFGHIJKLMNOPQRSTUVWXYZÆŒ

abcdefghijklmnopqrstuvwxyzæœfiffflffiffl

ABCDEFGHIJKLMNOPQRSTUVWXYZ&ÆŒ

abcdefghijklmnopqrstuvwxyzæœfiffflffiffl

.,:;!?‘’-()[]£ *:;!?* 1234567890

All normal European accents available

Available in composition sizes 9, 10, 11, 12, 14 *point*

Swash italic capitals available in 10 *and* 11 *point*

father to son, and from uncle to nephew, and, in one instance, from second cousin to second cousin, the sceptre had descended in the family of the Dales; and the acres had remained intact, growing in value and not decreasing in number, though guarded by no entail and protected by no wonderful amount of prudence or wisdom. The estate of Dale of Allington had been coterminous with the parish of Allington for some hundreds of years; and though, as I have said, the race of squires had possessed nothing of superhuman discretion and had perhaps been guided in their walks through life by no very distinct principles, still there had been with them so much of adherence to a sacred law, that no acre of the property had ever been parted from the hands of the existing squire. Some futile attempts had been made to increase the territory, as indeed had been done by Kit Dale, the father of Christopher Dale, who will appear as our squire of Allington when the persons of our drama are introduced. Old Kit Dale, who had married money, had bought outlying farms—a bit of ground here and a bit there—talking, as he did so, much of political influence and of the good old Tory cause. But these farms and bits of ground had gone again before our time. To them had been attached no religion. When old Kit had found himself pressed in that matter of the majority of the Nineteenth Dragoons, in which crack regiment his second son made for himself quite a career, he found it easier to sell than to save—seeing that that which he sold was his own and not the patrimony of the Dales. At his death the remainder of these purchases had gone. Family arrangements required completion, and Christopher Dale required ready money. The outlying farms flew away, as such new purchases had flown before; but the old patrimony of the Dales remained untouched, as it had ever remained.

It had been a religion among them; and seeing that the worship had been carried on without fail, that the vestal fire had never gone down upon the hearth, I should not have said that the Dales had walked their ways without high principle. To this religion they had all adhered, and the new heir had ever entered in upon his domain without other encumbrances than those with which he himself was then already burdened. And yet there had been no entail. The idea of an entail was not in accordance with the peculiarities of the Dale mind. It was necessary to the Dale religion that each squire should have the power of wasting them. I remember to have dined at a house, the whole glory and fortune of which depended on the safety of a glass goblet. We all know the story. If the luck of Edenhall should be shattered, the doom of the family would be sealed. Nevertheless I was bidden to drink out of the fatal glass, as were all guests in that house. It would not have contented the chivalrous mind of the master to protect his doom by lock and key and padded chest. And so it was with the Dales of Allington. To them an entail would have been a lock and key and a padded chest; but the old chivalry of their house denied to them the use of such protection.

I have spoken something slightingly of the acquirements and doings of the family; and indeed their acquirements had been few and their doings little. At Allington, Dale of Allington had always been known as a king. At Guest*wick, the neighbouring market-town, he was a great man—to be seen frequently on Saturdays, standing in the market-place, and laying down the law as to barley and oxen among men who knew usually more about barley and oxen than he did.*

MONOTYPE CASLON 128

10 point solid

FORMAT	PICAS	LINES	WPL	CPL	WPP	CPP
Royal 8vo	26×43	52	14.7	79	764	4108
Demy 8vo	24×40	48	13.6	73	653	3504
Large Crown 8vo	23×36	43	12.7	70	546	3010
Crown 8vo	21×34	41	11.8	63	484	2583

father to son, and from uncle to nephew, and, in one instance, from second cousin to second cousin, the sceptre had descended in the family of the Dales; and the acres had remained intact, growing in value and not decreasing in number, though guarded by no entail and protected by no wonderful amount of prudence or wisdom. The estate of Dale of Allington had been coterminous with the parish of Allington for some hundreds of years; and though, as I have said, the race of squires had possessed nothing of superhuman discretion and had perhaps been guided in their walks through life by no very distinct principles, still there had been with them so much of adherence to a sacred law, that no acre of the property had ever been parted from the hands of the existing squire. Some futile attempts had been made to increase the territory, as indeed had been done by Kit Dale, the father of Christopher Dale, who will appear as our squire of Allington when the persons of our drama are introduced. Old Kit Dale, who had married money, had bought outlying farms—a bit of ground here and a bit there—talking, as he did so, much of political influence and of the good old Tory cause. But these farms and bits of ground had gone again before our time. To them had been attached no religion. When old Kit had found himself pressed in that matter of the majority of the Nineteenth Dragoons, in which crack regiment his second son made for himself quite a career, he found it easier to sell than to save—seeing that that which he sold was his own and not the patrimony of the Dales. At his death the remainder of these purchases had gone. Family arrangements required completion, and Christopher Dale required ready money. The outlying farms flew away, as such new purchases had flown before; but the old patrimony of the Dales remained untouched, as it had ever remained.

It had been a religion among them; and seeing that the worship had been carried on without fail, that the vestal fire had never gone down upon the hearth, I should not have said that the Dales had walked their ways without high principle. To this religion they had all adhered, and the new heir had ever entered in upon his domain without other encumbrances than those with which he himself was then already burdened. And yet there had been no entail. The idea of an entail was not in accordance with the peculiarities of the Dale mind. It was necessary to the Dale religion that each squire should have the power of wasting them. I remember to have dined at a house, the whole glory and fortune of which depended on the safety of a glass goblet. We all know the story. If the luck of Edenhall should be shattered, the doom of the family would be sealed. Nevertheless I was bidden to drink out of the fatal glass, as were all guests in that house. It would not have contented the chivalrous mind of the master to protect his doom by lock and key and padded chest. And so it was with the Dales of Allington. To them an entail would have been a lock and key and a padded chest; but the old chivalry of *their house denied to them the use of such protection.*

I have spoken something slightingly of the acquirements and doings of the family; and indeed their acquirements had been few and their doings little. At

MONOTYPE CASLON 128

10 point, 1 point leaded

FORMAT	PICAS	LINES	WPL	CPL	WPP	CPP
Royal 8vo	26×43	47	14.7	79	690	3713
Demy 8vo	24×40	44	13.6	73	597	3212
Large Crown 8vo	23×36	39	12.7	70	496	2730
Crown 8vo	21×34	37	11.8	63	435	2331

father to son, and from uncle to nephew, and, in one instance, from second cousin to second cousin, the sceptre had descended in the family of the Dales; and the acres had remained intact, growing in value and not decreasing in number, though guarded by no entail, and protected by no wonderful amount of prudence or wisdom. The estate of Dale of Allington had been coterminous with the parish of Allington for some hundreds of years; and though, as I have said, the race of squires had possessed nothing of superhuman discretion and had perhaps been guided in their walks through life by no very distinct principles, still there had been with them so much of adherence to a sacred law, that no acre of the property had ever been parted from the hands of the existing squire. Some futile attempts had been made to increase the territory, as indeed had been done by Kit Dale, the father of Christopher Dale, who will appear as our squire of Allington when the persons of our drama are introduced. Old Kit Dale, who had married money, had bought outlying farms—a bit of ground here and a bit there—talking, as he did so, much of political influence and of the good old Tory cause. But these farms and bits of ground had gone again before our time. To them had been attached no religion. When old Kit had found himself pressed in that matter of the majority of the Nineteenth Dragoons, in which crack regiment his second son made for himself quite a career, he found it easier to sell than to save—seeing that that which he sold was his own and not the patrimony of the Dales. At his death the remainder of these purchases had gone. Family arrangements required completion, and Christopher Dale required ready money. The outlying farms flew away, as such new purchases had flown before; but the old patrimony of the Dales remained untouched, as it had ever remained.

It had been a religion among them; and seeing that the worship had been carried on without fail, that the vestal fire had never gone down upon the hearth, I should not have said that the Dales had walked their ways without high principle. To this religion they had all adhered, and the new heir had ever entered in upon his domain without other encumbrances than those with which he himself was then already burdened. And yet there had been no entail. The idea of an entail was not in accordance with the peculiarities of the Dale mind. It was necessary to the Dale religion that each squire should have the power of wasting them. I remember to have dined at a house, the whole glory and fortune of which depended on the safety of a glass goblet. We all know the story. If the luck of Edenhall should be shattered, the doom of the family would be sealed. Nevertheless I was bidden to drink out *of the fatal glass, as were all guests in that house. It would not have contented the chivalrous mind of the master to protect his doom by lock and key and padded chest. And so it was with the Dales of Allington. To them*

MONOTYPE CASLON 128

11 point solid

FORMAT	PICAS	LINES	WPL	CPL	WPP	CPP
Royal 8vo	26×43	47	13.3	71	625	3337
Demy 8vo	24×40	44	12.3	66	544	2904
Large Crown 8vo	23×36	39	11.3	63	440	2457
Crown 8vo	21×34	37	10.3	58	381	2146

father to son, and from uncle to nephew, and, in one instance, from second cousin to second cousin, the sceptre had descended in the family of the Dales; and the acres had remained intact, growing in value and not decreasing in number, though guarded by no entail, and protected by no wonderful amount of prudence or wisdom. The estate of Dale of Allington had been coterminous with the parish of Allington for some hundreds of years; and though, as I have said, the race of squires had possessed nothing of superhuman discretion and had perhaps been guided in their walks through life by no very distinct principles, still there had been with them so much of adherence to a sacred law, that no acre of the property had ever been parted from the hands of the existing squire. Some futile attempts had been made to increase the territory, as indeed had been done by Kit Dale, the father of Christopher Dale, who will appear as our squire of Allington when the persons of our drama are introduced. Old Kit Dale, who had married money, had bought outlying farms—a bit of ground here and a bit there—talking, as he did so, much of political influence and of the good old Tory cause. But these farms and bits of ground had gone again before our time. To them had been attached no religion. When old Kit had found himself pressed in that matter of the majority of the Nineteenth Dragoons, in which crack regiment his second son made for himself quite a career, he found it easier to sell than to save—seeing that that which he sold was his own and not the patrimony of the Dales. At his death the remainder of these purchases had gone. Family arrangements required completion, and Christopher Dale required ready money. The outlying farms flew away, as such purchases had flown before; but the old patrimony of the Dales remained untouched, as it had ever remained.

It had been a religion among them; and seeing that the worship had been carried on without fail, that the vestal fire had never gone down upon the hearth, I should not have said that the Dales had walked their ways without high principle. To this religion they had all adhered, and the new heir had ever entered in upon his domain without other encumbrances than those with which he himself was then already burdened. And yet there had been no entail. The idea of an entail was not in accordance with the peculiarities of the Dale mind. It was necessary to the Dale religion that each squire should have the power *of wasting them. I remember to have dined at a house, the whole glory and fortune of which depended on the safety of a glass goblet. We all know the story. If the luck of Edenhall should be shattered, the doom of the*

MONOTYPE CASLON 128

11 point, 1 point leaded

FORMAT	PICAS	LINES	WPL	CPL	WPP	CPP
Royal 8vo	26×43	43	13.3	71	571	3053
Demy 8vo	24×40	40	12.3	66	490	2640
Large Crown 8vo	23×36	36	11.3	63	409	2268
Crown 8vo	21×34	34	10.3	58	352	1972

father to son, and from uncle to nephew, and, in one instance, from second cousin to second cousin, the sceptre had descended in the family of the Dales; and the acres had remained intact, growing in value and not decreasing in number, though guarded by no entail and protected by no wonderful amount of prudence or wisdom. The estate of Dale of Allington had been coterminous with the parish of Allington for some hundreds of years; and though, as I have said, the race of squires had possessed nothing of superhuman discretion and had perhaps been guided in their walks through life by no very distinct principles, still there had been with them so much of adherence to a sacred law, that no acre of the property had ever been parted from the hands of the existing squire. Some futile attempts had been made to increase the territory, as indeed had been done by Kit Dale, the father of Christopher Dale, who will appear as our squire of Allington when the persons of our drama are introduced. Old Kit Dale, who had married money, had bought outlying farms—a bit of ground here and a bit there—talking, as he did so, much of political influence and of the good old Tory cause. But these farms and bits of ground had gone again before our time. To them had been attached no religion. When old Kit had found himself pressed in that matter of the majority of the Nineteenth Dragoons, in which crack regiment his second son made for himself quite a career, he found it easier to sell than to save—seeing that that which he sold was his own and not the patrimony of the Dales. At his death the remainder of these purchases had gone. Family arrangements required completion, and Christopher Dale required ready money. The outlying farms flew away, as such new purchases had flown before; but the old patrimony of the Dales remained untouched, as it had ever remained.

It had been a religion among them; and seeing that the worship had been carried on without fail, that the vestal fire had never gone down upon the hearth, I should not have said that the Dales had walked their ways without high *principle. To this religion they had all adhered, and the new heir had ever entered in upon his domain without other encumbrances than those with which he himself was then already burdened.*

MONOTYPE CASLON 128

12 point solid

FORMAT	PICAS	LINES	WPL	CPL	WPP	CPP
Royal 8vo	26×43	43	11.0	61	473	2623
Demy 8vo	24×40	40	10.2	56	409	2240
Large Crown 8vo	23×36	36	9.3	54	335	1944
Crown 8vo	21×34	34	8.4	49	284	1666

father to son, and from uncle to nephew, and, in one instance, from second cousin to second cousin, the sceptre had descended in the family of the Dales; and the acres had remained intact, growing in value and not decreasing in number, though guarded by no entail and protected by no wonderful amount of prudence or wisdom. The estate of Dale of Allington had been coterminous with the parish of Allington for some hundreds of years; and though, as I have said, the race of squires had possessed nothing of superhuman discretion and had perhaps been guided in their walks through life by no very distinct principles, still there had been with them so much of adherence to a sacred law, that no acre of the property had ever been parted from the hands of the existing squire. Some futile attempts had been made to increase the territory, as indeed had been done by Kit Dale, the father of Christopher Dale, who will appear as our squire of Allington when the persons of our drama are introduced. Old Kit Dale, who had married money, had bought outlying farms—a bit of ground here and a bit there—talking, as he did so, much of political influence and of the good old Tory cause. But these farms and bits of ground had gone again before our time. To them had been attached no religion. When old Kit had found himself pressed in that matter of the majority of the Nineteenth Dragoons, in which crack regiment his second son made for himself quite a career, he found it easier to sell than to save—seeing that that which he sold was his own and not the patrimony of the Dales. At his death the remainder of these purchases had gone. Family arrangements required completion, and Christopher Dale required ready money. The outlying farms flew away, as such new purchases had flown before; but the old patrimony of the Dales remained untouched, as it had ever remained.

It had been a religion among them; and seeing that the *worship had been carried on without fail, that the vestal fire had never gone down upon the hearth, I should not have said that the Dales had walked their ways without high principle. To this*

MONOTYPE CASLON 128

12 point, 1 point leaded

FORMAT	PICAS	LINES	WPL	CPL	WPP	CPP
Royal 8vo	26×43	40	11.0	61	440	2440
Demy 8vo	24×40	37	10.2	56	380	2072
Large Crown 8vo	23×36	33	9.3	54	307	1782
Crown 8vo	21×34	31	8.4	49	262	1519

father to son, and from uncle to nephew, and, in one instance, from second cousin to second cousin, the sceptre had descended in the family of the Dales; and the acres had remained intact, growing in value and not decreasing in number, though guarded by no entail and protected by no wonderful amount of prudence or wisdom. The estate of Dale of Allington had been coterminous with the parish of Allington for some hundreds of years; and though, as I have said, the race of squires had possessed nothing of superhuman discretion and had perhaps been guided in their walks through life by no very distinct principles, still there had been with them so much of adherence to a sacred law, that no acre of the property had ever been parted from the hands of the existing squire. Some futile attempts had been made to increase the territory, as indeed had been done by Kit Dale, the father of Christopher Dale, who will appear as our squire of Allington when the persons of our drama are introduced. Old Kit Dale, who had married money, had bought outlying farms—a bit of ground here and a bit there—talking, as he did so, much of political influence and of the good old Tory cause. But these farms and bits of ground had gone again before our time. To them had been attached no religion. When old Kit had found himself pressed in that matter of the majority of the Nineteenth Dragoons, in which crack regiment his second son made for himself quite a career, he found it easier to sell than to save—seeing that that which he sold was his own and not the patrimony of the Dales. At his death the remainder of these purchases had *gone. Family arrangements required completion, and Christopher Dale required ready money. The outlying farms flew away, as such new purchases had flown before;*

MONOTYPE CASLON 128

14 point (small face) solid

FORMAT	PICAS	LINES	WPL	CPL	WPP	CPP
Royal 8vo	26×43	37	10.1	56	374	2072
Demy 8vo	24×40	34	9.4	52	320	1768
Large Crown 8vo	23×36	31	8.8	50	274	1550
Crown 8vo	21×34	29	8.2	46	238	1334

MONOTYPE EHRHARDT 453

Synopsis in 10 point

ABCDEFGHIJKLMNOPQRSTUVWXYZ&ÆŒ

ABCDEFGHIJKLMNOPQRSTUVWXYZÆŒ

abcdefghijklmnopqrstuvwxyzæœfiffflffiffl

ABCDEFGHIJKLMNOPQRSTUVWXYZ&ÆŒ

abcdefghijklmnopqrstuvwxyzæœfiffflffiffl

.,:;!?"-()[]£ *:;!?*

1234567890 1234567890 *1234567890* *1234567890*

Related semi-bold · Series 573

ABCDEFGHIJKLMNOPQRSTUVWXYZ&ÆŒ

abcdefghijklmnopqrstuvwxyzæœfiffflffiffl

.,:;!?"-()£ 1234567890

All normal European accents available

Series 453 *and* 573 *available in composition sizes* 8, 9, 10, 11, 12 *point*

Series 573 *italic available in 11 point only*

father to son, and from uncle to nephew, and, in one instance, from second cousin to second cousin, the sceptre had descended in the family of the Dales; and the acres had remained intact, growing in value and not decreasing in number, though guarded by no entail and protected by no wonderful amount of prudence or wisdom. The estate of Dale of Allington had been coterminous with the parish of Allington for some hundreds of years; and though, as I have said, the race of squires had possessed nothing of superhuman discretion and had perhaps been guided in their walks through life by no very distinct principles, still there had been with them so much of adherence to a sacred law, that no acre of the property had ever been parted from the hands of the existing squire. Some futile attempts had been made to increase the territory, as indeed had been done by Kit Dale, the father of Christopher Dale, who will appear as our squire of Allington when the persons of our drama are introduced. Old Kit Dale, who had married money, had bought outlying farms—a bit of ground here and a bit there—talking, as he did so, much of political influence and of the good old Tory cause. But these farms and bits of ground had gone again before our time. To them had been attached no religion. When old Kit had found himself pressed in that matter of the majority of the Nineteenth Dragoons, in which crack regiment his second son made for himself quite a career, he found it easier to sell than to save—seeing that that which he sold was his own and not the patrimony of the Dales. At his death the remainder of these purchases had gone. Family arrangements required completion, and Christopher Dale required ready money. The outlying farms flew away, as such new purchases had flown before; but the old patrimony of the Dales remained untouched, as it had ever remained.

It had been a religion among them; and seeing that the worship had been carried on without fail, that the vestal fire had never gone down upon the hearth, I should not have said that the Dales had walked their ways without high principle. To this religion they had all adhered, and the new heir had ever entered in upon his domain without other encumbrances than those with which he himself was then already burdened. And yet there had been no entail. The idea of an entail was not in accordance with the peculiarities of the Dale mind. It was necessary to the Dale religion that each squire should have the power of wasting them. I remember to have dined at a house, the whole glory and fortune of which depended on the safety of a glass goblet. We all know the story. If the luck of Edenhall should be shattered, the doom of the family would be sealed. Nevertheless I was bidden to drink out of the fatal glass, as were all guests in that house. It would not have contented the chivalrous mind of the master to protect his doom by lock and key and padded chest. And so it was with the Dales of Allington. To them an entail would have been a lock and key and a padded chest; but the old chivalry of their house denied to them the use of such protection.

I have spoken something slightingly of the acquirements and doings of the family; and indeed their acquirements had been few and their doings little. At Allington, Dale of Allington had always been known as a king. At Guestwick, the neighbouring market town, he was a great man—to be seen frequently on *Saturdays, standing in the market-place, and laying down the law as to barley and oxen among men who knew usually more about barley and oxen than he did. At Hamersham, the assize town, he was generally in some repute, being a constant grand*

MONOTYPE EHRHARDT 453

9 point, 1 point leaded

FORMAT	PICAS	LINES	WPL	CPL	WPP	CPP
Royal 8vo	26×43	52	15.1	81	785	4212
Demy 8vo	24×40	48	14.0	75	669	3617
Large Crown 8vo	23×36	43	13.2	72	566	3077
Crown 8vo	21×34	41	12.0	65	494	2663

father to son, and from uncle to nephew, and, in one instance, from second cousin to second cousin, the sceptre had descended in the family of the Dales; and the acres had remained intact, growing in value and not decreasing in number, though guarded by no entail and protected by no wonderful amount of prudence or wisdom. The estate of Dale of Allington had been coterminous with the parish of Allington for some hundreds of years; and though, as I have said, the race of squires had possessed nothing of superhuman discretion and had perhaps been guided in their walks through life by no very distinct principles, still there had been with them so much of adherence to a sacred law, that no acre of the property had ever been parted from the hands of the existing squire. Some futile attempts had been made to increase the territory, as indeed had been done by Kit Dale, the father of Christopher Dale, who will appear as our squire of Allington when the persons of our drama are introduced. Old Kit Dale, who had married money, had bought outlying farms—a bit of ground here and a bit there—talking, as he did so, much of political influence and of the good old Tory cause. But these farms and bits of ground had gone again before our time. To them had been attached no religion. When old Kit had found himself pressed in that matter of the majority of the Nineteenth Dragoons, in which crack regiment his second son made for himself quite a career, he found it easier to sell than to save—seeing that that which he sold was his own and not the patrimony of the Dales. At his death the remainder of these purchases had gone. Family arrangements required completion, and Christopher Dale required ready money. The outlying farms flew away, as such new purchases had flown before; but the old patrimony of the Dales remained untouched, as it had ever remained.

It had been a religion among them; and seeing that the worship had been carried on without fail, that the vestal fire had never gone down upon the hearth, I should not have said that the Dales had walked their ways without high principle. To this religion they had all adhered, and the new heir had ever entered in upon his domain without other encumbrances than those with which he himself was then already burdened. And yet there had been no entail. The idea of an entail was not in accordance with the peculiarities of the Dale mind. It was necessary to the Dale religion that each squire should have the power of wasting them. I remember to have dined at a house, the whole glory and fortune of which depended on the safety of a glass goblet. We all know the story. If the luck of Edenhall should be shattered, the doom of the family would be sealed. Nevertheless I was bidden to drink out of the fatal glass, as were all guests in that house. It would not have contented the chivalrous mind of the master to protect his doom by lock and key and padded chest. And so it was with the Dales of Allington. To them an entail would have been a lock and key and a padded chest; but the old chivalry of their house denied to them the use of such protection.

I have spoken something slightingly of the acquirements and doings of the family; and indeed their acquirements had been few and their doings little. At Allington, Dale of Allington had always been known as a king. At

MONOTYPE EHRHARDT 453

10 point solid

FORMAT	PICAS	LINES	WPL	CPL	WPP	CPP
Royal 8vo	26×43	52	13.8	75	718	3900
Demy 8vo	24×40	48	12.8	69	614	3312
Large Crown 8vo	23×36	43	11.9	66	514	2838
Crown 8vo	21×34	41	10.7	60	437	2460

father to son, and from uncle to nephew, and in one instance, from second cousin to second cousin, the sceptre had descended in the family of the Dales; and the acres had remained intact, growing in value and not decreasing in number, though guarded by no entail and protected by no wonderful amount of prudence or wisdom. The estate of Dale of Allington had been coterminous with the parish of Allington for some hundreds of years; and though as I have said, the race of squires had possessed nothing of superhuman discretion and had perhaps been guided in their walks through life by no very distinct principles, still there had been with them so much of adherence to a sacred law, that no acre of the property had ever been parted from the hands of the existing squire. Some futile attempts had been made to increase the territory, as indeed had been done by Kit Dale, the father of Christopher Dale, who will appear as our squire of Allington when the persons of our drama are introduced. Old Kit Dale, who had married money, had bought outlying farms—a bit of ground here and a bit there—talking, as he did so, much of political influence and of the good old Tory cause. But these farms and bits of ground had gone again before our time. To them had been attached no religion. When old Kit had found himself pressed in that matter of the majority of the Nineteenth Dragoons, in which crack regiment his second son made for himself quite a career, he found it easier to sell than to save—seeing that that which he sold was his own and not the patrimony of the Dales. At his death the remainder of these purchases had gone. Family arrangements required completion, and Christopher Dale required ready money. The outlying farms flew away, as such new purchases had flown before; but the old patrimony of the Dales remained untouched, as it had ever remained.

It had been a religion among them; and seeing that the worship had been carried on without fail, that the vestal fire had never gone down upon the hearth, I should not have said that the Dales had walked their ways without high principle. To this religion they had all adhered, and the new heir had ever entered in upon his domain without other encumbrances than those with which he himself was then already burdened. And yet there had been no entail. The idea of an entail was not in accordance with the peculiarities of the Dale mind. It was necessary to the Dale religion that each squire should have the power of wasting them. I remember to have dined at a house, the whole glory and fortune of which depended on the safety of a glass goblet. We all know the story. If the luck of Edenhall should be shattered, the doom of the family would be sealed. Nevertheless I was bidden to drink out of the fatal glass, as were all guests in that house. It would not have contented the *chivalrous mind of the master to protect his doom by lock and key and padded chest. And so it was with the Dales of Allington. To them an entail would have been a lock and key and a padded chest; but the old chivalry of*

MONOTYPE EHRHARDT 453

10 point, 1 point leaded

FORMAT	PICAS	LINES	WPL	CPL	WPP	CPP
Royal 8vo	26×43	47	13.8	75	648	3525
Demy 8vo	24×40	44	12.8	69	565	3036
Large Crown 8vo	23×36	39	11.9	66	463	2574
Crown 8vo	21×34	37	10.7	60	396	2220

father to son, and from uncle to nephew, and, in one instance, from second cousin to second cousin, the sceptre had descended in the family of the Dales; and the acres had remained intact, growing in value and not decreasing in number, though guarded by no entail and protected by no wonderful amount of prudence or wisdom. The estate of Dale of Allington had been coterminous with the parish of Allington for some hundreds of years; and though, as I have said, the race of squires had possessed nothing of superhuman discretion and had perhaps been guided in their walks through life by no very distinct principles, still there had been with them so much of adherence to a sacred law, that no acre of the property had ever been parted from the hands of the existing squire. Some futile attempts had been made to increase the territory, as indeed had been done by Kit Dale, the father of Christopher Dale, who will appear as our squire of Allington when the persons of our drama are introduced. Old Kit Dale, who had married money, had bought outlying farms —a bit of ground here and a bit there—talking, as he did so, much of political influence and of the good old Tory cause. But these farms and bits of ground had gone again before our time. To them had been attached no religion. When old Kit had found himself pressed in that matter of the majority of the Nineteenth Dragoons, in which crack regiment his second son made for himself quite a career, he found it easier to sell than to save—seeing that that which he sold was his own and not the patrimony of the Dales. At his death the remainder of these purchases had gone. Family arrangements required completion, and Christopher Dale required ready money. The outlying farms flew away, as such new purchases had flown before; but the old patrimony of the Dales remained untouched, as it had ever remained.

It had been a religion among them; and seeing that the worship had been carried on without fail, that the vestal fire had never gone down upon the hearth, I should not have said that the Dales had walked their ways without high principle. To this religion they had all adhered, and the new heir had ever entered in upon his domain without other encumbrances than those with which he himself was then already burdened. And yet there had been no entail. The idea of an entail was not in accordance with the peculiarities of the Dale mind. It was necessary to the Dale religion that each squire should have the power of wasting them. I remember to have dined at a house, the whole glory and fortune of which depended on the safety of a glass goblet. We all know the story. If the luck of Edenhall *should be shattered, the doom of the family would be sealed. Nevertheless I was bidden to drink out of the fatal glass, as were all guests in that house. It would not have contented the chivalrous mind of the*

MONOTYPE EHRHARDT 453

11 point solid

FORMAT	PICAS	LINES	WPL	CPL	WPP	CPP
Royal 8vo	26×43	47	12.8	69	601	3243
Demy 8vo	24×40	44	11.9	64	524	2816
Large Crown 8vo	23×36	39	11.0	61	430	2379
Crown 8vo	21×34	37	10.2	56	378	2072

father to son, and from uncle to nephew, and, in one instance, from second cousin to second cousin, the sceptre had descended in the family of the Dales; and the acres had remained intact, growing in value and not decreasing in number, though guarded by no entail and protected by no wonderful amount of prudence or wisdom. The estate of Dale of Allington had been coterminous with the parish of Allington for some hundreds of years; and though, as I have said, the race of squires had possessed nothing of superhuman discretion and had perhaps been guided in their walks through life by no very distinct principles, still there had been with them so much of adherence to a sacred law, that no acre of the property had ever been parted from the hands of the existing squire. Some futile attempts had been made to increase the territory, as indeed had been done by Kit Dale, the father of Christopher Dale, who will appear as our squire of Allington when the persons of our drama are introduced. Old Kit Dale, who had married money, had bought outlying farms —a bit of ground here and a bit there—talking, as he did so, much of political influence and of the good old Tory cause. But these farms and bits of ground had gone again before our time. To them had been attached no religion. When old Kit had found himself pressed in that matter of the majority of the Nineteenth Dragoons, in which crack regiment his second son made for himself quite a career, he found it easier to sell than to save—seeing that that which he sold was his own and not the patrimony of the Dales. At his death the remainder of these purchases had gone. Family arrangements required completion, and Christopher Dale required ready money. The outlying farms flew away, as such new purchases had flown before; but the old patrimony of the Dales remained untouched, as it had ever remained.

It had been a religion among them; and seeing that the worship had been carried on without fail, that the vestal fire had never gone down upon the hearth, I should not have said that the Dales had walked their ways without high principle. To this religion they had all adhered, and the new heir had ever entered in upon his domain without other encumbrances than those with which he himself was then already burdened. And yet there had been no entail. The idea of an entail was not in accordance with the peculiarities of the Dale *mind. It was necessary to the Dale religion that each squire should have the power of wasting them. I remember to have dined at a house, the whole glory and fortune of which depended on the safety of a glass*

MONOTYPE EHRHARDT 453

11 point, 1 point leaded

FORMAT	PICAS	LINES	WPL	CPL	WPP	CPP
Royal 8vo	26×43	43	12.8	69	550	2967
Demy 8vo	24×40	40	11.9	64	478	2560
Large Crown 8vo	23×36	36	11.0	61	398	2196
Crown 8vo	21×34	34	10.2	56	350	1904

father to son, and from uncle to nephew, and, in one instance, from second cousin to second cousin, the sceptre had descended in the family of the Dales; and the acres had remained intact, growing in value and not decreasing in number, though guarded by no entail and protected by no wonderful amount of prudence or wisdom. The estate of Dale of Allington had been coterminous with the parish of Allington for some hundreds of years; and though, as I have said, the race of squires had possessed nothing of superhuman discretion and had perhaps been guided in their walks through life by no very distinct principles, still there had been with them so much of adherence to a sacred law, that no acre of the property had ever been parted from the hands of the existing squire. Some futile attempts had been made to increase the territory, as indeed had been done by Kit Dale, the father of Christopher Dale, who will appear as our squire of Allington when the persons of our drama are introduced. Old Kit Dale, who had married money, had bought outlying farms —a bit of ground here and a bit there—talking, as he did so, much of political influence and of the good old Tory cause. But these farms and bits of ground had gone again before our time. To them had been attached no religion. When old Kit had found himself pressed in that matter of the majority of the Nineteenth Dragoons, in which crack regiment his second son made for himself quite a career, he found it easier to sell than to save—seeing that that which he sold was his own and not the patrimony of the Dales. At his death the remainder of these purchases had gone. Family arrangements required completion, and Christopher Dale required ready money. The outlying farms flew away, as such new purchases had flown before; but the old patrimony of the Dales remained untouched, as it had ever remained.

It had been a religion among them; and seeing that the worship had been carried on without fail, that the vestal fire had never gone down upon the hearth, I should not have said that the Dales had walked their ways without high principle. To this religion they had all adhered, and the new heir had ever entered in upon his domain *without other encumbrances than those with which he himself was then already burdened. And yet there had been no entail. The idea of an entail was not in accordance with the peculiarities of the Dale mind.*

MONOTYPE EHRHARDT 453

11 point, 2 point leaded

FORMAT	PICAS	LINES	WPL	CPL	WPP	CPP
Royal 8vo	26×43	40	12.8	69	512	2760
Demy 8vo	24×40	37	11.9	64	438	2368
Large Crown 8vo	23×36	33	11.0	61	365	2013
Crown 8vo	21×34	31	10.2	56	317	1736

father to son, and from uncle to nephew, and, in one instance, from second cousin to second cousin, the sceptre had descended in the family of the Dales; and the acres had remained intact, growing in value and not decreasing in number, though guarded by no entail and protected by no wonderful amount of prudence or wisdom. The estate of Dale of Allington had been coterminous with the parish of Allington for some hundreds of years; and though, as I have said, the race of squires had possessed nothing of superhuman discretion and had perhaps been guided in their walks through life by no very distinct principles, still there had been with them so much of adherence to a sacred law, that no acre of property had ever been parted from the hands of the existing squire. Some futile attempts had been made to increase the territory, as indeed had been done by Kit Dale, the father of Christopher Dale, who will appear as our squire of Allington when the persons of our drama are introduced. Old Kit Dale, who had married money, had bought outlying farms—a bit of ground here and a bit there—talking, as he did so, much of political influence and of the good old Tory cause. But these farms and bits of ground had gone again before our time. To them had been attached no religion. When old Kit had found himself pressed in that matter of the majority of the Nineteenth Dragoons, in which crack regiment his second son made for himself quite a career, he found it easier to sell than to save—seeing that that which he sold was his own and not the patrimony of the Dales. At his death the remainder of these purchases had gone. Family arrangements required completion, and Christopher Dale required ready money. The outlying farms flew away, as such new purchases had flown before; but the old patrimony of the Dales remained untouched, as it had ever remained.

It had been a religion among them; and seeing that the worship had been carried on without fail, that the vestal fire had never gone down upon the hearth, I should not have said that *the Dales had walked their ways without high principle. To this religion they had all adhered, and the new heir had ever entered in upon his domain without other encumbrances than those with*

MONOTYPE EHRHARDT 453

12 point, 1 point leaded

FORMAT	PICAS	LINES	WPL	CPL	WPP	CPP
Royal 8vo	26×43	40	11.6	65	464	2600
Demy 8vo	24×40	37	10.7	60	396	2220
Large Crown 8vo	23×36	33	10.2	58	337	1914
Crown 8vo	21×34	31	9.4	53	291	1643

MONOTYPE FOURNIER 185

Synopsis in 10 *point*

ABCDEFGHIJKLMNOPQRSTUVWXYZ&ÆŒ

ABCDEFGHIJKLMNOPQRSTUVWXYZÆŒ

abcdefghijklmnopqrstuvwxyzæœfiffflffiffl

ABCDEFGHIJKLMNOPQRSTUVWXYZ&ÆŒ

abcdefghijklmnopqrstuvwxyzæœfiffflffiffl

.,:;!?‘’-()[]£ *:;!?*

1234567890 *1234567890*

Related shortened capitals · Series 285

ABCDEFGHIJKLMNOPQRSTUVWXYZ&ÆŒ

ABCDEFGHIJKLMNOPQRSTUVWXYZ&ÆŒ

All normal European accents available

Series 185 *available in composition sizes* 8, 9, 10, 11, 12 *point*

Series 285 *shortened caps available in composition sizes* 10, 11, 12 *point*

father to son, and from uncle to nephew, and, in one instance, from second cousin to second cousin, the sceptre had descended in the family of the Dales; and the acres had remained intact, growing in value and not decreasing in number, though guarded by no entail and protected by no wonderful amount of prudence or wisdom. The estate of Dale of Allington had been coterminous with the parish of Allington for some hundreds of years; and though, as I have said, the race of squires had possessed nothing of superhuman discretion and had perhaps been guided in their walks through life by no very distinct principles, still there had been with them so much of adherence to a sacred law, that no acre of the property had ever been parted from the hands of the existing squire. Some futile attempts had been made to increase the territory, as indeed had been done by Kit Dale, the father of Christopher Dale, who will appear as our squire of Allington when the persons of our drama are introduced. Old Kit Dale, who had married money, had bought outlying farms—a bit of ground here and a bit there—talking, as he did so, much of political influence and of the good old Tory cause. But these farms and bits of ground had gone again before our time. To them had been attached no religion. When old Kit had found himself pressed in that matter of the majority of the Nineteenth Dragoons, in which crack regiment his second son made for himself quite a career, he found it easier to sell than to save—seeing that that which he sold was his own and not the patrimony of the Dales. At his death the remainder of these purchases had gone. Family arrangements required completion, and Christopher Dale required ready money. The outlying farms flew away, as such new purchases had flown before; but the old patrimony of the Dales remained untouched, as it had ever remained.

It had been a religion among them; and seeing that the worship had been carried on without fail, that the vestal fire had never gone down upon the hearth, I should not have said that the Dales had walked their ways without high principle. To this religion they had all adhered, and the new heir had ever entered in upon his domain without other encumbrances than those with which he himself was then already burdened. And yet there had been no entail. The idea of an entail was not in accordance with the peculiarities of the Dale mind. It was necessary to the Dale religion that each squire should have the power of wasting them. I remember to have dined at a house, the whole glory and fortune of which depended on the safety of a glass goblet. We all know the story. If the luck of Edenhall should be shattered, the doom of the family would be sealed. Nevertheless, I was bidden to drink out of the fatal glass, as were all guests in that house. It would not have contented the chivalrous mind of the master to protect his doom by lock and key and padded chest. And so it was with the Dales of Allington. To them an entail would have been a lock and key and a padded chest; but the old chivalry of their house denied to them the use of such protection.

I have spoken something slightingly of the acquirements and doings of the family; and indeed their acquirements had been few and their doings little. At Allington, Dale of Allington had always been known as a king. At Guestwick, the neighbouring market town, he was a great man—to be seen frequently on Saturdays, standing in the market-place, and laying down the law as to barley *and oxen among men who knew usually more about barley and oxen than he did. At Hamersham, the assize town, he was generally in some repute, being a constant grand juror for the county, and a man who paid his way. But even at Hamersham the glory of*

MONOTYPE FOURNIER 185

9 point, 1 point leaded

FORMAT	PICAS	LINES	WPL	CPL	WPP	CPP
Royal 8vo	26×43	52	15.4	82	800	4264
Demy 8vo	24×40	48	14.3	76	686	3688
Large Crown 8vo	23×36	43	13.3	73	574	3149
Crown 8vo	21×34	41	12.1	67	498	2737

father to son, and from uncle to nephew, and, in one instance, from second cousin to second cousin, the sceptre had descended in the family of the Dales; and the acres had remained intact, growing in value and not decreasing in number, though guarded by no entail and protected by no wonderful amount of prudence or wisdom. The estate of Dale of Allington had been coterminous with the parish of Allington for some hundreds of years; and though, as I have said, the race of squires had possessed nothing of superhuman discretion and had perhaps been guided in their walks through life by no very distinct principles, still there had been with them so much of adherence to a sacred law, that no acre of the property had ever been parted from the hands of the existing squire. Some futile attempts had been made to increase the territory, as indeed had been done by Kit Dale, the father of Christopher Dale, who will appear as our squire of Allington when the persons of our drama are introduced. Old Kit Dale, who had married money, had bought outlying farms—a bit of ground here and a bit there—talking, as he did so, much of political influence and of the good old Tory cause. But these farms and bits of ground had gone again before our time. To them had been attached no religion. When old Kit had found himself pressed in that matter of the majority of the Nineteenth Dragoons, in which crack regiment his second son made for himself quite a career, he found it easier to sell than to save—seeing that that which he sold was his own and not the patrimony of the Dales. At his death the remainder of these purchases had gone. Family arrangements required completion, and Christopher Dale required ready money. The outlying farms flew away, as such new purchases had flown before; but the old patrimony of the Dales remained untouched, as it had ever remained.

It had been a religion among them; and seeing that the worship had been carried on without fail, that the vestal fire had never gone down upon the hearth, I should not have said that the Dales had walked their ways without high principle. To this religion they had all adhered, and the new heir had ever entered in upon his domain without other encumbrances than those with which he himself was then already burdened. And yet there had been no entail. The idea of an entail was not in accordance with the peculiarities of the Dale mind. It was necessary to the Dale religion that each squire should have the power of wasting them. I remember to have dined at a house, the whole glory and fortune of which depended on the safety of a glass goblet. We all know the story. If the luck of Edenhall should be shattered, the doom of the family would be sealed. Nevertheless I was bidden to drink out of the fatal glass, as were all guests in that house. It would not have contented the chivalrous mind of the master to protect his doom by lock and key and padded chest. And so it was with the Dales of Allington. To them an entail would have been a lock and key and a padded chest; but the old chivalry of their house denied to them the use of such protection.

I have spoken something slightingly of the acquirements and doings of the family; and indeed their acquirements had been few and their doings little. At Allington, Dale of Allington had always been known as a king. At *Guestwick, the neighbouring market town, he was a great man—to be seen frequently on Saturdays, standing in the market-place, and laying down the law as to barley and oxen among men who knew usually more about barley and oxen*

MONOTYPE FOURNIER 185

10 point solid

FORMAT	PICAS	LINES	WPL	CPL	WPP	CPP
Royal 8vo	26×43	52	14.6	78	759	4056
Demy 8vo	24×40	48	13.5	72	650	3456
Large Crown 8vo	22×36	43	12.7	69	544	2967
Crown 8vo	21×34	41	11.8	63	485	2583

father to son, and from uncle to nephew, and, in one instance, from second cousin to second cousin, the sceptre had descended in the family of the Dales; and the acres had remained intact, growing in value and not decreasing in number, though guarded by no entail and protected by no wonderful amount of prudence or wisdom. The estate of Dale of Allington had been coterminous with the parish of Allington for some hundreds of years; and though, as I have said, the race of squires had possessed nothing of superhuman discretion and had perhaps been guided in their walks through life by no very distinct principles, still there had been with them so much of adherence to a sacred law, that no acre of the property had ever been parted from the hands of the existing squire. Some futile attempts had been made to increase the territory, as indeed had been done by Kit Dale, the father of Christopher Dale, who will appear as our squire of Allington when the persons of our drama are introduced. Old Kit Dale, who had married money, had bought outlying farms—a bit of ground here and a bit there—talking, as he did so, much of political influence and of the good old Tory cause. But these farms and bits of ground had gone again before our time. To them had been attached no religion. When old Kit had found himself pressed in that matter of the majority of the Nineteenth Dragoons, in which crack regiment his second son made for himself quite a career, he found it easier to sell than to save—seeing that that which he sold was his own and not the patrimony of the Dales. At his death the remainder of these purchases had gone. Family arrangements required completion, and Christopher Dale required ready money. The outlying farms flew away, as such new purchases had flown before; but the old patrimony of the Dales remained untouched, as it had ever remained.

It had been a religion among them; and seeing that the worship had been carried on without fail, that the vestal fire had never gone down upon the hearth, I should not have said that the Dales had walked their ways without high principle. To this religion they had all adhered, and the new heir had ever entered in upon his domain without other encumbrances than those with which he himself was then already burdened. And yet there had been no entail. The idea of an entail was not in accordance with the peculiarities of the Dale mind. It was necessary to the Dale religion that each squire should have the power of wasting them. I remember to have dined at a house, the whole glory and fortune of which depended on the safety of a glass goblet. We all know the story. If the luck of Edenhall should be shattered, the doom of the family would be sealed. Nevertheless I was bidden to drink out of the fatal glass, as were all guests in that house. It would not have contented the chivalrous mind of the master to protect his doom by lock and key and padded chest. And so it was with the Dales of Allington. To them an entail would have been a lock and key and a padded chest; but the old chivalry of *their house denied to them the use of such protection.*

I have spoken something slightingly of the acquirements and doings of the family; and indeed their acquirements had been few and their doings little. At

MONOTYPE FOURNIER 185

10 point, 1 point leaded

FORMAT	PICAS	LINES	WPL	CPL	WPP	CPP
Royal 8vo	26×43	47	14.6	78	686	3666
Demy 8vo	24×40	44	13.5	72	597	3168
Large Crown 8vo	23×36	39	12.7	69	496	2691
Crown 8vo	21×34	37	11.8	63	437	2331

father to son, and from uncle to nephew, and, in one instance, from second cousin to second cousin, the sceptre had descended in the family of the Dales; and the acres had remained intact, growing in value and not decreasing in number, though guarded by no entail and protected by no wonderful amount of prudence or wisdom. The estate of Dale of Allington had been coterminous with the parish of Allington for some hundreds of years; and though, as I have said, the race of squires had possessed nothing of superhuman discretion, and had perhaps been guided in their walks through life by no very distinct principles, still there had been with them so much of adherence to a sacred law, that no acre of the property had ever been parted from the hands of the existing squire. Some futile attempts had been made to increase the territory, as indeed had been done by Kit Dale, the father of Christopher Dale, who will appear as our squire of Allington when the persons of our drama are introduced. Old Kit Dale, who had married money, had bought outlying farms—a bit of ground here and a bit there—talking, as he did so, much of political influence and of the good old Tory cause. But these farms and bits of ground had gone again before our time. To them had been attached no religion. When old Kit had found himself pressed in that matter of the majority of the Nineteenth Dragoons, in which crack regiment his second son made for himself quite a career, he found it easier to sell than to save—seeing that that which he sold was his own and not the patrimony of the Dales. At his death the remainder of these purchases had gone. Family arrangements required completion, and Christopher Dale required ready money. The outlying farms flew away, as such new purchases had flown before; but the old patrimony of the Dales remained untouched, as it had ever remained.

It had been a religion among them; and seeing that the worship had been carried on without fail, that the vestal fire had never gone down upon the hearth, I should not have said that the Dales had walked their ways without high principle. To this religion they had all adhered, and the new heir had ever entered in upon his domain without other encumbrances than those with which he himself was then already burdened. And yet there had been no entail. The idea of an entail was not in accordance with the peculiarities of the Dale mind. It was necessary to the Dale religion that each squire should have the power of wasting them. I remember to have dined at a house, the whole glory and fortune of which depended on the safety of a glass goblet. We all know the story. If the luck of Edenhall should be shattered, the doom of the family would be sealed. Nevertheless I was bidden to drink out of the *fatal glass, as were all guests in that house. It would not have contented the chivalrous mind of the master to protect his doom by lock and key and padded chest. And so it was with the Dales of Allington. To them an entail*

MONOTYPE FOURNIER 185

11 point solid

FORMAT	PICAS	LINES	WPL	CPL	WPP	CPP
Royal 8vo	26×43	47	13.4	71	629	3337
Demy 8vo	24×40	44	12.4	66	546	2904
Large Crown 8vo	23×36	39	11.4	63	447	2475
Crown 8vo	21×34	37	10.5	58	388	2146

father to son, and from uncle to nephew, and, in one instance, from second cousin to second cousin, the sceptre had descended in the family of the Dales; and the acres had remained intact, growing in value and not decreasing in number, though guarded by no entail and protected by no wonderful amount of prudence or wisdom. The estate of Dale of Allington had been coterminous with the parish of Allington for some hundreds of years; and though, as I have said, the race of squires had possessed nothing of superhuman discretion, and had perhaps been guided in their walks through life by no very distinct principles, still there had been with them so much of adherence to a sacred law, that no acre of the property had ever been parted from the hands of the existing squire. Some futile attempts had been made to increase the territory, as indeed had been done by Kit Dale, the father of Christopher Dale, who will appear as our squire of Allington when the persons of our drama are introduced. Old Kit Dale, who had married money, had bought outlying farms—a bit of ground here and a bit there—talking, as he did so, much of political influence and of the good old Tory cause. But these farms and bits of ground had gone again before our time. To them had been attached no religion. When old Kit had found himself pressed in that matter of the majority of the Nineteenth Dragoons, in which crack regiment his second son made for himself quite a career, he found it easier to sell than to save—seeing that that which he sold was his own and not the patrimony of the Dales. At his death the remainder of these purchases had gone. Family arrangements required completion, and Christopher Dale required ready money. The outlying farms flew away, as such new purchases had flown before; but the old patrimony of the Dales remained untouched, as it had ever remained.

It had been a religion among them; and seeing that the worship had been carried on without fail, that the vestal fire had never gone down upon the hearth, I should not have said that the Dales had walked their ways without high principle. To this religion they had all adhered, and the new heir had ever entered in upon his domain without other encumbrances than those with which he himself was then already burdened. And yet there had been no entail. The idea of an entail was not in accordance with the peculiarities of the Dale mind. It was necessary to the Dale religion that each squire should have the power of wasting *them. I remember to have dined at a house, the whole glory and fortune of which depended on the safety of a glass goblet. We all know the story. If the luck of Edenhall should be shattered, the doom of the family would*

MONOTYPE FOURNIER 185

11 point, 1 point leaded

FORMAT	PICAS	LINES	WPL	CPL	WPP	CPP
Royal 8vo	26×43	43	13.4	71	576	3053
Demy 8vo	24×40	40	12.4	66	491	2640
Large Crown 8vo	23×36	36	11.4	63	408	2268
Crown 8vo	21×34	34	10.5	58	355	1972

father to son, and from uncle to nephew, and, in one instance, from second cousin to second cousin, the sceptre had descended in the family of the Dales; and the acres had remained intact, growing in value and not decreasing in number, though guarded by no entail and protected by no wonderful amount of prudence or wisdom. The estate of Dale of Allington had been coterminous with the parish of Allington for some hundreds of years; and though, as I have said, the race of squires had possessed nothing of superhuman discretion, and had perhaps been guided in their walks through life by no very distinct principles, still there had been with them so much of adherence to a sacred law, that no acre of the property had ever been parted from the hands of the existing squire. Some futile attempts had been made to increase the territory, as indeed had been done by Kit Dale, the father of Christopher Dale, who will appear as our squire of Allington when the persons of our drama are introduced. Old Kit Dale, who had married money, had bought outlying farms—a bit of ground here and a bit there—talking, as he did so, much of political influence and of the good old Tory cause. But these farms and bits of ground had gone again before our time. To them had been attached no religion. When old Kit had found himself pressed in that matter of the majority of the Nineteenth Dragoons, in which crack regiment his second son made for himself quite a career, he found it easier to sell than to save—seeing that that which he sold was his own and not the patrimony of the Dales. At his death the remainder of these purchases had gone. Family arrangements required completion, and Christopher Dale required ready money. The outlying farms flew away, as such new purchases had flown before; but the old patrimony of the Dales remained untouched, as it had ever remained.

It had been a religion among them; and seeing that the worship had been carried on without fail, that the vestal fire had never gone down upon the hearth, I should not have said that the Dales had walked their ways without high principle. To this religion they had all adhered, and the new heir had ever entered in upon his domain without other encumbrances than those with which he himself was then already burdened. And yet there had been no *entail. The idea of an entail was not in accordance with the peculiarities of the Dale mind. It was necessary to the Dale religion that each squire should have the power of wasting them. I remember to*

MONOTYPE FOURNIER 185

12 point solid

FORMAT	PICAS	LINES	WPL	CPL	WPP	CPP
Royal 8vo	26×43	43	12.2	67	524	2881
Demy 8vo	24×40	40	11.3	62	452	2480
Large Crown 8vo	23×36	36	10.5	59	379	2124
Crown 8vo	21×34	34	9.7	54	330	1836

father to son, and from uncle to nephew, and, in one instance, from second cousin to second cousin, the sceptre had descended in the family of the Dales; and the acres had remained intact, growing in value and not decreasing in number, though guarded by no entail and protected by no wonderful amount of prudence or wisdom. The estate of Dale of Allington had been coterminous with the parish of Allington for some hundreds of years; and though, as I have said, the race of squires had possessed nothing of superhuman discretion, and had perhaps been guided in their walks through life by no very distinct principles, still there had been with them so much of adherence to a sacred law, that no acre of the property had ever been parted from the hands of the existing squire. Some futile attempts had been made to increase the territory, as indeed had been done by Kit Dale, the father of Christopher Dale, who will appear as our squire of Allington when the persons of our drama are introduced. Old Kit Dale, who had married money, had bought outlying farms—a bit of ground here and a bit there—talking, as he did so, much of political influence and of the good old Tory cause. But these farms and bits of ground had gone again before our time. To them had been attached no religion. When old Kit had found himself pressed in that matter of the majority of the Nineteenth Dragoons, in which crack regiment his second son made for himself quite a career, he found it easier to sell than to save—seeing that that which he sold was his own and not the patrimony of the Dales. At his death the remainder of these purchases had gone. Family arrangements required completion, and Christopher Dale required ready money. The outlying farms flew away, as such new purchases had flown before; but the old patrimony of the Dales remained untouched, as it had ever remained.

It had been a religion among them; and seeing that the worship had been carried on without fail, that the vestal fire had never gone down upon the hearth, I should not have said that the Dales had walked their ways without high principle. To this religion they *had all adhered, and the new heir had ever entered in upon his domain without other encumbrances than those with which he himself was then already burdened. And yet there had been no entail. The idea*

MONOTYPE FOURNIER 185

12 point, 1 point leaded

FORMAT	PICAS	LINES	WPL	CPL	WPP	CPP
Royal 8vo	26×43	40	12.2	67	488	2680
Demy 8vo	24×40	37	11.3	62	418	2294
Large Crown 8vo	23×36	33	10.5	59	346	1947
Crown 8vo	21×34	31	9.7	54	300	1674

MONOTYPE GARAMOND 156

Synopsis in 10 point

ABCDEFGHIJKLMNOPQRSTUVWXYZ&ÆŒ

ABCDEFGHIJKLMNOPQRSTUVWXYZÆŒ

abcdefghijklmnopqrstuvwxyzæœfiffflffiffl

ABCDEFGHIJKLMNOPQRSTUVWXYZÆŒ

abcdefghijklmnopqrstuvwxyzæœfiffflffiffl

.,:;!?"-()[]£ *;:!?*

1234567890 1234567890 *1234567890*

Related bold · *Series* 201

ABCDEFGHIJKLMNOPQRSTUVWXYZ&ÆŒ

abcdefghijklmnopqrstuvwxyzæœfiffflffiffl

.,:;!?"-()£ 1234567890

All normal European accents available

Series 156 *available in composition sizes* 8, 9, 10, 11, 12, 14, 18 *point*

(14 *and* 18 *point roman only*)

Series 201 *available in composition sizes* 8, 9, 10, 11, 12 *point*

father to son, and from uncle to nephew, and, in one instance, from second cousin to second cousin, the sceptre had descended in the family of the Dales; and the acres had remained intact, growing in value and not decreasing in number, though guarded by no entail and protected by no wonderful amount of prudence or wisdom. The estate of Dale of Allington had been coterminous with the parish of Allington for some hundreds of years; and though, as I have said, the race of squires had possessed nothing of superhuman discretion and had perhaps been guided in their walks through life by no very distinct principles, still there had been with them so much of adherence to a sacred law, that no acre of the property had ever been parted from the hands of the existing squire. Some futile attempts had been made to increase the territory, as indeed had been done by Kit Dale, the father of Christopher Dale, who will appear as our squire of Allington when the persons of our drama are introduced. Old Kit Dale, who had married money, had bought outlying farms—a bit of ground here and a bit there—talking, as he did so, much of political influence and of the good old Tory cause. But these farms and bits of ground had gone again before our time. To them had been attached no religion. When old Kit had found himself pressed in that matter of the majority of the Nineteenth Dragoons, in which crack regiment his second son made for himself quite a career, he found it easier to sell than to save—seeing that that which he sold was his own and not the patrimony of the Dales. At his death the remainder of these purchases had gone. Family arrangements required completion, and Christopher Dale required ready money. The outlying farms flew away, as such new purchases had flown before; but the old patrimony of the Dales remained untouched, as it had ever remained.

It had been a religion among them; and seeing that the worship had been carried on without fail, that the vestal fire had never gone down upon the hearth, I should not have said that the Dales had walked their ways without high principle. To this religion they had all adhered, and the new heir had ever entered in upon his domain without other encumbrances than those with which he himself was then already burdened. And yet there had been no entail. The idea of an entail was not in accordance with the peculiarities of the Dale mind. It was necessary to the Dale religion that each squire should have the power of wasting them. I remember to have dined at a house, the whole glory and fortune of which depended on the safety of a glass goblet. We all know the story. If the luck of Edenhall should be shattered, the doom of the family would be sealed. Nevertheless I was bidden to drink out of the fatal glass, as were all guests in that house. It would not have contented the chivalrous mind of the master to protect his doom by lock and key and padded chest. And so it was with the Dales of Allington. To them an entail would have been a lock and key and a padded chest; but the old chivalry of their house denied to them the use of such protection.

I have spoken something slightingly of the acquirements and doings of the family; and indeed their acquirements had been few and their doings little. *At Allington, Dale of Allington had always been known as a king. At Guestwick, the neighbouring market town, he was a great man—to be seen frequently on Saturdays, standing in the market-place, and laying down the law as to barley and oxen among men*

MONOTYPE GARAMOND 156

9 point. 1 point leaded

FORMAT	PICAS	LINES	WPL	CPL	WPP	CPP
Royal 8vo	26×43	52	14.5	78	754	4056
Demy 8vo	24×40	48	13.4	72	642	3456
Large Crown 8vo	23×36	43	12.4	69	535	2967
Crown 8vo	21×34	41	11.4	63	466	2583

father to son, and from uncle to nephew, and, in one instance, from second cousin to second cousin, the sceptre had descended in the family of the Dales; and the acres had remained intact, growing in value and not decreasing in number, though guarded by no entail and protected by no wonderful amount of prudence or wisdom. The estate of Dale of Allington had been coterminous with the parish of Allington for some hundreds of years; and though, as I have said, the race of squires had possessed nothing of superhuman discretion and had perhaps been guided in their walks through life by no very distinct principles, still there had been with them so much of adherence to a sacred law, that no acre of the property had ever been parted from the hands of the existing squire. Some futile attempts had been made to increase the territory, as indeed had been done by Kit Dale, the father of Christopher Dale, who will appear as our squire of Allington when the persons of our drama are introduced. Old Kit Dale, who had married money, had bought outlying farms—a bit of ground here and a bit there—talking, as he did so, much of political influence and of the good old Tory cause. But these farms and bits of ground had gone again before our time. To them had been attached no religion. When old Kit had found himself pressed in that matter of the majority of the Nineteenth Dragoons, in which crack regiment his second son made for himself quite a career, he found it easier to sell than to save—seeing that that which he sold was his own and not the patrimony of the Dales. At his death the remainder of these purchases had gone. Family arrangements required completion, and Christopher Dale required ready money. The outlying farms flew away, as such new purchases had flown before; but the old patrimony of the Dales remained untouched, as it had ever remained.

It had been a religion among them; and seeing that the worship had been carried on without fail, that the vestal fire had never gone down upon the hearth, I should not have said that the Dales had walked their ways without high principle. To this religion they had all adhered, and the new heir had ever entered in upon his domain without other encumbrances than those with which he himself was then already burdened. And yet there had been no entail. The idea of an entail was not in accordance with the peculiarities of the Dale mind. It was necessary to the Dale religion that each squire should have the power of wasting them. I remember to have dined at a house, the whole glory and fortune of which depended on the safety of a glass goblet. We all know the story. If the luck of Edenhall should be shattered, the doom of the family would be sealed. Nevertheless I was bidden to drink out of the fatal glass, as were all guests in that house. It would not have contented the chivalrous mind of the master to protect his doom by lock and key and padded chest. And so it was with the Dales of Allington. To them an entail would have been a lock and key and a padded chest; *but the old chivalry of their house denied to them the use of such protection.*

I have spoken something slightingly of the acquirements and doings of the family; and indeed their acquirements had been few and their doings little. At

MONOTYPE GARAMOND 156

10 point solid

FORMAT	PICAS	LINES	WPL	CPL	WPP	CPP
Royal 8vo	26×43	52	13.4	71	697	3692
Demy 8vo	24×40	48	12.4	66	597	3168
Large Crown 8vo	23×36	43	11.5	63	496	2709
Crown 8vo	21×34	41	10.4	58	427	2378

father to son, and from uncle to nephew, and, in one instance, from second cousin to second cousin, the sceptre had descended in the family of the Dales; and the acres had remained intact, growing in value and not decreasing in number, though guarded by no entail and protected by no wonderful amount of prudence or wisdom. The estate of Dale of Allington had been coterminous with the parish of Allington for some hundreds of years; and though, as I have said, the race of squires had possessed nothing of superhuman discretion and had perhaps been guided in their walks through life by no very distinct principles, still there had been with them so much of adherence to a sacred law, that no acre of the property had ever been parted from the hands of the existing squire. Some futile attempts had been made to increase the territory, as indeed had been done by Kit Dale, the father of Christopher Dale, who will appear as our squire of Allington when the persons of our drama are introduced. Old Kit Dale, who had married money, had bought outlying farms—a bit of ground here and a bit there—talking, as he did so, much of political influence and of the good old Tory cause. But these farms and bits of ground had gone again before our time. To them had been attached no religion. When old Kit had found himself pressed in that matter of the majority of the Nineteenth Dragoons, in which crack regiment his second son made for himself quite a career, he found it easier to sell than to save—seeing that that which he sold was his own and not the patrimony of the Dales. At his death the remainder of these purchases had gone. Family arrangements required completion, and Christopher Dale required ready money. The outlying farms flew away, as such new purchases had flown before; but the old patrimony of the Dales remained untouched, as it had ever remained.

It had been a religion among them; and seeing that the worship had been carried on without fail, that the vestal fire had never gone down upon the hearth, I should not have said that the Dales had walked their ways without high principle. To this religion they had all adhered, and the new heir had ever entered in upon his domain without other encumbrances than those with which he himself was then already burdened. And yet there had been no entail. The idea of an entail was not in accordance with the peculiarities of the Dale mind. It was necessary to the Dale religion that each squire should have the power of wasting them. I remember to have dined at a house, the whole glory and fortune of which depended on the safety of a glass goblet. We all know the story. If the luck of Edenhall should be shattered, the doom of the family would be sealed. Nevertheless I was bidden to drink out of the *fatal glass, as were all guests in that house. It would not have contented the chivalrous mind of the master to protect his doom by lock and key and padded chest. And so it was with the Dales of Allington. To them an entail would*

MONOTYPE GARAMOND 156

10 point, 1 point leaded

FORMAT	PICAS	LINES	WPL	CPL	WPP	CPP
Royal 8vo	26×43	47	13.4	71	629	3337
Demy 8vo	24×40	44	12.4	66	547	2904
Large Crown 8vo	23×36	39	11.5	63	448	2457
Crown 8vo	21×34	37	10.4	58	384	2146

father to son, and from uncle to nephew, and, in one instance, from second cousin to second cousin, the sceptre had descended in the family of the Dales; and the acres had remained intact, growing in value and not decreasing in number, though guarded by no entail and protected by no wonderful amount of prudence or wisdom. The estate of Dale of Allington had been coterminous with the parish of Allington for some hundreds of years; and though, as I have said, the race of squires had possessed nothing of superhuman discretion and had perhaps been guided in their walks through life by no very distinct principles, still there had been with them so much of adherence to a sacred law, that no acre of the property had ever been parted from the hands of the existing squire. Some futile attempts had been made to increase the territory, as indeed had been done by Kit Dale, the father of Christopher Dale, who will appear as our squire of Allington when the persons of our drama are introduced. Old Kit Dale, who had married money, had bought outlying farms—a bit of ground here and a bit there—talking, as he did so, much of political influence and of the good old Tory cause. But these farms and bits of ground had gone again before our time. To them had been attached no religion. When old Kit had found himself pressed in that matter of the majority of the Nineteenth Dragoons, in which crack regiment his second son made for himself quite a career, he found it easier to sell than to save—seeing that that which he sold was his own and not the patrimony of the Dales. At his death the remainder of these purchases had gone. Family arrangements required completion, and Christopher Dale required ready money. The outlying farms flew away, as such new purchases had flown before; but the old patrimony of the Dales remained untouched, as it had ever remained.

It had been a religion among them; and seeing that the worship had been carried on without fail, that the vestal fire had never gone down upon the hearth, I should not have said that the Dales had walked their ways without high principle. To this religion they had all adhered, and the new heir had ever entered in upon his domain without other encumbrances than those with which he himself was then already burdened. And yet there had been no entail. The idea of an entail was not in accordance with the peculiarities of the Dale mind. It was necessary to the Dale religion that each squire should have the power of wasting *them. I remember to have dined at a house, the whole glory and fortune of which depended on the safety of a glass goblet. We all know the story. If the luck of Edenhall should be shattered, the doom of the family would be sealed. Never-*

MONOTYPE GARAMOND 156

10 point, 2 point leaded

FORMAT	PICAS	LINES	WPL	CPL	WPP	CPP
Royal 8vo	26×43	43	13.4	71	576	3053
Demy 8vo	24×40	40	12.4	66	494	2640
Large Crown 8vo	23×36	36	11.5	63	414	2268
Crown 8vo	21×34	34	10.4	58	354	1972

father to son, and from uncle to nephew, and, in one instance, from second cousin to second cousin, the sceptre had descended in the family of the Dales; and the acres had remained intact, growing in value and not decreasing in number, though guarded by no entail and protected by no wonderful amount of prudence or wisdom. The estate of Dale of Allington had been coterminous with the parish of Allington for some hundreds of years; and though, as I have said, the race of squires had possessed nothing of superhuman discretion and had perhaps been guided in their walks through life by no very distinct principles, still there had been with them so much of adherence to a sacred law, that no acre of the property had ever been parted from the hands of the existing squire. Some futile attempts had been made to increase the territory, as indeed had been done by Kit Dale, the father of Christopher Dale, who will appear as our squire of Allington when the persons of our drama are introduced. Old Kit Dale, who had married money, had bought outlying farms—a bit of ground here and a bit there—talking, as he did so, much of political influence and of the good old Tory cause. But these farms and bits of ground had gone again before our time. To them had been attached no religion. When old Kit had found himself pressed in that matter of the majority of the Nineteenth Dragoons, in which crack regiment his second son made for himself quite a career, he found it easier to sell than to save—seeing that that which he sold was his own and not the patrimony of the Dales. At his death the remainder of these purchases had gone. Family arrangements required completion, and Christopher Dale required ready money. The outlying farms flew away, as such new purchases had flown before; but the old patrimony of the Dales remained untouched, as it had ever remained.

It had been a religion among them; and seeing that the worship had been carried on without fail, that the vestal fire had never gone down upon the hearth, I should not have said that the Dales had walked their ways without high principle. To this religion they had all adhered, and the new heir had ever entered in upon his domain without other encumbrances than those with which he himself was then already burdened. And yet there had been no entail. The idea of an entail was not in accordance with the peculiarities of the Dale mind. It was necessary to the Dale religion that each squire should have the power of wasting them. I remember to have dined at a house, the whole glory and fortune of which *depended on the safety of a glass goblet. We all know the story. If the luck of Edenhall should be shattered, the doom of the family would be sealed. Nevertheless I was bidden to drink out of the fatal glass, as were all guests*

MONOTYPE GARAMOND 156

11 point solid

FORMAT	PICAS	LINES	WPL	CPL	WPP	CPP
Royal 8vo	26×43	47	12.4	67	582	3149
Demy 8vo	24×40	44	11.5	62	508	2728
Large Crown 8vo	23×36	39	10.5	59	410	2301
Crown 8vo	21×34	37	9.8	54	361	1998

father to son, and from uncle to nephew, and, in one instance, from second cousin to second cousin, the sceptre had descended in the family of the Dales; and the acres had remained intact, growing in value and not decreasing in number, though guarded by no entail and protected by no wonderful amount of prudence or wisdom. The estate of Dale of Allington had been coterminous with the parish of Allington for some hundreds of years; and though, as I have said, the race of squires had possessed nothing of superhuman discretion and had perhaps been guided in their walks through life by no very distinct principles, still there had been with them so much of adherence to a sacred law, that no acre of the property had ever been parted from the hands of the existing squire. Some futile attempts had been made to increase the territory, as indeed had been done by Kit Dale, the father of Christopher Dale, who will appear as our squire of Allington when the persons of our drama are introduced. Old Kit Dale, who had married money, had bought outlying farms—a bit of ground here and a bit there—talking, as he did so, much of political influence and of the good old Tory cause. But these farms and bits of ground had gone again before our time. To them had been attached no religion. When old Kit had found himself pressed in that matter of the majority of the Nineteenth Dragoons, in which crack regiment his second son made for himself quite a career, he found it easier to sell than to save—seeing that that which he sold was his own and not the patrimony of the Dales. At his death the remainder of these purchases had gone. Family arrangements required completion, and Christopher Dale required ready money. The outlying farms flew away, as such new purchases had flown before; but the old patrimony of the Dales remained untouched, as it had ever remained.

It had been a religion among them; and seeing that the worship had been carried on without fail, that the vestal fire had never gone down upon the hearth, I should not have said that the Dales had walked their ways without high principle. To this religion they had all adhered, and the new heir had ever entered in upon his domain without other encumbrances than those with which he himself was then already burdened. And yet there had been no *entail. The idea of an entail was not in accordance with the peculiarities of the Dale mind. It was necessary to the Dale religion that each squire should have the power of wasting them. I remember to have dined at a*

MONOTYPE GARAMOND 156

11 point, 1 point leaded

FORMAT	PICAS	LINES	WPL	CPL	WPP	CPP
Royal 8vo	26×43	43	12.4	67	533	2881
Demy 8vo	24×40	40	11.5	62	456	2480
Large Crown 8vo	23×36	36	10.5	59	377	2124
Crown 8vo	21×34	34	9.8	54	334	1836

father to son, and from uncle to nephew, and, in one instance, from second cousin to second cousin, the sceptre had descended in the family of the Dales; and the acres had remained intact, growing in value and not decreasing in number, though guarded by no entail and protected by no wonderful amount of prudence or wisdom. The estate of Dale of Allington had been coterminous with the parish of Allington for some hundreds of years; and though, as I have said, the race of squires had possessed nothing of superhuman discretion and had perhaps been guided in their walks through life by no very distinct principles, still there had been with them so much of adherence to a sacred law, that no acre of the property had ever been parted from the hands of the existing squire. Some futile attempts had been made to increase the territory, as indeed had been done by Kit Dale, the father of Christopher Dale, who will appear as our squire of Allington when the persons of our drama are introduced. Old Kit Dale, who had married money, had bought outlying farms—a bit of ground here and a bit there —talking, as he did so, much of political influence and of the good old Tory cause. But these farms and bits of ground had gone again before our time. To them had been attached no religion. When old Kit had found himself pressed in that matter of the majority of the Nineteenth Dragoons, in which crack regiment his second son made for himself quite a career, he found it easier to sell than to save—seeing that that which he sold was his own and not the patrimony of the Dales. At his death the remainder of these purchases had gone. Family arrangements required completion, and Christopher Dale required ready money. The outlying farms flew away, as such new purchases had flown before; but the old patrimony of the Dales remained untouched, as it had ever remained.

It had been a religion among them; and seeing that the *worship had been carried on without fail, that the vestal fire had never gone down upon the hearth, I should not have said that the Dales had walked their ways without high principle. To this*

MONOTYPE GARAMOND 156

12 point, 1 point leaded

FORMAT	PICAS	LINES	WPL	CPL	WPP	CPP
Royal 8vo	26×43	40	11.1	61	444	2440
Demy 8vo	24×40	37	10.3	56	380	2072
Large Crown 8vo	23×36	33	9.3	53	306	1749
Crown 8vo	21×23	31	8.6	49	268	1519

father to son, and from uncle to nephew, and, in one instance, from second cousin to second cousin, the sceptre had descended in the family of the Dales; and the acres had remained intact, growing in value and not decreasing in number, though guarded by no entail and protected by no wonderful amount of prudence or wisdom. The estate of Dale of Allington had been coterminous with the parish of Allington for some hundreds of years; and though, as I have said, the race of squires had possessed nothing of superhuman discretion and had perhaps been guided in their walks through life by no very distinct principles, still there had been with them so much of adherence to a sacred law, that no acre of the property had ever been parted from the hands of the existing squire. Some futile attempts had been made to increase the territory, as indeed had been done by Kit Dale, the father of Christopher Dale, who will appear as our squire of Allington when the persons of our drama are introduced. Old Kit Dale, who had married money, had bought outlying farms—a bit of ground here and bit there—talking, as he did so, much of political influence and of the good old Tory cause. But these farms and bits of ground had gone again before our time. To them had been attached no religion. When old Kit had found himself pressed in that matter of the majority of the Nineteenth Dragoons, in which crack regiment his second son made for himself quite a career, he found it easier to sell than to save—seeing that that which he sold was his own and not the patrimony of the Dales. At his *death the remainder of these purchases had gone. Family arrangements required completion, aud Christopher Dale required ready money. The outlying farms flew away, as such*

MONOTYPE GARAMOND 156

14 point solid

FORMAT	PICAS	LINES	WPL	CPL	WPP	CCP
Royal 8vo	26×43	37	10.0	53	370	1961
Demy 8vo	24×40	34	9.3	49	315	1666
Large Crown 8vo	23×36	31	8.6	47	267	1457
Crown 8vo	21×34	29	7.7	43	224	1247

father to son, and from uncle to nephew, and, in one instance, from second cousin to the second cousin, the sceptre had descended in the family of the Dales; and the acres had remained intact, growing in value and not decreasing in number, though guarded by no entail and protected by no wonderful amount of prudence or wisdom. The estate of Dale of Allington had been coterminous with the parish of Allington for some hundreds of years; and though, as I have said, the race of squires had possessed nothing of superhuman discretion and had perhaps been guided in their walks through life by no very distinct principles, still there had been with them so much of adherence to a sacred law, that no acre of the property had ever been parted from the hands of the existing squire. Some futile attempts had been made to increase the territory, as indeed had been done by Kit Dale, the father of Christopher Dale, who will *appear as our squire of Allington when the persons of our drama are introduced. Old Kit Dale, who had married money, had bought outlying farms—a bit of ground here and bit*

MONOTYPE GARAMOND 156

18 point solid (italic hand-set)

FORMAT	PICAS	LINES	WPL	CPL	WPP	CPP
Royal 8vo	26×43	29	7.8	42	226	1218
Demy 8vo	24×40	27	7.2	39	194	1053
Large Crown 8vo	23×36	24	6.5	37	157	888
Crown 8vo	21×34	23	6.1	34	140	782

MONOTYPE GOUDY OLD STYLE 291

Synopsis in 10 point

ABCDEFGHIJKLMNOPQRSTUVWXYZ&ÆŒ

ABCDEFGHIJKLMNOPQRSTUVWXYZÆŒ

abcdefghijklmnopqrstuvwxyzæœfiffflffiffl

ABCDEFGHIJKLMNOPQRSTUVWXYZ&

abcdefghijklmnopqrstuvwxyzæœfiffflffiffl

.,:;!?‘’-()£ *:;!?*

1234567890 *1234567890*

Related bold · Series 269

ABCDEFGHIJKLMNOPQRSTUVWXYZ&ÆŒ

abcdefghijklmnopqrstuvwxyzæœfiffflffiffl

.,:;!?‘’-£ 1234567890

All normal European accents available

Series 291 *and* 269 *available in composition sizes* 8, 10, 12 *point* father to son, and from uncle to nephew, and, in one instance, from second cousin to second cousin, the sceptre had descended in the family of the Dales and the acres had remained intact, growing in value and not decreasing in number, though guarded by no entail and protected by no wonderful amount of prudence or wisdom. The estate of Dale of Allington had been coterminous with the parish of Allington for some hundreds of years; and though, as I have said, the race of squires had possessed nothing of superhuman discretion and had perhaps been guided in their walks through life by no very distinct principles, still there had been with them so much of adherence to a sacred law, that no acre of the property had ever been parted from the hands of the existing squire. Some futile attempts had been made to increase the territory, as indeed had been done by Kit Dale, the father of Christopher Dale, who will appear as our squire of Allington when the persons of our drama are introduced. Old Kit Dale, who had married money, had bought outlying farms—a bit of ground here and a bit there—talking, as he did so, much of political influence and of the good old Tory cause. But these farms and bits of ground had gone again before our time. To them had been attached no religion. When old Kit had found himself pressed in that matter of the majority of the Nineteenth Dragoons in which crack regiment his second son made for himself quite a career, he found it easier to sell than to save—seeing that that which he sold was his own and not the patrimony of the Dales. At his death the remainder of these purchases had gone. Family arrangements required completion, and Christopher Dale required ready money. The outlying farms flew away, as such new purchases had flown before; but the old patrimony of the Dales remained untouched, as it had ever remained.

It had been a religion among them; and seeing that the worship had been carried on without fail, that the vestal fire had never gone down upon the hearth, I should not have said that the Dales had walked their ways without high principle. To this religion they had all adhered, and the new heir had ever entered in upon his domain without other encumbrances than those with which he himself was then already burdened. And yet there had been no entail. The idea of an entail was not in accordance with the peculiarities of the Dale mind. It was necessary to the Dale religion that each squire should have the power of wasting them. I remember to have dined at a house, the whole glory and fortune of which depended on the safety of a glass goblet. We all know the story. If the luck of Edenhall should be shattered, the doom of the family would be sealed. Nevertheless I was bidden to drink out of the fatal glass, as were all guests in that house. It would not *have contented the chivalrous mind of the master to protect his doom by lock and key and padded chest. And so it was with the Dales of Allington. To them an entail would have been a lock and key and a padded*

MONOTYPE GOUDY O.S. 291

10 point solid

FORMAT	PICAS	LINES	WPL	CPL	WPP	CPP
Royal 8vo	26×43	52	12.4	67	645	3484
Demy 8vo	24×40	48	11.5	62	556	2976
Large Crown 8vo	23×36	43	10.6	59	458	2537
Crown 8vo	21×34	41	9.7	54	397	2214

father to son, and from uncle to nephew, and, in one instance, from second cousin to second cousin, the sceptre had descended in the family of the Dales and the acres had remained intact, growing in value and not decreasing in number, though guarded by no entail and protected by no wonderful amount of prudence or wisdom. The estate of Dale of Allington had been coterminous with the parish of Allington for some hundreds of years; and though, as I have said, the race of squires had possessed nothing of superhuman discretion and had perhaps been guided in their walks through life by no very distinct principles, still there had been with them so much of adherence to a sacred law, that no acre of the property had ever been parted from the hands of the existing squire. Some futile attempts had been made to increase the territory, as indeed had been done by Kit Dale, the father of Christopher Dale, who will appear as our squire of Allington when the persons of our drama are introduced. Old Kit Dale, who had married money, had bought outlying farms—a bit of ground here and a bit there—talking, as he did so, much of political influence and of the good old Tory cause. But these farms and bits of ground had gone again before our time. To them had been attached no religion. When old Kit had found himself pressed in that matter of the majority of the Nineteenth Dragoons in which crack regiment his second son made for himself quite a career, he found it easier to sell than to save—seeing that that which he sold was his own and not the patrimony of the Dales. At his death the remainder of these purchases had gone. Family arrangements required completion, and Christopher Dale required ready money. The outlying farms flew away, as such new purchases had flown before; but the old patrimony of the Dales remained untouched, as it had ever remained.

It had been a religion among them; and seeing that the worship had been carried on without fail, that the vestal fire had never gone down upon the hearth, I should not have said that the Dales had walked their ways without high principle. To this religion they had all adhered, and the new heir had ever entered in upon his domain without other encumbrances than those with which he himself was then already burdened. And yet there had been no entail. The idea of an entail was not in accordance with the peculiarities of the Dale mind. It was necessary to the Dale religion that each squire should have the power of wasting them. I remember to have dined at a house, the whole glory and fortune *of which depended on the safety of a glass goblet. We all know the story. If the luck of Edenhall should be shattered, the doom of the family would be sealed. Nevertheless I was bidden to drink out of the fatal*

MONOTYPE GOUDY O. S. 291

10 point, 1 point leaded

FORMAT	PICAS	LINES	WPL	CPL	WPP	CPP
Royal 8vo	26×43	47	12.4	67	582	3149
Demy 8vo	24×40	44	11.5	62	503	2728
Large Crown 8vo	23×36	39	10.6	59	412	2301
Crown 8vo	21×34	37	9.7	54	357	1998

father to son, and from uncle to nephew, and, in one instance, from second cousin to second cousin, the sceptre had descended in the family of the Dales; and the acres had remained intact, growing in value and not decreasing in number, though guarded by no entail and protected by no wonderful amount of prudence or wisdom. The estate of Dale of Allington had been coterminous with the parish of Allington for some hundreds of years; and though, as I have said, the race of squires had possessed nothing of superhuman discretion and had perhaps been guided in their walks through life by no very distinct principles, still there had been with them so much of adherence to a sacred law, that no acre of the property had ever been parted from the hands of the existing squire. Some futile attempts had been made to increase the territory, as indeed had been done by Kit Dale, the father of Christopher Dale, who will appear as our squire of Allington when the persons of our drama are introduced. Old Kit Dale, who had married money, had bought outlying farms—a bit of ground here and a bit there—talking, as he did so, much of political influence and of the good old Tory cause. But these farms and bits of ground had gone again before our time. To them had been attached no religion. When old Kit had found himself pressed in that matter of the majority of the Nineteenth Dragoons, in which crack regiment his second son made for himself quite a career, he found it easier to sell than to save—seeing that that which he sold was his own and not the patrimony of the Dales. At his death the remainder of these purchases had gone. Family arrangements required completion, and Christopher Dale required ready money. The outlying *farms flew away, as such new purchases had flown before; but the old patrimony of the Dales remained untouched, as it had ever remained.*

MONOTYPE GOUDY O.S. 291

12 point, 1 point leaded

FORMAT	PICAS	LINES	WPL	CPL	WPP	CPP
Royal 8vo	26×43	40	9.8	56	392	2240
Demy 8vo	24×40	37	9.1	52	334	1924
Large Crown 8vo	23×36	33	8.4	49	278	1617
Crown 8vo	21×34	31	7.6	45	238	1395

MONOTYPE IMPRINT 101

Synopsis in 10 point

ABCDEFGHIJKLMNOPQRSTUVWXYZ&ÆŒ

ABCDEFGHIJKLMNOPQRSTUVWXYZÆŒ

abcdefghijklmnopqrstuvwxyzæœfiffflffiffl

ABCDEFGHIJKLMNOPQRSTUVWXYZ&ÆŒ

abcdefghijklmnopqrstuvwxyzæœfiffflffiffl

.,:;!?‘’-()[]£ *:;!?*

1234567890 *1234567890* 1234567890 *1234567890*

Related bold · Series 310

ABCDEFGHIJKLMNOPQRSTUVWXYZ&ÆŒ

abcdefghijklmnopqrstuvwxyzæœfiffflffiffl

.,:;!?‘’-()£ 1234567890

All normal European accents available

Series 101 *available in composition sizes* 7, 8, 9, 10, 11, 12, 14, 18 *point*

(18 *point roman only*)

Series 310 *available in composition sizes* 8, 9, 10, 11, 12 *point*

father to son, and from uncle to nephew, and, in one instance, from second cousin to second cousin, the sceptre had descended in the family of the Dales; and the acres had remained intact, growing in value and not decreasing in number, though guarded by no entail and protected by no wonderful amount of prudence or wisdom. The estate of Dale of Allington had been coterminous with the parish of Allington for some hundreds of years; and though, as I have said, the race of squires had possessed nothing of superhuman discretion and had perhaps been guided in their walks through life by no very distinct principles, still there had been with them so much of adherence to a sacred law, that no acre of the property had ever been parted from the hands of the existing squire. Some futile attempts had been made to increase the territory, as indeed had been done by Kit Dale, the father of Christopher Dale, who will appear as our squire of Allington when the persons of our drama are introduced. Old Kit Dale, who had married money, had bought outlying farms—a bit of ground here and a bit there—talking, as he did so, much of political influence and of the good old Tory cause. But these farms and bits of ground had gone again before our time. To them had been attached no religion. When old Kit had found himself pressed in that matter of the majority of the Nineteenth Dragoons, in which crack regiment his second son made for himself quite a career, he found it easier to sell than to save—seeing that that which he sold was his own and not the patrimony of the Dales. At his death the remainder of these purchases had gone. Family arrangements required completion, and Christopher Dale required ready money. The outlying farms flew away, as such new purchases had flown before; but the old patrimony of the Dales remained untouched, as it had ever remained.

It had been a religion among them; and seeing that the worship had been carried on without fail, that the vestal fire had never gone down upon the hearth, I should not have said that the Dales had walked their ways without high principle. To this religion they had all adhered, and the new heir had ever entered in upon his domain without other encumbrances than those with which he himself was then already burdened. And yet there had been no entail. The idea of an entail was not in accordance with the peculiarities of the Dale mind. It was necessary to the Dale religion that each squire should have the power of wasting them. I remember to have dined at a house, the whole glory and fortune of which depended on the safety of a glass goblet. We all know the story. If the luck of Edenhall should be shattered, the doom of the family would be sealed. Nevertheless I was bidden to drink out of the fatal glass, as were all guests in that house. It would not have contented the chivalrous mind of the master to protect his doom by lock and key and padded chest. And so it was with the Dales of Allington. To them an entail would have been a lock and key and a padded chest; but the old chivalry of their house denied to them the use of such protection.

I have spoken something slightingly of the acquirements and doings of the family; and indeed their acquirements had been few and their doings little. At Allington, Dale of Allington had always been known as a king. At Guestwick,

MONOTYPE IMPRINT 101

9 point, 1 point leaded

FORMAT	PICAS	LINES	WPL	CPL	WPP	CPP
Royal 8vo	26×43	52	13.7	75	712	3900
Demy 8vo	24×40	48	12.7	69	610	3312
Large Crown 8vo	23×36	43	12.2	66	527	2871
Crown 8vo	21×34	41	11.2	60	460	2500

father to son, and from uncle to nephew, and, in one instance, from second cousin to second cousin, the sceptre had descended in the family of the Dales; and the acres had remained intact, growing in value and not decreasing in number, though guarded by no entail and protected by no wonderful amount of prudence or wisdom. The estate of Dale of Allington had been coterminous with the parish of Allington for some hundreds of years; and though, as I have said, the race of squires had possessed nothing of superhuman discretion and had perhaps been guided in their walks through life by no very distinct principles, still there had been with them so much of adherence to a sacred law, that no acre of the property had ever been parted from the hands of the existing squire. Some futile attempts had been made to increase the territory, as indeed had been done by Kit Dale, the father of Christopher Dale, who will appear as our squire of Allington when the persons of our drama are introduced. Old Kit Dale, who had married money, had bought outlying farms—a bit of ground here and a bit there—talking, as he did so, much of political influence and of the good old Tory cause. But these farms and bits of ground had gone again before our time. To them had been attached no religion. When old Kit had found himself pressed in that matter of the majority of the Nineteenth Dragoons, in which crack regiment his second son made for himself quite a career, he found it easier to sell than to save—seeing that that which he sold was his own and not the patrimony of the Dales. At his death the remainder of these purchases had gone. Family arrangements required completion, and Christopher Dale required ready money. The outlying farms flew away, as such new purchases had flown before; but the old patrimony of the Dales remained untouched, as it had ever remained.

It had been a religion among them; and seeing that the worship had been carried on without fail, that the vestal fire had never gone down upon the hearth, I should not have said that the Dales had walked their ways without high principle. To this religion they had all adhered, and the new heir had ever entered in upon his domain without other encumbrances than those with which he himself was then already burdened. And yet there had been no entail. The idea of an entail was not in accordance with the peculiarities of the Dale mind. It was necessary to the Dale religion that each squire should have the power of wasting them. I remember to have dined at a house, the whole glory and fortune of which depended on the safety of a glass goblet. We all know the story. If the luck of Endenhall should be shattered, the doom of the family would be sealed. Nevertheless I was bidden to drink out of the fatal glass, as were all guests in that house. It would not have contented the chivalrous mind of the master to protect his doom by lock and key and padded chest. And so it was with the Dales of Allington. To them an entail would have been a lock and key and a padded chest; but the old chivalry of their house denied to them the use of such protection.

I have spoken something slightingly of the acquirements and doings of the family; and indeed their acquirements had been few and their doings little. At Allington, Dale of Allington had always been known as a king. At

MONOTYPE IMPRINT 101

10 point solid

FORMAT	PICAS	LINES	WPL	CPL	WPP	CPP
Royal 8vo	26×43	52	13.7	73	712	3796
Demy 8vo	24×40	48	12.7	67	609	3216
Large Crown 8vo	23×36	43	11.8	64	509	2752
Crown 8vo	21×34	41	10.8	58	444	2378

father to son, and from uncle to nephew, and, in one instance, from second cousin to second cousin, the sceptre had descended in the family of the Dales; and the acres had remained intact, growing in value and not decreasing in number, though guarded by no entail and protected by no wonderful amount of prudence or wisdom. The estate of Dale of Allington had been coterminous with the parish of Allington for some hundreds of years; and though, as I have said, the race of squires had possessed nothing of superhuman discretion and had perhaps been guided in their walks through life by no very distinct principles, still there had been with them so much of adherence to a sacred law, that no acre of the property had ever been parted from the hands of the existing squire. Some futile attempts had been made to increase the territory, as indeed had been done by Kit Dale, the father of Christopher Dale, who will appear as our squire of Allington when the persons of our drama are introduced. Old Kit Dale, who had married money, had bought outlying farms—a bit of ground here and a bit there—talking, as he did so, much of political influence and of the good old Tory cause. But these farms and bits of ground had gone again before our time. To them had been attached no religion. When old Kit had found himself pressed in that matter of the majority of the Nineteenth Dragoons, in which crack regiment his second son made for himself quite a career, he found it easier to sell than to save—seeing that that which he sold was his own and not the patrimony of the Dales. At his death the remainder of these purchases had gone. Family arrangements required completion, and Christopher Dale required ready money. The outlying farms flew away, as such new purchases had flown before; but the old patrimony of the Dales remained untouched, as it had ever remained.

It had been a religion among them; and seeing that the worship had been carried on without fail, that the vestal fire had never gone down upon the hearth, I should not have said that the Dales had walked their ways without high principle. To this religion they had all adhered, and the new heir had ever entered in upon his domain without other encumbrances than those with which he himself was then already burdened. And yet there had been no entail. The idea of an entail was not in accordance with the peculiarities of the Dale mind. It was necessary to the Dale religion that each squire should have the power of wasting them. I remember to have dined at a house, the whole glory and fortune of which depended on the safety of a glass goblet. We all know the story. If the luck of Edenhall should be shattered, the doom of the family would be sealed. Nevertheless I was bidden to drink out of the fatal glass, as were all guests in that house. It would not have contented the *chivalrous mind of the master to protect his doom by lock and key and padded chest. And so it was with the Dales of Allington. To them an entail would have been a lock and key and a padded chest; but the old chivalry of*

MONOTYPE IMPRINT 101

10 point, 1 point leaded

FORMAT	PICAS	LINES	WPL	CPL	WPP	CPP
Royal 8vo	26×43	47	13.7	73	643	3431
Demy 8vo	24×40	44	12.7	67	562	2948
Large Crown 8vo	23×36	39	11.8	64	459	2496
Crown 8vo	21×34	37	10.8	58	399	2146

father to son, and from uncle to nephew, and, in one instance, from second cousin to second cousin, the sceptre had descended in the family of the Dales; and the acres had remained intact, growing in value and not decreasing in number, though guarded by no entail and protected by no wonderful amount of prudence or wisdom. The estate of Dale of Allington had been coterminous with the parish of Allington for some hundreds of years; and though, as I have said, the race of squires had possessed nothing of superhuman discretion and had perhaps been guided in their walks through life by no very distinct principles, still there had been with them so much of adherence to a sacred law, that no acre of the property had ever been parted from the hands of the existing squire. Some futile attempts had been made to increase the territory, as indeed had been done by Kit Dale, the father of Christopher Dale, who will appear as our squire of Allington when the persons of our drama are introduced. Old Kit Dale, who had married money, had bought outlying farms—a bit of ground here and a bit there—talking, as he did so, much of political influence and of the good old Tory cause. But these farms and bits of ground had gone again before our time. To them had been attached no religion. When old Kit had found himself pressed in that matter of the majority of the Nineteenth Dragoons, in which crack regiment his second son made for himself quite a career, he found it easier to sell than to save—seeing that that which he sold was his own and not the patrimony of the Dales. At his death the remainder of these purchases had gone. Family arrangements required completion, and Christopher Dale required ready money. The outlying farms flew away, as such new purchases had flown before; but the old patrimony of the Dales remained untouched, as it had ever remained.

It had been a religion among them; and seeing that the worship had been carried on without fail, that the vestal fire had never gone down upon the hearth, I should not have said that the Dales had walked their ways without high principle. To this religion they had all adhered, and the new heir had ever entered in upon his domain without other encumbrances than those with which he himself was then already burdened. And yet there had been no entail. The idea of an entail was not in accordance with the peculiarities of the Dale mind. It was necessary to the Dale religion that each squire should have the power of wasting them. I remember to have dined at a house, the whole glory and fortune *of which depended on the safety of a glass goblet. We all know the story. If the luck of Edenhall should be shattered, the doom of the family would be sealed. Nevertheless I was bidden to drink out of the*

MONOTYPE IMPRINT 101

11 point (small face) solid

FORMAT	PICAS	LINES	WPL	CPL	WPP	CPP
Royal 8vo	26×43	47	12.3	67	578	3149
Demy 8vo	24×40	44	11.4	62	502	2728
Large Crown 8vo	23×36	39	10.5	60	411	2340
Crown 8vo	21×34	37	9.7	55	360	2035

father to son, and from uncle to nephew, and, in one instance, from second cousin to second cousin, the sceptre had descended in the family of the Dales; and the acres had remained intact, growing in value and not decreasing in number, though guarded by no entail and protected by no wonderful amount of prudence or wisdom. The estate of Dale of Allington had been coterminous with the parish of Allington for some hundreds of years; and though, as I have said, the race of squires had possessed nothing of superhuman discretion and had perhaps been guided in their walks through life by no very distinct principles, still there had been with them so much of adherence to a sacred law, that no acre of the property had ever been parted from the hands of the existing squire. Some futile attempts had been made to increase the territory, as indeed had been done by Kit Dale, the father of Christopher Dale, who will appear as our squire of Allington when the persons of our drama are introduced. Old Kit Dale, who had married money, had bought outlying farms—a bit of ground here and a bit there—talking, as he did so, much of political influence and of the good old Tory cause. But these farms and bits of ground had gone again before our time. To them had been attached no religion. When old Kit had found himself pressed in that matter of the majority of the Nineteenth Dragoons, in which crack regiment his second son made for himself quite a career, he found it easier to sell than to save—seeing that that which he sold was his own and not the patrimony of the Dales. At his death the remainder of these purchases had gone. Family arrangements required completion, and Christopher Dale required ready money. The outlying farms flew away, as such new purchases had flown before; but the old patrimony of the Dales remained untouched, as it had ever remained.

It had been a religion among them; and seeing that the worship had been carried on without fail, that the vestal fire had never gone down upon the hearth, I should not have said that the Dales had walked their ways without high principle. To this religion they had all adhered, and the new heir had ever entered in upon his domain without other encumbrances than those with which he himself was then already burdened. And yet there had been no *entail. The idea of an entail was not in accordance with the peculiarities of the Dale mind. It was necessary to the Dale religion that each squire should have the power of wasting them. I remember to*

MONOTYPE IMPRINT 101

11 point (small face), 1 point leaded

FORMAT	PICAS	LINES	WPL	CPL	WPP	CPP
Royal 8vo	26×43	43	12.3	67	528	2881
Demy 8vo	24×40	40	11.4	62	452	2480
Large Crown 8vo	23×36	36	10.5	60	377	2160
Crown 8vo	21×34	34	9.7	55	330	1870

father to son, and from uncle to nephew, and, in one instance, from the second cousin to the second cousin, the sceptre had descended in the family of the Dales; and the acres had remained intact, growing in value and not decreasing in number, though guarded by no entail and protected by no wonderful amount of prudence or wisdom. The estate of Dale of Allington had been coterminous with the parish of Allington for some hundreds of years; and though, as I have said, the race of squires had possessed nothing of superhuman discretion and had perhaps been guided in their walks through life by no very distinct principles, still there had been with them so much of adherence to a sacred law, that no acre of the property had ever been parted from the hands of the existing squire. Some futile attempts had been made to increase the territory, as indeed had been done by Kit Dale, the father of Christopher Dale, who will appear as our squire of Allington when the persons of our drama are introduced. Old Kit Dale, who had married money, had bought outlying farms—a bit of ground here and a bit there—talking, as he did so, much of political influence and of the good old Tory cause. But these farms and bits of ground had gone again before our time. To them had been attached no religion. When old Kit had found himself pressed in that matter of the majority of the Nineteenth Dragoons, in which crack regiment his second son made for himself quite a career, he found it easier to sell than to save—seeing that that which he sold was his own and not the patrimony of the Dales. At his death the remainder of these purchases had gone. Family arrangements required completion, and Christopher Dale required ready money. The outlying farms flew away, as such new purchases had flown before; but the old patrimony of the Dales remained untouched, as it had ever remained.

It had been a religion among them; and seeing that the worship had been carried on without fail, that the vestal *fire had never gone down upon the hearth, I should not have said that the Dales had walked their ways without high principle. To this religion they had all adhered, and the new*

MONOTYPE IMPRINT 101

12 point solid

FORMAT	PICAS	LINES	WPL	CPL	WPP	CPP
Royal 8vo	26×43	43	10.5	58	451	2494
Demy 8vo	24×40	40	9.7	54	388	2160
Large Crown 8vo	23×36	36	8.9	52	319	1872
Crown 8vo	21×34	34	8.3	47	284	1598

father to son, and from uncle to nephew, and, in one instance, from the second cousin to the second cousin, the sceptre had descended in the family of the Dales; and the acres had remained intact, growing in value and not decreasing in number, though guarded by no entail and protected by no wonderful amount of prudence or wisdom. The estate of Dale of Allington had been coterminous with the parish of Allington for some hundreds of years; and though, as I have said, the race of squires had possessed nothing of superhuman discretion and had perhaps been guided in their walks through life by no very distinct principles, still there had been with them so much of adherence to a sacred law, that no acre of the property had ever been parted from the hands of the existing squire. Some futile attempts had been made to increase the territory, as indeed had been done by Kit Dale, the father of Christopher Dale, who will appear as our squire of Allington when the persons of our drama are introduced. Old Kit Dale, who had married money, had bought outlying farms—a bit of ground here and a bit there—talking, as he did so, much of political influence and of the good old Tory cause. But these farms and bits of ground had gone again before our time. To them had been attached no religion. When old Kit had found himself pressed in that matter of the majority of the Nineteenth Dragoons, in which crack regiment his second son made for himself quite a career, he found it easier to sell than to save—seeing that that which he sold was his own and not the patrimony of the Dales. At his death the remainder of these purchases had gone. Family arrangements required completion, and Christopher Dale required ready money. The outlying farms flew away, as such new purchases had flown before; but the old patrimony of the Dales remained untouched, as it had *ever remained.*

It had been a religion among them; and seeing that the worship had been carried on without fail, that the vestal

MONOTYPE IMPRINT 101

12 point, 1 point leaded

FORMAT	PICAS	LINES	WPL	CPL	WPP	CPP
Royal 8vo	26×43	40	10.5	58	420	2320
Demy 8vo	24×40	37	9.7	54	355	1998
Large Crown 8vo	23×36	33	8.9	52	295	1716
Crown 8vo	21×34	31	8.3	47	258	1457

father to son, and from uncle to nephew, and in one instance, from second cousin to second cousin, the sceptre had descended in the family of the Dales; and the acres had remained intact, growing in value and not decreasing in number, though guarded by no entail and protected by no wonderful amount of prudence or wisdom. The estate of Dale of Allington had been coterminous with the parish of Allington for some hundreds of years; and though, as I have said, the race of squires had possessed nothing of superhuman discretion and had perhaps been guided in their walks through life by no very distinct principles, still there had been with them so much of adherence to a sacred law, that no acre of the property had ever been parted from the hands of the existing squire. Some futile attempts had been made to increase the territory, as indeed had been done by Kit Dale, the father of Christopher Dale, who will appear as our squire of Allington when the persons of our drama are introduced. Old Kit Dale, who had married money, had bought outlying farms—a bit of ground here and a bit there—talking, as he did so, much of political influence and of the good old Tory cause. But these farms and bits of ground had gone again before our time. To them had been attached no religion. When old Kit had found himself pressed in that matter of the majority of the Nineteenth Dragoons, in which crack regiment his second son made for himself quite a career, he found it easier to sell than to save—seeing that that which he sold was his own *and not the patrimony of the Dales. At his death the remainder of these purchases had gone. Family arrangements required completion, and Christopher*

MONOTYPE IMPRINT 101

14 point solid

FORMAT	PICAS	LINES	WPL	CPL	WPP	CPP
Royal 8vo	26×43	37	9.7	52	360	1924
Demy 8vo	24×40	34	9.0	48	304	1632
Large Crown 8vo	23×36	31	8.4	46	261	1426
Crown 8vo	21×34	29	7.7	42	222	1218

father to son, and from uncle to nephew, and, in, one instance, from second cousin to second cousin, the sceptre had descended in the family of the Dales; and the acres had remained intact, growing in value and not decreasing in number, though guarded by no entail and protected by no wonderful amount of prudence or wisdom. The estate of Dale of Allington had been coterminous with the parish of Allington for some hundreds of years; and though, as I have said, the race of squires had possessed nothing of superhuman discretion and had perhaps been guided in their walks through life by no very distinct principles, still there had been with them so much of adherence to a sacred law, that no acre of the property had ever been parted from the hands of the existing squire. Some futile attempts had been made to increase the territory, *as indeed had been done by Kit Dale, the father of Christopher Dale, who will appear as our squire of Allington when the persons of our drama are*

MONOTYPE IMPRINT 101

18 point solid (italic hand-set)

FORMAT	PICAS	LINES	WPL	CPL	WPP	CPP
Royal 8vo	26×43	29	7.0	39	203	1131
Demy 8vo	24×40	27	6.6	36	178	972
Large Crown 8vo	23×36	24	6.0	34	145	816
Crown 8vo	21×34	23	5.8	31	133	713

MONOTYPE MODERN 7

Synopsis in 10 *point*

ABCDEFGHIJKLMNOPQRSTUVWXYZ&ÆŒ

ABCDEFGHIJKLMNOPQRSTUVWXYZÆŒ

abcdefghijklmnopqrstuvwxyzæœfiffflffiffl

ABCDEFGHIJKLMNOPQRSTUVWXYZ &ÆŒ

abcdefghijklmnopqrstuvwxyzæœfiffflffiffl

.,:;!?"-()[]£ *:;!?* 1234567890 *1234567890*

Related bold · Latin Antique Series 9

ABCDEFGHIJKLMNOPQRSTUVWXYZ &ÆŒ

abcdefghijklmnopqrstuvwxyzæœfiffflffiffl

.,:;!?"-()£ 1234567890

Related bold · Clarendon Series 12

ABCDEFGHIJKLMNOPQRSTUVWXYZ &ÆŒ

abcdefghijklmnopqrstuvwxyzæœfiffflffiffl

.,:;!?"-()£ 1234567890

Related bold · Grotesque Bold Condensed No. 2 *Series* 15

ABCDEFGHIJKLMNOPQRSTUVWXYZ &ÆŒ

abcdefghijklmnopqrstuvwxyzæœfiffflffiffl

.,:;!?"-()£ 1234567890

All normal European accents available

Series 7 *available in composition sizes* 6, 7, 8, 9, 10, 11, 12 *point*

Series 9 *available in composition sizes* 8, 10, 11, 12 *point*

Series 12 *available in composition sizes* 5, 6, 8, 10, 11 *point*

Series 15 *available in composition sizes* 6, 8, 10, 12 *point*

father to son, and from uncle to nephew, and, in one instance, from second cousin to second cousin, the sceptre had descended in the family of the Dales; and the acres had remained intact, growing in value and not decreasing in number, though guarded by no entail and protected by no wonderful amount of prudence or wisdom. The estate of Dale of Allington had been coterminous with the parish of Allington for some hundreds of years; and though, as I have said, the race of squires had possessed nothing of superhuman discretion and had perhaps been guided in their walks through life by no very distinct principles, still there had been with them so much of adherence to a sacred law, that no acre of the property had ever been parted from the hands of the existing squire. Some futile attempts had been made to increase the territory, as indeed had been done by Kit Dale, the father of Christopher Dale, who will appear as our squire of Allington when the persons of our drama are introduced. Old Kit Dale, who had married money, had bought outlying farms—a bit of ground here and a bit there—talking, as he did so, much of political influence and of the good old Tory cause. But these farms and bits of ground had gone again before our time. To them had been attached no religion. When old Kit had found himself pressed in that matter of the majority of the Nineteenth Dragoons, in which crack regiment his second son made for himself quite a career, he found it easier to sell than to save—seeing that that which he sold was his own and not the patrimony of the Dales. At his death the remainder of these purchases had gone. Family arrangements required completion, and Christopher Dale required ready money. The outlying farms flew away, as such new purchases had flown before; but the old patrimony of the Dales remained untouched, as it had ever remained.

It had been a religion among them; and seeing that the worship had been carried on without fail, that the vestal fire had never gone down upon the hearth, I should not have said that the Dales had walked their ways without high principle. To this religion they had all adhered, and the new heir had ever entered in upon his domain without other encumbrances than those with which he himself was then already burdened. And yet there had been no entail. The idea of an entail was not in accordance with the peculiarities of the Dale mind. It was necessary to the Dale religion that each squire should have the power of wasting them. I remember to have dined at a house, the whole glory and fortune of which depended on the safety of a glass goblet. We all know the story. If the luck of Edenhall should be shattered, the doom of the family would be sealed. Nevertheless I was bidden to drink out of the fatal glass, as were all guests in that house. It would not have contented the chivalrous mind of the master to protect his doom by lock and key and padded chest. *And so it was with the Dales of Allington. To them an entail would have been a lock and key and a padded chest; but the old chivalry of their house denied to them the use of such protection.*

MONOTYPE MODERN 7

10 point solid

FORMAT	PICAS	LINES	WPL	CPL	WPP	CPP
Royal 8vo	26×43	52	12.8	69	666	3588
Demy 8vo	24×40	48	11.9	64	571	3072
Large Crown 8vo	23×36	43	11.4	61	489	2623
Crown 8vo	21×34	41	10.5	56	429	2296

father to son, and from uncle to nephew, and, in one instance, from second cousin to second cousin, the sceptre had descended in the family of the Dales, and the acres had remained intact, growing in value and not decreasing in number, though guarded by no entail and protected by no wonderful amount of prudence or wisdom. The estate of Dale of Allington had been coterminous with the parish of Allington for some hundreds of years; and though, as I have said, the race of squires had pessessed nothing of superhuman discretion and had perhaps been guided in their walks through life by no very distinct principles, still there had been with them so much of adherence to a sacred law, that no acre of the property had ever been parted from the hands of the existing squire. Some futile attempts had been made to increase the territory, as indeed had been done by Kit Dale, the father of Christopher Dale, who will appear as our squire of Allington when the persons of our drama are introduced. Old Kit Dale, who had married money, had bought outlying farms—a bit of ground here and a bit there—talking, as he did so, much of political influence and of the good old Tory cause. But these farms and bits of ground had gone again before our time. To them had been attached no religion. When old Kit had found himself pressed in that matter of the majority of the Nineteenth Dragoons, in which crack regiment his second son made for himself quite a career, he found it easier to sell than to save—seeing that that which he sold was his own and not the patrimony of the Dales. At his death the remainder of these purchases had gone. Family arrangements required completion, and Christopher Dale required ready money. The outlying farms flew away, as such new purchases had flown before; but the old patrimony of the Dales remained untouched, as it had ever remained.

It had been a religion among them; and seeing that the worship had been carried on without fail, that the vestal fire had never gone down upon the hearth, I should not have said that the Dales had walked their ways without high principle. To this religion they had all adhered, and the new heir had ever entered in upon his domain without other encumbrances than those with which he himself was then already burdened. And yet there had been no entail. The idea of an entail was not in accordance with the peculiarities of the Dale mind. It was necessary to the Dale religion that each squire should have the power of wasting them, I remember to have dined at a house, the whole glory and fortune of which depended on the safety of a glass goblet. We all know the story. If the luck of Edenhall *should be shattered, the doom of the family would be sealed. Nevertheless I was bidden to drink out of the fatal glass, as were all guests in that house. It would not have contented the chivalrous mind of the master*

MONOTYPE MODERN 7

10 point, 1 point leaded

FORMAT	PICAS	LINES	WPL	CPL	WPP	CPP
Royal 8vo	26×43	47	12.8	69	601	3243
Demy 8vo	24×40	44	11.9	64	521	2816
Large Crown 8vo	23×36	39	11.4	61	445	2279
Crown 8vo	21×34	37	10.5	56	389	2072

father to son, and from uncle to nephew, and, in one instance, from second cousin to second cousin, the sceptre had descended in the family of the Dales; and the acres had remained intact, growing in value and not decreasing in number, though guarded by no entail and protected by no wonderful amount of prudence or wisdom. The estate of Dale of Allington had been coterminous with the parish of Allington for some hundreds of years; and though, as I have said, the race of squires had possessed nothing of superhuman discretion and had perhaps been guided in their walks through life by no very distinct principles, still there had been with them so much of adherence to a sacred law, that no acre of the property had ever been parted from the hands of the existing squire. Some futile attempts had been made to increase the territory, as indeed had been done by Kit Dale, the father of Christopher Dale, who will appear as our squire of Allington when the persons of our drama are introduced. Old Kit Dale, who had married money, had bought outlying farms—a bit of ground here and a bit there—talking, as he did so, much of political influence and of the good old Tory cause. But these farms and bits of ground had gone again before our time. To them had been attached no religion. When old Kit had found himself pressed in that matter of the majority of the Nineteenth Dragoons, in which crack regiment his second son made for himself quite a career, he found it easier to sell than to save—seeing that that which he sold was his own and not the patrimony of the Dales. At his death the remainder of these purchases had gone. Family arrangements required completion, and Christopher Dale required ready money. The outlying farms flew away, as such new purchases had flown before; but the old patrimony of the Dales remained untouched, as it had ever remained.

It had been a religion among them; and seeing that the worship had been carried on without fail, that the vestal fire had never gone down upon the hearth, I should not have said that the Dales had walked their ways without high principles. To this religion they had all adhered, and the new heir had ever entered in upon his domain without other encumbrances than those with which he himself was then already burdened. And yet there had been no entail. The idea of an entail was not in accordance with the peculiarities of the Dale mind. It was necessary to the Dale religion that each squire should have the power of wasting them. *I remember to have dined at a house, the whole glory and fortune of which depended on the safety of a glass goblet. We all know the story. If the luck of Edenhall should be shattered, the doom of the family*

MONOTYPE MODERN 7

11 point solid

FORMAT	PICAS	LINES	WPL	CPL	WPP	CPP
Royal 8vo	26×43	47	12.0	65	564	3055
Demy 8vo	24×40	44	11.1	60	490	2640
Large Crown 8vo	23×36	39	10.5	58	410	2262
Crown 8vo	21×34	37	9.5	53	350	1961

father to son, and from uncle to nephew, and, in one instance, from second cousin to second cousin, the sceptre had descended in the family of the Dales; and the acres had remained intact, growing in value and not decreasing in number, though guarded by no entail and protected by no wonderful amount of prudence or wisdom. The estate of Dale of Allington had been coterminous with the parish of Allington for some hundreds of years; and though, as I have said, the race of squires had possessed nothing of superhuman discretion and had perhaps been guided in their walks through life by no very distinct principles, still there had been with them so much of adherence to a sacred law, that no acre of the property had ever been parted from the hands of the existing squire. Some futile attempts had been made to increase the territory, as indeed had been done by Kit Dale, the father of Christopher Dale, who will appear as our squire of Allington when the persons of our drama are introduced. Old Kit Dale, who had married money, had bought outlying farms—a bit of ground here and a bit there—talking, as he did so, much of political influence and of the good old Tory cause. But these farms and bits of ground had gone again before our time. To them had been attached no religion. When old Kit had found himself pressed in that matter of the majority of the Nineteenth Dragoons, in which crack regiment his second son made for himself quite a career, he found it easier to sell than to save—seeing that that which he sold was his own and not the patrimony of the Dales. At his death the remainder of these purchases had gone. Family arrangements required completion, and Christopher Dale required ready money. The outlying farms flew away, as such new purchases had flown before; but the old patrimony of the Dales remained untouched, as it had ever remained.

It had been a religion among them; and seeing that the worship had been carried on without fail, that the vestal fire had never gone down upon the hearth, I should not have said that the Dales had walked their ways without high principles. To this religion they had all adhered, and the new heir had ever entered in upon his domain without other encumbrances than those with *which he himself was then already burdened. And yet there had been no entail. The idea of an entail was not in accordance with the peculiarities of the Dale mind. It was necessary to the Dale religion that*

MONOTYPE MODERN 7

11 point, 1 point leaded

FORMAT	PICAS	LINES	WPL	CPL	WPP	CPP
Royal 8vo	26×43	43	12.0	65	516	2795
Demy 8vo	24×40	40	11.1	60	440	2400
Large Crown 8vo	23×36	36	10.5	59	378	2088
Crown 8vo	21×34	34	9.5	53	323	1802

father to son, and from uncle to nephew, and, in one instance, from the second cousin to the second cousin, the sceptre had descended in the family of the Dales; and the acres had remained intact, growing in value and not decreasing in number, though guarded by no entail and protected by no wonderful amount of prudence or wisdom. The estate of Dale of Allington had been coterminous with the parish of Allington for some hundreds of years; and though, as I have said, the race of squires had possessed nothing of superhuman discretion and had perhaps been guided in their walks through life by no very distinct principles, still there had been with them so much of adherence to a sacred law, that no acre of the property had ever been parted from the hands of the existing squire. Some futile attempts had been made to increase the territory, as indeed had been done by Kit Dale, the father of Christopher Dale, who will appear as our squire of Allington when the persons of our drama are introduced. Old Kit Dale, who had married money, had bought some outlying farms—a bit of ground here and a bit there—talking, as he did so, much of political influence and of the good old Tory cause. But these farms and bits of ground had gone again before our time. To them had been attached no religion. When old Kit had found himself pressed in that matter of the majority of the Nineteenth Dragoons, in which crack regiment his second son made for himself quite a career, he found it easier to sell than to save—seeing that that which he sold was his own and not the patrimony of the Dales. At his death the remainder of these purchases had gone. Family arrangements required completion, and Christopher Dale required ready money. The outlying farms flew away, as such new purchases had flown before; but the old patrimony of *the Dales remained untouched, as it had ever remained.*

It had been a religion among them; and seeing that the worship had been carried on without fail, that the vestal

MONOTYPE MODERN 7

12 point, 1 point leaded

FORMAT	PICAS	LINES	WPL	CPL	WPP	CPP
Royal 8vo	26×43	40	10.4	56	416	2240
Demy 8vo	24×40	37	9.6	52	355	1924
Large Crown 8vo	23×36	33	9.2	50	304	1650
Crown 8vo	21×34	31	8.3	46	257	1426

MONOTYPE OLD STYLE 2

Synopsis in 10 point

ABCDEFGHIJKLMNOPQRSTUVWXYZ&ÆŒ

ABCDEFGHIJKLMNOPQRSTUVWXYZÆŒ

abcdefghijklmnopqrstuvwxyzæœfifffiffiffl

ABCDEFGHIJKLMNOPQRSTUVWXYZ &ÆŒ

abcdefghijklmnopqrstuvwxyzæœfiffflffiffl

.,:;!?''-()□£ *:;!?*

1234567890 *1234567890* 1234567890 *1234567890*

Related bold · Latin Antique Series 9

ABCDEFGHIJKLMNOPQRSTUVWXYZ &ÆŒ

abcdefghijklmnopqrstuvwxyzæœfiffflffiffl

.,:;!?''-()£ 1234567890

Related bold · Clarendon Series 12

ABCDEFGHIJKLMNOPQRSTUVWXYZ &ÆŒ

abcdefghijklmnopqrstuvwxyzæœfiffflffiffl

.,:;!?''-()£ 1234567890

Related bold · Old Style bold No. 1 Series 53

ABCDEFGHIJKLMNOPQRSTUVWXYZ&ÆŒ

abcdefghijklmnopqrstuvwxyzæœfiffflffiffl

.,:;! ?''-()£ 1234567890

Related bold · Old Style bold No. 5 Series 544

ABCDEFGHIJKLMNOPQRSTUVWXYZ &ÆŒ

abcdefghijklmnopqrstuvwxyzæœfiffflffiffl

.,:;!?''-()£ 1234567890

All normal European accents available

Series 2, 53 *and* 544 *available in composition sizes* 6, 8, 9, 10, 11, 12 *point*

Series 53 *italic available in* 8, 10, 12 *point*

Series 9 *available in composition sizes* 8, 10, 11, 12 *point*

Series 12 *available in composition sizes* 5, 6, 8, 10, 11 *point*

father to son, and from uncle to nephew, and, in one instance, from second cousin to second cousin, the sceptre had descended in the family of the Dales; and the acres had remained intact, growing in value and not decreasing in number, though guarded by no entail and protected by no wonderful amount of prudence or wisdom. The estate of Dale of Allington had been coterminous with the parish of Allington for some hundreds of years; and though, as I have said, the race of squires had possessed nothing of superhuman discretion and had perhaps been guided in their walks through life by no very distinct principles, still there had been with them so much of adherence to a sacred law, that no acre of the property had ever been parted from the hands of the existing squire. Some futile attempts had been made to increase the territory, as indeed had been done by Kit Dale, the father of Christopher Dale, who will appear as our squire of Allington when the persons of our drama are introduced. Old Kit Dale, who had married money, had bought outlying farms—a bit of ground here and a bit there—talking, as he did so, much of political influence and of the good old Tory cause. But these farms and bits of ground had gone again before our time. To them had been attached no religion. When old Kit had found himself pressed in that matter of the majority of the Nineteenth Dragoons, in which crack regiment his second son made for himself quite a career, he found it easier to sell than to save—seeing that that which he sold was his own and not the patrimony of the Dales. At his death the remainder of these purchases had gone. Family arrangements required completion, and Christopher Dale required ready money. The outlying farms flew away, as such new purchases had flown before; but the old patrimony of the Dales remained untouched, as it had ever remained.

It had been a religion among them; and seeing that the worship had been carried on without fail, that the vestal fire had never gone down upon the hearth, I should not have said that the Dales had walked their ways without high principle. To this religion they had all adhered, and the new heir had ever entered in upon his domain without other encumbrances than those with which he himself was then already burdened. And yet there had been no entail. The idea of an entail was not in accordance with the peculiarities of the Dale mind. It was necessary to the Dale religion that each squire should have the power of wasting them. I remember to have dined at a house, the whole glory and fortune of which depended on the safety of a glass goblet. We all know the story. If the luck of Edenhall should be shattered, the doom of the family would be sealed. Nevertheless I was bidden to drink out of the fatal glass, as were all guests in that house. It would not have contented the chivalrous mind of the master to protect his doom by lock and key and padded chest. And so it was with the Dales of Allington. To them an entail would have been a lock and key and a padded chest; but the old chivalry of their house denied to them the use of such protection.

I have spoken something slightingly of the acquirements and doings of the family; and indeed their acquirements had been few and their doings little. At Allington, Dale of Allington had always been known as a king. At

MONOTYPE OLD STYLE 2

9 point, 1 point leaded

FORMAT	PICAS	LINES	WPL	CPL	WPP	CPP
Royal 8vo	26×43	52	13.7	74	712	3848
Demy 8vo	24×40	48	12.7	68	609	3264
Large Crown 8vo	23×36	43	11.8	65	508	2795
Crown 8vo	21×34	41	10.8	59	441	2419

father to son, and from uncle to nephew, and, in one instance, from second cousin to second cousin, the sceptre had descended in the family of the Dales; and the acres had remained intact, growing in value and not decreasing in number, though guarded by no entail and protected by no wonderful amount of prudence or wisdom. The estate of Dale of Allington had been coterminous with the parish of Allington for some hundreds of years; and though, as I have said, the race of squires had possessed nothing of superhuman discretion and had perhaps been guided in their walks through life by no very distinct principles, still there had been with them so much of adherence to a sacred law, that no acre of the property had ever been parted from the hands of the existing squire. Some futile attempts had been made to increase the territory, as indeed had been done by Kit Dale, the father of Christopher Dale, who will appear as our squire of Allington when the persons of our drama are introduced. Old Kit Dale, who had married money, had bought outlying farms—a bit of ground here and a bit there—talking, as he did so, much of political influence and of the good old Tory cause. But these farms and bits of ground had gone again before our time. To them had been attached no religion. When old Kit had found himself pressed in that matter of the majority of the Nineteenth Dragoons, in which crack regiment his second son made for himself quite a career, he found it easier to sell than to save—seeing that that which he sold was his own and not the patrimony of the Dales. At his death the remainder of these purchases had gone. Family arrangements required completion, and Christopher Dale required ready money. The outlying farms flew away, as such new purchases had flown before; but the old patrimony of the Dales remained untouched, as it had ever remained.

It had been a religion among them; and seeing that the worship had been carried on without fail, that the vestal fire had never gone down upon the hearth, I should not have said that the Dales had walked their ways without high principle. To this religion they had all adhered, and the new heir had ever entered in upon his domain without other encumbrances than those with which he himself was then already burdened. And yet there had been no entail. The idea of an entail was not in accordance with the peculiarities of the Dale mind. It was necessary to the Dale religion that each squire should have the power of wasting them. I remember to have dined at a house, the whole glory and fortune of which depended on the safety of a glass goblet. We all know the story. If the luck of Edenhall should be shattered, the doom of the family would be sealed. Nevertheless I was bidden to drink out of the fatal glass, as were all guests in that house. It would not have contented the chivalrous mind of the master to protect his doom by lock and key and padded chest. *And so it was with the Dales of Allington. To them an entail would have been a lock and key and a padded chest; but the old chivalry of their house denied to them the use of such protection.*

MONOTYPE OLD STYLE 2

10 point solid

FORMAT	PICAS	LINES	WPL	CPL	WPP	CPP
Royal 8vo	26×43	52	12.8	69	667	3588
Demy 8vo	24×40	48	11.9	64	572	3072
Large Crown 8vo	23×36	43	11.0	61	473	2623
Crown 8vo	21×34	41	10.1	56	413	2296

father to son, and from uncle to nephew, and, in one instance, from second cousin to second cousin, the sceptre had descended in the family of the Dales; and the acres had remained intact, growing in value and not decreasing in number, though guarded by no entail and protected by no wonderful amount of prudence or wisdom. The estate of Dale of Allington had been coterminous with the parish of Allington for some hundreds of years; and though, as I have said, the race of squires had pessessed nothing of superhuman discretion and had perhaps been guided in their walks through life by no very distinct principles, still there had been with them so much of adherence to a sacred law, that no acre of the property had ever been parted from the hands of the existing squire. Some futile attempts had been made to increase the territory, as indeed had been done by Kit Dale, the father of Christopher Dale, who will appear as our squire of Allington when the persons of our drama are introduced. Old Kit Dale, who had married money, had bought outlying farms—a bit of ground here and a bit there—talking, as he did so, much of political influence and of the good old Tory cause. But these farms and bits of ground had gone again before our time. To them had been attached no religion. When old Kit had found himself pressed in that matter of the majority of the Nineteenth Dragoons, in which crack regiment his second son made for himself quite a career, he found it easier to sell than to save—seeing that that which he sold was his own and not the patrimony of the Dales. At his death the remainder of these purchases had gone. Family arrangements required completion, and Christopher Dale required ready money. The outlying farms flew away, as such new purchases had flown before; but the old patrimony of the Dales remained untouched, as it had ever remained.

It had been a religion among them; and seeing that the worship had been carried on without fail, that the vestal fire had never gone down upon the hearth, I should not have said that the Dales had walked their ways without high principle. To this religion they had all adhered, and the new heir had ever entered in upon his domain without other encumbrances than those with which he himself was then already burdened. And yet there had been no entail. The idea of an entail was not in accordance with the peculiarities of the Dale mind. It was necessary to the Dale religion that each squire should have the power of wasting them, I remember to have dined at a house, the whole glory and fortune of which depended on the safety of a glass goblet. We all know the story. If the luck of Edenhall *should be shattered, the doom of the family would be sealed. Nevertheless I was bidden to drink out of the fatal glass, as were all guests in that house. It would not have contented the chivalrous mind of the master*

MONOTYPE OLD STYLE 2

10 point, 1 point leaded

FORMAT	PICAS	LINES	WPL	CPL	WPP	CPP
Royal 8vo	26×43	47	12.8	69	601	3243
Demy 8vo	24×40	44	11.9	64	522	2816
Large Crown 8vo	23×36	39	11.0	61	427	2379
Crown 8vo	21×34	37	10.1	56	371	2072

father to son, and from uncle to nephew, and, in one instance, from second cousin to second cousin, the sceptre had descended in the family of the Dales; and the acres had remained intact, growing in value and not decreasing in number, though guarded by no entail and protected by no wonderful amount of prudence or wisdom. The estate of Dale of Allington had been coterminous with the parish of Allington for some hundreds of years; and though, as I have said, the race of squires had possessed nothing of superhuman discretion and had perhaps been guided in their walks through life by no very distinct principles, still there had been with them so much of adherence to a sacred law, that no acre of the property had ever been parted from the hands of the existing squire. Some futile attempts had been made to increase the territory, as indeed had been done by Kit Dale, the father of Christopher Dale, who will appear as our squire of Allington when the persons of our drama are introduced. Old Kit Dale, who had married money, had bought outlying farms—a bit of ground here and a bit there—talking, as he did so, much of political influence and of the good old Tory cause. But these farms and bits of ground had gone again before our time. To them had been attached no religion. When old Kit had found himself pressed in that matter of the majority of the Nineteenth Dragoons, in which crack regiment his second son made for himself quite a career, he found it easier to sell than to save—seeing that that which he sold was his own and not the patrimony of the Dales. At his death the remainder of these purchases had gone. Family arrangements required completion, and Christopher Dale required ready money. The outlying farms flew away, as such new purchases had flown before; but the old patrimony of the Dales remained untouched, as it had ever remained

It had been a religion among them; and seeing that the worship had been carried on without fail, that the vestal fire had never gone down upon the hearth, I should not have said that the Dales had walked their ways without high principles. To this religion they had all adhered, and the new heir had ever entered in upon his domain without other encumbrances than those with which he himself was then already burdened. And yet there had been no entail. The idea of an entail was not in accordance with the peculiarities of the Dale mind. It was necessary to the Dale religion that each squire should have the power of wasting them. *I remember to have dined at a house, the whole glory and fortune of which depended on the safety of a glass goblet. We all know the story. If the luck of Edenhall should be shattered, the doom of the family*

MONOTYPE OLD STYLE 2

11 point solid

FORMAT	PICAS	LINES	WPL	CPL	WPP	CPP
Royal 8vo	26×43	47	12.0	64	564	3008
Demy 8vo	24×40	44	11.1	59	490	2596
Large Crown 8vo	23×36	39	10.2	57	399	2223
Crown 8vo	21×34	37	9.3	52	346	1924

father to son, and from uncle to nephew, and, in one instance, from second cousin to second cousin, the sceptre had descended in the family of the Dales; and the acres had remained intact, growing in value and not decreasing in number, though guarded by no entail and protected by no wonderful amount of prudence or wisdom. The estate of Dale of Allington had been coterminous with the parish of Allington for some hundreds of years; and though, as I have said, the race of squires had possessed nothing of superhuman discretion and had perhaps been guided in their walks through life by no very distinct principles, still there had been with them so much of adherence to a sacred law, that no acre of the property had ever been parted from the hands of the existing squire. Some futile attempts had been made to increase the territory, as indeed had been done by Kit Dale, the father of Christopher Dale, who will appear as our squire of Allington when the persons of our drama are introduced. Old Kit Dale, who had married money, had bought outlying farms—a bit of ground here and a bit there—talking, as he did so, much of political influence and of the good old Tory cause. But these farms and bits of ground had gone again before our time. To them had been attached no religion. When old Kit had found himself pressed in that matter of the majority of the Nineteenth Dragoons, in which crack regiment his second son made for himself quite a career, he found it easier to sell than to save—seeing that that which he sold was his own and not the patrimony of the Dales. At his death the remainder of these purchases had gone. Family arrangements required completion, and Christopher Dale required ready money. The outlying farms flew away, as such new purchases had flown before; but the old patrimony of the Dales remained untouched, as it had ever remained.

It had been a religion among them; and seeing that the worship had been carried on without fail, that the vestal fire had never gone down upon the hearth, I should not have said that the Dales had walked their ways without high principles. To this religion they had all adhered, and the new heir had ever entered in upon his domain without other encumbrances than those with *which he himself was then already burdened. And yet there had been no entail. The idea of an entail was not in accordance with the peculiarities of the Dale mind. It was necessary to the Dale religion that*

MONOTYPE OLD STYLE 2

11 point, 1 point leaded

FORMAT	PICAS	LINES	WPL	CPL	WPP	CPP
Royal 8vo	26×43	43	12.0	64	516	2752
Demy 8vo	24×40	40	11.1	59	440	2360
Large Crown 8vo	23×36	36	10.2	57	368	2052
Crown 8vo	21×34	34	9.3	52	316	1768

father to son, and from uncle to nephew, and, in one instance, from the second cousin to the second cousin, the sceptre had descended in the family of the Dales; and the acres had remained intact, growing in value and not decreasing in number, though guarded by no entail and protected by no wonderful amount of prudence or wisdom. The estate of Dale of Allington had been coterminous with the parish of Allington for some hundreds of years; and though, as I have said, the race of squires had possessed nothing of superhuman discretion and had perhaps been guided in their walks through life by no very distinct principles, still there had been with them so much of adherence to a sacred law, that no acre of the property had ever been parted from the hands of the existing squire. Some futile attempts had been made to increase the territory, as indeed had been done by Kit Dale, the father of Christopher Dale, who will appear as our squire of Allington when the persons of our drama are introduced. Old Kit Dale, who had married money, had bought some outlying farms—a bit of ground here and a bit there—talking, as he did so, much of political influence and of the good old Tory cause. But these farms and bits of ground had gone again before our time. To them had been attached no religion. When old Kit had found himself pressed in that matter of the majority of the Nineteenth Dragoons, in which crack regiment his second son made for himself quite a career, he found it easier to sell than to save—seeing that that which he sold was his own and not the patrimony of the Dales. At his death the remainder of these purchases had gone. Family arrangements required completion, and Christopher Dale required ready money. The outlying farms flew away, as such new purchases had flown before; but the old patrimony of the Dales remained untouched, as it had ever remained.

It had been a religion among them; and seeing that the worship had been carried on without fail, that the *vestal fire had never gone down upon the hearth, I should not have said that the Dales had walked their ways without high principle. To this religion they had all adhered, and*

MONOTYPE OLD STYLE 2

12 point solid

FORMAT	PICAS	LINES	WPL	CPL	WPP	CPP
Royal 8vo	26×43	43	10.5	56	451	2408
Demy 8vo	24×40	40	9.7	52	386	2080
Large Crown 8vo	23×46	36	9.0	50	323	1800
Crown 8vo	21×34	34	8.3	46	281	1564

father to son, and from uncle to nephew, and, in one instance, from the second cousin to the second cousin, the sceptre had descended in the family of the Dales; and the acres had remained intact, growing in value and not decreasing in number, though guarded by no entail and protected by no wonderful amount of prudence or wisdom. The estate of Dale of Allington had been coterminous with the parish of Allington for some hundreds of years; and though, as I have said, the race of squires had possessed nothing of superhuman discretion and had perhaps been guided in their walks through life by no very distinct principles, still there had been with them so much of adherence to a sacred law, that no acre of the property had ever been parted from the hands of the existing squire. Some futile attempts had been made to increase the territory, as indeed had been done by Kit Dale, the father of Christopher Dale, who will appear as our squire of Allington when the persons of our drama are introduced. Old Kit Dale, who had married money, had bought some outlying farms—a bit of ground here and a bit there—talking, as he did so, much of political influence and of the good old Tory cause. But these farms and bits of ground had gone again before our time. To them had been attached no religion. When old Kit had found himself pressed in that matter of the majority of the Nineteenth Dragoons, in which crack regiment his second son made for himself quite a career, he found it easier to sell than to save—seeing that that which he sold was his own and not the patrimony of the Dales. At his death the remainder of these purchases had gone. Family arrangements required completion, and Christopher Dale required ready money. The outlying farms flew away, as such new purchases had flown before; but the old patrimony of *the Dales remained untouched, as it had ever remained.*

It had been a religion among them; and seeing that the worship had been carried on without fail, that the vestal

MONOTYPE OLD STYLE 2

12 point, 1 point leaded

FORMAT	PICAS	LINES	WPL	CPL	WPP	CPP
Royal 8vo	26×43	40	10.5	56	420	2240
Demy 8vo	24×40	37	9.7	52	355	1924
Large Crown 8vo	23×36	33	9.0	50	298	1650
Crown 8vo	21×34	31	8.3	46	260	1426

MONOTYPE PERPETUA 239

Synopsis in 10 point

ABCDEFGHIJKLMNOPQRSTUVWXYZ&ÆŒ

ABCDEFGHIJKLMNOPQRSTUVWXYZÆŒ

abcdefghijklmnopqrstuvwxyzæœfiffflffiffl

ABCDEFGHIJKLMNOPQRSTUVWXYZ&ÆŒ

abcdefghijklmnopqrstuvwxyzæœfiffflffiffl

.,:;!?''-()[]£ *:;!?*

1234567890 *1234567890* 1234567890 *1234567890*

Related bold · Series 461

ABCDEFGHIJKLMNOPQRSTUVWXYZ&ÆŒ

abcdefghijklmnopqrstuvwxyzæœfiffflffiffl

.,:;!?''-()£ 1234567890

All normal European accents available

Series 239 *available in composition sizes* 8, 10, 11, 12, 13, 14 *point*

Series 461 *available in composition sizes* 8, 10, 11, 12 *point*

father to son, and from uncle to nephew, and, in one instance, from second cousin to second cousin, the sceptre had descended in the family of the Dales; and the acres had remained intact, growing in value and not decreasing in number, though guarded by no entail and protected by no wonderful amount of prudence or wisdom. The estate of Dale of Allington had been coterminous with the parish of Allington for some hundreds of years; and though, as I have said, the race of squires had possessed nothing of superhuman discretion, and had perhaps been guided in their walks through life by no very distinct principles, still there had been with them so much of adherence to a sacred law, that no acre of the property had ever been parted from the hands of the existing squire. Some futile attempts had been made to increase the territory, as indeed had been done by Kit Dale, the father of Christopher Dale, who will appear as our squire of Allington when the persons of our drama are introduced. Old Kit Dale, who had married money, had bought outlying farms—a bit of ground here and a bit there—talking, as he did so, much of political influence and of the good old Tory cause. But these farms and bits of ground had gone again before our time. To them had been attached no religion. When old Kit had found himself pressed in that matter of the majority of the Nineteenth Dragoons, in which crack regiment his second son made for himself quite a career, he found it easier to sell than to save—seeing that that which he sold was his own and not the patrimony of the Dales. At his death the remainder of these purchases had gone. Family arrangements required completion, and Christopher Dale required ready money. The outlying farms flew away, as such new purchases had flown before; but the old patrimony of the Dales remained untouched, as it had ever remained.

It had been a religion among them; and seeing that the worship had been carried on without fail, that the vestal fire had never gone down upon the hearth, I should not have said that the Dales had walked their ways without high principle. To this religion they had all adhered, and the new heir had ever entered in upon his domain without other encumbrances than those with which he himself was then already burdened. And yet there had been no entail. The idea of an entail was not in accordance with the peculiarities of the Dale mind. It was necessary to the Dale religion that each squire should have the power of wasting them. I remember to have dined at a house, the whole glory and fortune of which depended on the safety of a glass goblet. We all know the story. If the luck of Edenhall should be shattered, the doom of the family would be sealed. Nevertheless I was bidden to drink out of the fatal glass, as were all guests in that house. It would not have contented the chivalrous mind of the master to protect his doom by lock and key and padded chest. And so it was with the Dales of Allington. To them an entail would have been a lock and key and a padded chest; but the old chivalry of their house denied to them the use of such protection.

I have spoken something slightingly of the acquirements and doings of the family; and indeed their acquirements had been few and their doings little. At Allington, Dale of Allington had always been known as a king. At Guestwick, *the neighbouring market town, he was a great man—to be seen frequently on Saturdays, in the market-place, and laying down the law as to barley and oxen among men who knew usually more about barley and oxen than he did. At Hamersham, the assize town,*

MONOTYPE PERPETUA 239

10 point solid

FORMAT	PICAS	LINES	WPL	CPL	WPP	CPP
Royal 8vo	26×43	52	14.8	80	770	4160
Demy 8vo	24×40	48	13.7	74	657	3552
Large Crown 8vo	23×36	43	12.9	71	551	3053
Crown 8vo	21×34	41	11.8	65	485	2665

father to son, and from uncle to nephew, and, in one instance, from second cousin to second cousin, the sceptre had descended in the family of the Dales; and the acres had remained intact, growing in value and not decreasing in number, though guarded by no entail and protected by no wonderful amount of prudence or wisdom. The estate of Dale of Allington had been coterminous with the parish of Allington for some hundreds of years; and though, as I have said, the race of squires had possessed nothing of superhuman discretion, and had perhaps been guided in their walks through life by no very distinct principles, still there had been with them so much of adherence to a sacred law, that no acre of the property had ever been parted from the hands of the existing squire. Some futile attempts had been made to increase the territory, as indeed had been done by Kit Dale, the father of Christopher Dale, who will appear as our squire of Allington when the persons of our drama are introduced. Old Kit Dale, who had married money, had bought outlying farms—a bit of ground here and a bit there—talking, as he did so, much of political influence and of the good old Tory cause. But these farms and bits of ground had gone again before our time. To them had been attached no religion. When old Kit had found himself pressed in that matter of the majority of the Nineteenth Dragoons, in which crack regiment his second son made for himself quite a career, he found it easier to sell than to save—seeing that that which he sold was his own and not the patrimony of the Dales. At his death the remainder of these purchases had gone. Family arrangements required completion, and Christopher Dale required ready money. The outlying farms flew away, as such new purchases had flown before; but the old patrimony of the Dales remained untouched, as it had ever remained.

It had been a religion among them; and seeing that the worship had been carried on without fail, that the vestal fire had never gone down upon the hearth, I should not have said that the Dales had walked their ways without high principle. To this religion they had all adhered, and the new heir had ever entered in upon his domain without other encumbrances than those with which he himself was then already burdened. And yet there had been no entail. The idea of an entail was not in accordance with the pecularities of the Dale mind. It was necessary to the Dale religion that each squire should have the power of wasting them. I remember to have dined at a house, the whole glory and fortune of which depended on the safety of a glass goblet. We all know the story If the luck of Edenhall should be shattered, the doom of the family would be sealed. Nevertheless I was bidden to drink out of the fatal glass, as were all guests in that house. It would not have contented the chivalrous mind of the master to protect his doom by lock and key and padded chest. And so it was with the Dales of Allington. To them an entail would have been a lock and key and a padded chest; but the old chivalry of their house denied to them the use *of such protection.*

I have spoken something slightingly of the acquirements and doings of the family; and indeed their acquirements had been few and their doings little. At Allington, Dale of

MONOTYPE PERPETUA 239

10 point, 1 point leaded

FORMAT	PICAS	LINES	WPL	CPL	WPP	CPP
Royal 8vo	26×43	47	14.8	80	695	3760
Demy 8vo	24×40	44	13.7	74	600	3256
Large Crown 8vo	23×36	39	12.9	71	506	2769
Crown 8vo	21×34	37	11.8	65	436	2405

father to son, and from uncle to nephew, and, in one instance, from second cousin to second cousin, the sceptre had descended in the family of the Dales; and the acres had remained intact, growing in value and not decreasing in number, though guarded by no entail and protected by no wonderful amount of prudence or wisdom. The estate of Dale of Allington had been coterminous with the parish of Allington for some hundreds of years; and though, as I have said, the race of squires had possessed nothing of superhuman discretion, and had perhaps been guided in their walks through life by no very distinct principles, still there had been with them so much of this adherence to a sacred law, that no acre of the property had ever been parted from the hands of the existing squire. Some futile attempts had been made to increase the territory, as indeed had been done by Kit Dale, the father of Christopher Dale, who will appear as our squire of Allington when the persons of our drama are introduced. Old Kit Dale, who had married money, had bought outlying farms—a bit of ground here and a bit there—talking, as he did so, much of political influence and of the good old Tory cause. But these farms and bits of ground had gone again before our time. To them had been attached no religion. When old Kit had found himself pressed in that matter of the majority of the Nineteenth Dragoons, in which crack regiment his second son made for himself quite a career, he found it easier to sell than to save—seeing that that which he sold was his own and not the patrimony of the Dales. At his death the remainder of these purchases had gone. Family arrangements required completion, and Christopher Dale required ready money. The outlying farms flew away, as such new purchases had flown before; but the old patrimony of the Dales remained untouched, as it had ever remained.

It had been a religion among them; and seeing that the worship had been carried on without fail, that the vestal fire had never gone down upon the hearth, I should not have said that the Dales had walked their ways without high principle. To this religion they had all adhered, and the new heir had ever entered in upon his domain without other encumbrances than those with which he himself was then already burdened. And yet there had been no entail. The idea of an entail was not in accordance with the peculiarities of the Dale mind. It was necessary to the Dale religion that each squire should have the power of wasting them. I remember to have dined at a house, the whole glory and fortune of which depended on the safety of a glass goblet. We all know the story. If the luck of Edenhall should be shattered, the doom of the family would be sealed. Nevertheless I was bidden to drink out of the fatal glass, as were all guests in that house. It would not have contented *the chivalrous mind of the master to protect his doom by lock and key and padded chest. And so it was with the Dales of Allington. To them an entail would have been a lock and key and a padded chest; but the old chivalry of their house denied*

MONOTYPE PERPETUA 239

11 point solid

FORMAT	PICAS	LINES	WPL	CPL	WPP	CPP
Royal 8vo	26×43	47	13.8	73	648	3431
Demy 8vo	24×40	44	12.8	67	565	2948
Large Crown 8vo	23×36	39	11.9	64	466	2496
Crown 8vo	21×34	37	10.9	58	402	2146

father to son, and from uncle to nephew, and, in one instance, from second cousin to second cousin, the sceptre had descended in the family of the Dales; and the acres had remained intact, growing in value and not decreasing in number, though guarded by no entail and protected by no wonderful amount of prudence or wisdom. The estate of Dale of Allington had been coterminous with the parish of Allington for some hundreds of years; and though, as I have said, the race of squires had possessed nothing of superhuman discretion, and had perhaps been guided in their walks through life by no very distinct principles, still there had been with them so much of this adherence to a sacred law, that no acre of the property had ever been parted from the hands of the existing squire. Some futile attempts had been made to increase the territory, as indeed had been done by Kit Dale, the father of Christopher Dale, who will appear as our squire of Allington when the persons of our drama are introduced. Old Kit Dale, who had married money, had bought outlying farms—a bit of ground here and a bit there—talking, as he did so, much of political influence and of the good old Tory cause. But these farms and bits of ground had gone again before our time. To them had been attached no religion. When old Kit had found himself pressed in that matter of the majority of the Nineteenth Dragoons, in which crack regiment his second son made for himself quite a career, he found it easier to sell than to save—seeing that that which he sold was his own and not the patrimony of the Dales. At his death the remainder of these purchases had gone. Family arrangements required completion, and Christopher Dale required ready money. The outlying farms flew away, as such new purchases had flown before; but the old patrimony of the Dales remained untouched, as it had ever remained.

It had been a religion among them; and seeing that the worship had been carried on without fail, that the vestal fire had never gone down upon the hearth, I should not have said that the Dales had walked their ways without high principle. To this religion they had all adhered, and the new heir had ever entered in upon his domain without other encumbrances than those with which he himself was then already burdened. And yet there had been no entail. The idea of an entail was not in accordance with the peculiarities of the Dale mind. It was necessary to the Dale religion that each squire should have the power of wasting them. I remember to have dined at a house, the whole glory and for-*tune of which depended on the safety of a glass goblet. We all know the story. If the luck of Edenhall should be shattered, the doom of the family would be sealed. Nevertheless I was bidden to drink out of the fatal glass, as were all*

MONOTYPE PERPETUA 239

11 point, 1 point leaded

FORMAT	PICAS	LINES	WPL	CPL	WPP	CPP
Royal 8vo	26×43	43	13.8	73	593	3139
Demy 8vo	24×40	40	12.8	67	507	2680
Large Crown 8vo	23×36	36	11.9	64	427	2304
Crown 8vo	21×34	34	10.9	58	370	1972

father to son, and from uncle to nephew, and, in one instance, from second cousin to second cousin, the sceptre had descended in the family of the Dales; and the acres had remained intact, growing in value and not decreasing in number, though guarded by no entail and protected by no wonderful amount of prudence or wisdom. The estate of Dale of Allington had been coterminous with the parish of Allington for some hundreds of years; and though, as I have said, the race of squires had possessed nothing of superhuman discretion, and had perhaps been guided in their walks through life by no very distinct principles, still there had been with them so much of adherence to a sacred law, that no acre of the property had ever been parted from the hands of the existing squire. Some futile attempts had been made to increase the territory, as indeed had been done by Kit Dale, the father of Christopher Dale, who will appear as our squire of Allington when the persons of our drama are introduced. Old Kit Dale, who had married money, had bought outlying farms—a bit of ground here and a bit there—talking, as he did so, much of political influence and of the good old Tory cause. But these farms and bits of ground had gone again before our time. To them had been attached no religion. When old Kit had found himself pressed in that matter of the majority of the Nineteenth Dragoons, in which crack regiment his second son made for himself quite a career, he found it easier to sell than to save—seeing that that which he sold was his own and not the patrimony of the Dales. At his death the remainder of these purchases had gone. Family arrangements required completion, and Christopher Dale required ready money. The outlying farms flew away, as such new purchases had flown before; but the old patrimony of the Dales remained untouched, as it had ever remained.

It had been a religion among them; and seeing that the worship had been carried on without fail, that the vestal fire had never gone down upon the hearth, I should not have said that the Dales had walked their ways without high principle. To this religion they had all adhered, and the new heir had ever entered in upon his domain without other encumbrances than those with which he himself was then already burdened. And yet there had been *no entail. The idea of an entail was not in accordance with the peculiarities of the Dale mind. It was necessary to the Dale religion that each squire should have the power of wasting them. I remember to have dined*

MONOTYPE PERPETUA 239

12 point solid

FORMAT	PICAS	LINES	WPL	CPL	WPP	CPP
Royal 8vo	26×43	43	12.2	66	524	2838
Demy 8vo	24×40	40	11.3	61	454	2440
Large Crown 8vo	23×36	36	10.5	58	378	2088
Crown 8vo	21×34	34	9.9	53	337	1802

father to son, and from uncle to nephew, and, in one instance, from second cousin to second cousin, the sceptre had descended in the family of the Dales; and the acres had remained intact, growing in value and not decreasing in number, though guarded by no entail and protected by no wonderful amount of prudence or wisdom. The estate of Dale of Allington had been coterminous with the parish of Allington for some hundreds of years; and though, as I have said, the race of squires had possessed nothing of superhuman discretion, and had perhaps been guided in their walks through life by no very distinct principles, still there had been with them so much of adherence to a sacred law, that no acre of the property had ever been parted from the hands of the existing squire. Some futile attempts had been made to increase the territory, as indeed had been done by Kit Dale, the father of Christopher Dale, who will appear as our squire of Allington when the persons of our drama are introduced. Old Kit Dale, who had married money, had bought outlying farms—a bit of ground here and a bit there—talking, as he did so, much of political influence and of the good old Tory cause. But these farms and bits of ground had gone again before our time. To them had been attached no religion. When old Kit had found himself pressed in that matter of the majority of the Nineteenth Dragoons, in which crack regiment his second son made for himself quite a career, he found it easier to sell than to save—seeing that that which he sold was his own and not the patrimony of the Dales. At his death the remainder of these purchases had gone. Family arrangements required completion, and Christopher Dale required ready money. The outlying farms flew away, as such new purchases had flown before; but the old patrimony of the Dales remained untouched, as it had ever remained.

It had been a religion among them; and seeing that the worship had been carried on without fail, that the vestal fire had never gone down upon the hearth, I should not have said that the Dales had walked their ways without high principle. To this religion *they had all adhered, and the new heir had ever entered in upon his domain without other encumbrances than those with which he himself was then already burdened. And yet there had been no entail. The idea*

MONOTYPE PERPETUA 239

12 point, 1 point leaded

FORMAT	PICAS	LINES	WPL	CPL	WPP	CPP
Royal 8vo	26×43	40	12.2	66	488	2640
Demy 8vo	24×40	37	11.3	61	418	2257
Large Crown 8vo	23×36	33	10.5	58	348	1914
Crown 8vo	21×34	31	9.9	53	305	1643

father to son, and from uncle to nephew, and, in one instance, from the second cousin to the second cousin, the sceptre had descended in the family of the Dales; and the acres had remained intact, growing in value and not decreasing in number, though guarded by no entail and protected by no wonderful amount of prudence or wisdom. The estate of Dale of Allington had been coterminous with the parish of Allington for some hundreds of years; and though, as I have said, the race of squires had possessed nothing of superhuman discretion and had perhaps been guided in their walks through life by no very distinct principles, still there had been with them so much of adherence to a sacred law, that no acre of the property had ever been parted from the hands of the existing squire. Some futile attempts had been made to increase the territory, as indeed had been done by Kit Dale, the father of Christopher Dale, who will appear as our squire of Allington when the persons of our drama are introduced. Old Kit Dale, who had married money, had bought outlying farms—a bit of ground here and a bit there—talking, as he did so, much of political influence and of the good old Tory cause. But these farms and bits of ground had gone again long before our time. To them had been attached no religion. When old Kit had found himself pressed in that matter of the majority of the Nineteenth Dragoons, in which crack regiment his second son made for himself quite a career, he found it easier to sell than to save—seeing that that which he sold was his own and not the patrimony of the Dales. At his death the remainder of these purchases had gone. Family arrangements required completion, and Christopher Dale required ready money. The outlying farms flew away, as such new purchases had flown before; but the old patrimony of the Dales remained untouched, as it had ever remained.

It had been a religion among them; and seeing that the *worship had been carried on without fail, that the vestal fire had never gone down upon the hearth, I should not have said that the Dales had walked their ways without high principle. To this*

MONOTYPE PERPETUA 239

13 point solid

FORMAT	PICAS	LINES	WPL	CPL	WPP	CPP
Royal 8vo	26×43	40	11.3	62	452	2480
Demy 8vo	24×40	37	10.5	57	386	2109
Large Crown 8vo	23×36	33	9.7	55	320	1815
Crown 8vo	21×34	31	8.8	50	271	1550

father to son, and from uncle to nephew, and, in one instance, from the second cousin to the second cousin, the sceptre had descended in the family of the Dales; and the acres had remained intact, growing in value and not decreasing in number, though guarded by no entail and protected by no wonderful amount of prudence or wisdom. The estate of Dale of Allington had been coterminous with the parish of Allington for some hundreds of years; and though, as I have said, the race of squires had possessed nothing of superhuman discretion and had perhaps been guided in their walks through life by no very distinct principles, still there had been with them so much of adherence to a sacred law, that no acre of the property had ever been parted from the hands of the existing squire. Some futile attempts had been made to increase the territory, as indeed had been done by Kit Dale, the father of Christopher Dale, who will appear as our squire of Allington when the persons of our drama are introduced. Old Kit Dale, who had married money, had bought outlying farms—a bit of ground here and a bit there—talking, as he did so, much of political influence and of the good old Tory cause. But these farms and bits of ground had gone again long before our time. To them had been attached no religion. When old Kit had found himself pressed in that matter of the majority of the Nineteenth Dragoons, in which crack regiment his second son made for himself quite a career, he found it easier to sell than to save—seeing that that which he sold was his own and not the patrimony of the Dales. At his death the remainder of these purchases had gone. Family arrangements required completion, and Christopher Dale required ready money. The outlying farms flew away, as such new purchases had flown before; but the old *patrimony of the Dales remained untouched, as it had ever remained.*

It had been a religion among them; and seeing that the worship had been carried on without fail, that the vestal fire had never gone

MONOTYPE PERPETUA 239

13 point, 1 point leaded

FORMAT	PICAS	LINES	WPL	CPL	WPP	CPP
Royal 8vo	26×43	37	11.3	62	418	2294
Demy 8vo	24×40	34	10.5	57	359	1938
Large Crown 8vo	23×36	31	9.7	55	301	1705
Crown 8vo	21×34	29	8.8	50	255	1450

father to son, and from uncle to nephew, and, in one instance, from second cousin to second cousin, the sceptre had descended in the family of the Dales; and the acres had remained intact, growing in value and not decreasing in number, though guarded by no entail and protected by no wonderful amount of prudence or wisdom. The estate of Dale of Allington had been coterminous with the parish of Allington for some hundreds of years; and though, as I have said, the race of squires had possessed nothing of superhuman discretion and had perhaps been guided in their walks through life by no very distinct principles, still there had been with them so much of adherence to a sacred law, that no acre of the property had ever been parted from the hands of the existing squire. Some futile attempts had been made to increase the territory, as indeed had been done by Kit Dale, the father of Christopher Dale, who will appear as our squire of Allington when the persons of our drama are introduced. Old Kit Dale, who had married money, had bought outlying farms—a bit of ground here and a bit there—talking, as he did so, much of political influence and of the good old Tory cause. But these farms and bits of ground had gone again before our time. To them had been attached no religion. When old Kit had found himself pressed in that matter of the majority of the Nineteenth Dragoons, in which crack regiment his second son made for himself quite a career, he found it easier to sell than to save—seeing that that which he sold was his own and not the patrimony of the Dales. At his death the remainder of these purchases had gone. Family arrangements required *completion, and Christopher Dale required ready money. The outlying farms flew away, as such new purchases had flown before; but the old patrimony of the Dales remained un-*

MONOTYPE PERPETUA 239

14 point solid

FORMAT	PICAS	LINES	WPL	CPL	WPP	CPP
Royal 8vo	26×43	37	10.4	56	385	2072
Demy 8vo	24×40	34	9.6	52	328	1768
Large Crown 8vo	23×36	31	9.0	49	279	1519
Crown 8vo	21×34	29	8.2	45	239	1305

MONOTYPE PLANTIN 110

Synopsis in 10 point

ABCDEFGHIJKLMNOPQRSTUVWXYZ&ÆŒ

ABCDEFGHIJKLMNOPQRSTUVWXYZÆŒ

abcdefghijklmnopqrstuvwxyzæœfiffflffiffl

ABCDEFGHIJKLMNOPQRSTUVWXYZ&ÆŒ

abcdefghijklmnopqrstuvwxyzæœfiffflffiffl

.,:;!?‘’-()[]£ *:;!?*

1234567890 *1234567890* 1234567890 *1234567890*

Related bold · Series 194

ABCDEFGHIJKLMNOPQRSTUVWXYZ&ÆŒ

abcdefghijklmnopqrstuvwxyzæœfiffflffiffl

.,:;!?‘’-()£ 1234567890

ABCDEFGHIJKLMNOPQRSTUVWXYZ&ÆŒ

abcdefghijklmnopqrstuvwxyzæœfiffflffiffl

.,:;!?‘’-()£ 1234567890

All normal European accents available

Series 110 *available in composition sizes* 8, 9, 10, 11, 12 *point*

Series 194 *available in composition sizes* 6, 8, 9, 10, 11, 12 *point*

Series 194 *italic available in composition sizes* 8, 10, 12 *point* father to son, and from uncle to nephew, and, in one instance, from second cousin to second cousin, the sceptre had descended in the family of the Dales; and the acres had remained intact, growing in value and not decreasing in number, though guarded by no entail and protected by no wonderful amount of prudence or wisdom. The estate of Dale of Allington had been coterminous with the parish of Allington for some hundreds of years; and though, as I have said, the race of squires had possessed nothing of superhuman discretion and had perhaps been guided in their walks through life by no very distinct principles, still there had been with them so much of adherence to a sacred law, that no acre of the property had ever been parted from the hands of the existing squire. Some futile attempts had been made to increase the territory, as indeed had been done by Kit Dale, the father of Christopher Dale, who will appear as our squire of Allington when the persons of our drama are introduced. Old Kit Dale, who had marreid money, had bought outlying farms—a bit of ground here and a bit there—talking, as he did so, much of political influence and of the good old Tory cause. But these farms and bits of ground had gone again before our time. To them had been attached no religion. When old Kit had found himself pressed in that matter of the majority of the Nineteenth Dragoons, in which crack regiment his second son made for himself quite a career, he found it easier to sell than to save—seeing that that which he sold was his own and not the patrimony of the Dales. At his death the remainder of these purchases had gone. Family arrangements required completion, and Christopher Dale required ready money. The outlying farms flew away, as such new purchases had flown before; but the old patrimony of the Dales remained untouched, as it had ever remained.

It had been a religion among them; and seeing that the worship had been carried on without fail, that the vestal fire had never gone down upon the hearth, I should not have said that the Dales had walked their ways without high principle. To this religion they had all adhered, and the new heir had ever entered in upon his domain without other encumbrances than those with which he himself was then already burdened. And yet there had been no entail. The idea of an entail was not in accordance with the peculiarities of the Dale mind. It was necessary to the Dale religion that each squire should have the power of wasting them. I remember to have dined at a house, the whole glory and fortune of which depended on the safety of a glass goblet. We all know the story. If the luck of Edenhall should be shattered, the doom of the family would be sealed. Nevertheless I was bidden to drink out of the fatal glass, as were all guests in that house. It would not have contented the chivalrous mind of the master to protect his doom by lock and key and padded chest. And so it was with the Dales of Allington. To them an entail would have been a lock and key and a padded chest; but the old chivalry of their house denied to them the use of such protection.

I have spoken something slightingly of the acquirements and doings of the family; and indeed their acquirements had been few and their doings little. At Allington, Dale of Allington had always been known as a king. At Guest-

MONOTYPE PLANTIN 110

9 point, 1 point leaded

FORMAT	PICAS	LINES	WPL	CPL	WPP	CPP
Royal 8vo	26×43	52	13.7	75	712	3900
Demy 8vo	24×40	48	12.7	69	610	3312
Large Crown 8vo	23×36	43	12.0	66	518	2838
Crown 8vo	21×34	41	11.0	60	451	2460

father to son, and from uncle to nephew, and, in one instance, from second cousin to second cousin, the sceptre had descended in the family of the Dales; and the acres had remained intact, growing in value and not decreasing in number, though guarded by no entail and protected by no wonderful amount of prudence or wisdom. The estate of Dale of Allington had been coterminous with the parish of Allington for some hundreds of years; and though, as I have said, the race of squires had possessed nothing of superhuman discretion and had perhaps been guided in their walks through life by no very distinct principles, still there had been with them so much of adherence to a sacred law, that no acre of the property had ever been parted from the hands of the existing squire. Some futile attempts had been made to increase the territory, as indeed had been done by Kit Dale, the father of Christopher Dale, who will appear as our squire of Allington when the persons of our drama are introduced. Old Kit Dale, who had married money, had bought outlying farms—a bit of ground here and a bit there—talking, as he did so, much of political influence and of the good old Tory cause. But these farms and bits of ground had gone again before our time. To them had been attached no religion. When old Kit had found himself pressed in that matter of the majority of the Nineteenth Dragoons, in which crack regiment his second son made for himself quite a career, he found it easier to sell than to save—seeing that that which he sold was his own and not the patrimony of the Dales. At his death the remainder of these purchases had gone. Family arrangements required completion, and Christopher Dale required ready money. The outlying farms flew away, as such new purchases had flown before; but the old patrimony of the Dales remained untouched, as it had ever remained.

It had been a religion among them; and seeing that the worship had been carried on without fail, that the vestal fire had never gone down upon the hearth, I should not have said that the Dales had walked their ways without high principle. To this religion they had all adhered, and the new heir had ever entered in upon his domain without other encumbrances than those with which he himself was then already burdened. And yet there had been no entail. The idea of an entail was not in accordance with the peculiarities of the Dale mind. It was necessary to the Dale religion that each squire should have the power of wasting them. I remember to have dined at a house, the whole glory and fortune of which depended on the safety of a glass goblet. We all know the story. If the luck of Edenhall should be shattered, the doom of the family would be sealed. Nevertheless I was bidden to drink out of the fatal glass, as were all guests in that house. It would not have contented the chivalrous mind of the master to protect his doom by lock and key and padded chest. And so it was with the Dales of Allington. To them an entail would have been a lock and key and a padded chest; but the old chivalry of their house denied to them the use of such protection.

I have spoken something slightingly of the acquirements and doings of the family; and indeed their acquirements had been few and their doings little. At Allington, Dale of Allington had always been known as a king. At

MONOTYPE PLANTIN 110

10 point solid

FORMAT	PICAS	LINES	WPL	CPL	WPP	CPP
Royal 8vo	26×43	52	13.7	73	712	3796
Demy 8vo	24×40	48	12.7	67	609	3216
Large Crown 8vo	23×36	43	11.8	64	510	2752
Crown 8vo	21×34	41	10.8	58	441	2378

father to son, and from uncle to nephew, and, in one instance, from second cousin to second cousin, the sceptre had descended in the family of the Dales; and the acres had remained intact, growing in value and not decreasing in number, though guarded by no entail and protected by no wonderful amount of prudence or wisdom. The estate of Dale of Allington had been coterminous with the parish of Allington for some hundreds of years; and though, as I have said, the race of squires had possessed nothing of superhuman discretion and had perhaps been guided in their walks through life by no very distinct principles, still there had been with them so much of adherence to a sacred law, that no acre of the property had ever been parted from the hands of the existing squire. Some futile attempts had been made to increase the territory, as indeed had been done by Kit Dale, the father of Christopher Dale, who will appear as our squire of Allington when the persons of our drama are introduced. Old Kit Dale, who had married money, had bought outlying farms—a bit of ground here and a bit there—talking, as he did so, much of political influence and of the good old Tory cause. But these farms and bits of ground had gone again before our time. To them had been attached no religion. When old Kit had found himself pressed in that matter of the majority of the Nineteenth Dragoons, in which crack regiment his second son made for himself quite a career, he found it easier to sell than to save—seeing that that which he sold was his own and not the patrimony of the Dales. At his death the remainder of these purchases had gone. Family arrangements required completion, and Christopher Dale required ready money. The outlying farms flew away, as such new purchases had flown before; but the old patrimony of the Dales remained untouched, as it had ever remained.

It had been a religion among them; and seeing that the worship had been carried on without fail, that the vestal fire had never gone down upon the hearth, I should not have said that the Dales had walked their ways without high principle. To this religion they had all adhered and the new heir had ever entered in upon his domain without other encumbrances than those with which he himself was then already burdened. And yet there had been no entail. The idea of an entail was not in accordance with the peculiarities of the Dale mind. It was necessary to the Dale religion that each squire should have the power of wasting them. I remember to have dined at a house, the whole glory and fortune of which depended on the safety of a glass goblet. We all know the story. If the luck of Edenhall should be shattered, the doom of the family would be sealed. Nevertheless I was bidden to drink out of the fatal glass, as were all guests in that house. It would not have contented the *chivalrous mind of the master to protect his doom by lock and key and padded chest. And so it was with the Dales of Allington. To them an entail would have been a lock and key and a padded chest; but the old chivalry of*

MONOTYPE PLANTIN 110

10 point, 1 point leaded

FORMAT	PICAS	LINES	WPL	CPL	WPP	CPP
Royal 8vo	26×43	47	13.7	73	643	3431
Demy 8vo	24×40	44	12.7	67	562	2948
Large Crown 8vo	23×36	39	11.8	64	460	2496
Crown 8vo	21×34	37	10.8	58	399	2146

father to son, and from uncle to nephew, and, in one instance, from second cousin to second cousin, the sceptre had descended in the family of the Dales; and the acres had remained intact, growing in value and not decreasing in number, though guarded by no entail and protected by no wonderful amount of prudence or wisdom. The estate of Dale of Allington had been coterminous with the parish of Allington for some hundreds of years; and though, as I have said, the race of squires had possessed nothing of superhuman discretion and had perhaps been guided in their walks through life by no very distinct principles, still there had been with them so much of adherence to a sacred law, that no acre of the property had ever been parted from the hands of the existing squire. Some futile attempts had been made to increase the territory, as indeed had been done by Kit Dale, the father of Christopher Dale, who will appear as our squire of Allington when the persons of our drama are introduced. Old Kit Dale, who had married money, had bought outlying farms—a bit of ground here and a bit there—talking, as he did so, much of political influence and of the good old Tory cause. But these farms and bits of ground had gone again before our time. To them had been attached no religion. When old Kit had found himself pressed in that matter of the majority of the Nineteenth Dragoons, in which crack regiment his second son made for himself quite a career, he found it easier to sell than to save—seeing that that which he sold was his own and not the patrimony of the Dales. At his death the remainder of these purchases had gone. Family arrangements required completion, and Christopher Dale required ready money. The outlying farms flew away, as such new purchases had flown before; but the old patrimony of the Dales remained untouched, as it had ever remained.

It had been a religion among them; and seeing that the worship had been carried on without fail, that the vestal fire had never gone down upon the hearth, I should not have said that the Dales had walked their ways without high principle. To this religion they had all adhered, and the new heir had ever entered in upon his domain without other encumbrances than those with which he himself was then already burdened. And yet there had been no entail. The idea of an entail was not in accordance with the peculiarities of the Dale mind. It was necessary to the Dale religion that each squire should have the power of wasting them. I remember to have dined at a house, the whole glory and fortune *of which depended on the safety of a glass goblet. We all know the story. If the luck of Edenhall should be shattered, the doom of the family would be sealed. Nevertheless I was bidden to drink out of the fatal glass, as were all*

MONOTYPE PLANTIN 110

10 point, 2 point leaded

FORMAT	PICAS	LINES	WPL	CPL	WPP	CPP
Royal 8vo	26×43	43	13.7	73	589	3139
Demy 8vo	24×40	40	12.7	67	507	2680
Large Crown 8vo	23×36	36	11.8	64	425	2304
Crown 8vo	21×34	34	10.8	58	367	1972

father to son, and from uncle to nephew, and, in one instance, from second cousin to second cousin, the sceptre had descended in the family of the Dales; and the acres had remained intact, growing in value and not decreasing in number, though guarded by no entail and protected by no wonderful amount of prudence or wisdom. The estate of Dale of Allington had been coterminous with the parish of Allington for some hundreds of years; and though, as I have said, the race of squires had possessed nothing of superhuman discretion and had perhaps been guided in their walks through life by no very distinct principles, still there had been with them so much of adherence to a sacred law, that no acre of the property had ever been parted from the hands of the existing squire. Some futile attempts had been made to increase the territory, as indeed had been done by Kit Dale, the father of Christopher Dale, who will appear as our squire of Allington when the persons of our drama are introduced. Old Kit Dale, who had married money, had bought outlying farms—a bit of ground here and a bit there—talking, as he did so, much of political influence and of the good old Tory cause. But these farms and bits of ground had gone again before our time. To them had been attached no religion. When old Kit had found himself pressed in that matter of the majority of the Nineteenth Dragoons, in which crack regiment his second son made for himself quite a career, he found it easier to sell than to save—seeing that that which he sold was his own and not the patrimony of the Dales. At his death the remainder of these purchases had gone. Family arrangements required completion, and Christopher Dale required ready money. The outlying farms flew away, as such new purchases had flown before; but the old patrimony of the Dales remained untouched, as it had ever remained.

It had been a religion among them; and seeing that the worship had been carried on without fail, that the vestal fire had never gone down upon the hearth, I should not have said that the Dales had walked their ways without high principle. To this religion they had all adhered, and the new heir had ever entered in upon his domain without other encumbrances than those with which he himself was then already burdened. And yet there had been no entail. The idea of an entail was not in accordance with the peculiarities of the Dale mind. It was necessary to the Dale religion that each squire should have the power of wasting them. I remember to have dined at a house, the whole glory and fortune *of which depended on the safety of a glass goblet. We all know the story. If the luck of Edenhall should be shattered, the doom of the family would be sealed. Nevertheless I was bidden to drink out of the*

MONOTYPE PLANTIN 110

11 point solid

FORMAT	PICAS	LINES	WPL	CPL	WPP	CPP
Royal 8vo	26×43	47	12.3	67	578	3149
Demy 8vo	24×40	44	11.4	62	502	2728
Large Crown 8vo	23×36	39	10.6	60	413	2340
Crown 8vo	21×34	37	9.6	55	356	2035

father to son, and from uncle to nephew, and, in one instance, from second cousin to second cousin, the sceptre had descended in the family of the Dales; and the acres had remained intact, growing in value and not decreasing in number, though guarded by no entail and protected by no wonderful amount of prudence or wisdom. The estate of Dale of Allington had been coterminous with the parish of Allington for some hundreds of years; and though, as I have said, the race of squires had possessed nothing of superhuman discretion and had perhaps been guided in their walks through life by no very distinct principles, still there had been with them so much of adherence to a sacred law, that no acre of the property had ever been parted from the hands of the existing squire. Some futile attempts had been made to increase the territory, as indeed had been done by Kit Dale, the father of Christopher Dale, who will appear as our squire of Allington when the persons of our drama are introduced. Old Kit Dale, who had married money, had bought outlying farms—a bit of ground here and a bit there—talking, as he did so, much of political influence and of the good old Tory cause. But these farms and bits of ground had gone again before our time. To them had been attached no religion. When old Kit had found himself pressed in that matter of the majority of the Nineteenth Dragoons, in which crack regiment his second son made for himself quite a career, he found it easier to sell than to save—seeing that that which he sold was his own and not the patrimony of the Dales. At his death the remainder of these purchases had gone. Family arrangements required completion, and Christopher Dale required ready money. The outlying farms flew away, as such new purchases had flown before; but the old patrimony of the Dales remained untouched, as it had ever remained.

It had been a religion among them; and seeing that the worship had been carried on without fail, that the vestal fire had never gone down upon the hearth, I should not have said that the Dales had walked their ways without high principle. To this religion they had all adhered, and the new heir had ever entered in upon his domain without other encumbrances than those with which he himself was then already burdened. And yet there had been no *entail. The idea of an entail was not in accordance with the peculiarities of the Dale mind. It was necessary to the Dale religion that each squire should have the power of wasting them. I remember to*

MONOTYPE PLANTIN 110

11 point, 1 point leaded

FORMAT	PICAS	LINES	WPL	CPL	WPP	CPP
Royal 8vo	26×43	43	12.3	67	528	2881
Demy 8vo	24×40	40	11.4	62	452	2480
Large Crown 8vo	23×36	36	10.6	60	380	2160
Crown 8vo	21×34	34	9.6	55	328	1870

father to son, and from uncle to nephew, and, in one instance, from second cousin to second cousin, the sceptre had descended in the family of the Dales; and the acres had remained intact, growing in value and not decreasing in number, though guarded by no entail and protected by no wonderful amount of prudence or wisdom. The estate of Dale of Allington had been coterminous with the parish of Allington for some hundreds of years; and though, as I have said, the race of squires had possessed nothing of superhuman discretion and had perhaps been guided in their walks through life by no very distinct principles, still there had been with them so much of adherence to a sacred law, that no acre of the property had ever been parted from the hands of the existing squire. Some futile attempts had been made to increase the territory, as indeed had been done by Kit Dale, the father of Christopher Dale, who will appear as our squire of Allington when the persons of our drama are introduced. Old Kit Dale, who had married money, had bought outlying farms—a bit of ground here and a bit there—talking, as he did so, much of political influence and of the good old Tory cause. But these farms and bits of ground had gone again before our time. To them had been attached no religion. When old Kit had found himself pressed in that matter of the majority of the Nineteenth Dragoons, in which crack regiment his second son made for himself quite a career, he found it easier to sell that to save—seeing that that which he sold was his own and not the patrimony of the Dales. At his death the remainder of these purchases had gone. Family arrangements required completion, and Christopher Dale required ready money. The outlying farms flew away, as such new purchases had flown before; but the old patrimony of the Dales remained untouched, as it *had ever remained.*

It had been a religion among them; and seeing that the worship had been carried on without fail, that the vestal

MONOTYPE PLANTIN 110

12 point, 1 point leaded

FORMAT	PICAS	LINES	WPL	CPL	WPP	CPP
Royal 8vo	26×43	40	10.5	58	420	2320
Demy 8vo	24×40	37	9.7	54	355	1998
Large Crown 8vo	23×36	33	8.8	52	293	1716
Crown 8vo	21×34	31	8.0	47	250	1457

MONOTYPE POLIPHILUS 170

Synopsis in 10 point

ABCDEFGHIJKLMNOPQRSTUVWXYZ&ÆŒ

ABCDEFGHIJKLMNOPQRSTUVWXYZÆŒ

abcdefghijklmnopqrstuvwxyzæœfiffflffiffl

Related italic · Blado Italic Series 119

ABCDEFGHIJKLMNOPQRSTUVWXYZ&ÆŒ

abcdefghijklmnopqrstuvwxyzæœfiffflffiffl

.,:;!?''-()[]£ *:;!?()* 1234567890 *1234567890*

All normal European accents available

Series 170 *and* 119 *available in composition sizes* 10, 11, 12, 13, 16 *point*

father to son, and from uncle to nephew, and, in one instance, from second cousin to second cousin, the sceptre had descended in the family of the Dales; and the acres had remained intact, growing in value and not decreasing in number, though guarded by no entail and protected by no wonderful amount of prudence or wisdom. The estate of Dale of Allington had been coterminous with the parish of Allington for some hundreds of years; and though, as I have said, the race of squires had possessed nothing of superhuman discretion and had perhaps been guided in their walks through life by no very distinct principles, still there had been with them so much of adherence to a sacred law, that no acre of the property had ever been parted from the hands of the existing squire. Some futile attempts had been made to increase the territory, as indeed had been done by Kit Dale, the father of Christopher Dale, who will appear as our squire of Allington when the persons of our drama are introduced. Old Kit Dale, who had married money, had bought outlying farms—a bit of ground here and a bit there—talking, as he did so, much of political influence and of the good old Tory cause. But these farms and bits of ground had gone again before our time. To them had been attached no religion. When old Kit had found himself pressed in that matter of the majority of the Nineteenth Dragoons, in which crack regiment his second son made for himself quite a career, he found it easier to sell than to save—seeing that that which he sold was his own and not the patrimony of the Dales. At his death the remainder of these purchases had gone. Family arrangements required completion, and Christopher Dale required ready money. The outlying farms flew away, as such new purchases had flown before; but the old patrimony of the Dales remained untouched, as it had ever remained.

It had been a religion among them; and seeing that the worship had been carried on without fail, that the vestal fire had never gone down upon the hearth, I should not have said that the Dales had walked their ways without high principle. To this religion they had all adhered, and the new heir had ever entered in upon his domain without other encumbrances than those with which he himself was then already burdened. And yet there had been no entail. The idea of an entail was not in accordance with the peculiarities of the Dale mind. It was necessary to the Dale religion that each squire should have the power of wasting them. I remember to have dined at a house, the whole glory and fortune of which depended on the safety of a glass goblet. We all know the story. If the luck of Edenhall should be shattered, the doom of the family would be sealed. Nevertheless I was bidden to drink out of the fatal glass, as were all guests in that house. It would not have contented the chivalrous mind of the master to protect his doom by lock and key and padded chest. And so it was with the Dales of Allington. To them an entail would have been a lock and key and a padded chest; but the old chivalry of their house denied to them the use of such protection.

I have spoken something slightingly of the acquirements and doings of the *family; and indeed their acquirements had been few and their doings little. At Allington, Dale of Allington had always been known as a king. At Guestwick, the neighbouring market town, he was a great man—to be seen frequently on Saturdays, standing in the market-place, and*

MONOTYPE POLIPHILUS 170

10 point, 1 point leaded

FORMAT	PICAS	LINES	WPL	CPL	WPP	CPP
Royal 8vo	26×43	47	15.6	83	733	3901
Demy 8vo	24×40	44	14.4	77	632	3388
Large Crown 8vo	23×36	39	13.3	74	521	2886
Crown 8vo	21×34	37	12 2	68	452	2516

father to son, and from uncle to nephew, and, in one instance, from second cousin to second cousin, the sceptre had descended in the family of the Dales; and the acres had remained intact, growing in value and not decreasing in number, though guarded by no entail and protected by no wonderful amount of prudence or wis-dom. The estate of Dale of Allington had been coterminous with the parish of Allington for some hundreds of years; and though, as I have said, the race of squires had possessed nothing of superhuman discretion and had perhaps been guided in their walks through life by no very distinct principles, still there had been with them so much of adherence to a sacred law, that no acre of the property had ever been parted from the hands of the existing squire. Some futile attempts had been made to increase the territory, as indeed had been done by Kit Dale, the father of Christopher Dale, who will appear as our squire of Allington when the persons of our drama are introduced. Old Kit Dale, who had married money, had bought outlying farms—a bit of ground here and a bit there—talking, as he did so, much of political influence and of the good old Tory cause. But these farms and bits of ground had gone again before our time. To them had been attached no religion. When old Kit had found himself pressed in that matter of the majority of the Nineteenth Dragoons, in which crack regiment his second son made for himself quite a career, he found it easier to sell than to save—seeing that that which he sold was his own and not the patrimony of the Dales. At his death the remainder of these purchases had gone. Family arrangements required completion, and Chris-topher Dale required ready money. The outlying farms flew away, as such new purchases had flown before; but the old patrimony of the Dales remained un-touched, as it had ever remained.

It had been a religion among them; and seeing that the worship had been carried on without fail, that the vestal fire had never gone down upon the hearth. I should not have said that the Dales had walked their ways without high principle. To this religion they had all adhered, and the new heir had ever entered in upon his domain without other encumbrances than those with which he himself was then already burdened. And yet there had been no entail. The idea of an entail was not in accordance with the peculiarities of the Dale mind. It was necessary to the Dale religion that each squire should have the power of wasting them. I remember to have dined at a house, the whole glory and fortune of which depended on the safety of a glass goblet. We all know the story. If the luck of Edenhall should be shattered, the doom of the family would be sealed. Nevertheless I was bidden to drink out of the fatal glass, as were all guests in that house. It would not have contented the chivalrous mind of the master to protect his doom by lock and key and padded *chest. And so it was with the Dales of Allington. To them an entail would have been a lock and key and a padded chest; but the old chivalry of their house denied to them the use of such protection.*

MONOTYPE POLIPHILUS 170

10 point, 2 point leaded

FORMAT	PICAS	LINES	WPL	CPL	WPP	CPP
Royal 8vo	26×43	43	15.6	83	670	3569
Demy 8vo	24×40	40	14.4	77	572	3080
Large Crown 8vo	23×36	36	13.3	74	479	2664
Crown 8vo	21×34	34	12.2	68	415	2312

father to son, and from uncle to nephew, and, in one instance, from second cousin to second cousin, the sceptre had descended in the family of the Dales; and the acres had remained intact, growing in value and not decreasing in number, though guarded by no entail and protected by no wonderful amount of prudence or wisdom. The estate of Dale of Allington had been coterminous with the parish of Allington for some hundreds of years; and though, as I have said, the race of squires had possessed nothing of superhuman discretion and had perhaps been guided in their walks through life by no very distinct principles, still there had been with them so much of adherence to a sacred law, that no acre of the property had ever been parted from the hands of the existing squire. Some futile attempts had been made to increase the territory, as indeed had been done by Kit Dale, the father of Christopher Dale, who will appear as our squire of Allington when the persons of our drama are introduced. Old Kit Dale, who had married money, had bought outlying farms—a bit of ground here and a bit there—talking, as he did so, much of political influence and of the good old Tory cause. But these farms and bits of ground had gone again before our time. To them had been attached no religion. When old Kit had found himself pressed in that matter of the majority of the Nineteenth Dragoons, in which crack regiment his second son made for himself quite a career, he found it easier to sell than to save—seeing that that which he sold was his own and not the patrimony of the Dales. At his death the remainder of these purchases had gone. Family arrangements required completion, and Christopher Dale required ready money. The outlying farms flew away, as such new purchases had flown before; but the old patrimony of the Dales remained untouched, as it had ever remained.

It had been a religion among them; and seeing that the worship had been carried on without fail, that the vestal fire had never gone down upon the hearth, I should not have said that the Dales had walked their ways without high principle. To this religion they had all adhered, and the new heir had ever entered in upon his domain without other encumbrances than those with which he himself was then already burdened. And yet there had been no entail. The idea of an entail was not in accordance with the peculiarities of the Dale mind. It was necessary to the Dale religion that each squire should have the power of wasting them. I remember to have dined at a house, the whole glory and fortune of which depended on the safety of a glass goblet. We all know the story. If the luck of Edenhall should be shattered, the doom of the family would be sealed. Nevertheless I was bidden to drink out of the fatal glass, as were all guests in that house. It would not have contented the chivalrous mind of the master to protect his doom by lock and key and padded chest. And so it was with the Dales of Allington. To them an entail *would have been a lock and key and a padded chest; but the old chivalry of their house denied to them the use of such protection.*

I have spoken something slightingly of the acquirements and doings of the family;

MONOTYPE POLIPHILUS 170

11 point solid

FORMAT	PICAS	LINES	WPL	CPL	WPP	CPP
Royal 8vo	26×43	47	14.4	78	676	3666
Demy 8vo	24×40	44	13.3	72	585	3168
Large Crown 8vo	23×36	39	12.5	69	487	2691
Crown 8vo	21×34	37	11.4	63	423	2331

father to son, and from uncle to nephew, and, in one instance, from second cousin to second cousin, the sceptre had descended in the family of the Dales; and the acres had remained intact, growing in value and not decreasing in number, though guarded by no entail and protected by no wonderful amount of prudence or wisdom. The estate of Dale of Allington had been coterminous with the parish of Allington for some hundreds of years; and though, as I have said, the race of squires had possessed nothing of superhuman discretion and had perhaps been guided in their walks through life by no very distinct principles, still there had been with them so much of adherence to a sacred law, that no acre of the property had ever been parted from the hands of the existing squire. Some futile attempts had been made to increase the territory, as indeed had been done by Kit Dale, the father of Christopher Dale, who will appear as our squire of Allington when the persons of our drama are introduced. Old Kit Dale, who had married money, had bought outlying farms—a bit of ground here and a bit there—talking, as he did so, much of political influence and of the good old Tory cause. But these farms and bits of ground had gone again before our time. To them had been attached no religion. When old Kit had found himself pressed in that matter of the majority of the Nineteenth Dragoons, in which crack regiment his second son made for himself quite a career, he found it easier to sell than to save—seeing that that which he sold was his own and not the patrimony of the Dales. At his death the remainder of these purchases had gone. Family arrangements required completion, and Christopher Dale required ready money. The outlying farms flew away, as such new purchases had flown before; but the old patrimony of the Dales remained untouched, as it had ever remained.

It had been a religion among them; and seeing that the worship had been carried on without fail, that the vestal fire had never gone down upon the hearth, I should not have said that the Dales had walked their ways without high principle. To this religion they had all adhered, and the new heir had ever entered in upon his domain without other encumbrances than those with which he himself was then already burdened. And yet there had been no entail. The idea of an entail was not in accordance with the peculiarities of the Dale mind. It was necessary to the Dale religion that each squire should have the power of wasting them. I remember to have dined at a house, the whole glory and fortune of which depended on the safety of a glass goblet. We all know the story. If the luck of Edenhall should be shattered, the doom *of the family would be sealed. Nevertheless I was bidden to drink out of the fatal glass, as were all guests in that house. It would not have contented the chivalrous mind of the master to protect his doom by lock and key and padded chest. And so it was with*

MONOTYPE POLIPHILUS 170

11 point, 1 point leaded

FORMAT	PICAS	LINES	WPL	CPL	WPP	CPP
Royal 8vo	26×43	43	14.4	78	619	3354
Demy 8vo	24×40	40	13.3	72	538	2880
Large Crown 8vo	23×36	36	12.5	69	448	2484
Crown 8vo	21×34	34	11.4	63	386	2142

father to son, and from uncle to nephew, and, in one instance, from second cousin to second cousin, the sceptre had descended in the family of the Dales; and the acres had remained intact, growing in value and not decreasing in number, though guarded by no entail and protected by no wonderful amount of prudence or wisdom. The estate of Dale of Allington had been coterminous with the parish of Allington for some hundreds of years; and though, as I have said, the race of squires had possessed nothing of superhuman discretion and had perhaps been guided in their walks through life by no very distinct principles, still there had been with them so much of adherence to a sacred law, that no acre of the property had ever been parted from the hands of the existing squire. Some futile attempts had been made to increase the territory, as indeed had been done by Kit Dale, the father of Christopher Dale, who will appear as our squire of Allington when the persons of our drama are introduced. Old Kit Dale, who had married money, had bought outlying farms—a bit of ground here and a bit there—talking, as he did so, much of political influence and of the good old Tory cause. But these farms and bits of ground had gone again before our time. To them had been attached no religion. When old Kit had found himself pressed in that matter of the majority of the Nineteenth Dragoons, in which crack regiment his second son made for himself quite a career, he found it easier to sell than to save—seeing that that which he sold was his own and not the patrimony of the Dales. At his death the remainder of these purchases had gone. Family arrangements required completion, and Christopher Dale required ready money. The outlying farms flew away, as such new purchases had flown before; but the old patrimony of the Dales remained untouched, as it had ever remained.

It had been a religion among them; and seeing that the worship had been carried on without fail, that the vestal fire had never gone down upon the hearth, I should not have said that the Dales had walked their ways without high principle. To this religion they had all adhered, and the new heir had ever entered in upon his domain without other encumbrances than those with which he himself was then already burdened. And yet there had been no *entail. The idea of an entail was not in accordance with the peculiarities of the Dale mind. It was necessary to the Dale religion that each squire should have the power of wasting them. I remember to have dined at a*

MONOTYPE POLIPHILUS 170

12 point solid

FORMAT	PICAS	LINES	WPL	CPL	WPP	CPP
Royal 8vo	26×43	43	12.3	67	528	2881
Demy 8vo	24×40	40	11.4	62	456	2480
Large Crown 8vo	23×36	36	10.5	59	378	2124
Crown 8vo	21×34	34	9.7	54	331	1836

father to son, and from uncle to nephew, and, in one instance, from second cousin to second cousin, the sceptre had descended in the family of the Dales; and the acres had remained intact, growing in value and not decreasing in number, though guarded by no entail and protected by no wonderful amount of prudence or wisdom. The estate of Dale of Allington had been coterminous with the parish of Allington for some hundreds of years; and though, as I have said, the race of squires had possessed nothing of superhuman discretion and had perhaps been guided in their walks through life by no very distinct principles, still there had been with them so much of adherence to a sacred law, that no acre of the property had ever been parted from the hands of the existing squire. Some futile attempts had been made to increase the territory, as indeed had been done by Kit Dale, the father of Christopher Dale, who will appear as our squire of Allington when the persons of our drama are introduced. Old Kit Dale, who had married money, had bought outlying farms—a bit of ground here and a bit there—talking, as he did so, much of political influence and of the good old Tory cause. But these farms and bits of ground had gone again before our time. To them had been attached no religion. When old Kit had found himself pressed in that matter of the majority of the Nineteenth Dragoons, in which crack regiment his second son made for himself quite a career, he found it easier to sell than to save—seeing that that which he sold was his own and not the patrimony of the Dales. At his death the remainder of these purchases had gone. Family arrangements required completion, and Christopher Dale required ready money. The outlying farms flew away, as such new purchases had flown before; but the old patrimony of the Dales remained untouched, as it had ever remained.

It had been a religion among them; and seeing that the worship had been carried on without fail, that the vestal fire had never gone down upon the hearth, I should not have said that the Dales had walked their ways without high principle. To this religion they *had all adhered, and the new heir had ever entered in upon his domain without other encumbrances than those with which he himself was then already burdened. And yet there had been no entail. The idea of an entail was not*

MONOTYPE POLIPHILUS 170

12 point, 1 point leaded

FORMAT	PICAS	LINES	WPL	CPL	WPP	CPP
Royal 8vo	26×43	40	12.3	67	492	2680
Demy 8vo	24×40	37	11.4	62	423	2294
Large Crown 8vo	23×36	33	10.5	59	348	1947
Crown 8vo	21×34	31	9.7	54	300	1674

father to son, and from uncle to nephew, and, in one instance, from the second cousin to the second cousin, the sceptre had descended in the family of the Dales; and the acres had remained intact, growing in value and not decreasing in num- ber, though guarded by no entail and protected by no won- derful amount of prudence or wisdom. The estate of Dale of Allington had been coterminous with the parish of Allington for some hundreds of years; and though, as I have said, the race of squires had possessed nothing of superhuman dis- cretion and had perhaps been guided in their walks through life by no very distinct principles, still there had been with them so much of adherence to a sacred law, that no acre of the property had ever been parted from the hands of the existing squire. Some futile attempts had been made to increase the territory, as indeed had been done by Kit Dale, the father of Christopher Dale, who will appear as our squire of Allington when the persons of our drama are introduced. Old Kit Dale, who had married money, had bought out- lying farms—a bit of ground here and a bit there—talking, as he did so, much of political influence and of the good old Tory cause. But these farms and bits of ground had gone again before our time. To them had been attached no re- ligion. When old Kit had found himself pressed in that matter of the majority of the Nineteenth Dragoons, in which crack regiment his second son made for himself quite a career, he found it easier to sell than to save—seeing that that which he sold was his own and not the patrimony of the Dales. At his death the remainder of these purchases had gone. Family arrangements required completion, and Chris- topher Dale required ready money. The outlying farms flew away, as such new purchases had flown before; but the old patrimony of the Dales remained untouched, as it had ever remained.

It had been a religion among them; and seeing that the *worship had been carried on without fail, that the vestal fire had never gone down upon the hearth, I should not have said that the Dales had walked their ways without high principle. To this religion they had all*

MONOTYPE POLIPHILUS 170

13 point solid

FORMAT	PICAS	LINES	WPL	CPL	WPP	CPP
Royal 8vo	26×43	40	11.3	62	452	2480
Demy 8vo	24×40	37	10.5	57	386	2109
Large Crown 8vo	23×36	33	9.6	55	315	1815
Crown 8vo	21×34	31	9.0	50	276	1550

father to son, and from uncle to nephew, and, in one instance, from the second cousin to the second cousin, the sceptre had descended in the family of the Dales; and the acres had remained intact, growing in value and not decreasing in number, though guarded by no entail and protected by no wonderful amount of prudence or wisdom. The estate of Dale of Allington had been coterminous with the parish of Allington for some hundreds of years; and though, as I have said, the race of squires had possessed nothing of superhuman discretion and had perhaps been guided in their walks through life by no very distinct principles, still there had been with them so much of adherence to a sacred law, that no acre of the property had ever been parted from the hands of the existing squire. Some futile attempts had been made to increase the territory, as indeed had been done by Kit Dale, the father of Christopher Dale, who will appear as our squire of Allington when the persons of our drama are introduced. Old Kit Dale, who had married money, had bought outlying farms—a bit of ground here and a bit there—talking, as he did so, much of political influence and of the good old Tory cause. But these farms and bits of ground had gone again before our time. To them had been attached no religion. When old Kit had found himself pressed in that matter of the majority of the Nineteenth Dragoons, in which crack regiment his second son made for himself quite a career, he found it easier to sell than to save—seeing that that which he sold was his own and not the patrimony of the Dales. At his death the remainder of these purchases had gone. Family arrangements required completion, and Christopher Dale required ready money. The outlying farms flew away, as such new purchases had flown before; but the old *patrimony of the Dales remained untouched, as it had ever remained.*

It had been a religion among them; and seeing that the worship had been carried on without fail, that the vestal fire had never gone down

MONOTYPE POLIPHILUS 170

13 point, 1 point leaded

FORMAT	PICAS	LINES	WPL	CPL	WPP	CPP
Royal 8vo	26×43	37	11.3	62	418	2294
Demy 8vo	24×40	34	10.5	57	359	1938
Large Crown 8vo	23×36	31	9.6	55	300	1705
Crown 8vo	21×34	29	9.0	50	260	1450

father to son, and from uncle to nephew, and, in one instance, from second cousin to second cousin, the sceptre had descended in the family of the Dales; and the acres had remained intact, growing in value and not decreasing in number, though guarded by no entail and protected by no wonderful amount of prudence or wisdom. The estate of Dale of Allington had been coterminous with the parish of Allington for some hundreds of years; and though, as I have said, the race of squires had possessed nothing of superhuman discretion and had perhaps been guided in their walks through life by no very distinct principles, still there had been with them so much of adherence to a sacred law, that no acre of the property had ever been parted from the hands of the existing squire. Some futile attempts had been made to increase the territory, as indeed had been done by Kit Dale, the father of Christopher Dale, who will appear as our squire of Allington when the persons of our drama are introduced. Old Kit Dale, who had married money, had bought outlying farms—a bit of ground here and a bit there—talking, as he did so, much of political influence and of the good old Tory cause. But these farms and bits of ground had gone again before our time. To them had been attached no religion. When old Kit had found himself pressed in that matter of the majority of the *Nineteenth Dragoons, in which crack regiment his second son made for himself quite a career, he found it easier to sell than to save—seeing that that which he sold was his own and not the*

MONOTYPE POLIPHILUS 170

16 point solid

FORMAT	PICAS	LINES	WPL	CPL	WPP	CPP
Royal 8vo	26×43	32	10.2	53	326	1696
Demy 8vo	24×40	30	9.5	49	284	1470
Large Crown 8vo	23×36	27	8.4	47	225	1269
Crown 8vo	21×34	25	7.7	43	193	1075

MONOTYPE SCOTCH ROMAN 46

Synopsis in 10 *point*

ABCDEFGHIJKLMNOPQRSTUVWXYZ&ÆŒ

ABCDEFGHIJKLMNOPQRSTUVWXYZÆŒ

abcdefghijklmnopqrstuvwxyzæœfiffflffiffl

ABCDEFGHIJKLMNOPQRSTUVWXYZ &ÆŒ

abcdefghijklmnopqrstuvwxyzæœfiffflffiffl

.,:;!?‘’-()[]£ *:;!?* 1234567890

All normal European accents available

Available in composition sizes 9, 10, 11, 12 *point*

father to son, and from uncle to nephew, and, in one instance, from second cousin to second cousin, the sceptre had descended in the family of the Dales; and the acres had remained intact, growing in value and not decreasing in number, though guarded by no entail and protected by no wonderful amount of prudence or wisdom. The estate of Dale of Allington had been coterminous with the parish of Allington for some hundreds of years; and though, as I have said, the race of squires had possessed nothing of superhuman discretion and had perhaps been guided in their walks through life by no very distinct principles, still there had been with them so much of adherence to a sacred law, that no acre of the property had ever been parted from the hands of the existing squire. Some futile attempts had been made to increase the territory, as indeed had been done by Kit Dale, the father of Christopher Dale, who will appear as our squire of Allington when the persons of our drama are introduced. Old Kit Dale, who had married money, had bought outlying farms—a bit of ground here and a bit there—talking, as he did so, much of political influence and of the good old Tory cause. But these farms and bits of ground had gone again before our time. To them had been attached no religion. When old Kit had found himself pressed in that matter of the majority of the Nineteenth Dragoons, in which crack regiment his second son made for himself quite a career, he found it easier to sell than to save—seeing that that which he sold was his own and not the patrimony of the Dales. At his death the remainder of these purchases had gone. Family arrangements required completion, and Christopher Dale required ready money. The outlying farms flew away, as such new purchases had flown before; but the old patrimony of the Dales remained untouched, as it had ever remained.

It had been a religion among them; and seeing that the worship had been carried on without fail, that the vestal fire had never gone down upon the hearth, I should not have said that the Dales had walked their ways without high principle. To this religion they had all adhered, and the new heir had ever entered in upon his domain without other encumbrances than those with which he himself was then already burdened. And yet there had been no entail. The idea of an entail was not in accordance with the peculiarities of the Dale mind. It was necessary to the Dale religion that each squire should have the power of wasting them. I remember to have dined at a house, the whole glory and fortune of which depended on the safety of a glass goblet. We all know the story. If the luck of Edenhall should be shattered, the doom of the family would be sealed. Nevertheless I was bidden to drink out of the fatal glass, as were all guests in that house. It would not have contented the chivalrous mind of the master to protect his doom by lock and key and padded chest. And so it was with the Dales of Allington. To them an entail would have been a lock and key and a padded chest; but the old chivalry of their house denied to them the use of such protection.

I have spoken something slightingly of the acquirements and doings of the family; and indeed their acquirements had been few and their doings little. At Allington, Dale of Allington had always been known as a king. At

MONOTYPE SCOTCH ROMAN 46

9 point, 1 point leaded

FORMAT	PICAS	LINES	WPL	CPL	WPP	CPP
Royal 8vo	26×43	52	13.7	74	712	3848
Demy 8vo	24×40	48	12.7	68	609	3264
Large Crown 8vo	23×36	43	11.9	65	511	2795
Crown 8vo	21×34	41	10.8	59	443	2419

father to son, and from uncle to nephew, and, in one instance, from second cousin to second cousin, the sceptre had descended in the family of the Dales; and the acres had remained intact, growing in value and not decreasing in number, though guarded by no entail and protected by no wonderful amount of prudence or wisdom. The estate of Dale of Allington had been coterminous with the parish of Allington for some hundreds of years; and though, as I have said, the race of squires had possessed nothing of superhuman discretion and had perhaps been guided in their walks through life by no very distinct principles, still there had been with them so much of adherence to a sacred law, that no acre of the property had ever been parted from the hands of the existing squire. Some futile attempts had been made to increase the territory, as indeed had been done by Kit Dale, the father of Christopher Dale, who will appear as our squire of Allington when the persons of our drama are introduced. Old Kit Dale, who had married money, had bought outlying farms—a bit of ground here and a bit there—talking, as he did so, much of political influence and of the good old Tory cause. But these farms and bits of ground had gone again before our time. To them had been attached no religion. When old Kit had found himself pressed in that matter of the majority of the Nineteenth Dragoons, in which crack regiment his second son made for himself quite a career, he found it easier to sell than to save—seeing that that which he sold was his own and not the patrimony of the Dales. At his death the remainder of these purchases had gone. Family arrangements required completion, and Christopher Dale required ready money. The outlying farms flew away, as such new purchases had flown before; but the old patrimony of the Dales remained untouched, as it had ever remained.

It had been a religion among them; and seeing that the worship had been carried on without fail, that the vestal fire had never gone down upon the hearth, I should not have said that the Dales had walked their ways without high principles. To this religion they had all adhered, and the new heir had ever entered in upon his domain without other encumbrances than those with which he himself was then already burdened. And yet there had been no entail. The idea of an entail was not in accordance with the peculiarities of the Dale mind. It was necessary to the Dale religion that each squire should have the power of wasting them. I remember to have dined at a house, the whole glory and fortune of which depended on the safety of a glass goblet. We all know the story. If the luck of Edenhall should be shattered, the doom of the family would be sealed. Nevertheless I was bidden to drink out of the fatal glass, as were all guests in that house. It would not have contented the chivalrous mind of the master to protect his doom by *lock and key and padded chest. And so it was with the Dales of Allington. To them an entail would have been a lock and key and a padded chest; but the old chivalry of their house denied to them the use of such*

MONOTYPE SCOTCH ROMAN 46

10 point solid

FORMAT	PICAS	LINES	WPL	CPL	WPP	CPP
Royal 8vo	26×43	52	12.8	67	666	3484
Demy 8vo	24×40	48	11.9	62	571	2976
Large Crown 8vo	23×36	43	10.9	60	468	2580
Crown 8vo	21×34	41	10.0	55	410	2255

father to son, and from uncle to nephew, and, in one instance, from second cousin to second cousin, the sceptre had descended in the family of the Dales; and the acres had remained intact, growing in value and not decreasing in number, though guarded by no entail and protected by no wonderful amount of prudence or wisdom. The estate of Dale of Allington had been coterminous with the parish of Allington for some hundreds of years; and though, as I have said, the race of squires had possessed nothing of superhuman discretion and had perhaps been guided in their walks through life by no very distinct principles, still there had been with them so much of adherence to a sacred law, that no acre of the property had ever been parted from the hands of the existing squire. Some futile attempts had been made to increase the territory, as indeed had been done by Kit Dale, the father of Christopher Dale, who will appear as our squire of Allington when the persons of our drama are introduced. Old Kit Dale, who had married money, had bought outlying farms—a bit of ground here and a bit there—talking, as he did so, much of political influence and of the good old Tory cause. But these farms and bits of ground had gone again before our time. To them had been attached no religion. When old Kit had found himself pressed in that matter of the majority of the Nineteenth Dragoons, in which crack regiment his second son made for himself quite a career, he found it easier to sell than to save—seeing that that which he sold was his own and not the patrimony of the Dales. At his death the remainder of these purchases had gone. Family arrangements required completion, and Christopher Dale required ready money. The outlying farms flew away, as such new purchases had flown before; but the old patrimony of the Dales remained untouched, as it had ever remained.

It had been a religion among them; and seeing that the worship had been carried on without fail, that the vestal fire had never gone down upon the hearth, I should not have said that the Dales had walked their ways without high principles. To this religion they had all adhered, and the new heir had ever entered in upon his domain without other encumbrances than those with which he himself was then already burdencd. And yet there had been no entail. The idea of an entail was not in accordance with the peculiarities of the Dale mind. It was necessary to the Dale religion that each squire should have the power of wasting them. I remember to have dined at a house, the whole glory and fortune of which depended on the safety of a glass goblet. We all know the story. If the luck *of Edenhall should be shattered, the doom of the family would be sealed. Nevertheless I was bidden to drink out of the fatal glass, as were all guests in that house. It would not have contented the chivalrous mind*

MONOTYPE SCOTCH ROMAN 46

10 point, 1 point leaded

FORMAT	PICAS	LINES	WPL	CPL	WPP	CPP
Royal 8vo	26×43	47	12.8	67	601	3149
Demy 8vo	24×40	44	11.9	62	519	2728
Large Crown 8vo	23×36	39	10.9	60	423	2340
Crown 8vo	21×34	37	10.0	55	368	2035

father to son, and from uncle to nephew, and, in one instance, from second cousin to second cousin, the sceptre had descended in the family of the Dales; and the acres had remained intact, but growing in value and not decreasing in number, though guarded by no entail and protected by no wonderful amount of prudence or wisdom. The estate of Dale of Allington had been coterminous with the parish of Allington for some hundreds of years; and though, as I have said, the race of squires had possessed nothing of superhuman discretion and had perhaps been guided in their walks through life by no very distinct principles, still there had been with them so much of adherence to a sacred law, that no acre of the property had ever been parted from the hands of the existing squire. Some futile attempts had been made to increase the territory, as indeed had been done by Kit Dale, the father of Christopher Dale, who will appear as our squire of Allington when the persons of our drama are introduced. Old Kit Dale, who had married money, had bought outlying farms—a bit of ground here and a bit there—talking, as he did so, much of political influence and of the good old Tory cause. But these farms and bits of ground had gone again before our time. To them had been attached no religion. When old Kit had found himself pressed in that matter of the majority of the Nineteenth Dragoons, in which crack regiment his second son made for himself quite a career, he found it easier to sell than to save—seeing that that which he sold was his own and not the patrimony of the Dales. At his death the remainder of these purchases had gone. Family arrangements required completion, and Christopher Dale required ready money. The outlying farms flew away, as such new purchases had flown before; but the old patrimony of the Dales remained untouched, as it had ever remained.

It had been a religion among them; and seeing that the worship had been carried on without fail, that the vestal fire had never gone down upon the hearth, I should not have said that the Dales had walked their ways without high principle. To this religion they had all adhered, and the new heir had ever entered in upon his domain without other encumbrances than those with which he himself was then already burdened. And yet there had been no entail. The idea of an entail was not in accordance with the peculiarities of the Dale mind. It was *necessary to the Dale religion that each squire should have the power of wasting them. I remember to have dined at a house, the whole glory and fortune of which depended on the safety of a glass*

MONOTYPE SCOTCH ROMAN 46

11 point solid

FORMAT	PICAS	LINES	WPL	CPL	WPP	CPP
Royal 8vo	26×43	47	11.5	63	540	2961
Demy 8vo	24×40	44	10.7	58	471	2552
Large Crown 8vo	23×36	39	10.0	55	390	2145
Crown 8vo	21×34	37	9.1	51	338	1887

father to son, and from uncle to nephew, and, in one instance, from second cousin to second cousin, the sceptre had descended in the family of the Dales; and the acres had remained intact, but growing in value and not decreasing in number, though guarded by no entail and protected by no wonderful amount of prudence or wisdom. The estate of Dale of Allington had been coterminous with the parish of Allington for some hundreds of years; and though, as I have said, the race of squires had possessed nothing of superhuman discretion and had perhaps been guided in their walks through life by no very distinct principles, still there had been with them so much of adherence to a sacred law, that no acre of the property had ever been parted from the hands of the existing squire. Some futile attempts had been made to increase the territory, as indeed had been done by Kit Dale, the father of Christopher Dale, who will appear as our squire of Allington when the persons of our drama are introduced. Old Kit Dale, who had married money, had bought outlying farms—a bit of ground here and a bit there—talking, as he did so, much of political influence and of the good old Tory cause. But these farms and bits of ground had gone again before our time. To them had been attached no religion. When old Kit had found himself pressed in that matter of the majority of the Nineteenth Dragoons, in which crack regiment his second son made for himself quite a career, he found it easier to sell than to save—seeing that that which he sold was his own and not the patrimony of the Dales. At his death the remainder of these purchases had gone. Family arrangements required completion, and Christopher Dale required ready money. The outlying farms flew away, as such new purchases had flown before; but the old patrimony of the Dales remained untouched, as it had ever remained.

It had been a religion among them; and seeing that the worship had been carried on without fail, that the vestal fire had never gone down upon the hearth, I should not have said that the Dales had walked their ways without high principle. To this religion they had all adhered, and the new heir had ever *entered in upon his domain without other encumbrances than those with which he himself was then already burdened. And yet there had been no entail. The idea of an entail was not in accord-*

MONOTYPE SCOTCH ROMAN 46

11 point, 1 point leaded

FORMAT	PICAS	LINES	WPL	CPL	WPP	CPP
Royal 8vo	26×43	43	11.5	63	494	2709
Demy 8vo	24×40	40	10.7	58	425	2320
Large Crown 8vo	23×36	36	10.0	55	362	1980
Crown 8vo	21×34	34	9.1	51	310	1734

father to son, and from uncle to nephew, and, in one instance, from second cousin to second cousin, the sceptre had descended in the family of the Dales; and the acres had remained intact, growing in value and not decreasing in number, though guarded by no entail and protected by no wonderful amount of prudence or wisdom. The estate of Dale of Allington had been coterminous with the parish of Allington for some hundreds of years; and though, as I have said, the race of squires had possessed nothing of superhuman discretion and had perhaps been guided in their walks through life by no very distinct principles, still there had been with them so much of adherence to a sacred law, that no acre of the property had ever been parted from the hands of the existing squire. Some futile attempts had been made to increase the territory, as indeed had been done by Kit Dale, the father of Christopher Dale, who will appear as our squire of Allington when the persons of our drama are introduced. Old Kit Dale, who had married money, had bought outlying farms—a bit of ground here and a bit there—talking, as he did so, much of political influence and of the good old Tory cause. But these farms and bits of ground had gone again before our time. To them had been attached no religion. When old Kit had found himself pressed in that matter of the majority of the Nineteenth Dragoons, in which crack regiment his second son made for himself quite a career, he found it easier to sell than to save—seeing that that which he sold was his own and not the patrimony of the Dales. At his death the remainder of these purchases had gone. Family arrangements required completion, and Christopher Dale required ready money. The outlying farms flew away, as such new purchases had flown before; but the old patrimony of the Dales remained untouched, as it had ever remained.

It had been a religion among them; and seeing that *the worship had been carried on without fail, that the vestal fire had never gone down upon the hearth, I should not have said that the Dales had walked their ways without*

MONOTYPE SCOTCH ROMAN 46

12 point solid

FORMAT	PICAS	LINES	WPL	CPL	WPP	CPP
Royal 8vo	26×43	43	10.1	55	434	2365
Demy 8vo	24×40	40	9.4	51	376	2040
Large Crown 8vo	23×36	36	8.8	49	317	1764
Crown 8vo	21×34	34	8.1	45	274	1530

father to son, and from uncle to nephew, and, in one instance, from second cousin to second cousin, the sceptre had descended in the family of the Dales; and the acres had remained intact, growing in value and not decreasing in number, though guarded by no entail and protected by no wonderful amount of prudence or wisdom. The estate of Dale of Allington had been coterminous with the parish of Allington for some hundreds of years; and though, as I have said, the race of squires had possessed nothing of superhuman discretion and had perhaps been guided in their walks through life by no very distinct principles, still there had been with them so much of adherence to a sacred law, that no acre of the property had ever been parted from the hands of the existing squire. Some futile attempts had been made to increase the territory, as indeed had been done by Kit Dale, the father of Christopher Dale, who will appear as our squire of Allington when the persons of our drama are introduced. Old Kit Dale, who had married money, had bought outlying farms—a bit of ground here and a bit there—talking, as he did so, much of political influence and of the good old Tory cause. But these farms and bits of ground had gone again before our time. To them had been attached no religion. When old Kit had found himself pressed in that matter of the majority of the Nineteenth Dragoons, in which crack regiment his second son made for himself quite a career, he found it easier to sell than to save—seeing that that which he sold was his own and not the patrimony of the Dales. At his death the remainder of these purchases had gone. Family arrangements required completion, and Christopher Dale required ready money. The outlying farms flew away, as such new purchases had flown before; *but the old patrimony of the Dales remained untouched, as it had ever remained.*

It had been a religion among them; and seeing that the

MONOTYPE SCOTCH ROMAN 46

12 point, 1 point leaded

FORMAT	PICAS	LINES	WPL	CPL	WPP	CPP
Royal 8vo	26×43	40	10.1	55	404	2200
Demy 8vo	24×40	37	9.4	51	345	1887
Large Crown 8vo	23×36	33	8.8	49	292	1617
Crown 8vo	21×34	31	8.1	45	253	1395

MONOTYPE SPECTRUM 556

Synopsis in 10 D *on* 11 *point*

ABCDEFGHIJKLMNOPQRSTUVWXYZ&ÆŒ

ABCDEFGHIJKLMNOPQRSTUVWXYZÆŒ

abcdefghijklmnopqrstuvwxyzæœfiffflffiffl

ABCDEFGHIJKLMNOPQRSTUVWXYZ&ÆŒ

abcdefghijklmnopqrstuvwxyzææfiffflffiffl

.,:;!?'-()[]£ *:;!?()[]*

1234567890 *1234567890* 1234567890

All normal European accents available

Available in composition sizes 8 *on* 9, 10 *on* 11, 12 *on* 13 *point*

father to son, and from uncle to nephew, and, in one instance, from second cousin to second cousin, the sceptre had descended in the family of the Dales; and the acres had remained intact, growing in value and not decreasing in number, though guarded by no entail and protected by no wonderful amount of prudence or wisdom. The estate of Dale of Allington had been coterminous with the parish of Allington for some hundreds of years; and though, as I have said, the race of squires had possessed nothing of superhuman discretion and had perhaps been guided in their walks through life by no very distinct principles, still there had been with them so much of adherence to a sacred law, that no acre of the property had ever been parted from the hands of the existing squire. Some futile attempts had been made to increase the territory, as indeed had been done by Kit Dale, the father of Christopher Dale, who will appear as our squire of Allington when the persons of our drama are introduced. Old Kit Dale, who had married money, had bought outlying farms—a bit of ground here and a bit there—talking, as he did so, much of political influence and of the good old Tory cause. But these farms and bits of ground had gone again before our time. To them had been attached no religion. When old Kit had found himself pressed in that matter of the majority of the Nineteenth Dragoons, in which crack regiment his second son made for himself quite a career, he found it easier to sell than to save—seeing that that which he sold was his own and not the patrimony of the Dales. At his death the remainder of these purchases had gone. Family arrangements required completion, and Christopher Dale required ready money. The outlying farms flew away, as such new purchases had flown before; but the old patrimony of the Dales remained untouched, as it had ever remained.

It had been a religion among them; and seeing that the worship had been carried on without fail, that the vestal fire had never gone down upon the hearth, I should not have said that the Dales had walked their ways without high principle. To this religion they had all adhered, and the new heir had ever entered in upon his domain without other encumbrances than those with which he himself was then already burdened. And yet there had been no entail. The idea of an entail was not in accordance with the peculiarities of the Dale mind. It was necessary to the Dale religion that each squire should have the power of wasting them. I remember to have dined at a house, the whole glory and fortune of which depended on the safety of a glass goblet. We all know the story. If the luck of Edenhall should be shattered, the doom of the family would be sealed. Nevertheless I was bidden *to drink out of the fatal glass, as were all guests in that house. It would not have contented the chivalrous mind of the master to protect his doom by lock and key and padded chest. And so it was with the Dales of Allington. To them an entail would have been a*

MONOTYPE SPECTRUM 556

10 point (D), 1 point leaded

FORMAT	PICAS	LINES	WPL	CPL	WPP	CPP
Royal 8vo	24×43	47	13.4	71	629	3337
Demy 8vo	24×40	44	12.4	66	548	2904
Large Crown 8vo	23×36	39	11.3	63	442	2457
Crown 8vo	21×34	37	10.4	58	385	2146

father to son, and from uncle to nephew, and, in one instance, from second cousin to second cousin, the sceptre had descended in the family of the Dales; and the acres had remained intact, growing in value and not decreasing in number, though guarded by no entail and protected by no wonderful amount of prudence or wisdom. The estate of Dale of Allington had been coterminous with the parish of Allington for some hundreds of years; and though, as I have said, the race of squires had possessed nothing of superhuman discretion and had perhaps been guided in their walks through life by no very distinct principles, still there had been with them so much of adherence to a sacred law, that no acre of the property had ever been parted from the hands of the existing squire. Some futile attempts had been made to increase the territory, as indeed had been done by Kit Dale, the father of Christopher Dale, who will appear as our squire of Allington when the persons of our drama are introduced. Old Kit Dale, who had married money, had bought outlying farms—a bit of ground here and a bit there—talking, as he did so, much of political influence and of the good old Tory cause. But these farms and bits of ground had gone again before our time. To them had been attached no religion. When old Kit had found himself pressed in that matter of the majority of the Nineteenth Dragoons, in which crack regiment his second son made for himself quite a career, he found it easier to sell than to save—seeing that that which he sold was his own and not the patrimony of the Dales. At his death the remainder of these purchases had gone. Family arrangements required completion, and Christopher Dale required ready money. The outlying farms flew away, as such new purchases had flown before; but the old patrimony of the Dales remained untouched, as it had ever remained.

It had been a religion among them; and seeing that the worship had been carried on without fail, that the vestal fire had never gone down upon the hearth, I should not have said that the Dales had walked their ways without high principle. To this religion they had all adhered, and the new heir had ever entered in upon his domain without other encumbrances than those with which he himself was then already burdened. And yet there had been no entail. The idea of an entail was not in accordance with the peculiarities of the Dale mind. It was necessary to the Dale religion that each squire should have the *power of wasting them. I remember to have dined at a house, the whole glory and fortune of which depended on the safety of a glass goblet. We all know the story. If the luck of Edenhall should be shattered, the doom of the family would be sealed. Nevertheless I*

MONOTYPE SPECTRUM 556

10 point (D), 2 point leaded

FORMAT	PICAS	LINES	WPL	CPL	WPP	CPP
Royal 8vo	26×43	43	13.4	71	576	3053
Demy 8vo	24×40	40	12.4	66	495	2640
Large Crown 8vo	23×36	36	11.3	63	406	2268
Crown 8vo	21×34	34	10.4	58	354	1972

father to son, and from uncle to nephew, and, in one instance, from second cousin to second cousin, the sceptre had descended in the family of the Dales; and the acres had remained intact, growing in value and not decreasing in number, though guarded by no entail and protected by no wonderful amount of prudence or wisdom. The estate of Dale of Allington had been coterminous with the parish of Allington for some hundreds of years; and though, as I have said, the race of squires had possessed nothing of superhuman discretion and had perhaps been guided in their walks through life by no very distinct principles, still there had been with them so much of adherence to a sacred law, that no acre of the property had ever been parted from the hands of the existing squire. Some futile attempts had been made to increase the territory, as indeed had been done by Kit Dale, the father of Christopher Dale, who will appear as our squire of Allington when the persons of our drama are introduced. Old Kit Dale, who had married money, had bought outlying farms—a bit of ground here and a bit there—talking, as he did so, much of political influence and of the good old Tory cause. But these farms and bits of ground had gone again before our time. To them had been attached no religion. When old Kit had found himself pressed in that matter of the majority of the Nineteenth Dragoons, in which crack regiment his second son made for himself quite a career, he found it easier to sell than to save—seeing that that which he sold was his own and not the patrimony of the Dales. At his death the remainder of these purchases had gone. Family arrangements required completion, and Christopher Dale required ready money. The outlying farms flew away, as such new purchases had flown before; but the old patrimony of the Dales remained untouched, as it had ever remained.

It had been a religion among them; and seeing that the worship had been carried on without fail, that the vestal fire had never gone down upon the hearth, I should not have said that the Dales had walked their ways without high principle. To this religion they had all adhered, and the new heir had ever entered in upon his domain without other encumbrances than those with which he himself was then already burdened. *And yet there had been no entail. The idea of an entail was not in accordance with the peculiarities of the Dale mind. It was necessary to the Dale religion that each squire should have the power of wasting them. I remember to have dined at a*

MONOTYPE SPECTRUM 556

10 point (D), 3 point leaded

FORMAT	PICAS	LINES	WPL	CPL	WPP	CPP
Royal 8vo	26×43	40	13.4	71	536	2840
Demy 8vo	24×40	37	12.4	66	458	2442
Large Crown 8vo	23×36	33	11.3	63	372	2079
Crown 8vo	21×34	31	10.4	58	323	1798

father to son, and from uncle to nephew, and, in one instance, from second cousin to second cousin, the sceptre had descended in the family of the Dales; and the acres had remained intact, growing in value and not decreasing in number, though guarded by no entail and protected by no wonderful amount of prudence or wisdom. The estate of Dale of Allington had been coterminous with the parish of Allington for some hundreds of years; and though, as I have said, the race of squires had possessed nothing of superhuman discretion and had perhaps been guided in their walks through life by no very distinct principles, still there had been with them so much of adherence to a sacred law, that no acre of the property had ever been parted from the hands of the existing squire. Some futile attempts had been made to increase the territory, as indeed had been done by Kit Dale, the father of Christopher Dale, who will appear as our squire of Allington when the persons of our drama are introduced. Old Kit Dale, who had married money, had bought outlying farms—a bit of ground here and a bit there—talking, as he did so, much of political influence and of the good old Tory cause. But these farms and bits of ground had gone again before our time. To them had been attached no religion. When old Kit had found himself pressed in that matter of the majority of the Nineteenth Dragoons, in which crack regiment his second son made for himself quite a career, he found it easier to sell than to save—seeing that that which he sold was his own and not the patrimony of the Dales. At his death the remainder of these purchases had gone. Family arrangements required completion, and Christopher Dale required ready money. The outlying farms flew away, as such new purchases had flown before; but the old patrimony of the Dales remained untouched, as it had ever remained.

It had been a religion among them; and seeing that the *worship had been carried on without fail, that the vestal fire had never gone down upon the hearth, I should not have said that the Dales had walked their ways without high principle. To this religion they had all*

MONOTYPE SPECTRUM 556

12 point (D), 1 point leaded

FORMAT	PICAS	LINES	WPL	CPL	WPP	CPP
Royal 8vo	26×43	40	11.0	62	440	2480
Demy 8vo	24×40	37	10.2	57	378	2109
Large Crown 8vo	23×36	33	9.5	53	316	1749
Crown 8vo	21×34	31	8.9	48	271	1488

father to son, and from uncle to nephew, and, in one instance, from second cousin to second cousin, the sceptre had descended in the family of the Dales; and the acres had remained intact, growing in value and not decreasing in number, though guarded by no entail and protected by no wonderful amount of prudence or wisdom. The estate of Dale of Allington had been coterminous with the parish of Allington for some hundreds of years; and though, as I have said, the race of squires had possessed nothing of superhuman discretion and had perhaps been guided in their walks through life by no very distinct principles, still there had been with them so much of adherence to a sacred law, that no acre of the property had ever been parted from the hands of the existing squire. Some futile attempts had been made to increase the territory, as indeed had been done by Kit Dale, the father of Christopher Dale, who will appear as our squire of Allington when the persons of our drama are introduced. Old Kit Dale, who had married money, had bought outlying farms—a bit of ground here and a bit there—talking, as he did so, much of political influence and of the good old Tory cause. But these farms and bits of ground had gone again before our time. To them had been attached no religion. When old Kit had found himself pressed in that matter of the majority of the Nineteenth Dragoons, in which crack regiment his second son made for himself quite a career, he found it easier to sell than to save—seeing that that which he sold was his own and not the patrimony of the Dales. At his death the remainder of these purchases had gone. Family arrangements required completion, and Christopher Dale required ready money. The outlying farms flew away, as such new purchases had flown *before; but the old patrimony of the Dales remained untouched, as it had ever remained.*

It had been a religion among them; and seeing that the worship had

MONOTYPE SPECTRUM 556

12 point (D), 2 point leaded

FORMAT	PICAS	LINES	WPL	CPL	WPP	CPP
Royal 8vo	26×43	37	11.0	62	407	2294
Demy 8vo	24×40	34	10.2	57	348	1938
Large Crown 8vo	23×36	31	9.5	53	297	1643
Crown 8vo	21×34	29	8.9	48	253	1392

MONOTYPE TIMES 327

Synopsis in 10 *point*

ABCDEFGHIJKLMNOPQRSTUVWXYZ&ÆŒ

ABCDEFGHIJKLMNOPQRSTUVWXYZÆŒ

abcdefghijklmnopqrstuvwxyzæœfifffflffiffl

ABCDEFGHIJKLMNOPQRSTUVWXYZ&ÆŒ

abcdefghijklmnopqrstuvwxyzæœfifffflffiffl

.,:;!?"-()£ *:;!?"*

1234567890 *1234567890* 1234567890 *1234567890*

Related bold · *Series* 334

ABCDEFGHIJKLMNOPQRSTUVWXYZ&ÆŒ

abcdefghijklmnopqrstuvwxyzæœfifffflffiffl

.,:;!?"-()£ 1234567890 1234567890

ABCDEFGHIJKLMNOPQRSTUVWXYZ&ÆŒ

abcdefghijklmnopqrstuvwxyzæœfifffflffiffl

,:;!?'-()£ 1234567890

All normal European accents available

Series 327 *available in composition sizes* 6, 7, 8, 9, 10, 11, 12 *point*

Series 334 *available in composition sizes* 6, 7, 8, 9, 10, 11, 12 *point*

Series 334 *italic available in composition sizes* 8, 9, 10, 11 *point*

father to son, and from uncle to nephew, and, in one instance, from second cousin to second cousin, the sceptre had descended in the family of the Dales; and the acres had remained intact, growing in value and not decreasing in number, though guarded by no entail and protected by no wonderful amount of prudence or wisdom. The estate of Dale of Allington had been coterminous with the parish of Allington for some hundreds of years; and though, as I have said, the race of squires had possessed nothing of superhuman discretion and had perhaps been guided in their walks through life by no very distinct principles, still there had been with them so much of adherence to a sacred law, that no acre of the property had ever been parted from the hands of the existing squire. Some futile attempts had been made to increase the territory, as indeed had been done by Kit Dale, the father of Christopher Dale, who will appear as our squire of Allington when the persons of our drama are introduced. Old Kit Dale, who had married money, had bought outlying farms—a bit of ground here and a bit there—talking, as he did so, much of political influence and of the good old Tory cause. But these farms and bits of ground had gone again before our time. To them had been attached no religion. When old Kit had found himself pressed in that matter of the majority of the Nineteenth Dragoons, in which crack regiment his second son made for himself quite a career, he found it easier to sell than to save—seeing that that which he sold was his own and not the patrimony of the Dales. At his death the remainder of these purchases had gone. Family arrangements required completion, and Christopher Dale required ready money. The outlying farms flew away, as such new purchases had flown before; but the old patrimony of the Dales remained untouched, as it had ever remained.

It had been a religion among them; and seeing that the worship had been carried on without fail, that the vestal fire had never gone down upon the hearth, I should not have said that the Dales had walked their ways without high principle. To this religion they had all adhered, and the new heir had ever entered in upon his domain without other encumbrances than those with which he himself was then already burdened. And yet there had been no entail. The idea of an entail was not in accordance with the peculiarities of the Dale mind. It was necessary to the Dale religion that each squire should have the power of wasting them. I remember to have dined at a house, the whole glory and fortune of which depended on the safety of a glass goblet. We all know the story. If the luck of Edenhall should be shattered, the doom of the family would be sealed. Nevertheless, I was bidden to drink out of the fatal glass, as were all guests in that house. It would not have contented the chivalrous mind of the master to protect his doom by lock and key and padded chest. And so it was with the Dales of Allington. To them an entail would have been a lock and key and a padded chest; but the old chivalry of their house denied to them the use of such protection.

I have spoken something slightingly of the acquirements and doings of *the family; and indeed their acquirements had been few and their doings little. At Allington, Dale of Allington had always been known as a king. At Guestwick, the neighbouring market town, he was a great man—to be seen fre-*

MONOTYPE TIMES 327 L.D.

9 point, 1 point leaded

FORMAT	PICAS	LINES	WPL	CPL	WPP	CPP
Royal 8vo	26×43	52	14.0	76	728	3952
Demy 8vo	24×40	48	13.0	70	623	3360
Large Crown 8vo	23×36	43	12.5	67	539	2881
Crown 8vo	21×34	41	11.3	61	463	2501

father to son, and from uncle to nephew, and, in one instance, from second cousin to second cousin, the sceptre had descended in the family of the Dales; and the acres had remained intact, growing in value and not decreasing in number, though guarded by no entail, and protected by no wonderful amount of prudence or wisdom. The estate of Dale of Allington had been coterminous with the parish of Allington for some hundreds of years; and though, as I have said, the race of squires had possessed nothing of superhuman discretion and had perhaps been guided in their walks through life by no very distinct principles, still there had been with them so much of adherence to a sacred law, that no acre of the property had ever been parted from the hands of the existing squire. Some futile attempts had been made to increase the territory, as indeed had been done by Kit Dale, the father of Christopher Dale, who will appear as our squire of Allington when the persons of our drama are introduced. Old Kit Dale, who had married money, had bought outlying farms—a bit of ground here and a bit there—talking, as he did so, much of political influence and of the good old Tory cause. But these farms and bits of ground had gone again before our time. To them had been attached no religion. When old Kit had found himself pressed in that matter of the majority of the Nineteenth Dragoons, in which crack regiment his second son made for himself quite a career, he found it easier to sell than to save—seeing that that which he sold was his own and not the patrimony of the Dales. At his death the remainder of these purchases had gone. Family arrangements required completion, and Christopher Dale required ready money. The outlying farms flew away, as such new purchases had flown before; but the old patrimony of the Dales remained untouched, as it had ever remained.

It had been a religion among them; and seeing that the worship had been carried on without fail, that the vestal fire had never gone down upon the hearth, I should not have said that the Dales had walked their ways without high principles. To this religion they had all adhered, and the new heir had ever entered in upon his domain without other encumbrances than those with which he himself was then already burdened. And yet there had been no entail. The idea of an entail was not in accordance with the peculiarities of the Dale mind. It was necessary to the Dale religion that each squire should have the power of wasting them. I remember to have dined at a house, the whole glory and fortune of which depended on the safety of a glass goblet. We all know the story. If the luck of Edenhall should be shattered, the doom of the family would be sealed. Nevertheless I was bidden to drink out of the fatal glass, as were all guests in that house. It would not have contented the chivalrous mind of the master to protect his doom by lock and key and padded chest. And so it was with the Dales of Allington. To them an entail would have been a *lock and key and a padded chest; but the old chivalry of their house denied to them the use of such protection.*

I have spoken something slightingly of the acquirements and doings

MONOTYPE TIMES 327 L.D.

10 point solid

FORMAT	PICAS	LINES	WPL	CPL	WPP	CPP
Royal 8vo	26×43	52	13.1	69	681	3588
Demy 8vo	24×40	48	12.1	64	582	3072
Large Crown 8vo	23×36	43	11.4	61	489	2623
Crown 8vo	21×34	41	10.2	56	419	2296

father to son, and from uncle to nephew, and, in one instance, from second cousin to second cousin, the sceptre had descended in the family of the Dales; and the acres had remained intact, growing in value and not decreasing in number, though guarded by no entail, and protected by no wonderful amount of prudence or wisdom. The estate of Dale of Allington had been coterminous with the parish of Allington for some hundreds of years; and though, as I have said, the race of squires had possessed nothing of superhuman discretion and had perhaps been guided in their walks through life by no very distinct principles, still there had been with them so much of adherence to a sacred law, that no acre of the property had ever been parted from the hands of the existing squire. Some futile attempts had been made to increase the territory, as indeed had been done by Kit Dale, the father of Christopher Dale, who will appear as our squire of Allington when the persons of our drama are introduced. Old Kit Dale, who had married money, had bought outlying farms—a bit of ground here and a bit there—talking, as he did so, much of political influence and of the good old Tory cause. But these farms and bits of ground had gone again before our time. To them had been attached no religion. When old Kit had found himself pressed in that matter of the majority of the Nineteenth Dragoons, in which crack regiment his second son made for himself quite a career, he found it easier to sell than to save—seeing that that which he sold was his own and not the patrimony of the Dales. At his death the remainder of these purchases had gone. Family arrangements required completion, and Christopher Dale required ready money. The outlying farms flew away, as such new purchases had flown before; but the old patrimony of the Dales remained untouched, as it had ever remained.

It had been a religion among them; and seeing that the worship had been carried on without fail, that the vestal fire had never gone down upon the hearth, I should not have said that the Dales had walked their ways without high principles. To this religion they had all adhered, and the new heir had ever entered in upon his domain without other encumbrances than those with which he himself was then already burdened. And yet there had been no entail. The idea of an entail was not in accordance with the peculiarities of the Dale mind. It was necessary to the Dale religion that each squire should have the power of wasting them. I remember to have dined at a house, the whole glory and fortune of which depended on the safety of a glass goblet. We all know the story. If the luck of Edenhall should be shattered, the doom of the family would be sealed. Nevertheless I was *bidden to drink out of the fatal glass, as were all guests in that house. It would not have contented the chivalrous mind of the master to protect his doom by lock and key and padded chest. And so it was with the*

MONOTYPE TIMES 327 L.D.

10 point, 1 point leaded

FORMAT	PICAS	LINES	WPL	CPL	WPP	CPP
Royal 8vo	26×43	47	13.1	69	615	3243
Demy 8vo	24×40	44	12.1	64	539	2816
Large Crown 8vo	23×36	39	11.4	61	443	2379
Crown 8vo	21×34	37	10.2	56	377	2072

father to son, and from uncle to nephew, and, in one instance, from second cousin to second cousin, the sceptre had descended in the family of the Dales; and the acres had remained intact, growing in value and not decreasing in number, though guarded by no entail, and protected by no wonderful amount of prudence or wisdom. The estate of Dale of Allington had been coterminous with the parish of Allington for some hundreds of years; and though, as I have said, the race of squires had possessed nothing of superhuman discretion and had perhaps been guided in their walks through life by no very distinct principles, still there had been with them so much of adherence to a sacred law, that no acre of the property had ever been parted from the hands of the existing squire. Some futile attempts had been made to increase the territory, as indeed had been done by Kit Dale, the father of Christopher Dale, who will appear as our squire of Allington when the persons of our drama are introduced. Old Kit Dale, who had married money, had bought outlying farms—a bit of ground here and a bit there—talking, as he did so, much of political influence and of the good old Tory cause. But these farms and bits of ground had gone again before our time. To them had been attached no religion. When old Kit had found himself pressed in that matter of the majority of the Nineteenth Dragoons, in which crack regiment his second son made for himself quite a career, he found it easier to sell than to save—seeing that that which he sold was his own and not the patrimony of the Dales. At his death the remainder of these purchases had gone. Family arrangements required completion, and Christopher Dale required ready money. The outlying farms flew away, as such new purchases had flown before; but the old patrimony of the Dales remained untouched, as it had ever remained.

It had been a religion among them; and seeing that the worship had been carried on without fail, that the vestal fire had never gone down upon the hearth, I should not have said that the Dales had walked their ways without high principles. To this religion they had all adhered, and the new heir had ever entered in upon his domain without other encumbrances than those with which he himself was then already burdened. And yet there had been no entail. The idea of an entail was not in accordance with the peculiarities of the Dale mind. It was necessary to the Dale religion that each squire should have the *power of wasting them. I remember to have dined at a house, the whole glory and fortune of which depended on the safety of a glass goblet. We all know the story. If the luck of Edenhall should be shattered, the*

MONOTYPE TIMES 327 L.D.

10 point, 2 point leaded

FORMAT	PICAS	LINES	WPL	CPL	WPP	CPP
Royal 8vo	26×43	43	13.1	69	563	2967
Demy 8vo	24×40	40	12.1	64	486	2560
Large Crown 8vo	23×36	36	11.4	61	410	2196
Crown 8vo	21×34	34	10.2	56	347	1904

father to son, and from uncle to nephew, and, in one instance, from second cousin to second cousin, the sceptre had descended in the family of the Dales; and the acres had remained intact, growing in value and not decreasing in number, though guarded by no entail and protected by no wonderful amount of prudence or wisdom. The estate of Dale of Allington had been coterminous with the parish of Allington for some hundreds of years; and though, as I have said, the race of squires had possessed nothing of superhuman discretion and had perhaps been guided in their walks through life by no very distinct principles, still there had been with them so much of adherence to a sacred law, that no acre of the property had ever been parted from the hands of the existing squire. Some futile attempts had been made to increase the territory, as indeed had been done by Kit Dale, the father of Christopher Dale, who will appear as our squire of Allington when the persons of our drama are introduced. Old Kit Dale, who had married money, had bought outlying farms —a bit of ground here and a bit there—talking, as he did so, much of political influence and of the good old Tory cause. But these farms and bits of ground had gone again before our time. To them had been attached no religion. When old Kit had found himself pressed in that matter of the majority of the Nineteenth Dragoons, in which crack regiment his second son made for himself quite a career, he found it easier to sell than to save —seeing that that which he sold was his own and not the patrimony of the Dales. At his death the remainder of these purchases had gone. Family arrangements required completion, and Christopher Dale required ready money. The outlying farms flew away, as such new purchases had flown before; but the old patrimony of the Dales remained untouched, as it had ever remained.

It had been a religion among them; and seeing that the worship had been carried on without fail, that the vestal fire had never gone down upon the hearth, I should not have said that the Dales had walked their ways without high principles. To this religion they had all adhered, and the new heir had ever entered in upon his domain without other encumbrances than those with which he himself was then already burdened. And yet there had been no entail. The idea of an entail was not in accordance with the peculiarities of the Dale mind. It was necessary to the Dale religion that each squire should have the power of wasting *them. I remember to have dined at a house, the whole glory and fortune of which depended on the safety of a glass goblet. We all know the story. If the luck of Edenhall should be shattered, the*

MONOTYPE TIMES 327

11 point solid

FORMAT	PICAS	LINES	WPL	CPL	WPP	CPP
Royal 8vo	26×43	47	11.9	65	559	3055
Demy 8vo	24×40	44	11.0	60	486	2640
Large Crown 8vo	23×36	39	10.2	58	398	2262
Crown 8vo	21×34	37	9.2	53	341	1961

father to son, and from uncle to nephew, and, in one instance, from second cousin to second cousin, the sceptre had descended in the family of the Dales; and the acres had remained intact, growing in value and not decreasing in number, though guarded by no entail and protected by no wonderful amount of prudence or wisdom. The estate of Dale of Allington had been coterminous with the parish of Allington for some hundreds of years; and though, as I have said, the race of squires had possessed nothing of superhuman discretion and had perhaps been guided in their walks through life by no very distinct principles, still there had been with them so much of adherence to a sacred law, that no acre of the property had ever been parted from the hands of the existing squire. Some futile attempts had been made to increase the territory, as indeed had been done by Kit Dale, the father of Christopher Dale, who will appear as our squire of Allington when the persons of our drama are introduced. Old Kit Dale, who had married money, had bought outlying farms —a bit of ground here and a bit there—talking, as he did so, much of political influence and of the good old Tory cause. But these farms and bits of ground had gone again before our time. To them had been attached no religion. When old Kit had found himself pressed in that matter of the majority of the Nineteenth Dragoons, in which crack regiment his second son made for himself quite a career, he found it easier to sell than to save —seeing that that which he sold was his own and not the patrimony of the Dales. At his death the remainder of these purchases had gone. Family arrangements required completion, and Christopher Dale required ready money. The outlying farms flew away, as such new purchases had flown before; but the old patrimony of the Dales remained untouched, as it had ever remained.

It had been a religion among them; and seeing that the worship had been carried on without fail, that the vestal fire had never gone down upon the hearth, I should not have said that the Dales had walked their ways without high principles. To this religion they had all adhered, and the new heir had ever entered in upon his domain without other encumbrances than those with *which he himself was then already burdened. And yet there had been no entail. The idea of an entail was not in accordance with the peculiarities of the Dale mind. It was necessary to the Dale religion*

MONOTYPE TIMES 327 L.D.

11 point, 1 point leaded

FORMAT	PICAS	LINES	WPL	CPL	WPP	CPP
Royal 8vo	26×43	43	11.9	65	511	2795
Demy 8vo	24×40	40	11.0	60	439	2400
Large Crown 8vo	23×36	36	10.2	58	367	2088
Crown 8vo	21×34	34	9.2	53	316	1802

father to son, and from uncle to nephew, and, in one instance, from second cousin to second cousin, the sceptre had descended in the family of the Dales; and the acres had remained intact, growing in value and not decreasing in number, though guarded by no entail and protected by no wonderful amount of prudence or wisdom. The estate of Dale of Allington had been coterminous with the parish of Allington for some hundreds of years; and though, as I have said, the race of squires had possessed nothing of superhuman discretion and had perhaps been guided in their walks through life by no very distinct principles, still there had been with them so much of adherence to a sacred law, that no acre of the property had ever been parted from the hands of the existing squire. Some futile attempts had been made to increase the territory, as indeed had been done by Kit Dale, the father of Christopher Dale, who will appear as our squire of Allington when the persons of our drama are introduced. Old Kit Dale, who had married money, had bought outlying farms —a bit of ground here and a bit there—talking, as he did so, much of the political influence and of the good old Tory cause. But these farms and bits of ground had gone again before our time. To them had been attached no religion. When old Kit had found himself pressed in that matter of the majority of the Nineteenth Dragoons, in which crack regiment his second son made for himself quite a career, he found it easier to sell than to save —seeing that that which he sold was his own and not the patrimony of the Dales. At his death the remainder of these purchases had gone. Family arrangements required completion, and Christopher Dale required ready money. The outlying farms flew away, as such new purchases had flown before; but the old patrimony of the Dales remained untouched, as it had ever remained.

It had been a religion among them; and seeing that the worship had been carried on without fail, that the vestal fire had never gone down upon the hearth, I should not have said that *the Dales had walked their ways without high principles. To this religion they had all adhered, and the new heir had ever entered in upon his domain without other encumbrances than those with which*

MONOTYPE TIMES 327 L.D.

11 point, 2 point leaded

FORMAT	PICAS	LINES	WPL	CPL	WPP	CPP
Royal 8vo	26×43	40	11.9	65	476	2600
Demy 8vo	24×40	37	11.0	60	407	2220
Large Crown 8vo	23×36	33	10.2	58	337	1914
Crown 8vo	21×34	31	9.2	53	285	1643

father to son, and from uncle to nephew, and, in one instance, from second cousin to second cousin, the sceptre had descended in the family of the Dales; and the acres had remained intact, growing in value and not decreasing in number, though guarded by no entail and protected by no wonderful amount of prudence or wisdom. The estate of Dale of Allington had been coterminous with the parish of Allington for some hundreds of years; and though, as I have said, the race of squires had possessed nothing of superhuman discretion and had perhaps been guided in their walks through life by no very distinct principles, still there had been with them so much of adherence to a sacred law, that no acre of the property had ever been parted from the hands of the existing squire. Some futile attempts had been made to increase the territory, as indeed had been done by Kit Dale, the father of Christopher Dale, who will appear as our squire of Allington when the persons of our drama are introduced. Old Kit Dale, who had married money, had bought outlying farms—a bit of ground here and a bit there—talking, as he did so, much of political influence and of the good old Tory cause. But these farms and bits of ground had gone again before our time. To them had been attached no religion. When old Kit had found himself pressed in that matter of the majority of the Nineteenth Dragoons, in which crack regiment his second son made for himself quite a career, he found it easier to sell than to save—seeing that that which he sold was his own and not the patrimony of the Dales. At his death the remainder of these purchases had gone. Family arrangements required completion, and Christopher Dale required ready money. The outlying farms flew away, as such new purchases had flown before; but the old patrimony of the Dales remained untouched, as it had ever remained.

It had been a religion among them; and seeing that the worship had been carried on without fail, that the *vestal fire had never gone down upon the hearth, I should not have said that the Dales had walked their ways without high principle. To this religion they had all adhered,*

MONOTYPE TIMES 327

12 point solid

FORMAT	PICAS	LINES	WPL	CPL	WPP	CPP
Royal 8vo	26×43	43	10.4	56	447	2408
Demy 8vo	24×40	40	9.6	52	385	2080
Large Crown 8vo	23×36	36	8.8	50	317	1800
Crown 8vo	21×34	34	8.1	46	275	1564

father to son, and from uncle to nephew, and, in one instance, from second cousin to second cousin, the sceptre had descended in the family of the Dales; and the acres had remained intact, growing in value and not decreasing in number, though guarded by no entail and protected by no wonderful amount of prudence or wisdom. The estate of Dale of Allington had been coterminous with the parish of Allington for some hundreds of years; and though, as I have said, the race of squires had possessed nothing of superhuman discretion and had perhaps been guided in their walks through life by no very distinct principles, still there had been with them so much of adherence to a sacred law, that no acre of the property had ever been parted from the hands of the existing squire. Some futile attempts had been made to increase the territory, as indeed had been done by Kit Dale, the father of Christopher Dale, who will appear as our squire of Allington when the persons of our drama are introduced. Old Kit Dale, who had married money, had bought outlying farms—a bit of ground here and a bit there—talking, as he did so, much of political influence and of the good old Tory cause. But these farms and bits of ground had gone again before our time. To them had been attached no religion. When old Kit had found himself pressed in that matter of the majority of the Nineteenth Dragoons, in which crack regiment his second son made for himself quite a career, he found it easier to sell than to save—seeing that that which he sold was his own and not the patrimony of the Dales. At his death the remainder of these purchases had gone. Family arrangements required completion, and Christopher Dale required ready money. The outlying farms flew away, as such new purchases had flown before; but the old patrimony of the Dales remained untouched, as *it had ever remained.*

It had been a religion among them; and seeing that the worship had been carried on without fail, that the vestal

MONOTYPE TIMES 327 L.D.

12 point, 1 point leaded

FORMAT	PICAS	LINES	WPL	CPL	WPP	CPP
Royal 8vo	26×43	40	10.4	56	416	2240
Demy 8vo	24×40	37	9.6	52	355	1924
Large Crown 8vo	23×36	33	8.8	50	293	1650
Crown 8vo	21×34	31	8.1	46	252	1426

MONOTYPE WALBAUM 374

Synopsis in 10D *on* 11 *point*

ABCDEFGHIJKLMNOPQRSTUVWXYZ&ÆŒ

ABCDEFGHIJKLMNOPQRSTUVWXYZÆŒ

abcdefghijklmnopqrstuvwxyzæœfifffflffiffl

ABCDEFGHIJKLMNOPQRSTUVWXYZ&ÆŒ

abcdefghijklmnopqrstuvwxyzæœfifffflffiffl

.,:;!?‘’-()[]£ *:;!?*

1234567890 *1234567890* 1234567890 *1234567890*

All normal European accents available

Available in composition sizes 8 *on* 9, 9 *on* 10, 10 *on* 11, 11 *on* 12, 12 *on* 13 *point*

father to son, and from uncle to nephew, and, in one instance, from second cousin to second cousin, the sceptre had descended in the family of the Dales; and the acres had remained intact, growing in value and not decreasing in number, though guarded by no entail and protected by no wonderful amount of prudence or wisdom. The estate of Dale of Allington had been coterminous with the parish of Allington for some hundreds of years; and though, as I have said, the race of squires had possessed nothing of superhuman discretion and had perhaps been guided in their walks through life by no very distinct principles, still there had been with them so much of adherence to a sacred law, that no acre of the property had ever been parted from the hands of the existing squire. Some futile attempts had been made to increase the territory, as indeed had been done by Kit Dale, the father of Christopher Dale, who will appear as our squire of Allington when the persons of our drama are introduced. Old Kit Dale, who had married money, had bought outlying farms—a bit of ground here and a bit there—talking, as he did so, much of political influence and of the good old Tory cause. But these farms and bits of ground had gone again before our time. To them had been attached no religion. When old Kit had found himself pressed in that matter of the majority of the Nineteenth Dragoons, in which crack regiment his second son made for himself quite a career, he found it easier to sell than to save—seeing that that which he sold was his own and not the patrimony of the Dales. At his death the remainder of these purchases had gone. Family arrangements required completion, and Christopher Dale required ready money. The outlying farms flew away, as such new purchases had flown before; but the old patrimony of the Dales remained untouched, as it had ever remained.

It had been a religion among them; and seeing that the worship had been carried on without fail, that the vestal fire had never gone down upon the hearth, I should not have said that the Dales had walked their ways without high principle. To this religion they had all adhered, and the new heir had ever entered in upon his domain without other encumbrances than those with which he himself was then already burdened. And yet there had been no entail. The idea of an entail was not in accordance with the peculiarities of the Dale mind. It was necessary to the Dale religion that each squire should have the power of wasting them. I remember to have dined at a house, the whole glory and fortune of which depended on the safety of a glass goblet. We all know the story. If the luck of Edenhall should be shattered, the doom of the family would be sealed. Nevertheless I was bidden to drink out of the fatal glass, as were all guests in that house. It would not have contented the chivalrous mind of the master to protect his doom by lock and key and padded chest. And so it was with the Dales of Allington. To them an entail would have been a lock and key and a padded chest; but the old chivalry of their house denied to them the use of such protection.

I have spoken something slightingly of the acquirements and doings of the family; and indeed their acquirements had been few and their doings little. At Allington, Dale of Allington had always been known as a king.

MONOTYPE WALBAUM 374

9 point (D), 1 point leaded

FORMAT	PICAS	LINES	WPL	CPL	WPP	CPP
Royal 8vo	26×43	52	13.7	73	712	3796
Demy 8vo	24×40	48	12.7	67	608	3216
Large Crown 8vo	23×36	43	12.0	64	514	2752
Crown 8vo	21×34	41	10.8	58	443	2378

father to son, and from uncle to nephew, and, in one instance, from second cousin to second cousin, the sceptre had descended in the family of the Dales; and the acres had remained intact, growing in value and not decreasing in number, though guarded by no entail, and protected by no wonderful amount of prudence or wisdom. The estate of Dale of Allington had been coterminous with the parish of Allington for some hundreds of years; and though, as I have said, the race of squires had possessed nothing of superhuman discretion and had perhaps been guided in their walks through life by no very distinct principles, still there had been with them so much of adherence to a sacred law, that no acre of the property had ever been parted from the hands of the existing squire. Some futile attempts had been made to increase the territory, as indeed had been done by Kit Dale, the father of Christopher Dale, who will appear as our squire of Allington when the persons of our drama are introduced. Old Kit Dale, who had married money, had bought outlying farms—a bit of ground here and a bit there—talking, as he did so, much of political influence and of the good old Tory cause. But these farms and bits of ground had gone again before our time. To them had been attached no religion. When old Kit had found himself pressed in that matter of the majority of the Nineteenth Dragoons, in which crack regiment his second son made for himself quite a career, he found it easier to sell than to save—seeing that that which he sold was his own and not the patrimony of the Dales. At his death the remainder of these purchases had gone. Family arrangements had required completion, and Christopher Dale required ready money. The outlying farms flew away, as such new purchases had flown before; but the old patrimony of the Dales remained untouched, as it had ever remained.

It had been a religion among them; and seeing that the worship had been carried on without fail, that the vestal fire had never gone down upon the hearth, I should not have said that the Dales had walked their ways without high principle. To this religion they had all adhered, and the new heir had ever entered in upon his domain without other encumbrances than those with which he himself was then already burdened. And yet there had been no entail. The idea of an entail was not in accordance with the peculiarities of the Dale mind. It was necessary to the Dale religion that each squire should have the power of wasting them. I remember to have dined at a house, the whole glory and fortune of which depended on the safety of a glass goblet. We all know the story. If the luck of Edenhall should be shattered, the doom of the family would be sealed. Nevertheless I was *bidden to drink out of the fatal glass, as were all guests in that house. It would not have contented the chivalrous mind of the master to protect his doom by lock and key and padded chest. And so it was with the Dales of*

MONOTYPE WALBAUM 374

10 point (D), 1 point leaded

FORMAT	PICAS	LINES	WPL	CPL	WPP	CPP
Royal 8vo	26×43	47	13.2	71	620	3337
Demy 8vo	24×40	44	12.2	66	539	2904
Large Crown 8vo	23×36	39	11.2	63	439	2457
Crown 8vo	21×34	37	10.4	58	384	2146

father to son, and from uncle to nephew, and, in one instance, from second cousin to second cousin, the sceptre had descended in the family of the Dales; and the acres had remained intact, growing in value and not decreasing in number, though guarded by no entail, and protected by no wonderful amount of prudence or wisdom. The estate of Dale of Allington had been coterminous with the parish of Allington for some hundreds of years; and though, as I have said, the race of squires had possessed nothing of superhuman discretion and had perhaps been guided in their walks through life by no very distinct principles, still there had been with them so much of adherence to a sacred law, that no acre of the property had ever been parted from the hands of the existing squire. Some futile attempts had been made to increase the territory, as indeed had been done by Kit Dale, the father of Christopher Dale, who will appear as our squire of Allington when the persons of our drama are introduced. Old Kit Dale, who had married money, had bought outlying farms—a bit of ground here and a bit there—talking, as he did so, much of political influence and of the good old Tory cause. But these farms and bits of ground had gone again before our time. To them had been attached no religion. When old Kit had found himself pressed in that matter of the majority of the Nineteenth Dragoons, in which crack regiment his second son made for himself quite a career, he found it easier to sell than to save—seeing that that which he sold was his own and not the patrimony of the Dales. At his death the remainder of these purchases had gone. Family arrangements had required completion, and Christopher Dale required ready money. The outlying farms flew away, as such new purchases had flown before; but the old patrimony of the Dales remained untouched, as it had ever remained.

It had been a religion among them; and seeing that the worship had been carried on without fail, that the vestal fire had never gone down upon the hearth, I should not have said that the Dales had walked their ways without high principle. To this religion they had all adhered, and the new heir had ever entered in upon his domain without other encumbrances than those with which he himself was then already burdened. And yet there had been no entail. The idea of an entail was not in accordance with the peculiarities of the Dale mind. It was necessary to the Dale religion that each squire should have the *power of wasting them. I remember to have dined at a house, the whole glory and fortune of which depended on the safety of a glass goblet. We all know the story. If the luck of Edenhall should be shattered,*

MONOTYPE WALBAUM 374

10 point (D), 2 point leaded

FORMAT	PICAS	LINES	WPL	CPL	WPP	CPP
Royal 8vo	26×43	43	13.2	71	567	3053
Demy 8vo	24×40	40	12.2	66	485	2640
Large Crown 8vo	23×36	36	11.2	63	403	2268
Crown 8vo	21×34	34	10.4	58	355	1972

father to son, and from uncle to nephew, and, in one instance, from second cousin to second cousin, the sceptre had descended in the family of the Dales; and the acres had remained intact, growing in value and not decreasing in number, though guarded by no entail and protected by no wonderful amount of prudence or wisdom. The estate of Dale of Allington had been coterminous with the parish of Allington for some hundreds of years; and though, as I have said, the race of squires had possessed nothing of superhuman discretion and had perhaps been guided in their walks through life by no very distinct principles, still there had been with them so much of adherence to a sacred law, that no acre of the property had ever been parted from the hands of the existing squire. Some futile attempts had been made to increase the territory, as indeed had been done by Kit Dale, the father of Christopher Dale, who will appear as our squire of Allington when the persons of our drama are introduced. Old Kit Dale, who had married money, had bought outlying farms—a bit of ground here and a bit there—talking, as he did so, much of political influence and of the good old Tory cause. But these farms and bits of ground had gone again before our time. To them had been attached no religion. When old Kit had found himself pressed in that matter of the majority of the Nineteenth Dragoons, in which crack regiment his second son made for himself quite a career, he found it easier to sell than to save—seeing that that which he sold was his own and not the patrimony of the Dales. At his death the remainder of these purchases had gone. Family arrangements required completion, and Christopher Dale required ready money. The outlying farms flew away, as such new purchases had flown before; but the old patrimony of the Dales remained untouched, as it had ever remained.

It had been a religion among them; and seeing that the worship had been carried on without fail, that the vestal fire had never gone down upon the hearth, I should not have said that the Dales had walked their ways without high principle. To this religion they had all adhered, and the new heir had ever entered in upon his domain without other encumbrances than those with which he himself was then already burdened. And yet there had *been no entail. The idea of an entail was not in accordance with the peculiarities of the Dale mind. It was necessary to the Dale religion that each squire should have the power of wasting them.*

MONOTYPE WALBAUM 374

11 point (D), 1 point leaded

FORMAT	PICAS	LINES	WPL	CPL	WPP	CPP
Royal 8vo	26×43	43	12.1	66	520	2838
Demy 8vo	24×40	40	11.2	61	449	2440
Large Crown 8vo	23×36	36	10.5	58	378	2088
Crown 8vo	21×34	34	9.6	53	327	1802

father to son, and from uncle to nephew, and, in one instance, from second cousin to second cousin, the sceptre had descended in the family of the Dales; and the acres had remained intact, growing in value and not decreasing in number, though guarded by no entail and protected by no wonderful amount of prudence or wisdom. The estate of Dale of Allington had been coterminous with the parish of Allington for some hundreds of years; and though, as I have said, the race of squires had possessed nothing of superhuman discretion and had perhaps been guided in their walks through life by no very distinct principles, still there had been with them so much of adherence to a sacred law, that no acre of the property had ever been parted from the hands of the existing squire. Some futile attempts had been made to increase the territory, as indeed had been done by Kit Dale, the father of Christopher Dale, who will appear as our squire of Allington when the persons of our drama are introduced. Old Kit Dale, who had married money, had bought outlying farms—a bit of ground here and a bit there—talking, as he did so, much of political influence and of the good old Tory cause. But these farms and bits of ground had gone again before our time. To them had been attached no religion. When old Kit had found himself pressed in that matter of the majority of the Nineteenth Dragoons, in which crack regiment his second son made for himself quite a career, he found it easier to sell than to save—seeing that that which he sold was his own and not the patrimony of the Dales. At his death the remainder of these purchases had gone. Family arrangements required completion, and Christopher Dale required ready money. The outlying farms flew away, as such new purchases had flown before; but the old patrimony of the Dales remained untouched, as it had ever remained.

It had been a religion among them; and seeing that the worship had been carried on without fail, that the vestal fire had never gone down upon the hearth, I should not have said that the Dales had walked their ways without high principle. To this *religion they had all adhered, and the new heir had ever entered in upon his domain without other encumbrances than those with which he himself was then already burdened. And yet there had*

MONOTYPE WALBAUM 374

11 point (D), 2 point leaded

FORMAT	PICAS	LINES	WPL	CPL	WPP	CPP
Royal 8vo	26×43	40	12.1	66	484	2640
Demy 8vo	24×40	37	11.2	61	413	2257
Large Crown 8vo	23×36	33	10.5	58	348	1914
Crown 8vo	21×34	31	9.6	53	298	1643

father to son, and from uncle to nephew, and, in one instance, from the second cousin to second cousin, the sceptre had descended in the family of the Dales; and the acres had remained intact, growing in value and not decreasing in number, though guarded by no entail and protected by no wonderful amount of prudence or wisdom. The estate of Dale of Allington had been coterminous with the parish of Allington for some hundreds of years; and though, as I have said, the race of squires had possessed nothing of superhuman discretion and had perhaps been guided in their walks through life by no very distinct principles, still there had been with them so much of adherence to a sacred law, that no acre of the property had ever been parted from the hands of the existing squire. Some futile attempts had been made to increase the territory, as indeed had been done by Kit Dale, the father of Christopher Dale, who will appear as our squire of Allington when the persons of our drama are introduced. Old Kit Dale, who had married money, had bought outlying farms—a bit of ground here and a bit there—talking, as he did so, much of political influence and of the good old Tory cause. But these farms and bits of ground had gone again before our time. To them had been attached no religion. When old Kit had found himself pressed in that matter of the majority of the Nineteenth Dragoons, in which crack regiment his second son made for himself quite a career, he found it easier to sell than to save—seeing that that which he sold was his own and not the patrimony of the Dales. At his death the remainder of these purchases had gone. Family arrangements required completion, and Christopher Dale required ready money. The outlying farms flew away, as such new purchases had flown before; but the old patrimony of the Dales remained untouched, as it had ever remained.

It had been a religion among them; and seeing that the *worship had been carried on without fail, that the vestal fire had never gone down upon the hearth, I should not have said that the Dales had walked their ways without high principle.*

MONOTYPE WALBAUM 374

12 point (D), 1 point leaded

FORMAT	PICAS	LINES	WPL	CPL	WPP	CPP
Royal 8vo	26×43	40	11.0	61	440	2440
Demy 8vo	24×40	37	10.2	56	378	2072
Large Crown 8vo	23×36	33	9.4	53	310	1749
Crown 8vo	21×34	31	8.5	49	263	1539

father to son, and from uncle to nephew, and, in one instance, from the second cousin to second cousin, the sceptre had descended in the family of the Dales; and the acres had remained intact, growing in value and not decreasing in number, though guarded by no entail and protected by no wonderful amount of prudence or wisdom. The estate of Dale of Allington had been coterminous with the parish of Allington for some hundreds of years; and though, as I have said, the race of squires had possessed nothing of superhuman discretion and had perhaps been guided in their walks through life by no very distinct principles, still there had been with them so much of adherence to a sacred law, that no acre of the property had ever been parted from the hands of the existing squire. Some futile attempts had been made to increase the territory, as indeed had been done by Kit Dale, the father of Christopher Dale, who will appear as our squire of Allington when the persons of our drama are introduced. Old Kit Dale, who had married money, had bought outlying farms—a bit of ground here and a bit there—talking, as he did so, much of political influence and of the good old Tory cause. But these farms and bits of ground had gone again before our time. To them had been attached no religion. When old Kit had found himself pressed in that matter of the majority of the Nineteenth Dragoons, in which crack regiment his second son made for himself quite a career, he found it easier to sell than to save—seeing that that which he sold was his own and not the patrimony of the Dales. At his death the remainder of these purchases had gone. Family arrangements required completion, and Christopher Dale required ready money. The outlying farms flew away, as such new purchases had flown *before; but the old patrimony of the Dales remained untouched, as it had ever remained.*

It had been a religion among them; and seeing that the

MONOTYPE WALBAUM 374

12 point (D), 2 point leaded

FORMAT	PICAS	LINES	WPL	CPL	WPP	CPP
Royal 8vo	26×43	37	11.0	61	407	2257
Demy 8vo	24×40	34	10.2	56	345	1904
Large Crown 8vo	23×36	31	9.4	53	293	1643
Crown 8vo	21×34	29	8.5	49	248	1421

2

SPECIMEN PAGES OF LINOTYPE & INTERTYPE FACES

INTERTYPE BASKERVILLE

Synopsis in 10 *point*

ABCDEFGHIJKLMNOPQRSTUVWXYZ&ÆŒ

ABCDEFGHIJKLMNOPQRSTUVWXYZÆŒ

abcdefghijklmnopqrstuvwxyzæœfiffflffiffl

ABCDEFGHIJKLMNOPQRSTUVWXYZ&ÆŒ

abcdefghijklmnopqrstuvwxyzæœfiffflffiffl

.,:;!?‘’-()[]£ *:;!?*

1234567890 *1234567890* 1234567890 *1234567890*

Related bold

ABCDEFGHIJKLMNOPQRSTUVWXYZ&ÆŒ

abcdefghijklmnopqrstuvwxyzæœfiffflffiffl

.,;!?-()£ 1234567890 1234567890

All normal European accents available

Available in composition sizes 8, 9, 10, 11, 12 *point*

Related bold available in composition sizes 8, 9, 10 *point* father to son, and from uncle to nephew, and, in one instance, from second cousin to second cousin, the sceptre had descended in the family of the Dales; and the acres had remained intact, growing in value and not decreasing in number, though guarded by no entail and protected by no wonderful amount of prudence or wisdom. The estate of Dale of Allington had been coterminous with the parish of Allington for some hundreds of years; and though, as I have said, the race of squires had possessed nothing of super-human discretion, and had perhaps been guided in their walks through life by no very distinct principles, still there had been with them so much of adherence to a sacred law, that no acre of the property had ever been parted from the hands of the existing squire. Some futile attempts had been made to increase the territory, as indeed had been done by Kit Dale, the father of Christopher Dale, who will appear as our squire of Allington when the persons of our drama are introduced. Old Kit Dale, who had married money, had bought outlying farms—a bit of ground here and a bit there—talking, as he did so, much of political influence and of the good old Tory cause. But these farms and bits of ground had gone again before our time. To them had been attached no religion. When old Kit had found himself pressed in that matter of the majority of the Nineteenth Dragoons, in which crack regiment his second son made for himself quite a career, he found it easier to sell than to save—seeing that that which he sold was his own and not the patrimony of the Dales. At his death the remainder of these purchases had gone. Family arrangements required completion, and Christopher Dale required ready money. The outlying farms flew away, as such new purchases had flown before; but the old patrimony of the Dales remained untouched, as it had ever remained.

It had been a religion among them; and seeing that the worship had been carried on without fail, that the vestal fire had never gone down upon the hearth, I should not have said that the Dales had walked their ways without high principle. To this religion they had all adhered, and the new heir had ever entered in upon his domain without other encumbrances than those with which he himself was then already burdened. And yet there had been no entail. The idea of an entail was not in accordance with the peculiarities of the Dale mind. It was necessary to the Dale religion that each squire should have the power of wasting them. I remember to have dined at a house, the whole glory and fortune of which depended on the safety of a glass goblet. We all know the story. If the luck of Edenhall should be shattered, the doom of the family would be sealed. Nevertheless I was bidden to drink out of the fatal glass, as were all guests in that house. It would not have contented the chivalrous mind of the master to protect his doom by lock and key and padded chest. And so it was with the Dales of Allington. To them an entail would have been a lock and key and a padded chest; but the old chivalry of their house denied to them the use of such protection.

I have spoken something slightingly of the acquirements and doings of the family; and indeed their acquirements had been few and their doings little. At Allington, Dale of Allington had always been known as a king.

INTERTYPE BASKERVILLE

9 point, 1 point leaded

FORMAT	PICAS	LINES	WPL	CPL	WPP	CPP
Royal 8vo	26×43	52	13.8	75	718	3900
Demy 8vo	24×40	48	12.8	69	610	3297
Large Crown 8vo	23×36	43	12.2	66	520	2849
Crown 8vo	21×34	41	11.1	61	458	2493

father to son, and from uncle to nephew, and, in one instance, from second cousin to second cousin, the sceptre had descended in the family of the Dales; and the acres had remained intact, growing in value and not decreasing in number, though guarded by no entail and protected by no wonderful amount of prudence or wisdom. The estate of Dale of Allington had been coterminous with the parish of Allington for some hundreds of years; and though, as I have said, the race of squires had possessed nothing of superhuman discretion, and had perhaps been guided in their walks through life by no very distinct principles, still there had been with them so much of adherence to a sacred law that no acre of the property had ever been parted from the hands of the existing squire. Some futile attempts had been made to increase the territory, as indeed had been done by Kit Dale, the father of Christopher Dale, who will appear as our squire of Allington when the persons of our drama are introduced. Old Kit Dale, who had married money, had bought outlying farms—a bit of ground here and a bit there—talking, as he did so, much of political influence and of the good old Tory cause. But these farms and bits of ground had gone again before our time. To them had been attached no religion. When old Kit had found himself pressed in that matter of the majority of the Nineteenth Dragoons, in which crack regiment his second son made for himself quite a career, he found it easier to sell than to save—seeing that that which he sold was his own and not the patrimony of the Dales. At his death the remainder of these purchases had gone. Family arrangements required completion, and Christopher Dale required ready money. The outlying farms flew away, as such new purchases had flown before; but the old patrimony of the Dales remained untouched, as it had ever remained.

It had been a religion among them; and seeing that the worship had been carried on without fail, that the vestal fire had never gone down upon the hearth, I should not have said that the Dales had walked their ways without high principle. To this religion they had all adhered, and the new heir had ever entered in upon his domain without other encumbrances than those with which he himself was then already burdened. And yet there had been no entail. The idea of an entail was not in accordance with the peculiarities of the Dale mind. It was necessary to the Dale religion that each squire should have the power of wasting them. I remember to have dined at a house, the whole glory and fortune of which depended on the safety of a glass goblet. We all know the story. If the luck of Edenhall should be shattered, the doom of the family would be sealed. Nevertheless I was bidden to drink out of the fatal glass, as were all guests in that house. It would not have contented the chivalrous mind of the master to protect his doom by lock and key and padded chest. And so it was with the Dales of Allington. To them an entail would *have been a lock and key and a padded chest; but the old chivalry of their house denied to them the use of such protection.*

I have spoken something slightly of the acquirements and doings

INTERTYPE BASKERVILLE

10 point solid

FORMAT	PICAS	LINES	WPL	CPL	WPP	CPP
Royal 8vo	26×43	52	13.1	74	681	3848
Demy 8vo	24×40	48	12.1	68	582	3264
Large Crown 8vo	23×36	43	11.3	64	487	2752
Crown 8vo	21×34	41	10.3	58	424	2378

father to son, and from uncle to nephew, and, in one instance, from second cousin to second cousin, the sceptre had descended in the family of the Dales; and the acres had remained intact, growing in value and not decreasing in number, though guarded by no entail and protected by no wonderful amount of prudence or wisdom. The estate of Dale of Allington had been coterminous with the parish of Allington for some hundreds of years; and though, as I have said, the race of squires had possesssed nothing of superhuman discretion, and had perhaps been guided in their walks through life by no very distinct principles, still there had been with them so much of adherence to a sacred law, that no acre of the property had ever been parted from the hands of the existing squire. Some futile attempts had been made to increase the territory, as indeed had been done by Kit Dale, the father of Christopher Dale, who will appear as our squire of Allington when the persons of our drama are introduced. Old Kit Dale, who had married money, had bought outlying farms—a bit of ground here and a bit there—talking, as he did so, much of political influence and of the good old Tory cause. But these farms and bits of ground had gone again before our time. To them had been attached no religion. When old Kit had found himself pressed in that matter of the majority of the Nineteenth Dragoons, in which crack regiment his second son made for himself quite a career, he found it easier to sell than to save—seeing that that which he sold was his own and not the patrimony of the Dales. At his death the remainder of these purchases had gone. Family arrangements required completion, and Christopher Dale required ready money. The outlying farms flew away, as such new purchases had flown before; but the old patrimony of the Dales remained untouched, as it had ever remained.

It had been a religion among them; and seeing that the worship had been carried on without fail, that the vestal fire had never gone down upon the hearth, I should not have said that the Dales had walked their ways without high principle. To this religion they had all adhered and the new heir had ever entered in upon his domain without other encumbrances than those with which he himself was then already burdened. And yet there had been no entail. The idea of an entail was not in accordance with the peculiarities of the Dale mind. It was necessary to the Dale religion that each squire should have the power of wasting them. I remember to have dined at a house, the whole glory and fortune of which depended on the safety of a glass goblet. We all know the story. If the luck of Edenhall should be shattered, the doom of the family would be sealed. Never*theless I was bidden to drink out of the fatal glass, as were all guests in that house. It would not have contented the chivalrous mind of the master to protect his doom by lock and key and padded*

INTERTYPE BASKERVILLE

10 point, 1 point leaded

FORMAT	PICAS	LINES	WPL	CPL	WPP	CPP
Royal 8vo	26×43	47	13.1	74	615	3478
Demy 8vo	24×40	44	12.1	68	532	2992
Large Crown 8vo	23×36	39	11.3	64	438	2496
Crown 8vo	21×34	37	10.3	58	379	2146

father to son, and from uncle to nephew, and, in one instance, from second cousin to second cousin, the sceptre had descended in the family of the Dales; and the acres had remained intact, growing in value and not decreasing in number, though guarded by no entail and protected by no wonderful amount of prudence or wisdom. The estate of Dale of Allington had been coterminous with the parish of Allington for some hundreds of years; and though, as I have said, the race of squires had possessed nothing of superhuman discretion, and had perhaps been guided in their walks through life by no very distinct principles, still there had been with them so much of adherence to a sacred law, that no acre of the property had ever been parted from the hands of the existing squire. Some futile attempts had been made to increase the territory, as indeed had been done by Kit Dale, the father of Christopher Dale, who will appear as our squire of Allington when the persons of our drama are introduced. Old Kit Dale, who had married money, had bought outlying farms—a bit of ground here and a bit there—talking, as he did so, much of political influence and of the good old Tory cause. But these farms and bits of ground had gone again before our time. To them had been attached no religion. When old Kit had found himself pressed in that matter of the majority of the Nineteenth Dragoons, in which crack regiment his second son made for himself quite a career, he found it easier to sell than to save—seeing that that which he sold was his own and not the patrimony of the Dales. At his death the remainder of these purchases had gone. Family arrangements required completion, and Christopher Dale required ready money. The outlying farms flew away, as such new purchases had flown before; but the old patrimony of the Dales remained untouched, as it had ever remained.

It had been a religion among them; and seeing that the worship had been carried on without fail, that the vestal fire had never gone down upon the hearth, I should not have said that the Dales had walked their ways without high principle. To this religion they had all adhered, and the new heir had ever entered in upon his domain without other encumbrances than those with which he himself was then already burdened. And yet there had been no entail. The idea of an entail was not in accordance with the peculiarities of the Dale mind. It was necessary to the Dale religion that each squire should have the power of wasting them. I remember to have dined at a house, the whole glory and fortune of which *depended on the safety of a glass goblet. We all know the story. If the luck of Edenhall should be shattered, the doom of the family would be sealed. Nevertheless I was bidden to drink out of the*

INTERTYPE BASKERVILLE

11 point solid

FORMAT	PICAS	LINES	WPL	CPL	WPP	CPP
Royal 8vo	26×43	47	12.2	69	573	3243
Demy 8vo	24×40	44	11.3	64	500	2816
Large Crown 8vo	23×36	39	10.6	62	413	2418
Crown 8vo	21×34	37	9.5	56	352	2072

father to son, and from uncle to nephew, and, in one instance, from second cousin to second cousin, the sceptre had descended in the family of the Dales; and the acres had remained intact, growing in value and not decreasing in number, though guarded by no entail and protected by no wonderful amount of prudence or wisdom. The estate of Dale of Allington had been coterminous with the parish of Allington for some hundreds of years; and though, as I have said, the race of squires had possessed nothing of superhuman discretion, and had perhaps been guided in their walks through life by no very distinct principles, still there had been with them so much of adherence to a sacred law, that no acre of property had ever been parted from the hands of the existing squire. Some futile attempts had been made to increase the territory, as indeed had been done by Kit Dale, the father of Christopher Dale, who will appear as our squire of Allington when the persons of our drama are introduced. Old Kit Dale, who had married money, had bought outlying farms—a bit of ground here and a bit there—talking, as he did so, much of political influence and of the good old Tory cause. But these farms and bits of ground had gone again before our time. To them had been attached no religion. When old Kit had found himself pressed in that matter of the majority of the Nineteenth Dragoons, in which crack regiment his second son made for himself quite a career, he found it easier to sell than to save—seeing that that which he sold was his own and not the patrimony of the Dales. At his death the remainder of these purchases had gone. Family arrangements required completion, and Christopher Dale required ready money. The outlying farms flew away, as such new purchases had flown before; but the old patrimony of the Dales remained untouched, as it had ever remained.

It had been a religion among them; and seeing that the worship had been carried on without fail, that the vestal fire had never gone down upon the hearth, I should not have said that the Dales had walked their ways without high principle. To this religion they had all adhered, and the new heir had ever entered in upon his domain without other encumbrances than those with which he himself was then already burdened. And yet there had been no *entail. The idea of an entail was not in accordance with the peculiarities of the Dale mind. It was necessary to the Dale religion that each squire should have the power of wasting them. I remem-*

INTERTYPE BASKERVILLE

11 point, 1 point leaded

FORMAT	PICAS	LINES	WPL	CPL	WPP	CPP
Royal 8vo	26×43	43	12.2	69	524	2967
Demy 8vo	24×40	40	11.3	64	451	2560
Large Crown 8vo	23×36	36	10.6	62	380	2232
Crown 8vo	21×34	34	9.5	56	324	1904

father to son, and from uncle to nephew, and, in one instance, from second cousin to second cousin, the sceptre had descended in the family of the Dales; and the acres had remained intact, growing in value and not decreasing in number, though guarded by no entail and protected by no wonderful amount of prudence or wisdom. The estate of Dale of Allington had been coterminous with the parish of Allington for some hundreds of years; and though, as I have said, the race of squires had possessed nothing of superhuman discretion, and had perhaps been guided in their walks through life by no very distinct principles, still there had been with them so much of adherence to a sacred law, that no acre of property had ever been parted from the hands of the existing squire. Some futile attempts had been made to increase the territory, as indeed had been done by Kit Dale, the father of Christopher Dale, who will appear as our squire of Allington when the persons of our drama are introduced. Old Kit Dale, who had married money, had bought outlying farms—a bit of ground here and a bit there—talking, as he did so, much of political influence and of the good old Tory cause. But these farms and bits of ground had gone again before our time. To them had been attached no religion. When old Kit had found himself pressed in that matter of the majority of the Nineteenth Dragoons, in which crack regiment his second son made for himself quite a career, he found it easier to sell than to save—seeing that that which he sold was his own and not the patrimony of the Dales. At his death the remainder of these purchases had gone. Family arrangements required completion, and Christopher Dale required ready money. The outlying farms flew away, as such new purchases had flown before; but the old patrimony of the Dales remained untouched, as it had ever remained.

It had been a religion among them; and seeing that the worship had been carried on without fail, that the vestal fire had never gone down upon the hearth, I should not have said that the Dales had walked their ways without high principle. To this religion they had all adhered, and the new heir had ever entered in upon *his domain without other encumbrances than those with which he himself was then already burdened. And yet there had been no entail. The idea of an entail was not in accordance with the pecu-*

INTERTYPE BASKERVILLE

11 point, 1½ point leaded

FORMAT	PICAS	LINES	WPL	CPL	WPP	CPP
Royal 8vo	26×43	41	12.2	69	500	2829
Demy 8vo	24×40	38	11.3	64	430	2432
Large Crcwn 8vo	23×36	35	10.6	62	371	2170
Crown 8vo	21×34	33	9.5	56	313	1848

father to son, and from uncle to nephew, and, in one instance, from second cousin to second cousin, the sceptre had descended in the family of the Dales; and the acres had remained intact, growing in value and not decreasing in number, though guarded by no entail and protected by no wonderful amount of prudence or wisdom. The estate of Dale of Allington had been coterminous with the parish of Allington for some hundreds of years; and though, as I have said, the race of squires had possessed nothing of superhuman discretion, and had perhaps been guided in their walks through life by no very distinct principles, still there had been with them so much of adherence to a sacred law, that no acre of the property had ever been parted from the hands of the existing squire. Some futile attempts had been made to increase the territory, as indeed had been done by Kit Dale, the father of Christopher Dale, who will appear as our squire of Allington when the persons of our drama are introduced. Old Kit Dale, who had married money, had bought outlying farms—a bit of ground here and a bit there—talking, as he did so, much of political influence and of the good old Tory cause. But these farms and bits of ground had gone again before our time. To them had been attached no religion. When old Kit had found himself pressed in that matter of the majority of the Nineteenth Dragoons, in which crack regiment his second son made for himself quite a career, he found it easier to sell than to save—seeing that that which he sold was his own and not the patrimony of the Dales. At his death the remainder of these purchases had gone. Family arrangements required completion, and Christopher Dale required ready money. The outlying farms flew away, as such new purchases had flown before; but the old patrimony of the Dales remained untouched, as it had ever remained.

It had been a religion among them; and seeing that the worship had been carried on without fail, that the vestal fire had never gone down upon the hearth, I should not

INTERTYPE BASKERVILLE

12 point, 1 point leaded

FORMAT	PICAS	LINES	WPL	CPL	WPP	CPP
Royal 8vo	26×43	40	10.7	59	428	2360
Demy 8vo	24×40	37	9.9	55	366	2035
Large Crown 8vo	23×36	33	9.1	53	302	1749
Crown 8vo	21×34	31	8.1	49	253	1519

LINOTYPE CALEDONIA

Synopsis in 10 *point*

ABCDEFGHIJKLMNOPQRSTUVWXYZ&ÆŒ

ABCDEFGHIJKLMNOPQRSTUVWXYZÆŒ

abcdefghijklmnopqrstuvwxyzæœfiffflffiffl

ABCDEFGHIJKLMNOPQRSTUVWXYZ&ÆŒ

abcdefghijklmnopqrstuvwxyzæœfiffflffiffl

.,:;;!?"-()[]£ *:;!?*

1234567890 *1234567890*

All normal European accents available

Available in composition sizes 8, 10, 11, 12 *point*

father to son, and from uncle to nephew, and, in one instance, from second cousin to second cousin, the sceptre had descended in the family of the Dales; and the acres had remained intact, growing in value and not decreasing in number, though guarded by no entail and protected by no wonderful amount of prudence or wisdom. The estate of Dale of Allington had been coterminous with the parish of Allington for some hundreds of years; and though, as I have said, the race of squires had possessed nothing of superhuman discretion, and had perhaps been guided in their walks through life by no very distinct principles, still there had been with them so much of adherence to a sacred law, that no acre of the property had ever been parted from the hands of the existing squire. Some futile attempts had been made to increase the territory, as indeed had been done by Kit Dale, the father of Christopher Dale, who will appear as our squire of Allington when the persons of our drama are introduced. Old Kit Dale, who had married money, had bought outlying farms—a bit of ground here and a bit there—talking, as he did so, much of political influence and of the good old Tory cause. But these farms and bits of ground had gone again before our time. To them had been attached no religion. When old Kit had found himself pressed in that matter of the majority of the Nineteenth Dragoons, in which crack regiment his second son made for himself quite a career, he found it easier to sell than to save—seeing that that which he sold was his own and not the patrimony of the Dales. At his death the remainder of these purchases had gone. Family arrangements required completion, and Christopher Dale required ready money. The outlying farms flew away, as such new purchases had flown before; but the old patrimony of the Dales remained untouched, as it had ever remained.

It had been a religion among them; and seeing that the worship had been carried on without fail, that the vestal fire had never gone down upon the hearth, I should not have said that the Dales had walked their ways without high principle. To this religion they had all adhered, and the new heir had ever entered in upon his domain without other encumbrances than those with which he himself was then already burdened. And yet there had been no entail. The idea of an entail was not in accordance with the peculiarities of the Dale mind. It was necessary to the Dale religion that each squire should have the power of wasting them. I remember to have dined at a house, the whole glory and fortune of which depended on the safety of a glass goblet. We all know the story. If the luck of Edenhall should be shattered, the doom of the family would be sealed. Nevertheless I was bidden to drink out of the fatal glass, as were all guests in that house. It would not *have contented the chivalrous mind of the master to protect his doom by lock and key and padded chest. And so it was with the Dales of Allington. To them an entail would have been a lock and*

LINOTYPE CALEDONIA

10 point solid

FORMAT	PICAS	LINES	WPL	CPL	WPP	CPP
Royal 8vo	26×43	52	12.4	67	645	3484
Demy 8vo	24×40	48	11.5	62	552	2976
Large Crown 8vo	23×36	43	10.7	59	460	2537
Crown 8vo	21×34	41	9.8	54	400	2214

father to son, and from uncle to nephew, and, in one instance, from second cousin to second cousin, the sceptre had descended in the family of the Dales; and the acres had remained intact, growing in value and not decreasing in number, though guarded by no entail and protected by no wonderful amount of prudence or wisdom. The estate of Dale of Allington had been coterminous with the parish of Allington for some hundreds of years; and though, as I have said, the race of squires had possessed nothing of superhuman discretion, and had perhaps been guided in their walks through life by no very distinct principles, still there had been with them so much of adherence to a sacred law, that no acre of the property had ever been parted from the hands of the existing squire. Some futile attempts had been made to increase the territory, as indeed had been done by Kit Dale, the father of Christopher Dale, who will appear as our squire of Allington when the persons of our drama are introduced. Old Kit Dale, who had married money, had bought outlying farms—a bit of ground here and a bit there—talking, as he did so, much of political influence and of the good old Tory cause. But these farms and bits of ground had gone again before our time. To them had been attached no religion. When old Kit had found himself pressed in that matter of the majority of the Nineteenth Dragoons, in which crack regiment his second son made for himself quite a career, he found it easier to sell than to save—seeing that that which he sold was his own and not the patrimony of the Dales. At his death the remainder of these purchases had gone. Family arrangements required completion, and Christopher Dale required ready money. The outlying farms flew away, as such new purchases had flown before; but the old patrimony of the Dales remained untouched, as it had ever remained.

It had been a religion among them; and seeing that the worship had been carried on without fail, that the vestal fire had never gone down upon the hearth, I should not have said that the Dales had walked their ways without high principle. To this religion they had all adhered, and the new heir had ever entered in upon his domain without other encumbrances than those with which he himself was then already burdened. And yet there had been no entail. The idea of an entail was not in accordance with the peculiarities of the Dale mind. It was necessary to the Dale religion that each squire should have the power of wasting them. I remember to have dined at a house, the whole glory and fortune of *which depended on the safety of a glass goblet. We all know the story. If the luck of Edenhall should be shattered, the doom of the family would be sealed. Nevertheless I was bidden to drink*

LINOTYPE CALEDONIA L.D.

10 point, 1 point leaded

FORMAT	PICAS	LINES	WPL	CPL	WPP	CPP
Royal 8vo	26×43	47	12.4	67	582	3149
Demy 8vo	24×40	44	11.5	62	499	2728
Large Crown 8vo	23×36	39	10.7	59	418	2301
Crown 8vo	21×34	37	9.8	54	366	1998

father to son, and from uncle to nephew, and, in one instance, from the second cousin to second cousin, the sceptre had descended in the family of the Dales; and the acres had remained intact, but growing in value and not decreasing in number, though guarded by no entail and protected by no wonderful amount of prudence or wisdom. The estate of Dale of Allington had been coterminous with the parish of Allington for some hundreds of years; and though, as I have said, the race of squires had possessed nothing of superhuman discretion, and had perhaps been guided in their walks through life by no very distinct principles, still there had been with them so much of adherence to a sacred law, that no acre of the property had ever been parted from the hands of the existing squire. Some futile attempts had been made to increase the territory, as indeed had been done by Kit Dale, the father of Christopher Dale, who will appear as our squire of Allington when the persons of our drama are introduced. Old Kit Dale, who had married money, had bought outlying farms—a bit of ground here and a bit there—talking, as he did so, much of political influence and of the good old Tory cause. But these farms and bits of ground had gone again before our time. To them had been attached no religion. When old Kit had found himself pressed in that matter of the majority of the Nineteenth Dragoons, in which crack regiment his second son made for himself quite a career, he found it easier to sell than to save—seeing that that which he sold was his own and not the patrimony of the Dales. At his death the remainder of these purchases had gone. Family arrangements required completion, and Christopher Dale required ready money. The outlying farms flew away, as such new purchases had flown before; but the old patrimony of the Dales remained untouched, as it had ever remained.

It had been a religion among them; and seeing that the worship had been carried on without fail, that the vestal fire had never gone down upon the hearth, I should not have said that the Dales had walked their ways without high principle. To this religion they had all adhered, and the new heir had ever entered in upon his domain without other encumbrances than those with which he himself was then already burdened. And yet there had been no entail. The idea of an entail was not in accordance with the peculiarities of the Dale mind. It *was necessary to the Dale religion that each squire should have the power of wasting them. I remember to have dined at a house the whole glory and fortune of which depended on*

LINOTYPE CALEDONIA

11 point solid

FORMAT	PICAS	LINES	WPL	CPL	WPP	CPP
Royal 8vo	26×43	47	11.4	63	535	2961
Demy 8vo	24×40	44	10.6	58	466	2552
Large Crown 8vo	23×36	39	9.9	56	386	2184
Crown 8vo	21×34	37	9.0	51	334	1887

father to son, and from uncle to nephew, and, in one instance, from the second cousin to second cousin, the sceptre had descended in the family of the Dales; and the acres had remained intact, but growing in value and not decreasing in number, though guarded by no entail and protected by no wonderful amount of prudence or wisdom. The estate of Dale of Allington had been coterminous with the parish of Allington for some hundreds of years; and though, as I have said, the race of squires had possessed nothing of superhuman discretion, and had perhaps been guided in their walks through life by no very distinct principles, still there had been with them so much of adherence to a sacred law, that no acre of the property had ever been parted from the hands of the existing squire. Some futile attempts had been made to increase the territory, as indeed had been done by Kit Dale, the father of Christopher Dale, who will appear as our squire of Allington when the persons of our drama are introduced. Old Kit Dale, who had married money, had bought outlying farms—a bit of ground here and a bit there—talking, as he did so, much of political influence and of the good old Tory cause. But these farms and bits of ground had gone again before our time. To them had been attached no religion. When old Kit had found himself pressed in that matter of the majority of the Nineteenth Dragoons, in which crack regiment his second son made for himself quite a career, he found it easier to sell than to save—seeing that that which he sold was his own and not the patrimony of the Dales. At his death the remainder of these purchases had gone. Family arrangements required completion, and Christopher Dale required ready money. The outlying farms flew away, as such new purchases had flown before; but the old patrimony of the Dales remained untouched, as it had ever remained.

It had been a religion among them; and seeing that the worship had been carried on without fail, that the vestal fire had never gone down upon the hearth, I should not have said that the Dales had walked their ways without high principle. To this religion they had all adhered, and the new heir had *ever entered in upon his domain without other encumbrances than those with which he himself was already burdened. And yet there had been no entail. The idea of an entail was*

LINOTYPE CALEDONIA L.D.

11 point, 1 point leaded

FORMAT	PICAS	LINES	WPL	CPL	WPP	CPP
Royal 8vo	26×43	43	11.4	63	490	2709
Demy 8vo	23×40	40	10.6	58	422	2320
Large Crown 8vo	23×36	36	9.9	56	355	2016
Crown 8vo	21×34	34	9.0	51	305	1734

father to son, and from uncle to nephew, and, in one instance, from second cousin to second cousin, the sceptre had descended in the family of the Dales; and the acres had remained intact, growing in value and not decreasing in number, though guarded by no entail and protected by no wonderful amount of prudence or wisdom. The estate of Dale of Allington had been coterminous with the parish of Allington for some hundreds of years; and though, as I have said, the race of squires had possessed nothing of superhuman discretion, and had perhaps been guided in their walks through life by no very distinct principles, still there had been with them so much of adherence to a sacred law, that no acre of the property had ever been parted from the hands of the existing squire. Some futile attempts had been made to increase the territory, as indeed had been done by Kit Dale, the father of Christopher Dale, who will appear as our squire of Allington when the persons of our drama are introduced. Old Kit Dale, who had married money, had bought outlying farms—a bit of ground here and a bit there—talking, as he did so, much of political influence and of the good old Tory cause. But these farms and bits of ground had gone again before our time. To them had been attached no religion. When old Kit had found himself pressed in that matter of the majority of the Nineteenth Dragoons, in which crack regiment his second son made for himself quite a career, he found it easier to sell than to save—seeing that that which he sold was his own and not the patrimony of the Dales. At his death the remainder of these purchases had gone. Family arrangements required completion, and Christopher Dale required ready money. The outlying farms flew away, as such new purchases had flown before; but the old patrimony of the Dales remained untouched, as it had ever *remained.*

It had been a religion among them; and seeing that the worship had been carried on without fail, that the vestal

LINOTYPE CALEDONIA L.D.

12 point, 1 point leaded

FORMAT	PICAS	LINES	WPL	CPL	WPP	CPP
Royal 8vo	26×43	40	10.5	59	420	2360
Demy 8vo	24×40	37	9.7	55	355	2035
Large Crown 8vo	23×36	33	9.1	53	302	1749
Crown 8vo	21×34	31	8.4	48	261	1488

LINOTYPE GRANJON

Synopsis in 10 point

ABCDEFGHIJKLMNOPQRSTUVWXYZ&ÆŒ
abcdefghijklmnopqrstuvwxyzæœfiffflffiffl
ABCDEFGHIJKLMNOPQRSTUVWXYZ&ÆŒ
.,:;!?'"-()[]£ *:;!?*
1234567890 *1234567890* 1234567890 *1234567890*

All normal European accents available
Available in composition sizes 9, 10, 11, 12 *point*

father to son, and from uncle to nephew, and, in one instance, from second cousin to second cousin, the sceptre had descended in the family of the Dales; and the acres had remained intact, growing in value and not decreasing in number, though guarded by no entail and protected by no wonderful amount of prudence or wisdom. The estate of Dale of Allington had been coterminous with the parish of Allington for some hundreds of years; and though, as I have said, the race of squires had possessed nothing of superhuman discretion, and had perhaps been guided in their walks through life by no very distinct principles, still there had been with them so much of adherence to a sacred law, that no acre of the property had ever been parted from the hands of the existing squire. Some futile attempts had been made to increase the territory, as indeed had been done by Kit Dale, the father of Christopher Dale, who will appear as our squire of Allington when the persons of our drama are introduced. Old Kit Dale, who had married money, had bought outlying farms—a bit of ground here and a bit there—talking, as he did so, much of political influence and the good old Tory cause. But these farms and bits of ground had gone again before our time. To them had been attached no religion. When old Kit had found himself pressed in that matter of the majority of the Nineteenth Dragoons, in which crack regiment his second son made for himself quite a career, he found it easier to sell than to save—seeing that that which he sold was his own and not the patrimony of the Dales. At his death the remainder of these purchases had gone. Family arrangements required completion, and Christopher Dale required ready money. The outlying farms flew away, as such new purchases had flown before; but the old patrimony of the Dales remained untouched as it had ever remained.

It had been a religion among them; and seeing that the worship had been carried on without fail, that the vestal fire had never gone down upon the hearth, I should not have said that the Dales had walked their ways without high principle. To this religion they had all adhered, and the new heir had ever entered in upon his domain without other encumbrances than those with which he himself was then already burdened. And yet there had been no entail. The idea of an entail was not in accordance with the peculiarities of the Dale mind. It was necessary to the Dale religion that each squire should have the power of wasting them. I remember to have dined at a house, the whole glory and fortune of which depended on the safety of a glass goblet. We all know the story. If the luck of Edenhall should be shattered, the doom of the family would be sealed. Nevertheless I was bidden to drink out of the fatal glass, as were all guests in that house. It would not have contented the chivalrous mind of the master to protect his doom by lock and key and padded chest. And so it was with the Dales of Allington. To them an entail would have been a lock and key and a padded chest; but the old chivalry of their house denied to them the use of such protection.

I have spoken somewhat slightingly of the acquirements and doings of the family; and indeed their acquirements had been few and their doings little. At Allington, Dale of Allington had always been known as a king.

LINOTYPE GRANJON

10 point solid

FORMAT	PICAS	LINES	WPL	CPL	WPP	CPP
Royal 8vo	26×43	52	13.8	75	718	3900
Demy 8vo	24×40	48	12.8	69	608	3312
Large Crown 8vo	23×36	43	11.9	66	512	2838
Crown 8vo	21×34	41	10.7	61	439	2051

father to son, and from uncle to nephew, and, in one instance, from second cousin to second cousin, the sceptre had descended in the family of the Dales; and the acres had remained intact, growing in value and not decreasing in number, though guarded by no entail and protected by no wonderful amount of prudence or wisdom. The estate of Dale of Allington had been coterminous with the parish of Allington for some hundreds of years; and though, as I have said, the race of squires had possessed nothing of superhuman discretion, and had perhaps been guided in their walks through life by no very distinct principles, still there had been with them so much of adherence to a sacred law, that no acre of the property had ever been parted from the hands of the existing squire. Some futile attempts had been made to increase the territory, as indeed had been done by Kit Dale, the father of Christopher Dale, who will appear as our squire of Allington when the persons of our drama are introduced. Old Kit Dale, who had married money, had bought outlying farms—a bit of ground here and a bit there—talking, as he did so, much of political influence and the good old Tory cause. But these farms and bits of ground had gone again before our time. To them had been attached no religion. When old Kit had found himself pressed in that matter of the majority of the Nineteenth Dragoons, in which crack regiment his second son made for himself quite a career, he found it easier to sell than to save—seeing that that which he sold was his own and not the patrimony of the Dales. At his death the remainder of these purchases had gone. Family arrangements required completion, and Christopher Dale required ready money. The outlying farms flew away, as such new purchases had flown before; but the old patrimony of the Dales remained untouched, as it had ever remained.

It had been a religion among them; and seeing that the worship had been carried on without fail, that the vestal fire had never gone down upon the hearth, I should not have said that the Dales had walked their ways without high principle. To this religion they had all adhered, and the new heir had entered in upon his domain without other encumbrances than those with which he himself was then already burdened. And yet there had been no entail. The idea of an entail was not in accordance with the peculiarities of the Dale mind. It was necessary to the Dale religion that each squire should have the power of wasting them. I remember to have dined at a house, the whole glory and fortune of which depended on the safety of a glass goblet. We all know the story. If the luck of Edenhall should be shattered, the doom of the family would be sealed. Nevertheless I was bidden to drink out of the fatal glass, as were all guests in that house. It would not have contented the chivalrous mind *of the master to protect his doom by lock and key and padded chest. And so it was with the Dales of Allington. To them an entail would have been a lock and key and a padded chest; but the old chivalry of their*

LINOTYPE GRANJON

10 point, 1 point leaded

FORMAT	PICAS	LINES	WPL	CPL	WPP	CPP
Royal 8vo	26×43	47	13.8	75	648	3525
Demy 8vo	24×40	44	12.8	69	563	3036
Large Crown 8vo	23×36	39	11.9	66	464	2574
Crown 8vo	21×34	37	10.7	61	394	2257

father to son, and from uncle to nephew, and, in one instance, from second cousin to second cousin, the sceptre had descended in the family of the Dales; and the acres had remained intact, growing in value and not decreasing in number, though guarded by no entail and protected by no wonderful amount of prudence or wisdom. The estate of Dale of Allington had been coterminous with the parish of Allington for some hundreds of years; and though, as I have said, the race of squires had possessed nothing of superhuman discretion, and had perhaps been guided in their walks through life by no very distinct principles, still there had been with them so much of adherence to a sacred law, that no acre of the property had ever been parted from the hands of the existing squire. Some futile attempts had been made to increase the territory, as indeed had been done by Kit Dale, the father of Christopher Dale, who will appear as our squire of Allington when the persons of our drama are introduced. Old Kit Dale, who had married money, had bought outlying farms —a bit of ground here and a bit there—talking, as he did so, much of political influence and of the good old Tory cause. But these farms and bits of ground had gone again before our time. To them had been attached no religion. When old Kit had found himself pressed in that matter of the majority of the Nineteenth Dragoons, in which crack regiment his second son made for himself quite a career, he found it easier to sell than to save—seeing that that which he sold was his own and not the patrimony of the Dales. At his death the remainder of these purchases had gone. Family arrangements required completion, and Christopher Dale required ready money. The outlying farms flew away, as such new purchases had flown before; but the old patrimony of the Dales remained untouched, as it had ever remained.

It had been a religion among them; and seeing that the worship had been carried on without fail, that the vestal fire had never gone down upon the hearth, I should not have said that the Dales had walked their ways without high principle. To this religion they had all adhered, and the new heir had ever entered in upon his domain without other encumbrances than those with which he himself was then already burdened. And yet there had been no entail. The idea of an entail was not in accordance with the peculiarities of the Dale mind. It was necessary to the Dale religion that each squire should have the power of wasting them. I remember to have dined at a house, the whole glory and fortune of which depended on the safety of a glass goblet. We all know the story. If the luck of Edenhall *should be shattered, the doom of the family would be sealed. Nevertheless I was bidden to drink out of the fatal glass, as were all guests in that house. It would not have contented the chivalrous mind of*

LINOTYPE GRANJON

11 point solid

FORMAT	PICAS	LINES	WPL	CPL	WPP	CPP
Royal 8vo	26×43	47	12.7	69	596	3243
Demy 8vo	24×40	44	11.8	64	520	2816
Large Crown 8vo	23×36	39	11.0	61	428	2379
Crown 8vo	21×34	37	10.0	55	369	2035

father to son, and from uncle to nephew, and, in one instance, from second cousin to second cousin, the sceptre had descended in the family of the Dales; and the acres had remained intact, growing in value and not decreasing in number, though guarded by no entail and protected by no wonderful amount of prudence or wisdom. The estate of Dale of Allington had been coterminous with the parish of Allington for some hundreds of years; and though, as I have said, the race of squires had possessed nothing of superhuman discretion, and had perhaps been guided in their walks through life by no very distinct principles, still there had been with them so much of adherence to a sacred law, that no acre of the property had ever been parted from the hands of the existing squire. Some futile attempts had been made to increase the territory, as indeed had been done by Kit Dale, the father of Christopher Dale, who will appear as our squire of Allington when the persons of our drama are introduced. Old Kit Dale, who had married money, had bought outlying farms —a bit of ground here and a bit there—talking, as he did so, much of political influence and of the good old Tory cause. But these farms and bits of ground had gone again before our time. To them had been attached no religion. When old Kit had found himself pressed in that matter of the majority of the Nineteenth Dragoons, in which crack regiment his second son made for himself quite a career, he found it easier to sell than to save—seeing that that which he sold was his own and not the patrimony of the Dales. At his death the remainder of these purchases had gone. Family arrangements required completion, and Christopher Dale required ready money. The outlying farms flew away, as such new purchases had flown before; but the old patrimony of the Dales remained untouched, as it had ever remained.

It had been a religion among them; and seeing that the worship had been carried on without fail, that the vestal fire had never gone down upon the hearth, I should not have said that the Dales had walked their ways without high principle. To this religion they had all adhered, and the new heir had ever entered in upon his domain without other encumbrances than those with which he himself was then already burdened. And yet there had been no entail. The idea of an entail was not in accordance with the peculiarities of the Dale *mind. It was necessary to the Dale religion that each squire should have the power of wasting them. I remember to have dined at a house, the whole glory and fortune of which depended on the safety*

LINOTYPE GRANJON

11 point, 1 point leaded

FORMAT	PICAS	LINES	WPL	CPL	WPP	CPP
Royal 8vo	26×43	43	12.7	69	546	2967
Demy 8vo	24×40	40	11.8	64	468	2560
Large Crown 8vo	23×36	36	11.0	61	394	2196
Crown 8vo	21×34	34	10.0	55	340	1870

father to son, and from uncle to nephew, and, in one instance, from second cousin to second cousin, the sceptre had descended in the family of the Dales; and the acres had remained intact, growing in value and not decreasing in number, though guarded by no entail and protected by no wonderful amount of prudence or wisdom. The estate of Dale of Allington had been coterminous with the parish of Allington for some hundreds of years; and though, as I have said before, the race of squires had possessed nothing of superhuman discretion, and had perhaps been guided in their walks through life by no very distinct principles, still there had been with them so much of adherence to a sacred law, that no acre of the property had ever been parted from the hands of the existing squire. Some futile attempts had been made to increase the territory, as indeed had been done by Kit Dale, the father of Christopher Dale, who will appear as our squire of Allington when the persons of our drama are introduced. Old Kit Dale, who had married money, had bought outlying farms—a bit of ground here and a bit there—talking, as he did so, much of political influence and of the good old Tory cause. But these farms and bits of ground had gone again before our time. To them had been attached no religion. When old Kit had found himself pressed in that matter of the majority of the Nineteenth Dragoons, in which crack regiment his second son made for himself quite a career, he found it easier to sell than to save—seeing that that which he sold was his own and not the patrimony of the Dales. At his death the remainder of these purchases had gone. Family arrangements required completion, and Christopher Dale required ready money. The outlying farms flew away, as such new purchases had flown before; but the old patrimony of the Dales remained untouched, as it had ever remained.

It had been a religion among them; and seeing that the worship had been carried on without fail, that the vestal fire had never gone down upon the hearth, I should not have said that *the Dales had walked their ways without high principle. To this religion they had all adhered, and the new heir had ever entered in upon his domain without other encumbrances than*

LINOTYPE GRANJON

12 point, 1 point leaded

FORMAT	PICAS	LINES	WPL	CPL	WPP	CPP
Royal 8vo	26×43	40	11.7	64	468	2560
Demy 8vo	24×40	37	10.8	59	400	2183
Large Crown 8vo	23×36	33	10.2	56	337	1848
Crown 8vo	21×34	31	9.3	51	288	1581

LINOTYPE JULIANA

Synopsis in 10 point

ABCDEFGHIJKLMNOPQRSTUVWXYZ&ÆŒ

ABCDEFGHIJKLMNOPQRSTUVWXYZÆŒ

abcdefghijklmnopqrstuvwxyzæœfiffflffiffl

ABCDEFGHIJKLMNOPQRSTUVWXYZ&ÆŒ

abcdefghijklmnopqrstuvwxyzæœfiffflffiffl

.,:;!?"-()[]£ *:;!?*

1234567890 1234567890 1234567890 *1234567890*

All normal European accents available

Available in composition sizes 8, 10, 11 point

father to son and from uncle to nephew, and, in one instance, from second cousin to second cousin, the sceptre had descended in the family of the Dales; and the acres had remained intact, growing in value and not decreasing in number, though guarded by no entail and protected by no wonderful amount of prudence or wisdom. The estate of Dale of Allington had been coterminous with the parish of Allington for some hundreds of years; and though, as I have said, the race of squires had possessed nothing of superhuman discretion, and had perhaps been guided in their walks through life by no very distinct principles, still there had been with them so much of adherence to a sacred law, that no acre of the property had ever been parted from the hands of the existing squire. Some futile attempts had been made to increase the territory, as indeed had been done by Kit Dale, the father of Christopher Dale, who will appear as our squire of Allington when the persons of our drama are introduced. Old Kit Dale, who had married money, had bought outlying farms—a bit of ground here and a bit there—talking, as he did so, much of political influence and of the good old Tory cause. But these farms and bits of ground had gone again before our time. To them had been attached no religion. When old Kit had found himself pressed in that matter of the majority of the Nineteenth Dragoons, in which crack regiment his second son made for himself quite a career, he found it easier to sell than to save—seeing that that which he sold was his own and not the patrimony of the Dales. At his death the remainder of these purchases had gone. Family arrangements required completion, and Christopher Dale required ready money. The outlying farms flew away, as such new purchases had flown before; but the old patrimony of the Dales remained untouched, as it had ever remained.

It had been a religion among them; and seeing that the worship had been carried on without fail, that the vestal fire had never gone down upon the hearth, I should not have said that the Dales had walked their ways without high principles. To this religion they had all adhered, and the new heir had ever entered in upon his domain without other encumbrances than those with which he himself was then already burdened. And yet there had been no entail. The idea of an entail was not in accordance with the peculiarities of the Dale mind. It was necessary to the Dale religion that each squire should have the power of wasting them. I remember to have dined at a house, the whole glory and fortune of which depended on the safety of a glass goblet. We all know the story. If the luck of Edenhall should be shattered, the doom of the family would be sealed. Nevertheless I was bidden to drink out of the fatal glass, as were all guests in that house. It would not have contented the chivalrous mind of the master to protect his doom by lock and key and padded chest. And so it was with the Dales of Allington. To them an entail would have *been a lock and key and a padded chest; but the old chivalry of their house denied to them the use of such protection.*

I have spoken something slightingly of the acquirements and

LINOTYPE JULIANA

10 point solid

FORMAT	PICAS	LINES	WPL	CPL	WPP	CPP
Royal 8vo	26×43	52	13.1	70	681	3640
Demy 8vo	24×40	48	12.1	65	581	3120
Large Crown 8vo	23×36	43	11.1	62	480	2666
Crown 8vo	21×34	41	10.3	56	424	2296

father to son and from uncle to nephew, and, in one instance, from second cousin to second cousin, the sceptre had descended in the family of the Dales; and the acres had remained intact, growing in value and not decreasing in number, though guarded by no entail and protected by no wonderful amount of prudence or wisdom. The estate of Dale of Allington had been coterminous with the parish of Allington for some hundreds of years; and though, as I have said, the race of squires had possessed nothing of a superhuman discretion, and had perhaps been guided in their walks through life by no very distinct principles, still there had been with them so much of adherence to a sacred law, that no acre of the property had ever been parted from the hands of the existing squire. Some futile attempts had been made to increase the territory, as indeed had been done by Kit Dale, the father of Christopher Dale, who will appear as our squire of Allington when the persons of our drama are introduced. Old Kit Dale, who had married money, had bought outlying farms—a bit of ground here and a bit there—talking, as he did so, much of political influence and of the good old Tory cause. But these farms and bits of ground had gone again before our time. To them had been attached no religion. When old Kit had found himself pressed in that matter of the majority of the Nineteenth Dragoons, in which crack regiment his second son made for himself quite a career, he found it easier to sell than to save—seeing that that which he sold was his own and not the patrimony of the Dales. At his death the remainder of these purchases had gone. Family arrangements required completion, and Christopher Dale required ready money. The outlying farms flew away, as such new purchases had flown before; but the old patrimony of the Dales remained untouched, as it had ever remained.

It had been a religion among them; and seeing that the worship had been carried on without fail, that the vestal fire had never gone down upon the hearth, I should not have said that the Dales had walked their ways without high principles. To this religion they had all adhered, and the new heir had ever entered in upon his domain without other encumbrances than those with which he himself was then already burdened. And yet there had been no entail. The idea of an entail was not in accordance with the peculiarities of the Dale mind. It was necessary to the Dale religion that each squire should have the power of wasting them. I remember to have dined at a house, the whole glory and fortune of which depended on the safety of a glass goblet. We all know the story. If the luck of Edenhall should be shattered, the doom of the family would be sealed. Nevertheless *I was bidden to drink out of the fatal glass, as were all guests in that house. It would not have contented the chivalrous mind of the master to protect his doom by lock and key and padded chest. And*

LINOTYPE JULIANA

10 point, 1 point leaded

FORMAT	PICAS	LINES	WPL	CPL	WPP	CPP
Royal 8vo	26×43	47	13.1	70	615	3290
Demy 8vo	24×40	44	12.1	65	534	2860
Large Crown 8vo	23×36	39	11.1	62	431	2418
Crown 8vo	21×34	37	10.3	56	380	2072

father to son and from uncle to nephew, and, in one instance, from second cousin to second cousin, the sceptre had descended in the family of the Dales; and the acres had remained intact, growing in value and not decreasing in number, though guarded by no entail and protected by no wonderful amount of prudence or wisdom. The estate of Dale of Allington had been coterminous with the parish of Allington for some hundreds of years; and though, as I have said, the race of squires had possessed nothing of superhuman discretion, and had perhaps been guided in their walks through life by no very distinct principles, still there had been with them so much of adherence to a sacred law, that no acre of the property had ever been parted from the hands of the existing squire. Some futile attempts had been made to increase the territory, as indeed had been done by Kit Dale, the father of Christopher Dale, who will appear as our squire of Allington when the persons of our drama are introduced. Old Kit Dale, who had married money, had bought outlying farms—a bit of ground here and a bit there—talking, as he did so, much of political influence and of the good old Tory cause. But these farms and bits of ground had gone again before our time. To them had been attached no religion. When old Kit had found himself pressed in that matter of the majority of the Nineteenth Dragoons, in which crack regiment his second son made for himself quite a career, he found it easier to sell than to save—seeing that that which he sold was his own and not the patrimony of the Dales. At his death the remainder of these purchases had gone. Family arrangements required completion, and Christopher Dale required ready money. The outlying farms flew away, as such new purchases had flown before; but the old patrimony of the Dales remained untouched, as it had ever remained.

It had been a religion among them; and seeing that the worship had been carried on without fail, that the vestal fire had never gone down upon the hearth, I should not have said that the Dales had walked their ways without high principles. To this religion they had all adhered, and the new heir had ever entered in upon his domain without other encumbrances than those with which he himself was then already burdened. And yet there had been no entail. The idea of an entail was not in accordance with the peculiarities of the Dale mind. It was necessary to the Dale religion that each squire should have the power of wasting them. I remember to have dined at a house, the whole glory and fortune of which depended on the safety *of a glass goblet. We all know the story. If the luck of Edenhall should be shattered, the doom of the family would be sealed. Nevertheless I was bidden to drink out of the fatal glass, as were all guests*

LINOTYPE JULIANA

10 point, $1\frac{1}{2}$ point leaded

FORMAT	PICAS	LINES	WPL	CPL	WPP	CPP
Royal 8vo	26×43	45	13.1	70	590	3150
Demy 8vo	24×40	42	12.1	65	508	2730
Large Crown 8vo	23×36	38	11.1	62	422	2356
Crown 8vo	21×34	35	10.3	56	359	1960

father to son, and from uncle to nephew, and, in one instance, from second cousin to second cousin, the sceptre had descended in the family of the Dales; and the acres had remained intact, growing in value and not decreasing in number, though guarded by no entail and protected by no wonderful amount of prudence or wisdom. The estate of Dale of Allington had been coterminous with the parish of Allington for some hundreds of years; and though, as I have said, the race of squires had possessed nothing of superhuman discretion, and they had perhaps been guided in their walks through life by no very distinct principles, still there had been with them so much of adherence to a sacred law, that no acre of the property had ever been parted from the hands of the existing squire. Some futile attempts had been made to increase the territory, as indeed had been done by Kit Dale, the father of Christopher Dale, who will appear as our squire of Allington when the persons of our drama are introduced. Old Kit Dale, who had married money, had bought outlying farms—a bit of ground here and a bit there—talking, as he did so, much of political influence and of the good old Tory cause. But these farms and bits of ground had gone again before our time. To them had been attached no religion. When old Kit had found himself pressed in that matter of the majority of the Nineteenth Dragoons, in which crack regiment his second son made for himself quite a career, he found it easier to sell than to save—seeing that that which he sold was his own and not the patrimony of the Dales. At his death the remainder of these purchases had gone. Family arrangements required completion, and Christopher Dale required ready money. The outlying farms flew away, as such new purchases had flown before, but the old patrimony of the Dales remained untouched, as it had ever remained.

It had been a religion among them; and seeing that the worship had been carried on without fail, that the vestal fire had never gone down upon the hearth, I should not have said that the Dales had walked their ways without high principle. To this religion they had all adhered, and the new heir had ever entered in upon his domain without other encumbrances than *those with which he himself was then already burdened. And yet there had been no entail. The idea of an entail was not in accordance with the peculiarities of the Dale mind. It was*

LINOTYPE JULIANA

11 point, 1 point leaded

FORMAT	PICAS	LINES	WPL	CPL	WPP	CPP
Royal 8vo	26×43	43	11.8	66	507	2838
Demy 8vo	24×40	40	10.9	61	436	2440
Large Crown 8vo	23×36	36	10.3	58	371	2088
Crown 8vo	21×34	34	9.3	53	316	1802

father to son, and from uncle to nephew, and, in one instance, from second cousin to second cousin, the sceptre had descended in the family of the Dales; and the acres had remained intact, growing in value and not decreasing in number, though guarded by no entail and protected by no wonderful amount of prudence or wisdom. The estate of Dale of Allington had been coterminous with the parish of Allington for some hundreds of years; and though, as I have said, the race of squires had possessed nothing of superhuman discretion, and they had perhaps been guided in their walks through life by no very distinct principles, still there had been with them so much of adherence to a sacred law, that no acre of the property had ever been parted from the hands of the existing squire. Some futile attempts had been made to increase the territory, as indeed had been done by Kit Dale, the father of Christopher Dale, who will appear as our squire of Allington when the persons of our drama are introduced. Old Kit Dale, who had married money, had bought outlying farms—a bit of ground here and a bit there—talking, as he did so, much of political influence and of the good old Tory cause. But these farms and bits of ground had gone again before our time. To them had been attached no religion. When old Kit had found himself pressed in that matter of the majority of the Nineteenth Dragoons, in which crack regiment his second son made for himself quite a career, he found it easier to sell than to save—seeing that that which he sold was his own and not the patrimony of the Dales. At his death the remainder of these purchases had gone. Family arrangements required completion, and Christopher Dale required ready money. The outlying farms flew away, as such new purchases had flown before; but the old patrimony of the Dales remained untouched, as it had ever remained.

It had been a religion among them; and seeing that the worship had been carried on without fail, that the vestal fire had never gone down upon the hearth, I should not have said that the Dales had walked their ways without high principle. To this *religion they had all adhered, and the new heir had ever entered in upon his domain without other encumbrances than those with which he himself was then already burdened. And*

LINOTYPE JULIANA

11 point, 1½ point leaded

FORMAT	PICAS	LINES	WPL	CPL	WPP	CPP
Royal 8vo	26×43	41	11.8	66	484	2706
Demy 8vo	24×40	38	10.9	61	413	2318
Large Crown 8vo	23×36	35	10.3	58	360	2030
Crown 8vo	21×34	33	9.3	53	307	1749

LINOTYPE TIMES

Synopsis in 10 *point*

ABCDEFGHIJKLMNOPQRSTUVWXYZ&ÆŒ

ABCDEFGHIJKLMNOPQRSTUVWXYZÆŒ

abcdefghijklmnopqrstuvwxyzææfiffflffiffl

ABCDEFGHIJKLMNOPQRSTUVWXYZ&ÆŒ

abcdefghijklmnopqrstuvwxyzææfiffflffiffl

.,:;!?‘’-()[]£ *:;!?*

1234567890 *1234567890*

Related bold

ABCDEFGHIJKLMNOPQRSTUVWXYZ&ÆŒ

abcdefghijklmnopqrstuvwxyzææfiffflffiffl

.,:;!?‘’-()£ 1234567890

All normal European accents available

Available in composition sizes 8, 10, 11 *point*

Related bold available in composition sizes 8, 10, 11 *point*

190 THE SMALL HOUSE AT ALLINGTON

father to son, and from uncle to nephew, and, in one instance, from second cousin to second cousin, the sceptre had descended in the family of the Dales; and the acres had remained intact, growing in value and not decreasing in number, though guarded by no entail and protected by no wonderful amount of prudence or wisdom. The estate of Dale of Allington had been coterminous with the parish of Allington for some hundreds of years; and though, as I have said, the race of squires had possessed nothing of superhuman discretion, and had perhaps been guided in their walks through life by no very distinct principles, still there had been with them so much of adherence to a sacred law, that no acre of the property had ever been parted from the hands of the existing squire. Some futile attempts had been made to increase the territory, as indeed had been done by Kit Dale, the father of Christopher Dale, who will appear as our squire of Allington when the persons of our drama are introduced. Old Kit Dale, who had married money, had bought outlying farms—a bit of ground here and a bit there—talking, as he did so, much of political influence and of the good old Tory cause. But these farms and bits of ground had gone again before our time. To them had been attached no religion. When old Kit had found himself pressed in that matter of the majority of the Nineteenth Dragoons, in which crack regiment his second son made for himself quite a career, he found it easier to sell than to save—seeing that that which he sold was his own and not the patrimony of the Dales. At his death the remainder of these purchases had gone. Family arrangements required completion, and Christopher Dale required ready money. The outlying farms flew away, as such new purchases had flown before; but the old patrimony of the Dales remained untouched, as it had ever remained.

It had been a religion among them; and seeing that the worship had been carried on without fail, that the vestal fire had never gone down upon the hearth, I should not have said that the Dales had walked their ways without high principles. To this religion they had all adhered, and the new heir had ever entered upon his domain without other encumbrances than those with which he himself was then already burdened. And yet there had been no entail. The idea of an entail was not in accordance with the peculiarities of the Dale mind. It was necessary to the Dale religion that each squire should have the power of wasting them. I remember to have dined at a house, the whole glory and fortune of which depended on the safety of a glass goblet. We all know the story. If the luck of Edenhall should be shattered, the doom of the family would be sealed. Nevertheless I was bidden to drink out of the fatal glass, as were all guests in that house. It would not have contented the chivalrous mind of the master to protect his doom by lock and key and padded chest. And so it was with the Dales of Allington. To them an entail would have *been a lock and key and a padded chest; but the old chivalry of their house denied to them the use of such protection.*

I have spoken something slightingly of the acquirements and

LINOTYPE TIMES

10 point solid

FORMAT	PICAS	LINES	WPL	CPL	WPP	CPP
Royal 8vo	26×43	52	13.1	70	681	3640
Demy 8vo	24×40	48	12.1	65	581	3120
Large Crown 8vo	23×36	43	11.1	62	480	2666
Crown 8vo	21×34	41	10.1	56	415	2296

father to son, and from uncle to nephew, and, in one instance, from second cousin to second cousin, the sceptre had descended in the family of the Dales; and the acres had remained intact, growing in value and not decreasing in number, though guarded by no entail and protected by no wonderful amount of prudence or wisdom. The estate of Dale of Allington had been coterminous with the parish of Allington for some hundreds of years; and though, as I have said, the race of squires had possessed nothing of superhuman discretion, and had perhaps been guided in their walks through life by no very distinct principles, still there had been with them so much of adherence to a sacred law, that no acre of the property had ever been parted from the hands of the existing squire. Some futile attempts had been made to increase the territory as indeed had been done by Kit Dale, the father of Christopher Dale, who will appear as our squire of Allington when the persons of our drama are introduced. Old Kit Dale, who had married money, had bought outlying farms—a bit of ground here and a bit there—talking, as he did so, much of political influence and of the good old Tory cause. But these farms and bits of ground had gone again before our time. To them had been attached no religion. When old Kit had found himself pressed in that matter of the majority of the Nineteenth Dragoons, in which crack regiment his second son made for himself quite a career, he found it easier to sell than to save—seeing that that which he sold was his own and not the patrimony of the Dales. At his death the remainder of these purchases had gone. Family arrangements required completion, and Christopher Dale required ready money. The outlying farms flew away, as such new purchases had flown before; but the old patrimony of the Dales remained untouched, as it had ever remained.

It had been a religion among them; and seeing that the worship had been carried on without fail, that the vestal fire had never gone down upon the hearth, I should not have said that the Dales had walked their ways without high principles. To this religion they had all adhered, and the new heir had ever entered in upon his domain without other encumbrances than those with which he himself was then already burdened. And yet there had been no entail. The idea of an entail was not in accordance with the peculiarities of the Dale mind. It was necessary to the Dale religion that each squire should have the power of wasting them. I remember to have dined at a house, the whole glory and fortune of which depended on the safety of a glass goblet. We all know the story. If the luck of Edenhall should be shattered, the doom of the family would be sealed. Never*theless I was bidden to drink out of the fatal glass, as were all guests in that house. It would not have contented the chivalrous mind of the master to protect his doom by lock and key and padded chest. And*

LINOTYPE TIMES L.D.

10 point, 1 point leaded

FORMAT	PICAS	LINES	WPL	CPL	WPP	CPP
Royal 8vo	26×43	47	13.1	70	615	3290
Demy 8vo	24×40	44	12.1	65	534	2860
Large Crown 8vo	23×36	39	11.1	62	433	2418
Crown 8vo	21×34	37	10.1	56	374	2072

father to son, and from uncle to nephew, and, in one instance, from second cousin to second cousin, the sceptre had descended in the family of the Dales; and the acres had remained intact, growing in value and not decreasing in number, though guarded by no entail and protected by no wonderful amount of prudence or wisdom. The estate of Dale of Allington had been coterminous with the parish of Allington for some hundreds of years; and though, as I have said, the race of squires had possessed nothing of superhuman discretion, and had perhaps been guided in their walks through life by no very distinct principles, still there had been with them so much of adherence to a sacred law, that no acre of the property had ever been parted from the hands of the existing squire. Some futile attempts had been made to increase the territory, as indeed had been done by Kit Dale, the father of Christopher Dale, who will appear as our squire of Allington when the persons of our drama are introduced. Old Kit Dale, who had married money, had bought outlying farms—a bit of ground here and a bit there—talking, as he did so, much of political influence and of the good old Tory cause. But these farms and bits of ground had gone again before our time. To them had been attached no religion. When old Kit had found himself pressed in that matter of the majority of the Nineteenth Dragoons, in which crack regiment his second son made for himself quite a career, he found it easier to sell than to save—seeing that that which he sold was his own and not the patrimony of the Dales. At his death the remainder of these purchases had gone. Family arrangements required completion, and Christopher Dale required ready money. The outlying farms flew away, as such new purchases had flown before; but the old patrimony of the Dales remained untouched, as it had ever remained.

It had been a religion among them; and seeing that the worship had been carried on without fail, that the vestal fire had never gone down upon the hearth, I should not have said that the Dales had walked their ways without high principles. To this religion they had all adhered, and the new heir had ever entered in upon his domain without other encumbrances than those with which he himself was then already burdened. And yet there had been no entail. The idea of an entail was not in accordance with the peculiarities of the Dale mind. It was necessary to the Dale religion that each squire should have the power of wasting them. I remember to have dined at a house, the whole glory and fortune of which depended on the safety *of a glass goblet. We all know the story. If the luck of Edenhall should be shattered, the doom of the family would be sealed. Nevertheless I was bidden to drink out of the fatal glass, as were all guests*

LINOTYPE TIMES L.D.

10 point, 1½ point leaded

FORMAT	PICAS	LINES	WPL	CPL	WPP	CPP
Royal 8vo	26×43	45	13.1	70	590	3150
Demy 8vo	24×40	42	12.1	65	509	2730
Large Crown 8vo	23×36	38	11.1	62	422	2356
Crown 8vo	21×34	35	10.1	56	356	1960

father to son, and from uncle to nephew, and, in one instance, from second cousin to second cousin, the sceptre had descended in the family of the Dales; and the acres had remained intact, growing in value and not decreasing in number, though guarded by no entail and protected by no wonderful amount of prudence or wisdom. The estate of Dale of Allington had been coterminous with the parish of Allington for some hundreds of years; and though, as I have said, the race of squires had possessed nothing of superhuman discretion, and they had perhaps been guided in their walks through life by no very distinct principles, still there had been with them so much of adherence to a sacred law, that no acre of the property had ever been parted from the hands of the existing squire. Some futile attempts had been made to increase the territory, as indeed had been done by Kit Dale, the father of Christopher Dale, who will appear as our squire of Allington when the persons of our drama are introduced. Old Kit Dale, who had married money, had bought outlying farms—a bit of ground here and a bit there—talking, as he did so, much of political influence and of the good old Tory cause. But these farms and bits of ground had gone again before our time. To them had been attached no religion. When old Kit had found himself pressed in that matter of the majority of the Nineteenth Dragoons, in which crack regiment his second son made for himself quite a career, he found it easier to sell than to save—seeing that that which he sold was his own and not the patrimony of the Dales. At his death the remainder of these purchases had gone. Family arrangements required completion, and Christopher Dale required ready money. The outlying farms flew away, as such new purchases had flown before; but the old patrimony of the Dales remained untouched, as it had ever remained.

It had been a religion among them; and seeing that the worship had been carried on without fail, that the vestal fire had never gone down upon the hearth, I should not have said that the Dales had walked their ways without high principle. To this religion they had all adhered and the new heir had ever entered in upon his domain without other encumbrances than *those with which he himself was then already burdened. And yet there had been no entail. The idea of an entail was not in accordance with the peculiarities of the Dale mind. It was*

LINOTYPE TIMES L.D.

11 point, 1 point leaded

FORMAT	PICAS	LINES	WPL	CPL	WPP	CPP
Royal 8vo	26×43	43	11.8	65	507	2795
Demy 8vo	24×40	40	10.9	60	436	2400
Large Crown 8vo	23×36	36	10.3	57	371	2052
Crown 8vo	21×34	34	9.1	52	309	1762

father to son, and from uncle to nephew, and, in one instance, from second cousin to second cousin, the sceptre had descended in the family of the Dales; and the acres had remained intact, growing in value and not decreasing in number, though guarded by no entail and protected by no wonderful amount of prudence or wisdom. The estate of Dale of Allington had been coterminous with the parish of Allington for some hundreds of years; and though, as I have said, the race of squires had possessed nothing of superhuman discretion, and they had perhaps been guided in their walks through life by no very distinct principles, still there had been with them so much of adherence to a sacred law, that no acre of the property had ever been parted from the hands of the existing squire. Some futile attempts had been made to increase the territory, as indeed had been done by Kit Dale, the father of Christopher Dale, who will appear as our squire of Allington when the persons of our drama are introduced. Old Kit Dale, who had married money, had bought outlying farms—a bit of ground here and a bit there— talking, as he did so, much of political influence and of the good old Tory cause. But these farms and bits of ground had gone again before our time. To them had been attached no religion. When old Kit had found himself pressed in that matter of the majority of the Nineteenth Dragoons, in which crack regiment his second son made for himself quite a career, he found it easier to sell than to save—seeing that that which he sold was his own and not the patrimony of the Dales. At his death the remainder of these purchases had gone. Family arrangements required completion, and Christopher Dale required ready money. The outlying farms flew away, as such new purchases had flown before; but the old patrimony of the Dales remained untouched, as it had ever remained.

It had been a religion among them; and seeing that the worship had been carried on without fail, that the vestal fire had never gone down upon the hearth, I should not have said that the Dales had walked their ways without high principle. To this *religion they had all adhered, and the new heir had ever entered in upon his domain without other encumbrances than those with which he himself was then already burdened. And*

LINOTYPE TIMES L.D.

11 point, 1½ point leaded

FORMAT	PICAS	LINES	WPL	CPL	WPP	CPP
Royal 8vo	26×43	41	11.8	65	483	2665
Demy 8vo	24×40	38	10.9	60	410	2280
Large Crown 8vo	23×36	35	10.3	57	361	1995
Crown 8vo	21×34	33	9.1	52	299	1716

3

TWELVE POINT ALPHABETS OF MONOTYPE, LINOTYPE & INTERTYPE FACES

MONOTYPE

Baskerville 169	ABCDEFGHIJKLMNOPQRSTUVWXYZ
Bell 341	ABCDEFGHIJKLMNOPQRSTUVWXYZ
Bembo 270	ABCDEFGHIJKLMNOPQRSTUVWXYZ
Bodoni 135	ABCDEFGHIJKLMNOPQRSTUVWXYZ
Caslon 128	ABCDEFGHIJKLMNOPQRSTUVWXYZ
Ehrhardt 453	ABCDEFGHIJKLMNOPQRSTUVWXYZ
Fournier 185	ABCDEFGHIJKLMNOPQRSTUVWXYZ
Garamond 156	ABCDEFGHIJKLMNOPQRSTUVWXYZ
Goudy O.S. 291	ABCDEFGHIJKLMNOPQRSTUVWXYZ
Imprint 101	ABCDEFGHIJKLMNOPQRSTUVWXYZ
Modern 7	ABCDEFGHIJKLMNOPQRSTUVWXYZ
Old Style 2	ABCDEFGHIJKLMNOPQRSTUVWXYZ
Perpetua 239	ABCDEFGHIJKLMNOPQRSTUVWXYZ
Plantin 110	ABCDEFGHIJKLMNOPQRSTUVWXYZ
Poliphilus 170	ABCDEFGHIJKLMNOPQRSTUVWXYZ
Scotch Roman 46	ABCDEFGHIJKLMNOPQRSTUVWXYZ
Spectrum 556	ABCDEFGHIJKLMNOPQRSTUVWXYZ
Times Roman 327	ABCDEFGHIJKLMNOPQRSTUVWXYZ
Walbaum 374	ABCDEFGHIJKLMNOPQRSTUVWXYZ

LINOTYPE & INTERTYPE

Inter. Baskerville	ABCDEFGHIJKLMNOPQRSTUVWXYZ
Lino Caledonia	ABCDEFGHIJKLMNOPQRSTUVWXYZ
Lino Granjon	ABCDEFGHIJKLMNOPQRSTUVWXYZ

12 Point Roman · *Small capitals & non-lining figures*

Monotype

Baskerville 169	ABCDEFGHIJKLMNOPQRSTUVWXYZ	1234567890
Bell 341	ABCDEFGHIJKLMNOPQRSTUVWXYZ	
Bembo 270	ABCDEFGHIJKLMNOPQRSTUVWXYZ	1234567890
Bodoni 135	ABCDEFGHIJKLMNOPQRSTUVWXYZ	
Caslon 128	ABCDEFGHIJKLMNOPQRSTUVWXYZ	1234567890
Ehrhardt 453	ABCDEFGHIJKLMNOPQRSTUVWXYZ	1234567890
Fournier 185	ABCDEFGHIJKLMNOPQRSTUVWXYZ	1234567890
Garamond 156	ABCDEFGHIJKLMNOPQRSTUVWXYZ	1234567890
Goudy O.S. 291	ABCDEFGHIJKLMNOPQRSTUVWXYZ	
Imprint 101	ABCDEFGHIJKLMNOPQRSTUVWXYZ	1234567890
Modern 7	ABCDEFGHIJKLMNOPQRSTUVWXYZ	
Old Style 2	ABCDEFGHIJKLMNOPQRSTUVWXYZ	1234567890
Perpetua 239	ABCDEFGHIJKLMNOPQRSTUVWXYZ	1234567890
Plantin 110	ABCDEFGHIJKLMNOPQRSTUVWXYZ	1234567890
Poliphilus 170	ABCDEFGHIJKLMNOPQRSTUVWXYZ	1234567890
Scotch Roman 46	ABCDEFGHIJKLMNOPQRSTUVWXYZ	
Spectrum 556	ABCDEFGHIJKLMNOPQRSTUVWXYZ	1234567890
Times Roman 327	ABCDEFGHIJKLMNOPQRSTUVWXYZ	
Walbaum 374	ABCDEFGHIJKLMNOPQRSTUVWXYZ	1234567890

Linotype & Intertype

Inter. Baskerville	ABCDEFGHIJKLMNOPQRSTUVWXYZ	1234567890
Lino Caledonia	ABCDEFGHIJKLMNOPQRSTUVWXYZ	
Lino Granjon	ABCDEFGHIJKLMNOPQRSTUVWXYZ	1234567890

MONOTYPE

Baskerville 169	abcdefghijklmnopqrstuvwxyz	1234567890
Bell 341	abcdefghijklmnopqrstuvwxyz	1234567890
Bembo 270	abcdefghijklmnopqrstuvwxyz	1234567890
Bodoni 135	abcdefghijklmnopqrstuvwxyz	1234567890
Caslon 128	abcdefghijklmnopqrstuvwxyz	
Ehrhardt 453	abcdefghijklmnopqrstuvwxyz	1234567890
Fournier 185	abcdefghijklmnopqrstuvwxyz	
Garamond 156	abcdefghijklmnopqrstuvwxyz	1234567890
Goudy O.S. 291	abcdefghijklmnopqrstuvwxyz	1234567890
Imprint 101	abcdefghijklmnopqrstuvwxyz	1234567890
Modern 7	abcdefghijklmnopqrstuvwxyz	1234567890
Old Style 2	abcdefghijklmnopqrstuvwxyz	1234567890
Perpetua 239	abcdefghijklmnopqrstuvwxyz	1234567890
Plantin 110	abcdefghijklmnopqrstuvwxyz	1234567890
Poliphilus 170	abcdefghijklmnopqrstuvwxyz	
Scotch Roman 46	abcdefghijklmnopqrstuvwxyz	1234567890
Spectrum 556	abcdefghijklmnopqrstuvwxyz	1234567890
Times Roman 327	abcdefghijklmnopqrstuvwxyz	1234567890
Walbaum 374	abcdefghijklmnopqrstuvwxyz	1234567890

LINOTYPE & INTERTYPE

Inter. Baskerville	abcdefghijklmnopqrstuvwxyz	1234567890
Lino Caledonia	abcdefghijklmnopqrstuvwxyz	1234567890
Lino Granjon	abcdefghijklmnopqrstuvwxyz	1234567890

Monotype

Baskerville 169	*ABCDEFGHIJKLMNOPQRSTUVWXYZ*
Bell 341	*ABCDEFGHIJKLMNOPQRSTUVWXYZ*
Bembo 270	*ABCDEFGHIJKLMNOPQRSTUVWXYZ*
Bodoni 135	*ABCDEFGHIJKLMNOPQRSTUVWXYZ*
Caslon 128	*ABCDEFGHIJKLMNOPQRSTUVWXYZ*
Ehrhardt 453	*ABCDEFGHIJKLMNOPQRSTUVWXYZ*
Fournier 185	*ABCDEFGHIJKLMNOPQRSTUVWXYZ*
Garamond 156	*ABCDEFGHIJKLMNOPQRSTUVWXYZ*
Goudy O.S. 291	*ABCDEFGHIJKLMNOPQRSTUVWXYZ*
Imprint 101	*ABCDEFGHIJKLMNOPQRSTUVWXYZ*
Modern 7	*ABCDEFGHIJKLMNOPQRSTUVWXYZ*
Old Style 2	*ABCDEFGHIJKLMNOPQRSTUVWXYZ*
Perpetua 239	*ABCDEFGHIJKLMNOPQRSTUVWXYZ*
Plantin 110	*ABCDEFGHIJKLMNOPQRSTUVWXYZ*
Blado 119	*ABCDEFGHIJKLMNOPQRSTUVWXYZ*
Scotch Roman 46	*ABCDEFGHIJKLMNOPQRSTUVWXYZ*
Spectrum 556	*ABCDEFGHIJKLMNOPQRSTUVWXYZ*
Times 327	*ABCDEFGHIJKLMNOPQRSTUVWXYZ*
Walbaum 374	*ABCDEFGHIJKLMNOPQRSTUVWXYZ*

Linotype & Intertype

Inter. Baskerville	*ABCDEFGHIJKLMNOPQRSTUVWXYZ*
Lino Caledonia	*ABCDEFGHIJKLMNOPQRSTUVWXYZ*
Lino Granjon	*ABCDEFGHIJKLMNOPQRSTUVWXYZ*

MONOTYPE

Baskerville 169	*abcdefghijklmnopqrstuvwxyz*	*1234567890*
Bell 341	*abcdefghijklmnopqrstuvwxyz*	*1234567890*
Bembo 270	*abcdefghijklmnopqrstuvwxyz*	*1234567890*
Bodoni 135	***abcdefghijklmnopqrstuvwxyz***	
Caslon 128	*abcdefghijklmnopqrstuvwxyz*	
Ehrhardt 453	*abcdefghijklmnopqrstuvwxyz*	*1234567890*
Fournier 185	*abcdefghijklmnopqrstuvwxyz*	*1234567890*
Garamond 156	*abcdefghijklmnopqrstuvwxyz*	*1234567890*
Goudy O.S. 291	*abcdefghijklmnopqrstuvwxyz*	*1234567890*
Imprint 101	*abcdefghijklmnopqrstuvwxyz*	*1234567890*
Modern 7	*abcdefghijklmnopqrstuvwxyz*	
Old Style 2	*abcdefghijklmnopqrstuvwxyz*	
Perpetua 239	*abcdefghijklmnopqrstuvwxyz*	*1234567890*
Plantin 110	*abcdefghijklmnopqrstuvwxyz*	*1234567890*
Poliphilus 170	*abcdefghijklmnopqrstuvwxyz*	*1234567890*
Scotch Roman 46	*abcdefghijklmnopqrstuvwxyz*	
Spectrum 556	*abcdefghijklmnopqrstuvwxyz*	*1234567890*
Times 327	*abcdefghijklmnopqrstuvwxyz*	*1234567890*
Walbaum 374	*abcdefghijklmnopqrstuvwxyz*	*1234567890*

LINOTYPE & INTERTYPE

Inter. Baskerville	*abcdefghijklmnopqrstuvwxyz*	*1234567890*
Lino Caledonia	*abcdefghijklmnopqrstuvwxyz*	*1234567890*
Lino Granjon	*abcdefghijklmnopqrstuvwxyz*	*1234567890*

ROMAN CAPITALS

Baskerville Bold 312	**ABCDEFGHIJKLMNOPQRSTUVWXYZ**
Bask. S/bold 313	ABCDEFGHIJKLMNOPQRSTUVWXYZ
Bembo Bold 428	**ABCDEFGHIJKLMNOPQRSTUVWXYZ**
Bodoni Bold 260	**ABCDEFGHIJKLMNOPQRSTUVWXYZ**
Ehrhardt S/bold 573	ABCDEFGHIJKLMNOPQRSTUVWXYZ
Goudy Bold 269	ABCDEFGHIJKLMNOPQRSTUVWX
Grot. Bold Cond. 15	**ABCDEFGHIJKLMNOPQRSTUVWXYZ**
Imprint Bold 310	**ABCDEFGHIJKLMNOPQRSTUVWXYZ**
Old Style Bold 53	ABCDEFGHIJKLMNOPQRSTUVWXYZ
Perpetua Bold 461	ABCDEFGHIJKLMNOPQRSTUVWXYZ
Plantin Bold 194	**ABCDEFGHIJKLMNOPQRSTUVWXYZ**
Times Bold 334	**ABCDEFGHIJKLMNOPQRSTUVWXYZ**

ITALIC CAPITALS

Bodoni Bold Italic 260	***ABCDEFGHIJKLMNOPQRSTUVWXYZ***
Old Style Bold Italic 53	***ABCDEFGHIJKLMNOPQRSTUVWXYZ***
Plantin Bold Italic 194	***ABCDEFGHIJKLMNOPQRSTUVWXYZ***

12 Point Bold · *Monotype Faces*

Roman Lower Case & Figures

Baskerville Bold 312	**abcdefghijklmnopqrstuvwxyz**	**1234567890**
Bask. S/bold 313	**abcdefghijklmnopqrstuvwxyz**	**1234567890**
Bembo Bold 428	**abcdefghijklmnopqrstuvwxyz**	**1234567890**
Bodoni Bold 260	**abcdefghijklmnopqrstuvwxyz**	**1234567890**
Ehrhardt S/bold 573	**abcdefghijklmnopqrstuvwxyz**	**1234567890**
Goudy Bold 269	**abcdefghijklmnopqrstuvwxyz**	**12345678**
Grot. Bold Cond. 15	**abcdefghijklmnopqrstuvwxyz**	**1234567890**
Imprint Bold 310	**abcdefghijklmnopqrstuvwxyz**	**1234567890**
Old Style Bold 53	**abcdefghijklmnopqrstuvwxyz**	**123456789**
Perpetua Bold 461	**abcdefghijklmnopqrstuvwxyz**	**1234567890**
Plantin Bold 194	**abcdefghijklmnopqrstuvwxyz**	**1234567890**
Times Bold 334	**abcdefghijklmnopqrstuvwxyz**	**1234567890**

Italic Lower Case & Figures

Bodoni Bold Italic 260	***abcdefghijklmnopqrstuvwxyz***	***123456789***
Old Style Bold Italic 53	***abcdefghijklmnopqrstuvwxyz***	***123456789***
Plantin Bold Italic 194	***abcdefghijklmnopqrstuvwxyz***	***123456789***

4

SPECIMEN PAGES OF VIP PHOTOSET FACES

VIP BASKERVILLE

Synopsis in 10 point

ABCDEFGHIJKLMNOPQRSTUVWXYZ&ÆŒ

ABCDEFGHIJKLMNOPQRSTUVWXYZ

abcdefghijklmnopqrstuvwxyzæœ

.,:;!?"-()£ 1234567890 1234567890

ABCDEFGHIJKLMNOPQRSTUVWXYZ&ÆŒ

abcdefghijklmnopqrstuvwxyzææ

.,:;!?"-()£ 1234567890 1234567890

Related bold

ABCDEFGHIJKLMNOPQRSTUVWXYZ&ÆŒ

abcdefghijklmnopqrstuvwxyzæœ

.,:;!?"-()£ 1234567890 1234567890

ABCDEFGHIJKLMNOPQRSTUVWXYZ&ÆŒ

abcdefghijklmnopqrstuvwxyzææ

.,:;!?"-() 1234567890

All normal European accents available

father to son, and from uncle to nephew, and, in one instance, from second cousin to second cousin, the sceptre had descended in the family of the Dales; and the acres had remained intact, growing in value and not decreasing in number, though guarded by no entail and protected by no wonderful amount of prudence or wisdom. The estate of Dale of Allington had been coterminous with the parish of Allington for some hundreds of years; and though, as I have said, the race of squires had possessed nothing of superhuman discretion and had perhaps been guided in their walks through life by no very distinct principles, still there had been with them so much of adherence to a sacred law, that no acre of the property had ever been parted from the hands of the existing squire. Some futile attempts had been made to increase the territory, as indeed had been done by Kit Dale, the father of Christopher Dale, who will appear as our squire of Allington when the persons of our drama are introduced. Old Kit Dale, who had married money, had bought outlying farms—a bit of ground here and a bit there—talking, as he did so, much of political influence and of the good old Tory cause. But these farms and bits of ground had gone again before our time. To them had been attached no religion. When old Kit had found himself pressed in that matter of the majority of the Nineteenth Dragoons, in which crack regiment his second son made for himself quite a career, he found it easier to sell than to save—seeing that that which he sold was his own and not the patrimony of the Dales. At his death the remainder of these purchases had gone. Family arrangements required completion, and Christopher Dale required ready money. The outlying farms flew away, as such new purchases had flown before; but the old patrimony of the Dales remained untouched, as it had ever remained.

It had been a religion among them; and seeing that the worship had been carried on without fail, that the vestal fire had never gone down upon the hearth, I should not have said that the Dales had walked their ways without high principle. To this religion they had all adhered, and the new heir had ever entered in upon his domain without other encumbrances than those with which he himself was then already burdened. And yet there had been no entail. The idea of an entail was not in accordance with the peculiarities of the Dale mind. It was necessary to the Dale religion that each squire should have the power of wasting them. I remember to have dined at a house, the whole glory and fortune of which depended on the safety of a glass goblet. We all know the story. If the luck of Edenhall should be shattered, the doom of the family would be sealed. Nevertheless I was bidden to drink out of the fatal glass, as were all guests in that house. It would not have contented the chivalrous mind of the master to protect his doom by lock and key and padded chest. And so it was with the Dales of Allington. To them an entail would have been a lock and key and a padded chest; but the old chivalry of their house denied to them the use of such protection.

I have spoken something slightingly of the acquirements and doings of the family; and indeed their acquirements had been few and their doings little. At Allington, Dale of Allington had always been known as a king. At Guestwick, *the neighbouring market town, he was a great man—to be seen frequently on Saturdays, standing in the market-place, and laying down the law as to barley and oxen among men who knew usually more about barley and oxen than he did. At Hamersham, the assize*

VIP BASKERVILLE

9 point, 1 point leaded

FORMAT	PICAS	LINES	WPL	CPL	WPP	CPP
Royal 8vo	26×43	52	15.0	81	780	4212
Demy 8vo	24×40	48	13.9	75	667	3600
Large Crown 8vo	23×36	43	13.3	72	572	3096
Crown 8vo	21×34	41	12.1	66	496	2706

father to son, and from uncle to nephew, and, in one instance, from second cousin to second cousin, the sceptre had descended in the family of the Dales; and the acres had remained intact, growing in value and not decreasing in number, though guarded by no entail and protected by no wonderful amount of prudence or wisdom. The estate of Dale of Allington had been coterminous with the parish of Allington for some hundreds of years; and though, as I have said, the race of squires had possessed nothing of superhuman discretion and had perhaps been guided in their walks through life by no very distinct principles, still there had been with them so much of adherence to a sacred law, that no acre of the property had ever been parted from the hands of the existing squire. Some futile attempts had been made to increase the territory, as indeed had been done by Kit Dale, the father of Christopher Dale, who will appear as our squire of Allington when the persons of our drama are introduced. Old Kit Dale, who had married money, had bought outlying farms—a bit of ground here and a bit there—talking, as he did so, much of political influence and of the good old Tory cause. But these farms and bits of ground had gone again before our time. To them had been attached no religion. When old Kit had found himself pressed in that matter of the majority of the Nineteenth Dragoons, in which crack regiment his second son made for himself quite a career, he found it easier to sell than to save—seeing that that which he sold was his own and not the patrimony of the Dales. At his death the remainder of these purchases had gone. Family arrangements required completion, and Christopher Dale required ready money. The outlying farms flew away, as such new purchases had flown before; but the old patrimony of the Dales remained untouched, as it had ever remained.

It had been a religion among them; and seeing that the worship had been carried on without fail, that the vestal fire had never gone down upon the hearth, I should not have said that the Dales had walked their ways without high principle. To this religion they had all adhered, and the new heir had ever entered in upon his domain without other encumbrances than those with which he himself was then already burdened. And yet there had been no entail. The idea of an entail was not in accordance with the peculiarities of the Dale mind. It was necessary to the Dale religion that each squire should have the power of wasting them. I remember to have dined at a house, the whole glory and fortune of which depended on the safety of a glass goblet. We all know the story. If the luck of Edenhall should be shattered, the doom of the family would be sealed. Nevertheless I was bidden to drink out of the fatal glass, as were all guests in that house. It would not have contented the chivalrous mind of the master to protect his doom by lock and key and padded chest. And so it was with the Dales of Allington. To them an entail would have been a lock and key and a padded chest; but the old chivalry of their house denied to them the use of such protection.

I have spoken something slightingly of the acquirements and doings of the *family; and indeed their acquirements had been few and their doings little. At Allington, Dale of Allington had always been known as a king. At Guestwick, the neighbouring market town, he was a great man—to be seen frequently on Saturdays, standing in the*

VIP BASKERVILLE

9 point, 1½ point leaded

FORMAT	PICAS	LINES	WPL	CPL	WPP	CPP
Royal 8vo	26×43	49	15.0	81	735	3969
Demy 8vo	24×40	46	13.9	75	639	3450
Large Crown 8vo	23×36	41	13.3	72	545	2952
Crown 8vo	21×34	39	12.1	66	472	2574

father to son, and from uncle to nephew, and, in one instance, from second cousin to second cousin, the sceptre had descended in the family of the Dales; and the acres had remained intact, growing in value and not decreasing in number, though guarded by no entail and protected by no wonderful amount of prudence or wisdom. The estate of Dale of Allington had been coterminous with the parish of Allington for some hundreds of years; and though, as I have said, the race of squires had possessed nothing of superhuman discretion and had perhaps been guided in their walks through life by no very distinct principles, still there had been with them so much of adherence to a sacred law, that no acre of the property had ever been parted from the hands of the existing squire. Some futile attempts had been made to increase the territory, as indeed had been done by Kit Dale, the father of Christopher Dale, who will appear as our squire of Allington when the persons of our drama are introduced. Old Kit Dale, who had married money, had bought outlying farms—a bit of ground here and a bit there—talking, as he did so, much of political influence and of the good old Tory cause. But these farms and bits of ground had gone again before our time. To them had been attached no religion. When old Kit had found himself pressed in that matter of the majority of the Nineteenth Dragoons, in which crack regiment his second son made for himself quite a career, he found it easier to sell than to save—seeing that that which he sold was his own and not the patrimony of the Dales. At his death the remainder of these purchases had gone. Family arrangements required completion, and Christopher Dale required ready money. The outlying farms flew away, as such new purchases had flown before; but the old patrimony of the Dales remained untouched, as it had ever remained.

It had been a religion among them; and seeing that the worship had been carried on without fail, that the vestal fire had never gone down upon the hearth, I should not have said that the Dales had walked their ways without high principle. To this religion they had all adhered, and the new heir had ever entered in upon his domain without other encumbrances than those with which he himself was then already burdened. And yet there had been no entail. The idea of an entail was not in accordance with the peculiarities of the Dale mind. It was necessary to the Dale religion that each squire should have the power of wasting them. I remember to have dined at a house, the whole glory and fortune of which depended on the safety of a glass goblet. We all know the story. If the luck of Edenhall should be shattered, the doom of the family would be sealed. Nevertheless I was bidden to drink out of the fatal glass, as were all guests in that house. It would not have contented the chivalrous mind of the master to protect his doom by lock and key and padded chest. And so it was with the Dales of Allington. To them an entail would have been a lock and key and a padded chest; but the old chivalry of their house *denied to them the use of such protection.*

I have spoken something slightingly of the acquirements and doings of the family; and indeed their acquirements had been few and their doings little. At Allington, Dale of

VIP BASKERVILLE

9 point, 2 point leaded

FORMAT	PICAS	LINES	WPL	CPL	WPP	CPP
Royal 8vo	26×43	47	15.0	81	705	3807
Demy 8vo	24×40	44	13.9	75	612	3300
Large Crown 8vo	23×36	39	13.3	71	519	2808
Crown 8vo	21×34	37	12.1	66	448	2442

father to son, and from uncle to nephew, and, in one instance, from second cousin to second cousin, the sceptre had descended in the family of the Dales; and the acres had remained intact, growing in value and not decreasing in number, though guarded by no entail and protected by no wonderful amount of prudence or wisdom. The estate of Dale of Allington had been coterminous with the parish of Allington for some hundreds of years; and though, as I have said, the race of squires had possessed nothing of superhuman discretion and had perhaps been guided in their walks through life by no very distinct principles, still there had been with them so much of adherence to a sacred law, that no acre of the property had ever been parted from the hands of the existing squire. Some futile attempts had been made to increase the territory, as indeed had been done by Kit Dale, the father of Christopher Dale, who will appear as our squire of Allington when the persons of our drama are introduced. Old Kit Dale, who had married money, had bought outlying farms—a bit of ground here and a bit there—talking, as he did so, much of political influence and of the good old Tory cause. But these farms and bits of ground had gone again before our time. To them had been attached no religion. When old Kit had found himself pressed in that matter of the majority of the Nineteenth Dragoons, in which crack regiment his second son made for himself quite a career, he found it easier to sell than to save—seeing that that which he sold was his own and not the patrimony of the Dales. At his death the remainder of these purchases had gone. Family arrangements required completion, and Christopher Dale required ready money. The outlying farms flew away, as such new purchases had flown before; but the old patrimony of the Dales remained untouched, as it had ever remained.

It had been a religion among them; and seeing that the worship had been carried on without fail, that the vestal fire had never gone down upon the hearth, I should not have said that the Dales had walked their ways without high principle. To this religion they had all adhered, and the new heir had ever entered in upon his domain without other encumbrances than those with which he himself was then already burdened. And yet there had been no entail. The idea of an entail was not in accordance with the peculiarities of the Dale mind. It was necessary to the Dale religion that each squire should have the power of wasting them. I remember to have dined at a house, the whole glory and fortune of which depended on the safety of a glass goblet. We all know the story. If the luck of Edenhall should be shattered, the doom of the family would be sealed. Nevertheless I was *bidden to drink out of the fatal glass, as were all guests in that house. It would not have contented the chivalrous mind of the master to protect his doom by lock and key and padded chest. And so it was with the Dales of Allington. To them an*

VIP BASKERVILLE

10 point, 1 point leaded

FORMAT	PICAS	LINES	WPL	CPL	WPP	CPP
Royal 8vo	26×43	47	13.1	73	616	3431
Demy 8vo	24×40	44	12.1	67	532	2948
Large Crown 8vo	23×36	39	11.5	64	449	2496
Crown 8vo	21×34	37	10.5	59	389	2183

father to son, and from uncle to nephew, and, in one instance, from second cousin to second cousin, the sceptre had descended in the family of the Dales; and the acres had remained intact, growing in value and not decreasing in number, though guarded by no entail and protected by no wonderful amount of prudence or wisdom. The estate of Dale of Allington had been coterminous with the parish of Allington for some hundreds of years; and though, as I have said, the race of squires had possessed nothing of superhuman discretion and had perhaps been guided in their walks through life by no very distinct principles, still there had been with them so much of adherence to a sacred law, that no acre of the property had ever been parted from the hands of the existing squire. Some futile attempts had been made to increase the territory, as indeed had been done by Kit Dale, the father of Christopher Dale, who will appear as our squire of Allington when the persons of our drama are introduced. Old Kit Dale, who had married money, had bought outlying farms—a bit of ground here and a bit there—talking, as he did so, much of political influence and of the good old Tory cause. But these farms and bits of ground had gone again before our time. To them had been attached no religion. When old Kit had found himself pressed in that matter of the majority of the Nineteenth Dragoons, in which crack regiment his second son made for himself quite a career, he found it easier to sell than to save—seeing that that which he sold was his own and not the patrimony of the Dales. At his death the remainder of these purchases had gone. Family arrangements required completion, and Christopher Dale required ready money. The outlying farms flew away, as such new purchases had flown before; but the old patrimony of the Dales remained untouched, as it had ever remained.

It had been a religion among them; and seeing that the worship had been carried on without fail, that the vestal fire had never gone down upon the hearth, I should not have said that the Dales had walked their ways without high principle. To this religion they had all adhered, and the new heir had ever entered in upon his domain without other encumbrances than those with which he himself was then already burdened. And yet there had been no entail. The idea of an entail was not in accordance with the peculiarities of the Dale mind. It was necessary to the Dale religion that each squire should have the power of wasting them. I remember to have dined at a house, the whole glory and fortune of which depended on the safety of a glass *goblet. We all know the story. If the luck of Edenhall should be shattered, the doom of the family would be sealed. Nevertheless I was bidden to drink out of the fatal glass, as were all guests in that house. It would not have contented the*

VIP BASKERVILLE

10 point, 1½ point leaded

FORMAT	PICAS	LINES	WPL	CPL	WPP	CPP
Royal 8vo	26×43	45	13.1	73	590	3285
Demy 8vo	24×40	42	12.1	67	508	2814
Large Crown 8vo	23×36	38	11.5	64	437	2432
Crown 8vo	21×34	35	10.5	59	368	2065

father to son, and from uncle to nephew, and, in one instance, from second cousin to second cousin, the sceptre had descended in the family of the Dales; and the acres had remained intact, growing in value and not decreasing in number, though guarded by no entail and protected by no wonderful amount of prudence or wisdom. The estate of Dale of Allington had been coterminous with the parish of Allington for some hundreds of years; and though, as I have said, the race of squires had possessed nothing of superhuman discretion and had perhaps been guided in their walks through life by no very distinct principles, still there had been with them so much of adherence to a sacred law, that no acre of the property had ever been parted from the hands of the existing squire. Some futile attempts had been made to increase the territory, as indeed had been done by Kit Dale, the father of Christopher Dale, who will appear as our squire of Allington when the persons of our drama are introduced. Old Kit Dale, who had married money, had bought outlying farms—a bit of ground here and a bit there—talking, as he did so, much of political influence and of the good old Tory cause. But these farms and bits of ground had gone again before our time. To them had been attached no religion. When old Kit had found himself pressed in that matter of the majority of the Nineteenth Dragoons, in which crack regiment his second son made for himself quite a career, he found it easier to sell than to save—seeing that that which he sold was his own and not the patrimony of the Dales. At his death the remainder of these purchases had gone. Family arrangements required completion, and Christopher Dale required ready money. The outlying farms flew away, as such new purchases had flown before; but the old patrimony of the Dales remained untouched, as it had ever remained.

It had been a religion among them; and seeing that the worship had been carried on without fail, that the vestal fire had never gone down upon the hearth, I should not have said that the Dales had walked their ways without high principle. To this religion they had all adhered, and the new heir had ever entered in upon his domain without other encumbrances than those with which he himself was then already burdened. And yet there had been no entail. The idea of an entail was not in accordance with the peculiarities of the Dale mind. It was necessary to the Dale religion that each squire should *have the power of wasting them. I remember to have dined at a house, the whole glory and fortune of which depended on the safety of a glass goblet. We all know the story. If the luck of Edenhall should be shattered, the doom of the family*

VIP BASKERVILLE

10 point, 2 point leaded

FORMAT	PICAS	LINES	WPL	CPL	WPP	CPP
Royal 8vo	26×43	43	13.1	73	563	3139
Demy 8vo	24×40	40	12.1	67	484	2680
Large Crown 8vo	23×36	36	11.5	64	414	2304
Crown 8vo	21×34	34	10.5	59	357	2006

father to son, and from uncle to nephew, and, in one instance, from second cousin to second cousin, the sceptre had descended in the family of the Dales; and the acres had remained intact, growing in value and not decreasing in number, though guarded by no entail and protected by no wonderful amount of prudence or wisdom. The estate of Dale of Allington had been coterminous with the parish of Allington for some hundreds of years; and though, as I have said, the race of squires had possessed nothing of superhuman discretion and had perhaps been guided in their walks through life by no very distinct principles, still there had been with them so much of adherence to a sacred law, that no acre of the property had ever been parted from the hands of the existing squire. Some futile attempts had been made to increase the territory, as indeed had been done by Kit Dale, the father of Christopher Dale, who will appear as our squire of Allington when the persons of our drama are introduced. Old Kit Dale, who had married money, had bought outlying farms—a bit of ground here and a bit there—talking, as he did so, much of political influence and of the good old Tory cause. But these farms and bits of ground had gone again before our time. To them had been attached no religion. When old Kit had found himself pressed in that matter of the majority of the Nineteenth Dragoons, in which crack regiment his second son made for himself quite a career, he found it easier to sell than to save—seeing that that which he sold was his own and not the patrimony of the Dales. At his death the remainder of these purchases had gone. Family arrangements required completion, and Christopher Dale required ready money. The outlying farms flew away, as such new purchases had flown before; but the old patrimony of the Dales remained untouched, as it had ever remained.

It had been a religion among them; and seeing that the worship had been carried on without fail, that the vestal fire had never gone down upon the hearth, I should not have said that the Dales had walked their ways without high principle. To this religion they had all adhered, and the new heir had ever entered in upon his domain without other encumbrances than *those with which he himself was then already burdened. And yet there had been no entail. The idea of an entail was not in accordance with the peculiarities of the Dale mind. It was necessary to the Dale religion that*

VIP BASKERVILLE

11 point, 1 point leaded

FORMAT	PICAS	LINES	WPL	CPL	WPP	CPP
Royal 8vo	26×43	43	11.7	65	503	2795
Demy 8vo	24×40	40	10.8	60	432	2400
Large Crown 8vo	23×36	36	10.3	58	371	2088
Crown 8vo	21×34	34	9.4	53	320	1802

father to son, and from uncle to nephew, and, in one instance, from second cousin to second cousin, the sceptre had descended in the family of the Dales; and the acres had remained intact, growing in value and not decreasing in number, though guarded by no entail and protected by no wonderful amount of prudence or wisdom. The estate of Dale of Allington had been coterminous with the parish of Allington for some hundreds of years; and though, as I have said, the race of squires had possessed nothing of superhuman discretion and had perhaps been guided in their walks through life by no very distinct principles, still there had been with them so much of adherence to a sacred law, that no acre of the property had ever been parted from the hands of the existing squire. Some futile attempts had been made to increase the territory, as indeed had been done by Kit Dale, the father of Christopher Dale, who will appear as our squire of Allington when the persons of our drama are introduced. Old Kit Dale, who had married money, had bought outlying farms—a bit of ground here and a bit there—talking, as he did so, much of political influence and of the good old Tory cause. But these farms and bits of ground had gone again before our time. To them had been attached no religion. When old Kit had found himself pressed in that matter of the majority of the Nineteenth Dragoons, in which crack regiment his second son made for himself quite a career, he found it easier to sell than to save—seeing that that which he sold was his own and not the patrimony of the Dales. At his death the remainder of these purchases had gone. Family arrangements required completion, and Christopher Dale required ready money. The outlying farms flew away, as such new purchases had flown before; but the old patrimony of the Dales remained untouched, as it had ever remained.

It had been a religion among them; and seeing that the worship had been carried on without fail, that the vestal fire had never gone down upon the hearth, I should not have said that the Dales had walked their ways without high principle. *To this religion they had all adhered, and the new heir had ever entered in upon his domain without other encumbrances than those with which he himself was then already burdened. And yet there had been no entail. The*

VIP BASKERVILLE

11 point, 1½ point leaded

FORMAT	PICAS	LINES	WPL	CPL	WPP	CPP
Royal 8vo	26×43	41	11.7	65	480	2665
Demy 8vo	24×40	38	10.8	60	410	2280
Large Crown 8vo	23×36	35	10.3	58	361	2030
Crown 8vo	21×34	33	9.4	53	310	1749

father to son, and from uncle to nephew, and, in one instance, from second cousin to second cousin, the sceptre had descended in the family of the Dales; and the acres had remained intact, growing in value and not decreasing in number, though guarded by no entail and protected by no wonderful amount of prudence or wisdom. The estate of Dale of Allington had been coterminous with the parish of Allington for some hundreds of years; and though, as I have said, the race of squires had possessed nothing of superhuman discretion and had perhaps been guided in their walks through life by no very distinct principles, still there had been with them so much of adherence to a sacred law, that no acre of the property had ever been parted from the hands of the existing squire. Some futile attempts had been made to increase the territory, as indeed had been done by Kit Dale, the father of Christopher Dale, who will appear as our squire of Allington when the persons of our drama are introduced. Old Kit Dale, who had married money, had bought outlying farms—a bit of ground here and a bit there—talking, as he did so, much of political influence and of the good old Tory cause. But these farms and bits of ground had gone again before our time. To them had been attached no religion. When old Kit had found himself pressed in that matter of the majority of the Nineteenth Dragoons, in which crack regiment his second son made for himself quite a career, he found it easier to sell than to save—seeing that that which he sold was his own and not the patrimony of the Dales. At his death the remainder of these purchases had gone. Family arrangements required completion, and Christopher Dale required ready money. The outlying farms flew away, as such new purchases had flown before; but the old patrimony of the Dales remained untouched, as it had ever remained.

It had been a religion among them; and seeing that the worship had been carried on without fail, that the vestal fire had never gone down upon the hearth, I should not have said *that the Dales had walked their ways without high principle. To this religion they had all adhered, and the new heir had ever entered in upon his domain without other encumbrances than those with which he himself was*

VIP BASKERVILLE

11 point, 2 point leaded

FORMAT	PICAS	LINES	WPL	CPL	WPP	CPP
Royal 8vo	26×43	40	11.7	65	468	2600
Demy 8vo	24×40	37	10.8	60	400	2220
Large Crown 8vo	23×36	33	10.3	58	340	1914
Crown 8vo	21×34	31	9.4	53	291	1643

VIP BEMBO

Synopsis in 10 point

ABCDEFGHIJKLMNOPQRSTUVWXYZ&ÆŒ

ABCDEFGHIJKLMNOPQRSTUVWXYZ

abcdefghijklmnopqrstuvwxyzæœ

.,:;!?“”-()£ 1234567890 1234567890

ABCDEFGHIJKLMNOPQRSTUVWXYZ&ÆŒ

abcdefghijklmnopqrstuvwxyzæœ

.,:;!?“”-()£ 1234567890

Related bold

ABCDEFGHIJKLMNOPQRSTUVWXYZ&ÆŒ

abcdefghijklmnopqrstuvwxyzæœ

.,:;!?“”-()£ 1234567890

ABCDEFGHIJKLMNOPQRSTUVWXYZ&ÆŒ

abcdefghijklmnopqrstuvwxyzæœ

.,:;!?“”-()£ 1234567890

All normal European accents available

father to son, and from uncle to nephew, and, in one instance, from second cousin to second cousin, the sceptre had descended in the family of the Dales; and the acres had remained intact, growing in value and not decreasing in number, though guarded by no entail and protected by no wonderful amount of prudence or wisdom. The estate of Dale of Allington had been coterminous with the parish of Allington for some hundreds of years; and though, as I have said, the race of squires had possessed nothing of superhuman discretion and had perhaps been guided in their walks through life by no very distinct principles, still there had been with them so much of adherence to a sacred law, that no acre of the property had ever been parted from the hands of the existing squire. Some futile attempts had been made to increase the territory, as indeed had been done by Kit Dale, the father of Christopher Dale, who will appear as our squire of Allington when the persons of our drama are introduced. Old Kit Dale, who had married money, had bought outlying farms—a bit of ground here and a bit there—talking, as he did so, much of political influence and of the good old Tory cause. But these farms and bits of ground had gone again before our time. To them had been attached no religion. When old Kit had found himself pressed in that matter of the majority of the Nineteenth Dragoons, in which crack regiment his second son made for himself quite a career, he found it easier to sell than to save—seeing that that which he sold was his own and not the patrimony of the Dales. At his death the remainder of these purchases had gone. Family arrangements required completion, and Christopher Dale required ready money. The outlying farms flew away, as such new purchases had flown before; but the old patrimony of the Dales remained untouched, as it had ever remained.

It had been a religion among them; and seeing that the worship had been carried on without fail, that the vestal fire had never gone down upon the hearth, I should not have said that the Dales had walked their ways without high principle. To this religion they had all adhered, and the new heir had ever entered in upon his domain without other encumbrances than those with which he himself was then already burdened. And yet there had been no entail. The idea of an entail was not in accordance with the peculiarities of the Dale mind. It was necessary to the Dale religion that each squire should have the power of wasting them. I remember to have dined at a house, the whole glory and fortune of which depended on the safety of a glass goblet. We all know the story. If the luck of Edenhall should be shattered, the doom of the family would be sealed. Nevertheless I was bidden to drink out of the fatal glass, as were all guests in that house. It would not have contented the chivalrous mind of the master to protect his doom by lock and key and padded chest. And so it was with the Dales of Allington. To them an entail would have been a lock and key and a padded chest; but the old chivalry of their house denied to them the use of such protection.

I have spoken something slightingly of the acquirements and doings of the family; and indeed their acquirements had been few and their doings little. *At Allington, Dale of Allington had always been known as a king. At Guestwick, the neighbouring market town, he was a great man—to be seen frequently on Saturdays, standing in the market-place, and laying down the law as to barley and*

VIP BEMBO

9 point, 1 point leaded

FORMAT	PICAS	LINES	WPL	CPL	WPP	CPP
Royal 8vo	26×43	52	14.7	79	764	4108
Demy 8vo	24×40	48	13.6	73	653	3504
Large Crown 8vo	23×36	43	13.0	70	559	3010
Crown 8vo	21×34	41	11.9	64	487	2624

father to son, and from uncle to nephew, and, in one instance, from second cousin to second cousin, the sceptre had descended in the family of the Dales; and the acres had remained intact, growing in value and not decreasing in number, though guarded by no entail and protected by no wonderful amount of prudence or wisdom. The estate of Dale of Allington had been coterminous with the parish of Allington for some hundreds of years; and though, as I have said, the race of squires had possessed nothing of superhuman discretion and had perhaps been guided in their walks through life by no very distinct principles, still there had been with them so much of adherence to a sacred law, that no acre of the property had ever been parted from the hands of the existing squire. Some futile attempts had been made to increase the territory, as indeed had been done by Kit Dale, the father of Christopher Dale, who will appear as our squire of Allington when the persons of our drama are introduced. Old Kit Dale, who had married money, had bought outlying farms—a bit of ground here and a bit there—talking, as he did so, much of political influence and of the good old Tory cause. But these farms and bits of ground had gone again before our time. To them had been attached no religion. When old Kit had found himself pressed in that matter of the majority of the Nineteenth Dragoons, in which crack regiment his second son made for himself quite a career, he found it easier to sell than to save—seeing that that which he sold was his own and not the patrimony of the Dales. At his death the remainder of these purchases had gone. Family arrangements required completion, and Christopher Dale required ready money. The outlying farms flew away, as such new purchases had flown before; but the old patrimony of the Dales remained untouched, as it had ever remained.

It had been a religion among them; and seeing that the worship had been carried on without fail, that the vestal fire had never gone down upon the hearth, I should not have said that the Dales had walked their ways without high principle. To this religion they had all adhered, and the new heir had ever entered in upon his domain without other encumbrances than those with which he himself was then already burdened. And yet there had been no entail. The idea of an entail was not in accordance with the peculiarities of the Dale mind. It was necessary to the Dale religion that each squire should have the power of wasting them. I remember to have dined at a house, the whole glory and fortune of which depended on the safety of a glass goblet. We all know the story. If the luck of Edenhall should be shattered, the doom of the family would be sealed. Nevertheless I was bidden to drink out of the fatal glass, as were all guests in that house. It would not have contented the chivalrous mind of the master to protect his doom by lock and key and padded chest. And so it was with the Dales of Allington. To them an entail would have been a lock and key and a padded chest; but the old chivalry of their house denied to them the use of such protection.

I have spoken something slightingly of the acquirements and doings of the family; and indeed their acquirements had been few and their doings little. At Allington, Dale of Allington had always been known as a king. At Guestwick, the neighbour-

VIP BEMBO

9 point, $1\frac{1}{2}$ point leaded

FORMAT	PICAS	LINES	WPL	CPL	WPP	CPP
Royal 8vo	26×43	49	14.7	79	720	3871
Demy 8vo	24×40	46	13.6	73	625	3358
Large Crown 8vo	23×36	41	13.0	70	533	2870
Crown 8vo	21×34	39	11.9	64	464	2496

father to son, and from uncle to nephew, and, in one instance, from second cousin to second cousin, the sceptre had descended in the family of the Dales; and the acres had remained intact, growing in value and not decreasing in number, though guarded by no entail and protected by no wonderful amount of prudence or wisdom. The estate of Dale of Allington had been coterminous with the parish of Allington for some hundreds of years; and though, as I have said, the race of squires had possessed nothing of super-human discretion and had perhaps been guided in their walks through life by no very distinct principles, still there had been with them so much of adherence to a sacred law, that no acre of the property had ever been parted from the hands of the existing squire. Some futile attempts had been made to increase the territory, as indeed had been done by Kit Dale, the father of Christopher Dale, who will appear as our squire of Allington when the persons of our drama are introduced. Old Kit Dale, who had married money, had bought outlying farms—a bit of ground here and a bit there—talking, as he did so, much of political influence and of the good old Tory cause. But these farms and bits of ground had gone again before our time. To them had been attached no religion. When old Kit had found himself pressed in that matter of the majority of the Nineteenth Dragoons, in which crack regiment his second son made for himself quite a career, he found it easier to sell than to save—seeing that that which he sold was his own and not the patrimony of the Dales. At his death the remainder of these purchases had gone. Family arrangements required completion, and Christopher Dale required ready money. The outlying farms flew away, as such new purchases had flown before; but the old patrimony of the Dales remained untouched, as it had ever remained.

It had been a religion among them; and seeing that the worship had been carried on without fail, that the vestal fire had never gone down upon the hearth, I should not have said that the Dales had walked their ways without high principle. To this religion they had all adhered, and the new heir had ever entered in upon his domain without other encumbrances than those with which he himself was then already burdened. And yet there had been no entail. The idea of an entail was not in accordance with the peculiarities of the Dale mind. It was necessary to the Dale religion that each squire should have the power of wasting them. I remember to have dined at a house, the whole glory and fortune of which depended on the safety of a glass goblet. We all know the story. If the luck of Edenhall should be shattered, the doom of the family would be sealed. Nevertheless I was bidden to drink out of the fatal glass, as were all guests in that house. It would not have contented the chivalrous mind of the master to protect his doom by lock and key and padded chest. And so it was with the Dales of Allington. To them an entail *would have been a lock and key and a padded chest; but the old chivalry of their house denied to them the use of such protection.*

I have spoken something slightingly of the acquirements and doings of the family;

VIP BEMBO

9 point, 2 point leaded

FORMAT	PICAS	LINES	WPL	CPL	WPP	CPP
Royal 8vo	26×43	47	14.7	79	691	3713
Demy 8vo	24×40	44	13.6	73	598	3212
Large Crown 8vo	23×36	39	13.0	70	507	2730
Crown 8vo	21×34	37	11.9	64	440	2368

father to son, and from uncle to nephew, and, in one instance, from second cousin to second cousin, the sceptre had descended in the family of the Dales; and the acres had remained intact, growing in value and not decreasing in number, though guarded by no entail and protected by no wonderful amount of prudence or wisdom. The estate of Dale of Allington had been coterminous with the parish of Allington for some hundreds of years; and though, as I have said, the race of squires had possessed nothing of superhuman discretion and had perhaps been guided in their walks through life by no very distinct principles, still there had been with them so much of adherence to a sacred law, that no acre of the property had ever been parted from the hands of the existing squire. Some futile attempts had been made to increase the territory, as indeed had been done by Kit Dale, the father of Christopher Dale, who will appear as our squire of Allington when the persons of our drama are introduced. Old Kit Dale, who had married money, had bought outlying farms—a bit of ground here and a bit there—talking, as he did so, much of political influence and of the good old Tory cause. But these farms and bits of ground had gone again before our time. To them had been attached no religion. When old Kit had found himself pressed in that matter of the majority of the Nineteenth Dragoons, in which crack regiment his second son made for himself quite a career, he found it easier to sell than to save—seeing that that which he sold was his own and not the patrimony of the Dales. At his death the remainder of these purchases had gone. Family arrangements required completion, and Christopher Dale required ready money. The outlying farms flew away, as such new purchases had flown before; but the old patrimony of the Dales remained untouched, as it had ever remained.

It had been a religion among them; and seeing that the worship had been carried on without fail, that the vestal fire had never gone down upon the hearth, I should not have said that the Dales had walked their ways without high principle. To this religion they had all adhered, and the new heir had ever entered in upon his domain without other encumbrances than those with which he himself was then already burdened. And yet there had been no entail. The idea of an entail was not in accordance with the peculiarities of the Dale mind. It was necessary to the Dale religion that each squire should have the power of wasting them. I remember to have dined at a house, the whole glory and fortune of which depended on the safety of a glass goblet. We all know the story. If the luck of Edenhall should be shattered, the doom of the family would be sealed. *Nevertheless I was bidden to drink out of the fatal glass, as were all guests in that house. It would not have contented the chivalrous mind of the master to protect his doom by lock and key and padded chest. And so it was with the*

VIP BEMBO

10 point, 1 point leaded

FORMAT	PICAS	LINES	WPL	CPL	WPP	CPP
Royal 8vo	26×43	47	14.4	72	677	3384
Demy 8vo	24×40	44	13.3	66	585	2904
Large Crown 8vo	23×36	39	12.7	63	495	2457
Crown 8vo	21×34	37	11.6	58	429	2146

father to son, and from uncle to nephew, and, in one instance, from second cousin to second cousin, the sceptre had descended in the family of the Dales; and the acres had remained intact, growing in value and not decreasing in number, though guarded by no entail and protected by no wonderful amount of prudence or wisdom. The estate of Dale of Allington had been coterminous with the parish of Allington for some hundreds of years; and though, as I have said, the race of squires had possessed nothing of superhuman discretion and had perhaps been guided in their walks through life by no very distinct principles, still there had been with them so much of adherence to a sacred law, that no acre of the property had ever been parted from the hands of the existing squire. Some futile attempts had been made to increase the territory, as indeed had been done by Kit Dale, the father of Christopher Dale, who will appear as our squire of Allington when the persons of our drama are introduced. Old Kit Dale, who had married money, had bought outlying farms—a bit of ground here and a bit there—talking, as he did so, much of political influence and of the good old Tory cause. But these farms and bits of ground had gone again before our time. To them had been attached no religion. When old Kit had found himself pressed in that matter of the majority of the Nineteenth Dragoons, in which crack regiment his second son made for himself quite a career, he found it easier to sell than to save—seeing that that which he sold was his own and not the patrimony of the Dales. At his death the remainder of these purchases had gone. Family arrangements required completion, and Christopher Dale required ready money. The outlying farms flew away, as such new purchases had flown before; but the old patrimony of the Dales remained untouched, as it had ever remained.

It had been a religion among them; and seeing that the worship had been carried on without fail, that the vestal fire had never gone down upon the hearth, I should not have said that the Dales had walked their ways without high principle. To this religion they had all adhered, and the new heir had ever entered in upon his domain without other encumbrances than those with which he himself was then already burdened. And yet there had been no entail. The idea of an entail was not in accordance with the peculiarities of the Dale mind. It was necessary to the Dale religion that each squire should have the power of wasting them. I remember to have dined at a house, the whole glory and fortune of which depended on the safety *of a glass goblet. We all know the story. If the luck of Edenhall should be shattered, the doom of the family would be sealed. Nevertheless I was bidden to drink out of the fatal glass, as were all guests in that house. It would not*

VIP BEMBO

10 point, 1½ point leaded

FORMAT	PICAS	LINES	WPL	CPL	WPP	CPP
Royal 8vo	26×43	45	14.4	72	648	3240
Demy 8vo	24×40	42	13.3	66	559	2772
Large Crown 8vo	23×36	38	12.7	63	483	2394
Crown 8vo	21×34	35	11.6	58	406	2030

father to son, and from uncle to nephew, and, in one instance, from second cousin to second cousin, the sceptre had descended in the family of the Dales; and the acres had remained intact, growing in value and not decreasing in number, though guarded by no entail and protected by no wonderful amount of prudence or wisdom. The estate of Dale of Allington had been coterminous with the parish of Allington for some hundreds of years; and though, as I have said, the race of squires had possessed nothing of superhuman discretion and had perhaps been guided in their walks through life by no very distinct principles, still there had been with them so much of adherence to a sacred law, that no acre of the property had ever been parted from the hands of the existing squire. Some futile attempts had been made to increase the territory, as indeed had been done by Kit Dale, the father of Christopher Dale, who will appear as our squire of Allington when the persons of our drama are introduced. Old Kit Dale, who had married money, had bought outlying farms—a bit of ground here and a bit there—talking, as he did so, much of political influence and of the good old Tory cause. But these farms and bits of ground had gone again before our time. To them had been attached no religion. When old Kit had found himself pressed in that matter of the majority of the Nineteenth Dragoons, in which crack regiment his second son made for himself quite a career, he found it easier to sell than to save—seeing that that which he sold was his own and not the patrimony of the Dales. At his death the remainder of these purchases had gone. Family arrangements required completion, and Christopher Dale required ready money. The outlying farms flew away, as such new purchases had flown before; but the old patrimony of the Dales remained untouched, as it had ever remained.

It had been a religion among them; and seeing that the worship had been carried on without fail, that the vestal fire had never gone down upon the hearth, I should not have said that the Dales had walked their ways without high principle. To this religion they had all adhered, and the new heir had ever entered in upon his domain without other encumbrances than those with which he himself was then already burdened. And yet there had been no entail. The idea of an entail was not in accordance with the peculiarities of the Dale mind. It was necessary to the Dale religion that each squire should *have the power of wasting them. I remember to have dined at a house, the whole glory and fortune of which depended on the safety of a glass goblet. We all know the story. If the luck of Edenhall should be shattered, the doom of*

VIP BEMBO

10 point, 2 point leaded

FORMAT	PICAS	LINES	WPL	CPL	WPP	CPP
Royal 8vo	26×43	43	14.4	72	619	3096
Demy 8vo	24×40	40	13.3	66	532	2640
Large Crown 8vo	23×36	36	12.7	63	457	2268
Crown 8vo	21×34	34	11.6	58	394	1972

father to son, and from uncle to nephew, and, in one instance, from second cousin to second cousin, the sceptre had descended in the family of the Dales; and the acres had remained intact, growing in value and not decreasing in number, though guarded by no entail and protected by no wonderful amount of prudence or wisdom. The estate of Dale of Allington had been coterminous with the parish of Allington for some hundreds of years; and though, as I have said, the race of squires had possessed nothing of superhuman discretion and had perhaps been guided in their walks through life by no very distinct principles, still there had been with them so much of adherence to a sacred law, that no acre of the property had ever been parted from the hands of the existing squire. Some futile attempts had been made to increase the territory, as indeed had been done by Kit Dale, the father of Christopher Dale, who will appear as our squire of Allington when the persons of our drama are introduced. Old Kit Dale, who had married money, had bought outlying farms—a bit of ground here and a bit there—talking, as he did so, much of political influence and of the good old Tory cause. But these farms and bits of ground had gone again before our time. To them had been attached no religion. When old Kit had found himself pressed in that matter of the majority of the Nineteenth Dragoons, in which crack regiment his second son made for himself quite a career, he found it easier to sell than to save—seeing that that which he sold was his own and not the patrimony of the Dales. At his death the remainder of these purchases had gone. Family arrangements required completion, and Christopher Dale required ready money. The outlying farms flew away, as such new purchases had flown before; but the old patrimony of the Dales remained untouched, as it had ever remained.

It had been a religion among them; and seeing that the worship had been carried on without fail, that the vestal fire had never gone down upon the hearth, I should not have said that the Dales had walked their ways without high principle. To this religion they had all adhered, and the new heir had ever *entered in upon his domain without other encumbrances than those with which he himself was then already burdened. And yet there had been no entail. The idea of an entail was not in accordance with the*

VIP BEMBO

11 point, 1 point leaded

FORMAT	PICAS	LINES	WPL	CPL	WPP	CPP
Royal 8vo	26×43	43	11.7	64	503	2752
Demy 8vo	24×40	40	10.8	59	432	2360
Large Crown 8vo	23×36	36	10.3	57	371	2052
Crown 8vo	21×34	34	9.4	52	320	1768

father to son, and from uncle to nephew, and, in one instance, from second cousin to second cousin, the sceptre had descended in the family of the Dales; and the acres had remained intact, growing in value and not decreasing in number, though guarded by no entail and protected by no wonderful amount of prudence or wisdom. The estate of Dale of Allington had been coterminous with the parish of Allington for some hundreds of years; and though, as I have said, the race of squires had possessed nothing of superhuman discretion and had perhaps been guided in their walks through life by no very distinct principles, still there had been with them so much of adherence to a sacred law, that no acre of the property had ever been parted from the hands of the existing squire. Some futile attempts had been made to increase the territory, as indeed had been done by Kit Dale, the father of Christopher Dale, who will appear as our squire of Allington when the persons of our drama are introduced. Old Kit Dale, who had married money, had bought outlying farms—a bit of ground here and a bit there—talking, as he did so, much of political influence and of the good old Tory cause. But these farms and bits of ground had gone again before our time. To them had been attached no religion. When old Kit had found himself pressed in that matter of the majority of the Nineteenth Dragoons, in which crack regiment his second son made for himself quite a career, he found it easier to sell than to save—seeing that that which he sold was his own and not the patrimony of the Dales. At his death the remainder of these purchases had gone. Family arrangements required completion, and Christopher Dale required ready money. The outlying farms flew away, as such new purchases had flown before; but the old patrimony of the Dales remained untouched, as it had ever remained.

It had been a religion among them; and seeing that the worship had been carried on without fail, that the vestal fire had never gone down upon the hearth, I should not have said *that the Dales had walked their ways without high principle. To this religion they had all adhered, and the new heir had ever entered in upon his domain without other encumbrances than those with which*

VIP BEMBO

11 point, 1½ point leaded

FORMAT	PICAS	LINES	WPL	CPL	WPP	CPP
Royal 8vo	26×43	41	11.7	64	480	2624
Demy 8vo	24×40	38	10.8	59	410	2242
Large Crown 8vo	23×36	35	10.3	57	361	1995
Crown 8vo	21×34	33	9.4	52	304	1716

father to son, and from uncle to nephew, and, in one instance, from second cousin to second cousin, the sceptre had descended in the family of the Dales; and the acres had remained intact, growing in value and not decreasing in number, though guarded by no entail and protected by no wonderful amount of prudence or wisdom. The estate of Dale of Allington had been coterminous with the parish of Allington for some hundreds of years; and though, as I have said, the race of squires had possessed nothing of superhuman discretion and had perhaps been guided in their walks through life by no very distinct principles, still there had been with them so much of adherence to a sacred law, that no acre of the property had ever been parted from the hands of the existing squire. Some futile attempts had been made to increase the territory, as indeed had been done by Kit Dale, the father of Christopher Dale, who will appear as our squire of Allington when the persons of our drama are introduced. Old Kit Dale, who had married money, had bought outlying farms—a bit of ground here and a bit there—talking, as he did so, much of political influence and of the good old Tory cause. But these farms and bits of ground had gone again before our time. To them had been attached no religion. When old Kit had found himself pressed in that matter of the majority of the Nineteenth Dragoons, in which crack regiment his second son made for himself quite a career, he found it easier to sell than to save—seeing that that which he sold was his own and not the patrimony of the Dales. At his death the remainder of these purchases had gone. Family arrangements required completion, and Christopher Dale required ready money. The outlying farms flew away, as such new purchases had flown before; but the old patrimony of the Dales remained untouched, as it had ever remained.

It had been a religion among them; and seeing that the worship had been carried on without fail, that the vestal fire *had never gone down upon the hearth, I should not have said that the Dales had walked their ways without high principle. To this religion they had all adhered, and the new heir had ever entered in upon his*

VIP BEMBO

11 point, 2 point leaded

FORMAT	PICAS	LINES	WPL	CPL	WPP	CPP
Royal 8vo	26×43	40	11.7	64	468	2560
Demy 8vo	24×40	37	10.8	59	400	2183
Large Crown 8vo	23×36	33	10.3	57	340	1881
Crown 8vo	21×34	31	9.4	52	291	1612

VIP CENTURY SCHOOLBOOK

Synopsis in 10 *point*

ABCDEFGHIJKLMNOPQRSTUVWXYZ&ÆŒ
abcdefghijklmnopqrstuvwxyzæœ
.,:;!?"-()£ 1234567890
ABCDEFGHIJKLMNOPQRSTUVWXYZ&ÆŒ
abcdefghijklmnopqrstuvwxyzæœ
.,:;!?"-()£ 1234567890

Related bold

ABCDEFGHIJKLMNOPQRSTUVWXYZ&ÆŒ
abcdefghijklmnopqrstuvwxyzæœ
.,:;!?"-()£ 1234567890

All normal European accents available

father to son, and from uncle to nephew, and, in one instance, from second cousin to second cousin, the sceptre had descended in the family of the Dales; and the acres had remained intact, growing in value and not decreasing in number, though guarded by no entail and protected by no wonderful amount of prudence or wisdom. The estate of Dale of Allington had been coterminous with the parish of Allington for some hundreds of years; and though, as I have said, the race of squires had possessed nothing of superhuman discretion and had perhaps been guided in their walks through life by no very distinct principles, still there had been with them so much of adherence to a sacred law, that no acre of the property had ever been parted from the hands of the existing squire. Some futile attempts had been made to increase the territory, as indeed had been done by Kit Dale, the father of Christopher Dale, who will appear as our squire of Allington when the persons of our drama are introduced. Old Kit Dale, who had married money, had bought outlying farms—a bit of ground here and a bit there—talking, as he did so, much of political influence and of the good old Tory cause. But these farms and bits of ground had gone again before our time. To them had been attached no religion. When old Kit had found himself pressed in that matter of the majority of the Nineteenth Dragoons, in which crack regiment his second son made for himself quite a career, he found it easier to sell than to save—seeing that that which he sold was his own and not the patrimony of the Dales. At his death the remainder of these purchases had gone. Family arrangements required completion, and Christopher Dale required ready money. The outlying farms flew away, as such new purchases had flown before; but the old patrimony of the Dales remained untouched, as it had ever remained.

It had been a religion among them; and seeing that the worship had been carried on without fail, that the vestal fire had never gone down upon the hearth, I should not have said that the Dales had walked their ways without high principle. To this religion they had all adhered, and the new heir had ever entered in upon his domain without other encumbrances than those with which he himself was then already burdened. And yet there had been no entail. The idea of an entail was not in accordance with the peculiarities of the Dale mind. It was necessary to the Dale religion that each squire should have the power of wasting them. I remember to have dined at a house, the whole glory and fortune of which depended on the safety of a glass goblet. We all know the story. If the luck of Edenhall should be shattered, the doom of the family would be sealed. Nevertheless I was bidden to drink out of the fatal glass, as were all guests in that house. It would not have contented the chivalrous mind of the master to protect his doom by lock and key and padded chest. And so it was with the Dales of Allington. To them an entail would have been a lock and key and a padded chest; but the old chivalry of their house denied to them the use of such protection.

I have spoken something slightingly of the acquirements and doings of the family; and indeed their acquirements had been few and their doings little. At Allington, Dale of Allington had always been known as a king.

VIP CENTURY SCHOOLBOOK

9 point, 1 point leaded

FORMAT	PICAS	LINES	WPL	CPL	WPP	CPP
Royal 8vo	26×43	52	13.5	75	702	3900
Demy 8vo	24×40	48	12.5	69	600	3312
Large Crown 8vo	23×36	43	11.9	66	512	2838
Crown 8vo	21×34	41	10.9	60	447	2460

father to son, and from uncle to nephew, and, in one instance, from second cousin to second cousin, the sceptre had descended in the family of the Dales; and the acres had remained intact, growing in value and not decreasing in number, though guarded by no entail and protected by no wonderful amount of prudence or wisdom. The estate of Dale of Allington had been coterminous with the parish of Allington for some hundreds of years; and though, as I have said, the race of squires had possessed nothing of superhuman discretion and had perhaps been guided in their walks through life by no very distinct principles, still there had been with them so much of adherence to a sacred law, that no acre of the property had ever been parted from the hands of the existing squire. Some futile attempts had been made to increase the territory, as indeed had been done by Kit Dale, the father of Christopher Dale, who will appear as our squire of Allington when the persons of our drama are introduced. Old Kit Dale, who had married money, had bought outlying farms—a bit of ground here and a bit there—talking, as he did so, much of political influence and of the good old Tory cause. But these farms and bits of ground had gone again before our time. To them had been attached no religion. When old Kit had found himself pressed in that matter of the majority of the Nineteenth Dragoons, in which crack regiment his second son made for himself quite a career, he found it easier to sell than to save—seeing that that which he sold was his own and not the patrimony of the Dales. At his death the remainder of these purchases had gone. Family arrangements required completion, and Christopher Dale required ready money. The outlying farms flew away, as such new purchases had flown before; but the old patrimony of the Dales remained untouched, as it had ever remained.

It had been a religion among them; and seeing that the worship had been carried on without fail, that the vestal fire had never gone down upon the hearth, I should not have said that the Dales had walked their ways without high principle. To this religion they had all adhered, and the new heir had ever entered in upon his domain without other encumbrances than those with which he himself was then already burdened. And yet there had been no entail. The idea of an entail was not in accordance with the peculiarities of the Dale mind. It was necessary to the Dale religion that each squire should have the power of wasting them. I remember to have dined at a house, the whole glory and fortune of which depended on the safety of a glass goblet. We all know the story. If the luck of Edenhall should be shattered, the doom of the family would be sealed. Nevertheless I was bidden to drink out of the fatal glass, as were all guests in that house. It would not have contented the chivalrous mind of the master to protect his doom by lock and key and padded chest. And so it was with the Dales of Allington. To *them an entail would have been a lock and key and a padded chest; but the old chivalry of their house denied to them the use of such protection.*

I have spoken something slightingly of the acquirements and doings of

VIP CENTURY SCHOOLBOOK

9 point, $1\frac{1}{2}$ point leaded

FORMAT	PICAS	LINES	WPL	CPL	WPP	CPP
Royal 8vo	26×43	49	13.5	75	661	3675
Demy 8vo	24×40	46	12.5	69	575	3174
Large Crown 8vo	23×36	41	11.9	66	488	2706
Crown 8vo	21×34	39	10.9	60	425	2340

father to son, and from uncle to nephew, and, in one instance, from second cousin to second cousin, the sceptre had descended in the family of the Dales; and the acres had remained intact, growing in value and not decreasing in number, though guarded by no entail and protected by no wonderful amount of prudence or wisdom. The estate of Dale of Allington had been coterminous with the parish of Allington for some hundreds of years; and though, as I have said, the race of squires had possessed nothing of superhuman discretion and had perhaps been guided in their walks through life by no very distinct principles, still there had been with them so much of adherence to a sacred law, that no acre of the property had ever been parted from the hands of the existing squire. Some futile attempts had been made to increase the territory, as indeed had been done by Kit Dale, the father of Christopher Dale, who will appear as our squire of Allington when the persons of our drama are introduced. Old Kit Dale, who had married money, had bought outlying farms—a bit of ground here and a bit there—talking, as he did so, much of political influence and of the good old Tory cause. But these farms and bits of ground had gone again before our time. To them had been attached no religion. When old Kit had found himself pressed in that matter of the majority of the Nineteenth Dragoons, in which crack regiment his second son made for himself quite a career, he found it easier to sell than to save—seeing that that which he sold was his own and not the patrimony of the Dales. At his death the remainder of these purchases had gone. Family arrangements required completion, and Christopher Dale required ready money. The outlying farms flew away, as such new purchases had flown before; but the old patrimony of the Dales remained untouched, as it had ever remained.

It had been a religion among them; and seeing that the worship had been carried on without fail, that the vestal fire had never gone down upon the hearth, I should not have said that the Dales had walked their ways without high principle. To this religion they had all adhered, and the new heir had ever entered in upon his domain without other encumbrances than those with which he himself was then already burdened. And yet there had been no entail. The idea of an entail was not in accordance with the peculiarities of the Dale mind. It was necessary to the Dale religion that each squire should have the power of wasting them. I remember to have dined at a house, the whole glory and fortune of which depended on the safety of a glass goblet. We all know the story. If the luck of Edenhall should be shattered, the doom of the family would be sealed. Nevertheless I was bidden to drink out of the fatal glass, as were all guests in that house. It would not have *contented the chivalrous mind of the master to protect his doom by lock and key and padded chest. And so it was with the Dales of Allington. To them an entail would have been a lock and key and a padded chest; but*

VIP CENTURY SCHOOLBOOK

9 point, 2 point leaded

FORMAT	PICAS	LINES	WPL	CPL	WPP	CPP
Royal 8vo	26×43	47	13.5	75	635	3525
Demy 8vo	24×40	44	12.5	69	550	3036
Large Crown 8vo	23×36	39	11.9	66	464	2574
Crown 8vo	21×34	37	10.9	60	403	2220

father to son, and from uncle to nephew, and, in one instance, from second cousin to second cousin, the sceptre had descended in the family of the Dales; and the acres had remained intact, growing in value and not decreasing in number, though guarded by no entail and protected by no wonderful amount of prudence or wisdom. The estate of Dale of Allington had been coterminous with the parish of Allington for some hundreds of years; and though, as I have said, the race of squires had possessed nothing of superhuman discretion and had perhaps been guided in their walks through life by no very distinct principles, still there had been with them so much of adherence to a sacred law, that no acre of the property had ever been parted from the hands of the existing squire. Some futile attempts had been made to increase the territory, as indeed had been done by Kit Dale, the father of Christopher Dale, who will appear as our squire of Allington when the persons of our drama are introduced. Old Kit Dale, who had married money, had bought outlying farms—a bit of ground here and a bit there—talking, as he did so, much of political influence and of the good old Tory cause. But these farms and bits of ground had gone again before our time. To them had been attached no religion. When old Kit had found himself pressed in that matter of the majority of the Nineteenth Dragoons, in which crack regiment his second son made for himself quite a career, he found it easier to sell than to save—seeing that that which he sold was his own and not the patrimony of the Dales. At his death the remainder of these purchases had gone. Family arrangements required completion, and Christopher Dale required ready money. The outlying farms flew away, as such new purchases had flown before; but the old patrimony of the Dales remained untouched, as it had ever remained.

It had been a religion among them; and seeing that the worship had been carried on without fail, that the vestal fire had never gone down upon the hearth, I should not have said that the Dales had walked their ways without high principle. To this religion they had all adhered, and the new heir had ever entered in upon his domain without other encumbrances than those with which he himself was then already burdened. And yet there had been no entail. The idea of an entail was not in accordance with the peculiarities of the Dale mind. It was necessary to the Dale religion that each squire should have the power *of wasting them. I remember to have dined at a house, the whole glory and fortune of which depended on the safety of a glass goblet. We all know the story. If the luck of Edenhall should be*

VIP CENTURY SCHOOLBOOK

10 point, 1 point leaded

FORMAT	PICAS	LINES	WPL	CPL	WPP	CPP
Royal 8vo	26×43	47	12.4	66	583	3102
Demy 8vo	24×40	44	11.5	61	493	2684
Large Crown 8vo	23×36	39	11.0	58	429	2262
Crown 8vo	21×34	37	10.0	53	370	1961

father to son, and from uncle to nephew, and, in one instance, from second cousin to second cousin, the sceptre had descended in the family of the Dales; and the acres had remained intact, growing in value and not decreasing in number, though guarded by no entail and protected by no wonderful amount of prudence or wisdom. The estate of Dale of Allington had been coterminous with the parish of Allington for some hundreds of years; and though, as I have said, the race of squires had possessed nothing of superhuman discretion and had perhaps been guided in their walks through life by no very distinct principles, still there had been with them so much of adherence to a sacred law, that no acre of the property had ever been parted from the hands of the existing squire. Some futile attempts had been made to increase the territory, as indeed had been done by Kit Dale, the father of Christopher Dale, who will appear as our squire of Allington when the persons of our drama are introduced. Old Kit Dale, who had married money, had bought outlying farms—a bit of ground here and a bit there—talking, as he did so, much of political influence and of the good old Tory cause. But these farms and bits of ground had gone again before our time. To them had been attached no religion. When old Kit had found himself pressed in that matter of the majority of the Nineteenth Dragoons, in which crack regiment his second son made for himself quite a career, he found it easier to sell than to save—seeing that that which he sold was his own and not the patrimony of the Dales. At his death the remainder of these purchases had gone. Family arrangements required completion, and Christopher Dale required ready money. The outlying farms flew away, as such new purchases had flown before; but the old patrimony of the Dales remained untouched, as it had ever remained.

It had been a religion among them; and seeing that the worship had been carried on without fail, that the vestal fire had never gone down upon the hearth, I should not have said that the Dales had walked their ways without high principle. To this religion they had all adhered, and the new heir had ever entered in upon his domain without other encumbrances than those with which he himself was then already burdened. And yet there had been no entail. The idea of an entail was not in *accordance with the peculiarities of the Dale mind. It was necessary to the Dale religion that each squire should have the power of wasting them. I remember to have dined at a house, the whole*

VIP CENTURY SCHOOLBOOK

10 point, 1½ point leaded

FORMAT	PICAS	LINES	WPL	CPL	WPP	CPP
Royal 8vo	26×43	45	12.4	66	558	2970
Demy 8vo	24×40	42	11.5	61	483	2562
Large Crown 8vo	23×36	38	11.0	58	418	2204
Crown 8vo	21×34	35	10.0	53	350	1855

father to son, and from uncle to nephew, and, in one instance, from second cousin to second cousin, the sceptre had descended in the family of the Dales; and the acres had remained intact, growing in value and not decreasing in number, though guarded by no entail and protected by no wonderful amount of prudence or wisdom. The estate of Dale of Allington had been coterminous with the parish of Allington for some hundreds of years; and though, as I have said, the race of squires had possessed nothing of superhuman discretion and had perhaps been guided in their walks through life by no very distinct principles, still there had been with them so much of adherence to a sacred law, that no acre of the property had ever been parted from the hands of the existing squire. Some futile attempts had been made to increase the territory, as indeed had been done by Kit Dale, the father of Christopher Dale, who will appear as our squire of Allington when the persons of our drama are introduced. Old Kit Dale, who had married money, had bought outlying farms—a bit of ground here and a bit there—talking, as he did so, much of political influence and of the good old Tory cause. But these farms and bits of ground had gone again before our time. To them had been attached no religion. When old Kit had found himself pressed in that matter of the majority of the Nineteenth Dragoons, in which crack regiment his second son made for himself quite a career, he found it easier to sell than to save—seeing that that which he sold was his own and not the patrimony of the Dales. At his death the remainder of these purchases had gone. Family arrangements required completion, and Christopher Dale required ready money. The outlying farms flew away, as such new purchases had flown before; but the old patrimony of the Dales remained untouched, as it had ever remained.

It had been a religion among them; and seeing that the worship had been carried on without fail, that the vestal fire had never gone down upon the hearth, I should not have said that the Dales had walked their ways without high principle. To this religion they had all adhered, and the new heir had ever entered in upon his domain without other encumbrances than those *with which he himself was then already burdened. And yet there had been no entail. The idea of an entail was not in accordance with the peculiarities of the Dale mind. It was necessary to the*

VIP CENTURY SCHOOLBOOK

10 point, 2 point leaded

FORMAT	PICAS	LINES	WPL	CPL	WPP	CPP
Royal 8vo	26×43	43	12.4	66	533	2838
Demy 8vo	24×40	40	11.5	61	460	2440
Large Crown 8vo	23×36	36	11.0	58	396	2088
Crown 8vo	21×34	34	10.0	53	340	1802

father to son, and from uncle to nephew, and, in one instance, from second cousin to second cousin, the sceptre had descended in the family of the Dales; and the acres had remained intact, growing in value and not decreasing in number, though guarded by no entail and protected by no wonderful amount of prudence or wisdom. The estate of Dale of Allington had been coterminous with the parish of Allington for some hundreds of years; and though, as I have said, the race of squires had possessed nothing of superhuman discretion and had perhaps been guided in their walks through life by no very distinct principles, still there had been with them so much of adherence to a sacred law, that no acre of the property had ever been parted from the hands of the existing squire. Some futile attempts had been made to increase the territory, as indeed had been done by Kit Dale, the father of Christopher Dale, who will appear as our squire of Allington when the persons of our drama are introduced. Old Kit Dale, who had married money, had bought outlying farms—a bit of ground here and a bit there—talking, as he did so, much of political influence and of the good old Tory cause. But these farms and bits of ground had gone again before our time. To them had been attached no religion. When old Kit had found himself pressed in that matter of the majority of the Nineteenth Dragoons, in which crack regiment his second son made for himself quite a career, he found it easier to sell than to save—seeing that that which he sold was his own and not the patrimony of the Dales. At his death the remainder of these purchases had gone. Family arrangements required completion, and Christopher Dale required ready money. The outlying farms flew away, as such new purchases had flown before; but the old patrimony of the Dales remained untouched, as it had ever remained.

It had been a religion among them; and seeing that the worship had been carried on without fail, that the vestal fire had never gone down upon the hearth, I should not *have said that the Dales had walked their ways without high principle. To this religion they had all adhered, and the new heir had ever entered in upon his domain without*

VIP CENTURY SCHOOLBOOK

11 point, 1 point leaded

FORMAT	PICAS	LINES	WPL	CPL	WPP	CPP
Royal 8vo	26×43	43	10.9	61	469	2623
Demy 8vo	24×40	40	10.1	56	404	2240
Large Crown 8vo	23×36	36	9.6	54	346	1944
Crown 8vo	21×34	34	8.8	49	299	1666

father to son, and from uncle to nephew, and, in one instance, from second cousin to second cousin, the sceptre had descended in the family of the Dales; and the acres had remained intact, growing in value and not decreasing in number, though guarded by no entail and protected by no wonderful amount of prudence or wisdom. The estate of Dale of Allington had been coterminous with the parish of Allington for some hundreds of years; and though, as I have said, the race of squires had possessed nothing of superhuman discretion and had perhaps been guided in their walks through life by no very distinct principles, still there had been with them so much of adherence to a sacred law, that no acre of the property had ever been parted from the hands of the existing squire. Some futile attempts had been made to increase the territory, as indeed had been done by Kit Dale, the father of Christopher Dale, who will appear as our squire of Allington when the persons of our drama are introduced. Old Kit Dale, who had married money, had bought outlying farms—a bit of ground here and a bit there—talking, as he did so, much of political influence and of the good old Tory cause. But these farms and bits of ground had gone again before our time. To them had been attached no religion. When old Kit had found himself pressed in that matter of the majority of the Nineteenth Dragoons, in which crack regiment his second son made for himself quite a career, he found it easier to sell than to save—seeing that that which he sold was his own and not the patrimony of the Dales. At his death the remainder of these purchases had gone. Family arrangements required completion, and Christopher Dale required ready money. The outlying farms flew away, as such new purchases had flown before; but the old patrimony of the Dales remained untouched, as it had ever remained.

It had been a religion among them; and seeing that the *worship had been carried on without fail, that the vestal fire had never gone down upon the hearth, I should not have said that the Dales had walked their ways without*

VIP CENTURY SCHOOLBOOK

11 point, 1½ point leaded

FORMAT	PICAS	LINES	WPL	CPL	WPP	CPP
Royal 8vo	26×43	41	10.9	61	447	2501
Demy 8vo	24×40	38	10.1	56	384	2128
Large Crown 8vo	23×36	35	9.6	54	336	1890
Crown 8vo	21×34	33	8.8	49	290	1617

father to son, and from uncle to nephew, and, in one instance, from second cousin to second cousin, the sceptre had descended in the family of the Dales; and the acres had remained intact, growing in value and not decreasing in number, though guarded by no entail and protected by no wonderful amount of prudence or wisdom. The estate of Dale of Allington had been coterminous with the parish of Allington for some hundreds of years; and though, as I have said, the race of squires had possessed nothing of superhuman discretion and had perhaps been guided in their walks through life by no very distinct principles, still there had been with them so much of adherence to a sacred law, that no acre of the property had ever been parted from the hands of the existing squire. Some futile attempts had been made to increase the territory, as indeed had been done by Kit Dale, the father of Christopher Dale, who will appear as our squire of Allington when the persons of our drama are introduced. Old Kit Dale, who had married money, had bought outlying farms—a bit of ground here and a bit there—talking, as he did so, much of political influence and of the good old Tory cause. But these farms and bits of ground had gone again before our time. To them had been attached no religion. When old Kit had found himself pressed in that matter of the majority of the Nineteenth Dragoons, in which crack regiment his second son made for himself quite a career, he found it easier to sell than to save—seeing that that which he sold was his own and not the patrimony of the Dales. At his death the remainder of these purchases had gone. Family arrangements required completion, and Christopher Dale required ready money. The outlying farms flew away, as such new purchases had flown before; but the old patrimony of the Dales remained untouched, as it had ever remained.

It had been a religion among them; and seeing that the worship had been carried on without fail, that the vestal fire had never gone down upon the hearth, I should not

VIP CENTURY SCHOOLBOOK

11 point, 2 point leaded

FORMAT	PICAS	LINES	WPL	CPL	WPP	CPP
Royal 8vo	26×43	40	10.9	61	436	2440
Demy 8vo	24×40	37	10.1	56	374	2072
Large Crown 8vo	23×36	33	9.6	54	317	1782
Crown 8vo	21×34	31	8.8	49	273	1519

VIP GARAMOND

Synopsis in 10 point

ABCDEFGHIJKLMNOPQRSTUVWXYZ&ÆŒ

ABCDEFGHIJKLMNOPQRSTUVWXYZ

abcdefghijklmnopqrstuvwxyzæœ

.,:;!?''-()£ 1234567890 1234567890

ABCDEFGHIJKLMNOPQRSTUVWXYZ&ÆŒ

abcdefghijklmnopqrstuvwxyzæœ

.,:;!?''-()£ 1234567890 1234567890

Related bold

ABCDEFGHIJKLMNOPQRSTUVWXYZ&ÆŒ

abcdefghijklmnopqrstuvwxyzæœ

.,:;!?''-()£ 1234567890 1234567890

ABCDEFGHIJKLMNOPQRSTUVWXYZ&ÆŒ

abcdefghijklmnopqrstuvwxyzæœ

.,:;!?''-()£ 1234567890

All normal European accents available

father to son, and from uncle to nephew, and, in one instance, from second cousin to second cousin, the sceptre had descended in the family of the Dales; and the acres had remained intact, growing in value and not decreasing in number, though guarded by no entail and protected by no wonderful amount of prudence or wisdom. The estate of Dale of Allington had been coterminous with the parish of Allington for some hundreds of years; and though, as I have said, the race of squires had possessed nothing of superhuman discretion and had perhaps been guided in their walks through life by no very distinct principles, still there had been with them so much of adherence to a sacred law, that no acre of the property had ever been parted from the hands of the existing squire. Some futile attempts had been made to increase the territory, as indeed had been done by Kit Dale, the father of Christopher Dale, who will appear as our squire of Allington when the persons of our drama are introduced. Old Kit Dale, who had married money, had bought outlying farms—a bit of ground here and a bit there—talking, as he did so, much of political influence and of the good old Tory cause. But these farms and bits of ground had gone again before our time. To them had been attached no religion. When old Kit had found himself pressed in that matter of the majority of the Nineteenth Dragoons, in which crack regiment his second son made for himself quite a career, he found it easier to sell than to save—seeing that that which he sold was his own and not the patrimony of the Dales. At his death the remainder of these purchases had gone. Family arrangements required completion, and Christopher Dale required ready money. The outlying farms flew away, as such new purchases had flown before; but the old patrimony of the Dales remained untouched, as it had ever remained.

It had been a religion among them; and seeing that the worship had been carried on without fail, that the vestal fire had never gone down upon the hearth, I should not have said that the Dales had walked their ways without high principle. To this religion they had all adhered, and the new heir had ever entered in upon his domain without other encumbrances than those with which he himself was then already burdened. And yet there had been no entail. The idea of an entail was not in accordance with the peculiarities of the Dale mind. It was necessary to the Dale religion that each squire should have the power of wasting them. I remember to have dined at a house, the whole glory and fortune of which depended on the safety of a glass goblet. We all know the story. If the luck of Edenhall should be shattered, the doom of the family would be sealed. Nevertheless I was bidden to drink out of the fatal glass, as were all guests in that house. It would not have contented the chivalrous mind of the master to protect his doom by lock and key and padded chest. And so it was with the Dales of Allington. To them an entail would have been a lock and key and a padded chest; but the old chivalry of their house denied to them the use of such protection.

I have spoken something slightingly of the acquirements and doings of the family; and indeed their acquirements had been few and their doings little. At Allington, Dale of Allington had always been known as a king. At Guestwick, the neighbouring market town, he was a great man—to be seen frequently on Saturdays, standing in the market-place, and laying down the law as to barley and oxen among men who knew usually more about barley and oxen than he did. At Hamersham, the assize *town, he was generally in some repute, being a constant grand juror for the county, and a man who paid his way. But even at Hamersham the glory of the Dales had, at most periods, begun to pale.*

VIP GARAMOND

9 point, 1 point leaded

FORMAT	PICAS	LINES	WPL	CPL	WPP	CPP
Royal 8vo	26×43	52	16.4	89	853	4628
Demy 8vo	24×40	48	15.2	82	730	3936
Large Crown 8vo	23×36	43	14.5	79	624	3397
Crown 8vo	21×34	41	13.2	72	541	2952

father to son, and from uncle to nephew, and, in one instance, from second cousin to second cousin, the sceptre had descended in the family of the Dales; and the acres had remained intact, growing in value and not decreasing in number, though guarded by no entail and protected by no wonderful amount of prudence or wisdom. The estate of Dale of Allington had been coterminous with the parish of Allington for some hundreds of years; and though, as I have said, the race of squires had possessed nothing of superhuman discretion and had perhaps been guided in their walks through life by no very distinct principles, still there had been with them so much of adherence to a sacred law, that no acre of the property had ever been parted from the hands of the existing squire. Some futile attempts had been made to increase the territory, as indeed had been done by Kit Dale, the father of Christopher Dale, who will appear as our squire of Allington when the persons of our drama are introduced. Old Kit Dale, who had married money, had bought outlying farms—a bit of ground here and a bit there—talking, as he did so, much of political influence and of the good old Tory cause. But these farms and bits of ground had gone again before our time. To them had been attached no religion. When old Kit had found himself pressed in that matter of the majority of the Nineteenth Dragoons, in which crack regiment his second son made for himself quite a career, he found it easier to sell than to save—seeing that that which he sold was his own and not the patrimony of the Dales. At his death the remainder of these purchases had gone. Family arrangements required completion, and Christopher Dale required ready money. The outlying farms flew away, as such new purchases had flown before; but the old patrimony of the Dales remained untouched, as it had ever remained.

It had been a religion among them; and seeing that the worship had been carried on without fail, that the vestal fire had never gone down upon the hearth, I should not have said that the Dales had walked their ways without high principle. To this religion they had all adhered, and the new heir had ever entered in upon his domain without other encumbrances than those with which he himself was then already burdened. And yet there had been no entail. The idea of an entail was not in accordance with the peculiarities of the Dale mind. It was necessary to the Dale religion that each squire should have the power of wasting them. I remember to have dined at a house, the whole glory and fortune of which depended on the safety of a glass goblet. We all know the story. If the luck of Edenhall should be shattered, the doom of the family would be sealed. Nevertheless I was bidden to drink out of the fatal glass, as were all guests in that house. It would not have contented the chivalrous mind of the master to protect his doom by lock and key and padded chest. And so it was with the Dales of Allington. To them an entail would have been a lock and key and a padded chest; but the old chivalry of their house denied to them the use of such protection.

I have spoken something slightingly of the acquirements and doings of the family; and indeed their acquirements had been few and their doings little. At Allington, Dale of Allington had always been known as a king. At Guestwick, the neighbouring market town, he was a great man—to be seen frequently on Saturdays, standing in *the market-place, and laying down the law as to barley and oxen among men who knew usually more about barley and oxen than he did. At Hamersham, the assize town, he was generally in some repute, being a constant grand juror for the county, and a man who paid his way. But even*

VIP GARAMOND

9 point, 1½ point leaded

FORMAT	PICAS	LINES	WPL	CPL	WPP	CPP
Royal 8vo	26×43	49	16.4	89	804	4361
Demy 8vo	24×40	46	15.2	82	699	3772
Large Crown 8vo	23×36	41	14.5	79	595	3239
Crown 8vo	21×34	39	13.2	72	515	2808

father to son, and from uncle to nephew, and, in one instance, from second cousin to second cousin, the sceptre had descended in the family of the Dales; and the acres had remained intact, growing in value and not decreasing in number, though guarded by no entail and protected by no wonderful amount of prudence or wisdom. The estate of Dale of Allington had been coterminous with the parish of Allington for some hundreds of years; and though, as I have said, the race of squires had possessed nothing of superhuman discretion and had perhaps been guided in their walks through life by no very distinct principles, still there had been with them so much of adherence to a sacred law, that no acre of the property had ever been parted from the hands of the existing squire. Some futile attempts had been made to increase the territory, as indeed had been done by Kit Dale, the father of Christopher Dale, who will appear as our squire of Allington when the persons of our drama are introduced. Old Kit Dale, who had married money, had bought outlying farms—a bit of ground here and a bit there—talking, as he did so, much of political influence and of the good old Tory cause. But these farms and bits of ground had gone again before our time. To them had been attached no religion. When old Kit had found himself pressed in that matter of the majority of the Nineteenth Dragoons, in which crack regiment his second son made for himself quite a career, he found it easier to sell than to save—seeing that that which he sold was his own and not the patrimony of the Dales. At his death the remainder of these purchases had gone. Family arrangements required completion, and Christopher Dale required ready money. The outlying farms flew away, as such new purchases had flown before; but the old patrimony of the Dales remained untouched, as it had ever remained.

It had been a religion among them; and seeing that the worship had been carried on without fail, that the vestal fire had never gone down upon the hearth, I should not have said that the Dales had walked their ways without high principle. To this religion they had all adhered, and the new heir had ever entered in upon his domain without other encumbrances than those with which he himself was then already burdened. And yet there had been no entail. The idea of an entail was not in accordance with the peculiarities of the Dale mind. It was necessary to the Dale religion that each squire should have the power of wasting them. I remember to have dined at a house, the whole glory and fortune of which depended on the safety of a glass goblet. We all know the story. If the luck of Edenhall should be shattered, the doom of the family would be sealed. Nevertheless I was bidden to drink out of the fatal glass, as were all guests in that house. It would not have contented the chivalrous mind of the master to protect his doom by lock and key and padded chest. And so it was with the Dales of Allington. To them an entail would have been a lock and key and a padded chest; but the old chivalry of their house denied to them the use of such protection.

I have spoken something slightingly of the acquirements and doings of the family; and indeed their acquirements had been few and their doings little. At Allington, Dale of Allington had always been known as a king. At Guestwick, the neighbouring market town, he was a great

VIP GARAMOND

9 point, 2 point leaded

FORMAT	PICAS	LINES	WPL	CPL	WPP	CPP
Royal 8vo	26×43	47	16.4	89	771	4183
Demy 8vo	24×40	44	15.2	82	669	3608
Large Crown 8vo	23×36	39	14.5	79	566	3081
Crown 8vo	21×34	37	13.2	72	488	2664

father to son, and from uncle to nephew, and, in one instance, from second cousin to second cousin, the sceptre had descended in the family of the Dales; and the acres had remained intact, growing in value and not decreasing in number, though guarded by no entail and protected by no wonderful amount of prudence or wisdom. The estate of Dale of Allington had been coterminous with the parish of Allington for some hundreds of years; and though, as I have said, the race of squires had possessed nothing of superhuman discretion and had perhaps been guided in their walks through life by no very distinct principles, still there had been with them so much of adherence to a sacred law, that no acre of the property had ever been parted from the hands of the existing squire. Some futile attempts had been made to increase the territory, as indeed had been done by Kit Dale, the father of Christopher Dale, who will appear as our squire of Allington when the persons of our drama are introduced. Old Kit Dale, who had married money, had bought outlying farms—a bit of ground here and a bit there—talking, as he did so, much of political influence and of the good old Tory cause. But these farms and bits of ground had gone again before our time. To them had been attached no religion. When old Kit had found himself pressed in that matter of the majority of the Nineteenth Dragoons, in which crack regiment his second son made for himself quite a career, he found it easier to sell than to save—seeing that that which he sold was his own and not the patrimony of the Dales. At his death the remainder of these purchases had gone. Family arrangements required completion, and Christopher Dale required ready money. The outlying farms flew away, as such new purchases had flown before; but the old patrimony of the Dales remained untouched, as it had ever remained.

It had been a religion among them; and seeing that the worship had been carried on without fail, that the vestal fire had never gone down upon the hearth, I should not have said that the Dales had walked their ways without high principle. To this religion they had all adhered, and the new heir had ever entered in upon his domain without other encumbrances than those with which he himself was then already burdened. And yet there had been no entail. The idea of an entail was not in accordance with the peculiarities of the Dale mind. It was necessary to the Dale religion that each squire should have the power of wasting them. I remember to have dined at a house, the whole glory and fortune of which depended on the safety of a glass goblet. We all know the story. If the luck of Edenhall should be shattered, the doom of the family would be sealed. Nevertheless I was bidden to drink out of the fatal glass, as were all guests in that house. It would not have contented the *chivalrous mind of the master to protect his doom by lock and key and padded chest. And so it was with the Dales of Allington. To them an entail would have been a lock and key and a padded chest; but the old chivalry of their house denied to them the use of*

VIP GARAMOND

10 point, 1 point leaded

FORMAT	PICAS	LINES	WPL	CPL	WPP	CPP
Royal 8vo	26×43	47	14.4	80	677	3760
Demy 8vo	24×40	44	13.3	74	585	3256
Large Crown 8vo	23×36	39	12.7	71	495	2769
Crown 8vo	21×34	37	11.6	65	429	2405

father to son, and from uncle to nephew, and, in one instance, from second cousin to second cousin, the sceptre had descended in the family of the Dales; and the acres had remained intact, growing in value and not decreasing in number, though guarded by no entail and protected by no wonderful amount of prudence or wisdom. The estate of Dale of Allington had been coterminous with the parish of Allington for some hundreds of years; and though, as I have said, the race of squires had possessed nothing of super-human discretion and had perhaps been guided in their walks through life by no very distinct principles, still there had been with them so much of adherence to a sacred law, that no acre of the property had ever been parted from the hands of the existing squire. Some futile attempts had been made to increase the territory, as indeed had been done by Kit Dale, the father of Christopher Dale, who will appear as our squire of Allington when the persons of our drama are introduced. Old Kit Dale, who had married money, had bought outlying farms—a bit of ground here and a bit there—talking, as he did so, much of political influence and of the good old Tory cause. But these farms and bits of ground had gone again before our time. To them had been attached no religion. When old Kit had found himself pressed in that matter of the majority of the Nineteenth Dragoons, in which crack regiment his second son made for himself quite a career, he found it easier to sell than to save—seeing that that which he sold was his own and not the patrimony of the Dales. At his death the remainder of these purchases had gone. Family arrangements required completion, and Christopher Dale required ready money. The outlying farms flew away, as such new purchases had flown before; but the old patrimony of the Dales remained untouched, as it had ever remained.

It had been a religion among them; and seeing that the worship had been carried on without fail, that the vestal fire had never gone down upon the hearth, I should not have said that the Dales had walked their ways without high principle. To this religion they had all adhered, and the new heir had ever entered in upon his domain without other encumbrances than those with which he himself was then already burdened. And yet there had been no entail. The idea of an entail was not in accordance with the peculiarities of the Dale mind. It was necessary to the Dale religion that each squire should have the power of wasting them. I remember to have dined at a house, the whole glory and fortune of which depended on the safety of a glass goblet. We all know the story. If the luck of Edenhall should be shattered, the doom of the family would be sealed. Nevertheless I was bidden to drink out of the fatal glass, as were all guests in that house. It would not have contented the *chivalrous mind of the master to protect his doom by lock and key and padded chest. And so it was with the Dales of Allington. To them an entail would have been a lock and key and a padded chest; but the old chivalry of their house denied to them the use of*

VIP GARAMOND

10 point, 1½ point leaded

FORMAT	PICAS	LINES	WPL	CPL	WPP	CPP
Royal 8vo	26×43	45	14.4	80	648	3600
Demy 8vo	24×40	42	13.3	74	559	3108
Large Crown 8vo	22×36	38	12.7	71	483	2698
Crown 8vo	21×34	35	11.6	65	406	2275

father to son, and from uncle to nephew, and, in one instance, from second cousin to second cousin, the sceptre had descended in the family of the Dales; and the acres had remained intact, growing in value and not decreasing in number, though guarded by no entail and protected by no wonderful amount of prudence or wisdom. The estate of Dale of Allington had been coterminous with the parish of Allington for some hundreds of years; and though, as I have said, the race of squires had possessed nothing of superhuman discretion and had perhaps been guided in their walks through life by no very distinct principles, still there had been with them so much of adherence to a sacred law, that no acre of the property had ever been parted from the hands of the existing squire. Some futile attempts had been made to increase the territory, as indeed had been done by Kit Dale, the father of Christopher Dale, who will appear as our squire of Allington when the persons of our drama are introduced. Old Kit Dale, who had married money, had bought outlying farms—a bit of ground here and a bit there—talking, as he did so, much of political influence and of the good old Tory cause. But these farms and bits of ground had gone again before our time. To them had been attached no religion. When old Kit had found himself pressed in that matter of the majority of the Nineteenth Dragoons, in which crack regiment his second son made for himself quite a career, he found it easier to sell than to save—seeing that that which he sold was his own and not the patrimony of the Dales. At his death the remainder of these purchases had gone. Family arrangements required completion, and Christopher Dale required ready money. The outlying farms flew away, as such new purchases had flown before; but the old patrimony of the Dales remained untouched, as it had ever remained.

It had been a religion among them; and seeing that the worship had been carried on without fail, that the vestal fire had never gone down upon the hearth, I should not have said that the Dales had walked their ways without high principle. To this religion they had all adhered, and the new heir had ever entered in upon his domain without other encumbrances than those with which he himself was then already burdened. And yet there had been no entail. The idea of an entail was not in accordance with the peculiarities of the Dale mind. It was necessary to the Dale religion that each squire should have the power of wasting them. I remember to have dined at a house, the whole glory and fortune of which depended on the safety of a glass goblet. We all know the story. If the luck of Edenhall should be shattered, the doom *of the family would be sealed. Nevertheless I was bidden to drink out of the fatal glass, as were all guests in that house. It would not have contented the chivalrous mind of the master to protect his doom by lock and key and padded chest. And so it was with the*

VIP GARAMOND

10 point, 2 point leaded

FORMAT	PICAS	LINES	WPL	CPL	WPP	CPP
Royal 8vo	26×43	43	14.4	80	619	3440
Demy 8vo	24×40	40	13.3	74	532	2960
Large Crown 8vo	23×36	36	12.7	71	457	2556
Crown 8vo	21×34	34	11.6	65	394	2210

father to son, and from uncle to nephew, and, in one instance, from second cousin to second cousin, the sceptre had descended in the family of the Dales; and the acres had remained intact, growing in value and not decreasing in number, though guarded by no entail and protected by no wonderful amount of prudence or wisdom. The estate of Dale of Allington had been coterminous with the parish of Allington for some hundreds of years; and though, as I have said, the race of squires had possessed nothing of superhuman discretion and had perhaps been guided in their walks through life by no very distinct principles, still there had been with them so much of adherence to a sacred law, that no acre of the property had ever been parted from the hands of the existing squire. Some futile attempts had been made to increase the territory, as indeed had been done by Kit Dale, the father of Christopher Dale, who will appear as our squire of Allington when the persons of our drama are introduced. Old Kit Dale, who had married money, had bought outlying farms—a bit of ground here and a bit there—talking, as he did so, much of political influence and of the good old Tory cause. But these farms and bits of ground had gone again before our time. To them had been attached no religion. When old Kit had found himself pressed in that matter of the majority of the Nineteenth Dragoons, in which crack regiment his second son made for himself quite a career, he found it easier to sell than to save—seeing that that which he sold was his own and not the patrimony of the Dales. At his death the remainder of these purchases had gone. Family arrangements required completion, and Christopher Dale required ready money. The outlying farms flew away, as such new purchases had flown before; but the old patrimony of the Dales remained untouched, as it had ever remained.

It had been a religion among them; and seeing that the worship had been carried on without fail, that the vestal fire had never gone down upon the hearth, I should not have said that the Dales had walked their ways without high principle. To this religion they had all adhered, and the new heir had ever entered in upon his domain without other encumbrances than those with which he himself was then already burdened. And yet there had been no entail. The idea of an entail was not in accordance with the peculiarities of the Dale mind. It was necessary to the Dale religion that each squire should *have the power of wasting them. I remember to have dined at a house, the whole glory and fortune of which depended on the safety of a glass goblet. We all know the story. If the luck of Edenhall should be shattered, the doom of the*

VIP GARAMOND

11 point, 1 point leaded

FORMAT	PICAS	LINES	WPL	CPL	WPP	CPP
Royal 8vo	26×43	43	13.1	72	563	3096
Demy 8vo	24×40	40	12.1	66	484	2640
Large Crown 8vo	23×36	36	11.6	63	418	2268
Crown 8vo	21×34	34	10.9	58	371	1972

father to son, and from uncle to nephew, and, in one instance, from second cousin to second cousin, the sceptre had descended in the family of the Dales; and the acres had remained intact, growing in value and not decreasing in number, though guarded by no entail and protected by no wonderful amount of prudence or wisdom. The estate of Dale of Allington had been coterminous with the parish of Allington for some hundreds of years; and though, as I have said, the race of squires had possessed nothing of superhuman discretion and had perhaps been guided in their walks through life by no very distinct principles, still there had been with them so much of adherence to a sacred law, that no acre of the property had ever been parted from the hands of the existing squire. Some futile attempts had been made to increase the territory, as indeed had been done by Kit Dale, the father of Christopher Dale, who will appear as our squire of Allington when the persons of our drama are introduced. Old Kit Dale, who had married money, had bought outlying farms—a bit of ground here and a bit there—talking, as he did so, much of political influence and of the good old Tory cause. But these farms and bits of ground had gone again before our time. To them had been attached no religion. When old Kit had found himself pressed in that matter of the majority of the Nineteenth Dragoons, in which crack regiment his second son made for himself quite a career, he found it easier to sell than to save—seeing that that which he sold was his own and not the patrimony of the Dales. At his death the remainder of these purchases had gone. Family arrangements required completion, and Christopher Dale required ready money. The outlying farms flew away, as such new purchases had flown before; but the old patrimony of the Dales remained untouched, as it had ever remained.

It had been a religion among them; and seeing that the worship had been carried on without fail, that the vestal fire had never gone down upon the hearth, I should not have said that the Dales had walked their ways without high principle. To this religion they had all adhered, and the new heir had ever entered in upon his domain without other encumbrances than those with which he himself was then already burdened. And yet there had been no entail. The idea of *an entail was not in accordance with the peculiarities of the Dale mind. It was necessary to the Dale religion that each squire should have the power of wasting them. I remember to have dined at a house, the whole glory and fortune of*

VIP GARAMOND

11 point, 1½ point leaded

FORMAT	PICAS	LINES	WPL	CPL	WPP	CPP
Royal 8vo	26×43	41	13.1	72	537	2952
Demy 8vo	24×40	38	12.1	66	460	2508
Large Crown 8vo	23×36	35	11.6	63	394	2142
Crown 8vo	21×34	33	10.9	58	349	1856

father to son, and from uncle to nephew, and, in one instance, from second cousin to second cousin, the sceptre had descended in the family of the Dales; and the acres had remained intact, growing in value and not decreasing in number, though guarded by no entail and protected by no wonderful amount of prudence or wisdom. The estate of Dale of Allington had been coterminous with the parish of Allington for some hundreds of years; and though, as I have said, the race of squires had possessed nothing of superhuman discretion and had perhaps been guided in their walks through life by no very distinct principles, still there had been with them so much of adherence to a sacred law, that no acre of the property had ever been parted from the hands of the existing squire. Some futile attempts had been made to increase the territory, as indeed had been done by Kit Dale, the father of Christopher Dale, who will appear as our squire of Allington when the persons of our drama are introduced. Old Kit Dale, who had married money, had bought outlying farms—a bit of ground here and a bit there—talking, as he did so, much of political influence and of the good old Tory cause. But these farms and bits of ground had gone again before our time. To them had been attached no religion. When old Kit had found himself pressed in that matter of the majority of the Nineteenth Dragoons, in which crack regiment his second son made for himself quite a career, he found it easier to sell than to save—seeing that that which he sold was his own and not the patrimony of the Dales. At his death the remainder of these purchases had gone. Family arrangements required completion, and Christopher Dale required ready money. The outlying farms flew away, as such new purchases had flown before; but the old patrimony of the Dales remained untouched, as it had ever remained.

It had been a religion among them; and seeing that the worship had been carried on without fail, that the vestal fire had never gone down upon the hearth, I should not have said that the Dales had walked their ways without high principle. To this religion they had all adhered, and the new heir had ever entered in upon his domain without other encumbrances than those with which he himself was *then already burdened. And yet there had been no entail. The idea of an entail was not in accordance with the peculiarities of the Dale mind. It was necessary to the Dale religion that each squire should have the power of wasting them. I*

VIP GARAMOND

11 point, 2 point leaded

FORMAT	PICAS	LINES	WPL	CPL	WPP	CPP
Royal 8vo	26×43	40	13.1	72	524	2880
Demy 8vo	24×40	37	12.1	66	448	2442
Large Crown 8vo	23×36	33	11.6	63	383	2079
Crown 8vo	21×34	31	10.9	58	338	1798

father to son, and from uncle to nephew, and, in one instance, from second cousin to second cousin, the sceptre had descended in the family of the Dales; and the acres had remained intact, growing in value and not decreasing in number, though guarded by no entail and protected by no wonderful amount of prudence or wisdom. The estate of Dale of Allington had been coterminous with the parish of Allington for some hundreds of years; and though, as I have said, the race of squires had possessed nothing of superhuman discretion and had perhaps been guided in their walks through life by no very distinct principles, still there had been with them so much of adherence to a sacred law, that no acre of the property had ever been parted from the hands of the existing squire. Some futile attempts had been made to increase the territory, as indeed had been done by Kit Dale, the father of Christopher Dale, who will appear as our squire of Allington when the persons of our drama are introduced. Old Kit Dale, who had married money, had bought outlying farms—a bit of ground here and a bit there—talking, as he did so, much of political influence and of the good old Tory cause. But these farms and bits of ground had gone again before our time. To them had been attached no religion. When old Kit had found himself pressed in that matter of the majority of the Nineteenth Dragoons, in which crack regiment his second son made for himself quite a career, he found it easier to sell than to save—seeing that that which he sold was his own and not the patrimony of the Dales. At his death the remainder of these purchases had gone. Family arrangements required completion, and Christopher Dale required ready money. The outlying farms flew away, as such new purchases had flown before; but the old patrimony of the Dales remained untouched, as it had ever remained.

It had been a religion among them; and seeing that the worship had been carried on without fail, that the vestal fire had never gone down upon the hearth, I should not have said that *the Dales had walked their ways without high principle. To this religion they had all adhered, and the new heir had ever entered in upon his domain without other encumbrances than those with which he*

VIP GARAMOND

12 point, 1 point leaded

FORMAT	PICAS	LINES	WPL	CPL	WPP	CPP
Royal 8vo	26×43	40	12.0	68	480	2720
Demy 8vo	24×40	37	11.1	63	411	2331
Large Crown 8vo	23×36	33	10.6	60	350	1980
Crown 8vo	21×34	31	9.7	55	301	1705

father to son, and from uncle to nephew, and, in one instance, from second cousin to second cousin, the sceptre had descended in the family of the Dales; and the acres had remained intact, growing in value and not decreasing in number, though guarded by no entail and protected by no wonderful amount of prudence or wisdom. The estate of Dale of Allington had been coterminous with the parish of Allington for some hundreds of years; and though, as I have said, the race of squires had possessed nothing of superhuman discretion and had perhaps been guided in their walks through life by no very distinct principles, still there had been with them so much of adherence to a sacred law, that no acre of the property had ever been parted from the hands of the existing squire. Some futile attempts had been made to increase the territory, as indeed had been done by Kit Dale, the father of Christopher Dale, who will appear as our squire of Allington when the persons of our drama are introduced. Old Kit Dale, who had married money, had bought outlying farms—a bit of ground here and a bit there—talking, as he did so, much of political influence and of the good old Tory cause. But these farms and bits of ground had gone again before our time. To them had been attached no religion. When old Kit had found himself pressed in that matter of the majority of the Nineteenth Dragoons, in which crack regiment his second son made for himself quite a career, he found it easier to sell than to save—seeing that that which he sold was his own and not the patrimony of the Dales. At his death the remainder of these purchases had gone. Family arrangements required completion, and Christopher Dale required ready money. The outlying farms flew away, as such new purchases had flown before; but the old patrimony of the Dales remained untouched, as it had ever remained.

It had been a religion among them; and seeing that the *worship had been carried on without fail, that the vestal fire had never gone down upon the hearth, I should not have said that the Dales had walked their ways without high principle. To this religion they had all*

VIP GARAMOND

12 point, 1½ point leaded

FORMAT	PICAS	LINES	WPL	CPL	WPP	CPP
Royal 8vo	26×43	38	12.0	68	456	2584
Demy 8vo	24×40	36	11.1	63	400	2268
Large Crown 8vo	23×36	32	10.6	60	339	1920
Crown 8vo	21×34	30	9.7	55	291	1650

VIP HELVETICA

Synopsis in 10 point

ABCDEFGHIJKLMNOPQRSTUVWXYZ&ÆŒ
abcdefghijklmnopqrstuvwxyzæœ
.,:;!?"-()£ 1234567890
ABCDEFGHIJKLMNOPQRSTUVWXYZ&ÆŒ
abcdefghijklmnopqrstuvwxyzæœ
.,:;!?"-()£ 1234567890

Related bold

ABCDEFGHIJKLMNOPQRSTUVWXYZ&ÆŒ
abcdefghijklmnopqrstuvwxyzæœ
.,:;!?"-()£ 1234567890
ABCDEFGHIJKLMNOPQRSTUVWXYZ&ÆŒ
abcdefghijklmnopqrstuvwxyzæœ
.,:;!?"-()£ 1234567890

All normal European accents available

father to son, and from uncle to nephew, and, in one instance, from second cousin to second cousin, the sceptre had descended in the family of the Dales; and the acres had remained intact, growing in value and not decreasing in number, though guarded by no entail and protected by no wonderful amount of prudence or wisdom. The estate of Dale of Allington had been coterminous with the parish of Allington for some hundreds of years; and though, as I have said, the race of squires had possessed nothing of superhuman discretion and had perhaps been guided in their walks through life by no very distinct principles, still there had been with them so much of adherence to a sacred law, that no acre of the property had ever been parted from the hands of the existing squire. Some futile attempts had been made to increase the territory, as indeed had been done by Kit Dale, the father of Christopher Dale, who will appear as our squire of Allington when the persons of our drama are introduced. Old Kit Dale, who had married money, had bought outlying farms—a bit of ground here and a bit there—talking, as he did so, much of political influence and of the good old Tory cause. But these farms and bits of ground had gone again before our time. To them had been attached no religion. When old Kit had found himself pressed in that matter of the majority of the Nineteenth Dragoons, in which crack regiment his second son made for himself quite a career, he found it easier to sell than to save—seeing that that which he sold was his own and not the patrimony of the Dales. At his death the remainder of these purchases had gone. Family arrangements required completion, and Christopher Dale required ready money. The outlying farms flew away, as such new purchases had flown before; but the old patrimony of the Dales remained untouched, as it had ever remained.

It had been a religion among them; and seeing that the worship had been carried on without fail, that the vestal fire had never gone down upon the hearth, I should not have said that the Dales had walked their ways without high principle. To this religion they had all adhered, and the new heir had ever entered in upon his domain without other encumbrances than those with which he himself was then already burdened. And yet there had been no entail. The idea of an entail was not in accordance with the peculiarities of the Dale mind. It was necessary to the Dale religion that each squire should have the power of wasting them. I remember to have dined at a house, the whole glory and fortune of which depended on the safety of a glass goblet. We all know the story. If the luck of Edenhall should be shattered, the doom of the family would be sealed. Nevertheless I was bidden to drink out of the fatal glass, as were all guests in that house. It would not have contented the chivalrous mind of the master to protect his doom by lock and key and padded chest. And so it was with the Dales of Allington. To them an entail would have been a lock and key and a padded chest; but the old chivalry of their house denied to them the use of such *protection.*

I have spoken something slightingly of the acquirements and doings of the family; and indeed their acquirements had been few and their doings

VIP HELVETICA

9 point, 1½ point leaded

FORMAT	PICAS	LINES	WPL	CPL	WPP	CPP
Royal 8vo	26×43	49	13.6	78	666	3822
Demy 8vo	24×40	46	12.6	72	580	3312
Large Crown 8vo	23×36	41	12.0	69	492	2829
Crown 8vo	21×34	39	11.0	63	429	2457

father to son, and from uncle to nephew, and, in one instance, from second cousin to second cousin, the sceptre had descended in the family of the Dales; and the acres had remained intact, growing in value and not decreasing in number, though guarded by no entail and protected by no wonderful amount of prudence or wisdom. The estate of Dale of Allington had been coterminous with the parish of Allington for some hundreds of years; and though, as I have said, the race of squires had possessed nothing of superhuman discretion and had perhaps been guided in their walks through life by no very distinct principles, still there had been with them so much of adherence to a sacred law, that no acre of the property had ever been parted from the hands of the existing squire. Some futile attempts had been made to increase the territory, as indeed had been done by Kit Dale, the father of Christopher Dale, who will appear as our squire of Allington when the persons of our drama are introduced. Old Kit Dale, who had married money, had bought outlying farms—a bit of ground here and a bit there—talking, as he did so, much of political influence and of the good old Tory cause. But these farms and bits of ground had gone again before our time. To them had been attached no religion. When old Kit had found himself pressed in that matter of the majority of the Nineteenth Dragoons, in which crack regiment his second son made for himself quite a career, he found it easier to sell than to save—seeing that that which he sold was his own and not the patrimony of the Dales. At his death the remainder of these purchases had gone. Family arrangements required completion, and Christopher Dale required ready money. The outlying farms flew away, as such new purchases had flown before; but the old patrimony of the Dales remained untouched, as it had ever remained.

It had been a religion among them; and seeing that the worship had been carried on without fail, that the vestal fire had never gone down upon the hearth, I should not have said that the Dales had walked their ways without high principle. To this religion they had all adhered, and the new heir had ever entered in upon his domain without other encumbrances than those with which he himself was then already burdened. And yet there had been no entail. The idea of an entail was not in accordance with the peculiarities of the Dale mind. It was necessary to the Dale religion that each squire should have the power of wasting them. I remember to have dined at a house, the whole glory and fortune of which depended on the safety of a glass goblet. We all know the story. If the luck of Edenhall should be shattered, the doom of the family would be sealed. Nevertheless I was bidden to drink out of the fatal glass, as were all guests in that house. It would not have contented the chivalrous mind of the master to protect his doom by lock and key and padded chest. And so it was with the Dales of *Allington. To them an entail would have been a lock and key and a padded chest; but the old chivalry of their house denied to them the use of such protection.*

VIP HELVETICA

9 point, 2 point leaded

FORMAT	PICAS	LINES	WPL	CPL	WPP	CPP
Royal 8vo	26×43	47	13.6	78	639	3666
Demy 8vo	24×40	44	12.6	72	554	3168
Large Crown 8vo	23×36	39	12.0	69	468	2691
Crown 8vo	21×34	37	11.0	63	407	2331

father to son, and from uncle to nephew, and, in one instance, from second cousin to second cousin, the sceptre had descended in the family of the Dales; and the acres had remained intact, growing in value and not decreasing in number, though guarded by no entail and protected by no wonderful amount of prudence or wisdom. The estate of Dale of Allington had been coterminous with the parish of Allington for some hundreds of years; and though, as I have said, the race of squires had possessed nothing of superhuman discretion and had perhaps been guided in their walks through life by no very distinct principles, still there had been with them so much of adherence to a sacred law, that no acre of the property had ever been parted from the hands of the existing squire. Some futile attempts had been made to increase the territory, as indeed had been done by Kit Dale, the father of Christopher Dale, who will appear as our squire of Allington when the persons of our drama are introduced. Old Kit Dale, who had married money, had bought outlying farms—a bit of ground here and a bit there—talking, as he did so, much of political influence and of the good old Tory cause. But these farms and bits of ground had gone again before our time. To them had been attached no religion. When old Kit had found himself pressed in that matter of the majority of the Nineteenth Dragoons, in which crack regiment his second son made for himself quite a career, he found it easier to sell than to save—seeing that that which he sold was his own and not the patrimony of the Dales. At his death the remainder of these purchases had gone. Family arrangements required completion, and Christopher Dale required ready money. The outlying farms flew away, as such new purchases had flown before; but the old patrimony of the Dales remained untouched, as it had ever remained.

It had been a religion among them; and seeing that the worship had been carried on without fail, that the vestal fire had never gone down upon the hearth, I should not have said that the Dales had walked their ways without high principle. To this religion they had all adhered, and the new heir had ever entered in upon his domain without other encumbrances than those with which he himself was then already burdened. And yet there had been no entail. The idea of an entail was not in accordance with the peculiarities of the Dale mind. It was necessary to the Dale religion that each squire should have the power of wasting them. I remember to have dined at a *house, the whole glory and fortune of which depended on the safety of a glass goblet. We all know the story. If the luck of Edenhall should be shattered, the doom of the family would be*

VIP HELVETICA

10 point, 1½ point leaded

FORMAT	PICAS	LINES	WPL	CPL	WPP	CPP
Royal 8vo	26×43	45	12.8	70	576	3150
Demy 8vo	24×40	42	11.8	65	496	2730
Large Crown 8vo	23×36	38	11.3	62	429	2356
Crown 8vo	21×34	35	10.3	57	361	1995

father to son, and from uncle to nephew, and, in one instance, from second cousin to second cousin, the sceptre had descended in the family of the Dales; and the acres had remained intact, growing in value and not decreasing in number, though guarded by no entail and protected by no wonderful amount of prudence or wisdom. The estate of Dale of Allington had been coterminous with the parish of Allington for some hundreds of years; and though, as I have said, the race of squires had possessed nothing of superhuman discretion and had perhaps been guided in their walks through life by no very distinct principles, still there had been with them so much of adherence to a sacred law, that no acre of the property had ever been parted from the hands of the existing squire. Some futile attempts had been made to increase the territory, as indeed had been done by Kit Dale, the father of Christopher Dale, who will appear as our squire of Allington when the persons of our drama are introduced. Old Kit Dale, who had married money, had bought outlying farms—a bit of ground here and a bit there—talking, as he did so, much of political influence and of the good old Tory cause. But these farms and bits of ground had gone again before our time. To them had been attached no religion. When old Kit had found himself pressed in that matter of the majority of the Nineteenth Dragoons, in which crack regiment his second son made for himself quite a career, he found it easier to sell than to save—seeing that that which he sold was his own and not the patrimony of the Dales. At his death the remainder of these purchases had gone. Family arrangements required completion, and Christopher Dale required ready money. The outlying farms flew away, as such new purchases had flown before; but the old patrimony of the Dales remained untouched, as it had ever remained.

It had been a religion among them; and seeing that the worship had been carried on without fail, that the vestal fire had never gone down upon the hearth, I should not have said that the Dales had walked their ways without high principle. To this religion they had all adhered, and the new heir had ever entered in upon his domain without other encumbrances than those with which he himself was then already burdened. And yet there had been no entail. The idea of an entail was not in accordance with the peculiarities of the Dale *mind. It was necessary to the Dale religion that each squire should have the power of wasting them. I remember to have dined at a house, the whole glory and fortune of which depended on the*

VIP HELVETICA

10 point, 2 point leaded

FORMAT	PICAS	LINES	WPL	CPL	WPP	CPP
Royal 8vo	26×43	43	12.8	70	550	3010
Demy 8vo	24×40	40	11.8	65	472	2600
Large Crown 8vo	23×36	36	11.3	62	407	2232
Crown 8vo	21×34	34	10.3	57	350	1938

father to son, and from uncle to nephew, and, in one instance, from second cousin to second cousin, the sceptre had descended in the family of the Dales; and the acres had remained intact, growing in value and not decreasing in number, though guarded by no entail and protected by no wonderful amount of prudence or wisdom. The estate of Dale of Allington had been coterminous with the parish of Allington for some hundreds of years; and though, as I have said, the race of squires had possessed nothing of superhuman discretion and had perhaps been guided in their walks through life by no very distinct principles, still there had been with them so much of adherence to a sacred law, that no acre of the property had ever been parted from the hands of the existing squire. Some futile attempts had been made to increase the territory, as indeed had been done by Kit Dale, the father of Christopher Dale, who will appear as our squire of Allington when the persons of our drama are introduced. Old Kit Dale, who had married money, had bought outlying farms—a bit of ground here and a bit there—talking, as he did so, much of political influence and of the good old Tory cause. But these farms and bits of ground had gone again before our time. To them had been attached no religion. When old Kit had found himself pressed in that matter of the majority of the Nineteenth Dragoons, in which crack regiment his second son made for himself quite a career, he found it easier to sell than to save—seeing that that which he sold was his own and not the patrimony of the Dales. At his death the remainder of these purchases had gone. Family arrangements required completion, and Christopher Dale required ready money. The outlying farms flew away, as such new purchases had flown before; but the old patrimony of the Dales remained untouched, as it had ever remained.

It had been a religion among them; and seeing that the worship had been carried on without fail, that the vestal fire *had never gone down upon the hearth, I should not have said that the Dales had walked their ways without high principle. To this religion they had all adhered, and the new*

VIP HELVETICA

11 point, 2 point leaded

FORMAT	PICAS	LINES	WPL	CPL	WPP	CPP
Royal 8vo	26× 43	40	11.6	64	464	2560
Demy 8vo	24× 40	37	10.7	59	396	2183
Large Crown 8vo	23× 36	33	10.2	57	337	1881
Crown 8vo	21× 34	31	9.3	52	288	1612

VIP MELIOR

Synopsis in 10 point

ABCDEFGHIJKLMNOPQRSTUVWXYZ&ÆŒ
abcdefghijklmnopqrstuvwxyzæœ
.,:;!?'‘-()£ 1234567890
ABCDEFGHIJKLMNOPQRSTUVWXYZ&ÆŒ
abcdefghijklmnopqrstuvwxyzæœ
.,:;!?'‘-()£ 1234567890

Related bold

ABCDEFGHIJKLMNOPQRSTUVWXYZ&ÆŒ
abcdefghijklmnopqrstuvwxyzæœ
.,:;!?'‘-()£ 1234567890

All normal European accents available

father to son, and from uncle to nephew, and, in one instance, from second cousin to second cousin, the sceptre had descended in the family of the Dales; and the acres had remained intact, growing in value and not decreasing in number, though guarded by no entail and protected by no wonderful amount of prudence or wisdom. The estate of Dale of Allington had been coterminous with the parish of Allington for some hundreds of years; and though, as I have said, the race of squires had possessed nothing of superhuman discretion and had perhaps been guided in their walks through life by no very distinct principles, still there had been with them so much of adherence to a sacred law, that no acre of the property had ever been parted from the hands of the existing squire. Some futile attempts had been made to increase the territory, as indeed had been done by Kit Dale, the father of Christopher Dale, who will appear as our squire of Allington when the persons of our drama are introduced. Old Kit Dale, who had married money, had bought outlying farms—a bit of ground here and a bit there—talking, as he did so, much of political influence and of the good old Tory cause. But these farms and bits of ground had gone again before our time. To them had been attached no religion. When old Kit had found himself pressed in that matter of the majority of the Nineteenth Dragoons, in which crack regiment his second son made for himself quite a career, he found it easier to sell than to save—seeing that that which he sold was his own and not the patrimony of the Dales. At his death the remainder of these purchases had gone. Family arrangements required completion, and Christopher Dale required ready money. The outlying farms flew away, as such new purchases had flown before; but the old patrimony of the Dales remained untouched, as it had ever remained.

It had been a religion among them; and seeing that the worship had been carried on without fail, that the vestal fire had never gone down upon the hearth, I should not have said that the Dales had walked their ways without high principle. To this religion they had all adhered, and the new heir had ever entered in upon his domain without other encumbrances than those with which he himself was then already burdened. And yet there had been no entail. The idea of an entail was not in accordance with the peculiarities of the Dale mind. It was necessary to the Dale religion that each squire should have the power of wasting them. I remember to have dined at a house, the whole glory and fortune of which depended on the safety of a glass goblet. We all know the story. If the luck of Edenhall should be shattered, the doom of the family would be sealed. Nevertheless I was bidden to drink out of the fatal glass, as were all guests in that house. It would not have contented the chivalrous mind of the master to protect his doom by lock and key and padded chest. And so it was with the Dales of Allington. To them an entail would have been a lock and key and a padded chest; but the old chivalry of their house denied to them the use of such protection.

I have spoken something slightingly of the acquirements and doings of the family; and indeed their acquirements had been few and their doings little. At Allington, Dale of Allington had always been known as

VIP MELIOR

9 point, 1 point leaded

FORMAT	PICAS	LINES	WPL	CPL	WPP	CPP
Royal 8vo	26×43	52	13.8	75	718	3900
Demy 8vo	24×40	48	12.8	69	614	3312
Large Crown 8vo	23×36	43	12.2	66	525	2838
Crown 8vo	21×34	41	11.1	60	455	2460

father to son, and from uncle to nephew, and, in one instance, from second cousin to second cousin, the sceptre had descended in the family of the Dales; and the acres had remained intact, growing in value and not decreasing in number, though guarded by no entail and protected by no wonderful amount of prudence or wisdom. The estate of Dale of Allington had been coterminous with the parish of Allington for some hundreds of years; and though, as I have said, the race of squires had possessed nothing of superhuman discretion and had perhaps been guided in their walks through life by no very distinct principles, still there had been with them so much of adherence to a sacred law, that no acre of the property had ever been parted from the hands of the existing squire. Some futile attempts had been made to increase the territory, as indeed had been done by Kit Dale, the father of Christopher Dale, who will appear as our squire of Allington when the persons of our drama are introduced. Old Kit Dale, who had married money, had bought outlying farms—a bit of ground here and a bit there—talking, as he did so, much of political influence and of the good old Tory cause. But these farms and bits of ground had gone again before our time. To them had been attached no religion. When old Kit had found himself pressed in that matter of the majority of the Nineteenth Dragoons, in which crack regiment his second son made for himself quite a career, he found it easier to sell than to save—seeing that that which he sold was his own and not the patrimony of the Dales. At his death the remainder of these purchases had gone. Family arrangements required completion, and Christopher Dale required ready money. The outlying farms flew away, as such new purchases had flown before; but the old patrimony of the Dales remained untouched, as it had ever remained.

It had been a religion among them; and seeing that the worship had been carried on without fail, that the vestal fire had never gone down upon the hearth, I should not have said that the Dales had walked their ways without high principle. To this religion they had all adhered, and the new heir had ever entered in upon his domain without other encumbrances than those with which he himself was then already burdened. And yet there had been no entail. The idea of an entail was not in accordance with the peculiarities of the Dale mind. It was necessary to the Dale religion that each squire should have the power of wasting them. I remember to have dined at a house, the whole glory and fortune of which depended on the safety of a glass goblet. We all know the story. If the luck of Edenhall should be shattered, the doom of the family would be sealed. Nevertheless I was bidden to drink out of the fatal glass, as were all guests in that house. It would not have contented the chivalrous mind of the master to protect his doom by lock and key and padded chest. And so it was with the Dales of Allington. To them an *entail would have been a lock and key and a padded chest; but the old chivalry of their house denied to them the use of such protection.*

I have spoken something slightingly of the acquirements and doings

VIP MELIOR

9 point, 1½ point leaded

FORMAT	PICAS	LINES	WPL	CPL	WPP	CPP
Royal 8vo	26×43	49	13.8	75	676	3675
Demy 8vo	24×40	46	12.8	69	589	3174
Large Crown 8vo	23×36	41	12.2	66	500	2706
Crown 8vo	21×34	39	11.1	60	433	2340

father to son, and from uncle to nephew, and, in one instance, from second cousin to second cousin, the sceptre had descended in the family of the Dales; and the acres had remained intact, growing in value and not decreasing in number, though guarded by no entail and protected by no wonderful amount of prudence or wisdom. The estate of Dale of Allington had been coterminous with the parish of Allington for some hundreds of years; and though, as I have said, the race of squires had possessed nothing of superhuman discretion and had perhaps been guided in their walks through life by no very distinct principles, still there had been with them so much of adherence to a sacred law, that no acre of the property had ever been parted from the hands of the existing squire. Some futile attempts had been made to increase the territory, as indeed had been done by Kit Dale, the father of Christopher Dale, who will appear as our squire of Allington when the persons of our drama are introduced. Old Kit Dale, who had married money, had bought outlying farms—a bit of ground here and a bit there—talking, as he did so, much of political influence and of the good old Tory cause. But these farms and bits of ground had gone again before our time. To them had been attached no religion. When old Kit had found himself pressed in that matter of the majority of the Nineteenth Dragoons, in which crack regiment his second son made for himself quite a career, he found it easier to sell than to save—seeing that that which he sold was his own and not the patrimony of the Dales. At his death the remainder of these purchases had gone. Family arrangements required completion, and Christopher Dale required ready money. The outlying farms flew away, as such new purchases had flown before; but the old patrimony of the Dales remained untouched, as it had ever remained.

It had been a religion among them; and seeing that the worship had been carried on without fail, that the vestal fire had never gone down upon the hearth, I should not have said that the Dales had walked their ways without high principle. To this religion they had all adhered, and the new heir had ever entered in upon his domain without other encumbrances than those with which he himself was then already burdened. And yet there had been no entail. The idea of an entail was not in accordance with the peculiarities of the Dale mind. It was necessary to the Dale religion that each squire should have the power of wasting them. I remember to have dined at a house, the whole glory and fortune of which depended on the safety of a glass goblet. We all know the story. If the luck of Edenhall should be shattered, the doom of the family would be sealed. Nevertheless I was bidden to drink out of the fatal glass, as were all guests in that house. It would not have contented *the chivalrous mind of the master to protect his doom by lock and key and padded chest. And so it was with the Dales of Allington. To them an entail would have been a lock and key and a padded chest; but the*

VIP MELIOR

9 point, 2 point leaded

FORMAT	PICAS	LINES	WPL	CPL	WPP	CPP
Royal 8vo	26×43	47	13.8	75	649	3525
Demy 8vo	24×40	44	12.8	69	563	3036
Large Crown 8vo	23×36	39	12.2	66	476	2574
Crown 8vo	21×34	37	11.1	60	411	2220

father to son, and from uncle to nephew, and, in one instance, from second cousin to second cousin, the sceptre had descended in the family of the Dales; and the acres had remained intact, growing in value and not decreasing in number, though guarded by no entail and protected by no wonderful amount of prudence or wisdom. The estate of Dale of Allington had been coterminous with the parish of Allington for some hundreds of years; and though, as I have said, the race of squires had possessed nothing of superhuman discretion and had perhaps been guided in their walks through life by no very distinct principles, still there had been with them so much of adherence to a sacred law, that no acre of the property had ever been parted from the hands of the existing squire. Some futile attempts had been made to increase the territory, as indeed had been done by Kit Dale, the father of Christopher Dale, who will appear as our squire of Allington when the persons of our drama are introduced. Old Kit Dale, who had married money, had bought outlying farms—a bit of ground here and a bit there—talking, as he did so, much of political influence and of the good old Tory cause. But these farms and bits of ground had gone again before our time. To them had been attached no religion. When old Kit had found himself pressed in that matter of the majority of the Nineteenth Dragoons, in which crack regiment his second son made for himself quite a career, he found it easier to sell than to save—seeing that that which he sold was his own and not the patrimony of the Dales. At his death the remainder of these purchases had gone. Family arrangements required completion, and Christopher Dale required ready money. The outlying farms flew away, as such new purchases had flown before; but the old patrimony of the Dales remained untouched, as it had ever remained.

It had been a religion among them; and seeing that the worship had been carried on without fail, that the vestal fire had never gone down upon the hearth, I should not have said that the Dales had walked their ways without high principle. To this religion they had all adhered, and the new heir had ever entered in upon his domain without other encumbrances than those with which he himself was then already burdened. And yet there had been no entail. The idea of an entail was not in accordance with the peculiarities of the Dale mind. It was necessary to the Dale religion that each squire should have the power *of wasting them. I remember to have dined at a house, the whole glory and fortune of which depended on the safety of a glass goblet. We all know the story. If the luck of Edenhall should be*

VIP MELIOR

10 point, 1 point leaded

FORMAT	PICAS	LINES	WPL	CPL	WPP	CPP
Royal 8vo	26×43	47	12.1	66	569	3102
Demy 8vo	24×40	44	11.2	61	493	2684
Large Crown 8vo	23×36	39	10.7	58	417	2262
Crown 8vo	21×34	37	9.7	53	359	1961

father to son, and from uncle to nephew, and, in one instance, from second cousin to second cousin, the sceptre had descended in the family of the Dales; and the acres had remained intact, growing in value and not decreasing in number, though guarded by no entail and protected by no wonderful amount of prudence or wisdom. The estate of Dale of Allington had been coterminous with the parish of Allington for some hundreds of years; and though, as I have said, the race of squires had possessed nothing of superhuman discretion and had perhaps been guided in their walks through life by no very distinct principles, still there had been with them so much of adherence to a sacred law, that no acre of the property had ever been parted from the hands of the existing squire. Some futile attempts had been made to increase the territory, as indeed had been done by Kit Dale, the father of Christopher Dale, who will appear as our squire of Allington when the persons of our drama are introduced. Old Kit Dale, who had married money, had bought outlying farms—a bit of ground here and a bit there—talking, as he did so, much of political influence and of the good old Tory cause. But these farms and bits of ground had gone again before our time. To them had been attached no religion. When old Kit had found himself pressed in that matter of the majority of the Nineteenth Dragoons, in which crack regiment his second son made for himself quite a career, he found it easier to sell than to save—seeing that that which he sold was his own and not the patrimony of the Dales. At his death the remainder of these purchases had gone. Family arrangements required completion, and Christopher Dale required ready money. The outlying farms flew away, as such new purchases had flown before; but the old patrimony of the Dales remained untouched, as it had ever remained.

It had been a religion among them; and seeing that the worship had been carried on without fail, that the vestal fire had never gone down upon the hearth, I should not have said that the Dales had walked their ways without high principle. To this religion they had all adhered, and the new heir had ever entered in upon his domain without other encumbrances than those with which he himself was then already burdened. And yet there had been no entail. The idea of an entail was not in *accordance with the peculiarities of the Dale mind. It was necessary to the Dale religion that each squire should have the power of wasting them. I remember to have dined at a house, the*

VIP MELIOR

10 point, 1½ point leaded

FORMAT	PICAS	LINES	WPL	CPL	WPP	CPP
Royal 8vo	26×43	45	12.1	66	545	2970
Demy 8vo	24×40	42	11.2	61	470	2562
Large Crown 8vo	23×36	38	10.7	58	407	2204
Crown 8vo	21×34	35	9.7	53	340	1855

father to son, and from uncle to nephew, and, in one instance, from second cousin to second cousin, the sceptre had descended in the family of the Dales; and the acres had remained intact, growing in value and not decreasing in number, though guarded by no entail and protected by no wonderful amount of prudence or wisdom. The estate of Dale of Allington had been coterminous with the parish of Allington for some hundreds of years; and though, as I have said, the race of squires had possessed nothing of superhuman discretion and had perhaps been guided in their walks through life by no very distinct principles, still there had been with them so much of adherence to a sacred law, that no acre of the property had ever been parted from the hands of the existing squire. Some futile attempts had been made to increase the territory, as indeed had been done by Kit Dale, the father of Christopher Dale, who will appear as our squire of Allington when the persons of our drama are introduced. Old Kit Dale, who had married money, had bought outlying farms—a bit of ground here and a bit there—talking, as he did so, much of political influence and of the good old Tory cause. But these farms and bits of ground had gone again before our time. To them had been attached no religion. When old Kit had found himself pressed in that matter of the majority of the Nineteenth Dragoons, in which crack regiment his second son made for himself quite a career, he found it easier to sell than to save—seeing that that which he sold was his own and not the patrimony of the Dales. At his death the remainder of these purchases had gone. Family arrangements required completion, and Christopher Dale required ready money. The outlying farms flew away, as such new purchases had flown before; but the old patrimony of the Dales remained untouched, as it had ever remained.

It had been a religion among them; and seeing that the worship had been carried on without fail, that the vestal fire had never gone down upon the hearth, I should not have said that the Dales had walked their ways without high principle. To this religion they had all adhered, and the new heir had ever entered in upon his domain without other encumbrances than those *with which he himself was then already burdened. And yet there had been no entail. The idea of an entail was not in accordance with the peculiarities of the Dale mind. It was*

VIP MELIOR

10 point, 2 point leaded

FORMAT	PICAS	LINES	WPL	CPL	WPP	CPP
Royal 8vo	26×43	43	12.1	66	520	2838
Demy 8vo	24×40	40	11.2	61	448	2440
Large Crown 8vo	23×36	36	10.7	58	385	2088
Crown 8vo	21×34	34	9.7	53	330	1802

father to son, and from uncle to nephew, and, in one instance, from second cousin to second cousin, the sceptre had descended in the family of the Dales; and the acres had remained intact, growing in value and not decreasing in number, though guarded by no entail and protected by no wonderful amount of prudence or wisdom. The estate of Dale of Allington had been coterminous with the parish of Allington for some hundreds of years; and though, as I have said, the race of squires had possessed nothing of superhuman discretion and had perhaps been guided in their walks through life by no very distinct principles, still there had been with them so much of adherence to a sacred law, that no acre of the property had ever been parted from the hands of the existing squire. Some futile attempts had been made to increase the territory, as indeed had been done by Kit Dale, the father of Christopher Dale, who will appear as our squire of Allington when the persons of our drama are introduced. Old Kit Dale, who had married money, had bought outlying farms—a bit of ground here and a bit there—talking, as he did so, much of political influence and of the good old Tory cause. But these farms and bits of ground had gone again before our time. To them had been attached no religion. When old Kit had found himself pressed in that matter of the majority of the Nineteenth Dragoons, in which crack regiment his second son made for himself quite a career, he found it easier to sell than to save—seeing that that which he sold was his own and not the patrimony of the Dales. At his death the remainder of these purchases had gone. Family arrangements required completion, and Christopher Dale required ready money. The outlying farms flew away, as such new purchases had flown before; but the old patrimony of the Dales remained untouched, as it had ever remained.

It had been a religion among them; and seeing that the worship had been carried on without fail, that the vestal fire had never gone down upon the hearth, I should not *have said that the Dales had walked their ways without high principle. To this religion they had all adhered, and the new heir had ever entered in upon his domain without*

VIP MELIOR

11 point, 1 point leaded

FORMAT	PICAS	LINES	WPL	CPL	WPP	CPP
Royal 8vo	26×43	43	10.9	61	469	2623
Demy 8vo	24×40	40	10.1	56	404	2240
Large Crown 8vo	23×36	36	9.6	54	346	1944
Crown 8vo	21×34	34	8.8	49	299	1666

father to son, and from uncle to nephew, and, in one instance, from second cousin to second cousin, the sceptre had descended in the family of the Dales; and the acres had remained intact, growing in value and not decreasing in number, though guarded by no entail and protected by no wonderful amount of prudence or wisdom. The estate of Dale of Allington had been coterminous with the parish of Allington for some hundreds of years; and though, as I have said, the race of squires had possessed nothing of superhuman discretion and had perhaps been guided in their walks through life by no very distinct principles, still there had been with them so much of adherence to a sacred law, that no acre of the property had ever been parted from the hands of the existing squire. Some futile attempts had been made to increase the territory, as indeed had been done by Kit Dale, the father of Christopher Dale, who will appear as our squire of Allington when the persons of our drama are introduced. Old Kit Dale, who had married money, had bought outlying farms—a bit of ground here and a bit there—talking, as he did so, much of political influence and of the good old Tory cause. But these farms and bits of ground had gone again before our time. To them had been attached no religion. When old Kit had found himself pressed in that matter of the majority of the Nineteenth Dragoons, in which crack regiment his second son made for himself quite a career, he found it easier to sell than to save—seeing that that which he sold was his own and not the patrimony of the Dales. At his death the remainder of these purchases had gone. Family arrangements required completion, and Christopher Dale required ready money. The outlying farms flew away, as such new purchases had flown before; but the old patrimony of the Dales remained untouched, as it had ever remained.

It had been a religion among them; and seeing that the *worship had been carried on without fail, that the vestal fire had never gone down upon the hearth, I should not have said that the Dales had walked their ways without*

VIP MELIOR

11 point, 1½ point leaded

FORMAT	PICAS	LINES	WPL	CPL	WPP	CPP
Royal 8vo	26×43	41	10.9	61	447	2501
Demy 8vo	24×40	38	10.1	56	384	2128
Large Crown 8vo	23×36	35	9.6	54	336	1890
Crown 8vo	21×34	33	8.8	49	290	1617

father to son, and from uncle to nephew, and, in one instance, from second cousin to second cousin, the sceptre had descended in the family of the Dales; and the acres had remained intact, growing in value and not decreasing in number, though guarded by no entail and protected by no wonderful amount of prudence or wisdom. The estate of Dale of Allington had been coterminous with the parish of Allington for some hundreds of years; and though, as I have said, the race of squires had possessed nothing of superhuman discretion and had perhaps been guided in their walks through life by no very distinct principles, still there had been with them so much of adherence to a sacred law, that no acre of the property had ever been parted from the hands of the existing squire. Some futile attempts had been made to increase the territory, as indeed had been done by Kit Dale, the father of Christopher Dale, who will appear as our squire of Allington when the persons of our drama are introduced. Old Kit Dale, who had married money, had bought outlying farms—a bit of ground here and a bit there—talking, as he did so, much of political influence and of the good old Tory cause. But these farms and bits of ground had gone again before our time. To them had been attached no religion. When old Kit had found himself pressed in that matter of the majority of the Nineteenth Dragoons, in which crack regiment his second son made for himself quite a career, he found it easier to sell than to save—seeing that that which he sold was his own and not the patrimony of the Dales. At his death the remainder of these purchases had gone. Family arrangements required completion, and Christopher Dale required ready money. The outlying farms flew away, as such new purchases had flown before; but the old patrimony of the Dales remained untouched, as it had ever remained.

It had been a religion among them; and seeing that the worship had been carried on without fail, that the vestal fire had never gone down upon the hearth, I should not

VIP MELIOR

11 point, 2 point leaded

FORMAT	PICAS	LINES	WPL	CPL	WPP	CPP
Royal 8vo	26×43	40	10.9	61	436	2440
Demy 8vo	24×40	37	10.1	56	374	2072
Large Crown 8vo	23×36	33	9.6	54	317	1782
Crown 8vo	21×34	31	8.8	49	273	1519

VIP OPTIMA

Synopsis in 10 point

ABCDEFGHIJKLMNOPQRSTUVWXYZ&ÆŒ

abcdefghijklmnopqrstuvwxyzæœ

.,:;!?''-()£ 1234567890

ABCDEFGHIJKLMNOPQRSTUVWXYZ&ÆŒ

abcdefghijklmnopqrstuvwxyzæœ

.,:;!?''-()£ 1234567890

Related bold

ABCDEFGHIJKLMNOPQRSTUVWXYZ&ÆŒ

abcdefghijklmnopqrstuvwxyzæœ

.,:;!?''-()£ 1234567890

All normal European accents available

father to son, and from uncle to nephew, and, in one instance, from second cousin to second cousin, the sceptre had descended in the family of the Dales; and the acres had remained intact, growing in value and not decreasing in number, though guarded by no entail and protected by no wonderful amount of prudence or wisdom. The estate of Dale of Allington had been coterminous with the parish of Allington for some hundreds of years; and though, as I have said, the race of squires had possessed nothing of superhuman discretion and had perhaps been guided in their walks through life by no very distinct principles, still there had been with them so much of adherence to a sacred law, that no acre of the property had ever been parted from the hands of the existing squire. Some futile attempts had been made to increase the territory, as indeed had been done by Kit Dale, the father of Christopher Dale, who will appear as our squire of Allington when the persons of our drama are introduced. Old Kit Dale, who had married money, had bought outlying farms—a bit of ground here and a bit there—talking, as he did so, much of political influence and of the good old Tory cause. But these farms and bits of ground had gone again before our time. To them had been attached no religion. When old Kit had found himself pressed in that matter of the majority of the Nineteenth Dragoons, in which crack regiment his second son made for himself quite a career, he found it easier to sell than to save—seeing that that which he sold was his own and not the patrimony of the Dales. At his death the remainder of these purchases had gone. Family arrangements required completion, and Christopher Dale required ready money. The outlying farms flew away, as such new purchases had flown before; but the old patrimony of the Dales remained untouched, as it had ever remained.

It had been a religion among them; and seeing that the worship had been carried on without fail, that the vestal fire had never gone down upon the hearth, I should not have said that the Dales had walked their ways without high principle. To this religion they had all adhered, and the new heir had ever entered in upon his domain without other encumbrances than those with which he himself was then already burdened. And yet there had been no entail. The idea of an entail was not in accordance with the peculiarities of the Dale mind. It was necessary to the Dale religion that each squire should have the power of wasting them. I remember to have dined at a house, the whole glory and fortune of which depended on the safety of a glass goblet. We all know the story. If the luck of Edenhall should be shattered, the doom of the family would be sealed. Nevertheless I was bidden to drink out of the fatal glass, as were all guests in that house. It would not have contented the chivalrous mind of the master to protect his doom by lock and key and padded chest. And so it was with the Dales of Allington. To them an entail would have been a lock and key and a padded chest; but the old chivalry of their house denied to them the use of such protection.

I have spoken something slightingly of the acquirements and doings of the family; and indeed their acquirements had been few and their doings little. *At Allington, Dale of Allington had always been known as a king. At Guestwick, the neighbouring market town, he was a great man—to be seen frequently on Saturdays, standing in the market-place, and laying down the*

VIP OPTIMA

9 point, 1 point leaded

FORMAT	PICAS	LINES	WPL	CPL	WPP	CPP
Royal 8vo	26×43	52	14.8	80	770	4160
Demy 8vo	24×40	48	13.7	74	658	3552
Large Crown 8vo	23×36	43	13.1	71	563	3053
Crown 8vo	21×34	41	11.9	65	488	2665

father to son, and from uncle to nephew, and, in one instance, from second cousin to second cousin, the sceptre had descended in the family of the Dales; and the acres had remained intact, growing in value and not decreasing in number, though guarded by no entail and protected by no wonderful amount of prudence or wisdom. The estate of Dale of Allington had been coterminous with the parish of Allington for some hundreds of years; and though, as I have said, the race of squires had possessed nothing of superhuman discretion and had perhaps been guided in their walks through life by no very distinct principles, still there had been with them so much of adherence to a sacred law, that no acre of the property had ever been parted from the hands of the existing squire. Some futile attempts had been made to increase the territory, as indeed had been done by Kit Dale, the father of Christopher Dale, who will appear as our squire of Allington when the persons of our drama are introduced. Old Kit Dale, who had married money, had bought outlying farms—a bit of ground here and a bit there—talking, as he did so, much of political influence and of the good old Tory cause. But these farms and bits of ground had gone again before our time. To them had been attached no religion. When old Kit had found himself pressed in that matter of the majority of the Nineteenth Dragoons, in which crack regiment his second son made for himself quite a career, he found it easier to sell than to save—seeing that that which he sold was his own and not the patrimony of the Dales. At his death the remainder of these purchases had gone. Family arrangements required completion, and Christopher Dale required ready money. The outlying farms flew away, as such new purchases had flown before; but the old patrimony of the Dales remained untouched, as it had ever remained.

It had been a religion among them; and seeing that the worship had been carried on without fail, that the vestal fire had never gone down upon the hearth, I should not have said that the Dales had walked their ways without high principle. To this religion they had all adhered, and the new heir had ever entered in upon his domain without other encumbrances than those with which he himself was then already burdened. And yet there had been no entail. The idea of an entail was not in accordance with the peculiarities of the Dale mind. It was necessary to the Dale religion that each squire should have the power of wasting them. I remember to have dined at a house, the whole glory and fortune of which depended on the safety of a glass goblet. We all know the story. If the luck of Edenhall should be shattered, the doom of the family would be sealed. Nevertheless I was bidden to drink out of the fatal glass, as were all guests in that house. It would not have contented the chivalrous mind of the master to protect his doom by lock and key and padded chest. And so it was with the Dales of Allington. To them an entail would have been a lock and key and a padded chest; but the old chivalry of their house denied to them the use of such protection.

I have spoken something slightingly of the acquirements and doings of the family; and indeed their acquirements had been few and their doings little. At Allington, Dale of Allington had always been known as a king. At

VIP OPTIMA

9 point, 1½ point leaded

FORMAT	PICAS	LINES	WPL	CPL	WPP	CPP
Royal 8vo	26×43	49	14.8	80	725	3920
Demy 8vo	24×40	46	13.7	74	630	3404
Large Crown 8vo	23×36	41	13.1	71	537	2911
Crown 8vo	21×34	39	11.9	65	464	2535

father to son, and from uncle to nephew, and, in one instance, from second cousin to second cousin, the sceptre had descended in the family of the Dales; and the acres had remained intact, growing in value and not decreasing in number, though guarded by no entail and protected by no wonderful amount of prudence or wisdom. The estate of Dale of Allington had been coterminous with the parish of Allington for some hundreds of years; and though, as I have said, the race of squires had possessed nothing of superhuman discretion and had perhaps been guided in their walks through life by no very distinct principles, still there had been with them so much of adherence to a sacred law, that no acre of the property had ever been parted from the hands of the existing squire. Some futile attempts had been made to increase the territory, as indeed had been done by Kit Dale, the father of Christopher Dale, who will appear as our squire of Allington when the persons of our drama are introduced. Old Kit Dale, who had married money, had bought outlying farms—a bit of ground here and a bit there—talking, as he did so, much of political influence and of the good old Tory cause. But these farms and bits of ground had gone again before our time. To them had been attached no religion. When old Kit had found himself pressed in that matter of the majority of the Nineteenth Dragoons, in which crack regiment his second son made for himself quite a career, he found it easier to sell than to save—seeing that that which he sold was his own and not the patrimony of the Dales. At his death the remainder of these purchases had gone. Family arrangements required completion, and Christopher Dale required ready money. The outlying farms flew away, as such new purchases had flown before; but the old patrimony of the Dales remained untouched, as it had ever remained.

It had been a religion among them; and seeing that the worship had been carried on without fail, that the vestal fire had never gone down upon the hearth, I should not have said that the Dales had walked their ways without high principle. To this religion they had all adhered, and the new heir had ever entered in upon his domain without other encumbrances than those with which he himself was then already burdened. And yet there had been no entail. The idea of an entail was not in accordance with the peculiarities of the Dale mind. It was necessary to the Dale religion that each squire should have the power of wasting them. I remember to have dined at a house, the whole glory and fortune of which depended on the safety of a glass goblet. We all know the story. If the luck of Edenhall should be shattered, the doom of the family would be sealed. Nevertheless I was bidden to drink out of the fatal glass, as were all guests in that house. It would not have contented the chivalrous mind of the master to protect his doom by lock and key and padded chest. And so it was with the Dales of Allington. To them an entail *would have been a lock and key and a padded chest; but the old chivalry of their house denied to them the use of such protection.*

I have spoken something slightingly of the acquirements and doings of the

VIP OPTIMA

9 point, 2 point leaded

FORMAT	PICAS	LINES	WPL	CPL	WPP	CPP
Royal 8vo	26×43	47	14.8	80	696	3760
Demy 8vo	24×40	44	13.7	74	603	3256
Large Crown 8vo	23×36	39	13.1	71	511	2769
Crown 8vo	21×34	37	11.9	65	440	2405

father to son, and from uncle to nephew, and, in one instance, from second cousin to second cousin, the sceptre had descended in the family of the Dales; and the acres had remained intact, growing in value and not decreasing in number, though guarded by no entail and protected by no wonderful amount of prudence or wisdom. The estate of Dale of Allington had been coterminous with the parish of Allington for some hundreds of years; and though, as I have said, the race of squires had possessed nothing of superhuman discretion and had perhaps been guided in their walks through life by no very distinct principles, still there had been with them so much of adherence to a sacred law, that no acre of the property had ever been parted from the hands of the existing squire. Some futile attempts had been made to increase the territory, as indeed had been done by Kit Dale, the father of Christopher Dale, who will appear as our squire of Allington when the persons of our drama are introduced. Old Kit Dale, who had married money, had bought outlying farms—a bit of ground here and a bit there—talking, as he did so, much of political influence and of the good old Tory cause. But these farms and bits of ground had gone again before our time. To them had been attached no religion. When old Kit had found himself pressed in that matter of the majority of the Nineteenth Dragoons, in which crack regiment his second son made for himself quite a career, he found it easier to sell than to save—seeing that that which he sold was his own and not the patrimony of the Dales. At his death the remainder of these purchases had gone. Family arrangements required completion, and Christopher Dale required ready money. The outlying farms flew away, as such new purchases had flown before; but the old patrimony of the Dales remained untouched, as it had ever remained.

It had been a religion among them; and seeing that the worship had been carried on without fail, that the vestal fire had never gone down upon the hearth, I should not have said that the Dales had walked their ways without high principle. To this religion they had all adhered, and the new heir had ever entered in upon his domain without other encumbrances than those with which he himself was then already burdened. And yet there had been no entail. The idea of an entail was not in accordance with the peculiarities of the Dale mind. It was necessary to the Dale religion that each squire should have the power of wasting them. I remember to have dined at a house, the whole glory and fortune of which depended on the safety of a glass goblet. We all know the story. If the luck of Edenhall should be shattered, the doom of the family would be sealed. Nevertheless I *was bidden to drink out of the fatal glass, as were all guests in that house. It would not have contented the chivalrous mind of the master to protect his doom by lock and key and padded chest. And so it was*

VIP OPTIMA

10 point, 1 point leaded

FORMAT	PICAS	LINES	WPL	CPL	WPP	CPP
Royal 8vo	26×43	47	13.1	72	616	3384
Demy 8vo	24×40	44	12.1	66	532	2904
Large Crown 8vo	23×36	39	11.6	63	452	2457
Crown 8vo	21×34	37	10.5	58	389	2146

father to son, and from uncle to nephew, and, in one instance, from second cousin to second cousin, the sceptre had descended in the family of the Dales; and the acres had remained intact, growing in value and not decreasing in number, though guarded by no entail and protected by no wonderful amount of prudence or wisdom. The estate of Dale of Allington had been coterminous with the parish of Allington for some hundreds of years; and though, as I have said, the race of squires had possessed nothing of superhuman discretion and had perhaps been guided in their walks through life by no very distinct principles, still there had been with them so much of adherence to a sacred law, that no acre of the property had ever been parted from the hands of the existing squire. Some futile attempts had been made to increase the territory, as indeed had been done by Kit Dale, the father of Christopher Dale, who will appear as our squire of Allington when the persons of our drama are introduced. Old Kit Dale, who had married money, had bought outlying farms—a bit of ground here and a bit there—talking, as he did so, much of political influence and of the good old Tory cause. But these farms and bits of ground had gone again before our time. To them had been attached no religion. When old Kit had found himself pressed in that matter of the majority of the Nineteenth Dragoons, in which crack regiment his second son made for himself quite a career, he found it easier to sell than to save—seeing that that which he sold was his own and not the patrimony of the Dales. At his death the remainder of these purchases had gone. Family arrangements required completion, and Christopher Dale required ready money. The outlying farms flew away, as such new purchases had flown before; but the old patrimony of the Dales remained untouched, as it had ever remained.

It had been a religion among them; and seeing that the worship had been carried on without fail, that the vestal fire had never gone down upon the hearth, I should not have said that the Dales had walked their ways without high principle. To this religion they had all adhered, and the new heir had ever entered in upon his domain without other encumbrances than those with which he himself was then already burdened. And yet there had been no entail. The idea of an entail was not in accordance with the peculiarities of the Dale mind. It was necessary to the Dale religion that each squire should have the power of wasting them. I remember to have dined at a house, the whole glory and fortune of which depended on the safety *of a glass goblet. We all know the story. If the luck of Edenhall should be shattered, the doom of the family would be sealed. Nevertheless I was bidden to drink out of the fatal glass, as were all guests in that*

VIP OPTIMA

10 point, 1½ point leaded

FORMAT	PICAS	LINES	WPL	CPL	WPP	CPP
Royal 8vo	26×43	45	13.1	72	590	3240
Demy 8vo	24×40	42	12.1	66	508	2772
Large Crown 8vo	23×36	38	11.6	63	441	2394
Crown 8vo	21×34	35	10.5	58	368	2030

father to son, and from uncle to nephew, and, in one instance, from second cousin to second cousin, the sceptre had descended in the family of the Dales; and the acres had remained intact, growing in value and not decreasing in number, though guarded by no entail and protected by no wonderful amount of prudence or wisdom. The estate of Dale of Allington had been coterminous with the parish of Allington for some hundreds of years; and though, as I have said, the race of squires had possessed nothing of superhuman discretion and had perhaps been guided in their walks through life by no very distinct principles, still there had been with them so much of adherence to a sacred law, that no acre of the property had ever been parted from the hands of the existing squire. Some futile attempts had been made to increase the territory, as indeed had been done by Kit Dale, the father of Christopher Dale, who will appear as our squire of Allington when the persons of our drama are introduced. Old Kit Dale, who had married money, had bought outlying farms—a bit of ground here and a bit there—talking, as he did so, much of political influence and of the good old Tory cause. But these farms and bits of ground had gone again before our time. To them had been attached no religion. When old Kit had found himself pressed in that matter of the majority of the Nineteenth Dragoons, in which crack regiment his second son made for himself quite a career, he found it easier to sell than to save—seeing that that which he sold was his own and not the patrimony of the Dales. At his death the remainder of these purchases had gone. Family arrangements required completion, and Christopher Dale required ready money. The outlying farms flew away, as such new purchases had flown before; but the old patrimony of the Dales remained untouched, as it had ever remained.

It had been a religion among them; and seeing that the worship had been carried on without fail, that the vestal fire had never gone down upon the hearth, I should not have said that the Dales had walked their ways without high principle. To this religion they had all adhered, and the new heir had ever entered in upon his domain without other encumbrances than those with which he himself was then already burdened. And yet there had been no entail. The idea of an entail was not in accordance with the peculiarities of the Dale mind. It was necessary to the Dale religion that each squire should *have the power of wasting them. I remember to have dined at a house, the whole glory and fortune of which depended on the safety of a glass goblet. We all know the story. If the luck of Edenhall should*

VIP OPTIMA

10 point, 2 point leaded

FORMAT	PICAS	LINES	WPL	CPL	WPP	CPP
Royal 8vo	26×43	43	13.1	72	563	3096
Demy 8vo	24×40	40	12.1	66	484	2640
Large Crown 8vo	23×36	36	11.6	63	418	2268
Crown 8vo	21×34	34	10.5	58	357	1972

father to son, and from uncle to nephew, and, in one instance, from second cousin to second cousin, the sceptre had descended in the family of the Dales; and the acres had remained intact, growing in value and not decreasing in number, though guarded by no entail and protected by no wonderful amount of prudence or wisdom. The estate of Dale of Allington had been coterminous with the parish of Allington for some hundreds of years; and though, as I have said, the race of squires had possessed nothing of superhuman discretion and had perhaps been guided in their walks through life by no very distinct principles, still there had been with them so much of adherence to a sacred law, that no acre of the property had ever been parted from the hands of the existing squire. Some futile attempts had been made to increase the territory, as indeed had been done by Kit Dale, the father of Christopher Dale, who will appear as our squire of Allington when the persons of our drama are introduced. Old Kit Dale, who had married money, had bought outlying farms—a bit of ground here and a bit there—talking, as he did so, much of political influence and of the good old Tory cause. But these farms and bits of ground had gone again before our time. To them had been attached no religion. When old Kit had found himself pressed in that matter of the majority of the Nineteenth Dragoons, in which crack regiment his second son made for himself quite a career, he found it easier to sell than to save—seeing that that which he sold was his own and not the patrimony of the Dales. At his death the remainder of these purchases had gone. Family arrangements required completion, and Christopher Dale required ready money. The outlying farms flew away, as such new purchases had flown before; but the old patrimony of the Dales remained untouched, as it had ever remained.

It had been a religion among them; and seeing that the worship had been carried on without fail, that the vestal fire had never gone down upon the hearth, I should not have said that the Dales had walked their ways without high principle. To this religion they had all adhered, and the new heir had ever *entered in upon his domain without other encumbrances than those with which he himself was then already burdened. And yet there had been no entail. The idea of an entail was not in*

VIP OPTIMA

11 point, 1 point leaded

FORMAT	PICAS	LINES	WPL	CPL	WPP	CPP
Royal 8vo	26×43	43	11.6	63	499	2709
Demy 8vo	24×40	40	10.7	58	428	2320
Large Crown 8vo	23×36	36	10.2	56	367	2016
Crown 8vo	21×34	34	9.3	51	316	1734

father to son, and from uncle to nephew, and, in one instance, from second cousin to second cousin, the sceptre had descended in the family of the Dales; and the acres had remained intact, growing in value and not decreasing in number, though guarded by no entail and protected by no wonderful amount of prudence or wisdom. The estate of Dale of Allington had been coterminous with the parish of Allington for some hundreds of years; and though, as I have said, the race of squires had possessed nothing of superhuman discretion and had perhaps been guided in their walks through life by no very distinct principles, still there had been with them so much of adherence to a sacred law, that no acre of the property had ever been parted from the hands of the existing squire. Some futile attempts had been made to increase the territory, as indeed had been done by Kit Dale, the father of Christopher Dale, who will appear as our squire of Allington when the persons of our drama are introduced. Old Kit Dale, who had married money, had bought outlying farms—a bit of ground here and a bit there—talking, as he did so, much of political influence and of the good old Tory cause. But these farms and bits of ground had gone again before our time. To them had been attached no religion. When old Kit had found himself pressed in that matter of the majority of the Nineteenth Dragoons, in which crack regiment his second son made for himself quite a career, he found it easier to sell than to save—seeing that that which he sold was his own and not the patrimony of the Dales. At his death the remainder of these purchases had gone. Family arrangements required completion, and Christopher Dale required ready money. The outlying farms flew away, as such new purchases had flown before; but the old patrimony of the Dales remained untouched, as it had ever remained.

It had been a religion among them; and seeing that the worship had been carried on without fail, that the vestal fire had never gone down upon the hearth, I should not have said *that the Dales had walked their ways without high principle. To this religion they had all adhered, and the new heir had ever entered in upon his domain without other encumbrances than*

VIP OPTIMA

11 point, 1½ point leaded

FORMAT	PICAS	LINES	WPL	CPL	WPP	CPP
Royal 8vo	26×43	41	11.6	63	476	2583
Demy 8vo	24×40	38	10.7	58	407	2204
Large Crown 8vo	23×36	35	10.2	56	357	1960
Crown 8vo	21×34	33	9.3	51	307	1683

father to son, and from uncle to nephew, and, in one instance, from second cousin to second cousin, the sceptre had descended in the family of the Dales; and the acres had remained intact, growing in value and not decreasing in number, though guarded by no entail and protected by no wonderful amount of prudence or wisdom. The estate of Dale of Allington had been coterminous with the parish of Allington for some hundreds of years; and though, as I have said, the race of squires had possessed nothing of superhuman discretion and had perhaps been guided in their walks through life by no very distinct principles, still there had been with them so much of adherence to a sacred law, that no acre of the property had ever been parted from the hands of the existing squire. Some futile attempts had been made to increase the territory, as indeed had been done by Kit Dale, the father of Christopher Dale, who will appear as our squire of Allington when the persons of our drama are introduced. Old Kit Dale, who had married money, had bought outlying farms—a bit of ground here and a bit there—talking, as he did so, much of political influence and of the good old Tory cause. But these farms and bits of ground had gone again before our time. To them had been attached no religion. When old Kit had found himself pressed in that matter of the majority of the Nineteenth Dragoons, in which crack regiment his second son made for himself quite a career, he found it easier to sell than to save—seeing that that which he sold was his own and not the patrimony of the Dales. At his death the remainder of these purchases had gone. Family arrangements required completion, and Christopher Dale required ready money. The outlying farms flew away, as such new purchases had flown before; but the old patrimony of the Dales remained untouched, as it had ever remained.

It had been a religion among them; and seeing that the worship had been carried on without fail, that the vestal fire *had never gone down upon the hearth, I should not have said that the Dales had walked their ways without high principle. To this religion they had all adhered, and the new heir had ever*

VIP OPTIMA

11 point, 2 point leaded

FORMAT	PICAS	LINES	WPL	CPL	WPP	CPP
Royal 8vo	26×43	40	11.6	63	464	2520
Demy 8vo	24×40	37	10.7	58	396	2204
Large Crown 8vo	23×36	33	10.2	56	337	1848
Crown 8vo	21×34	31	9.3	51	288	1581

VIP PALATINO

Synopsis in 10 point

ABCDEFGHIJKLMNOPQRSTUVWXYZ&ÆŒ

ABCDEFGHIJKLMNOPQRSTUVWXYZ

abcdefghijklmnopqrstuvwxyzæœ

.,:;!?"-()£ 1234567890 1234567890

ABCDEFGHIJKLMNOPQRSTUVWXYZ&ÆŒ

abcdefghijklmnopqrstuvwxyzæœ

.,:;!?"-()£ 1234567890

Related bold

ABCDEFGHIJKLMNOPQRSTUVWXYZ&ÆŒ

abcdefghijklmnopqrstuvwxyzæœ

.,:;!?"-()£ 1234567890

ABCDEFGHIJKLMNOPQRSTUVWXYZ&ÆŒ

abcdefghijklmnopqrstuvwxyzæœ

.,:;!?"-()£ 1234567890

All normal European accents available

father to son, and from uncle to nephew, and, in one instance, from second cousin to second cousin, the sceptre had descended in the family of the Dales; and the acres had remained intact, growing in value and not decreasing in number, though guarded by no entail and protected by no wonderful amount of prudence or wisdom. The estate of Dale of Allington had been coterminous with the parish of Allington for some hundreds of years; and though, as I have said, the race of squires had possessed nothing of superhuman discretion and had perhaps been guided in their walks through life by no very distinct principles, still there had been with them so much of adherence to a sacred law, that no acre of the property had ever been parted from the hands of the existing squire. Some futile attempts had been made to increase the territory, as indeed had been done by Kit Dale, the father of Christopher Dale, who will appear as our squire of Allington when the persons of our drama are introduced. Old Kit Dale, who had married money, had bought outlying farms—a bit of ground here and a bit there—talking, as he did so, much of political influence and of the good old Tory cause. But these farms and bits of ground had gone again before our time. To them had been attached no religion. When old Kit had found himself pressed in that matter of the majority of the Nineteenth Dragoons, in which crack regiment his second son made for himself quite a career, he found it easier to sell than to save—seeing that that which he sold was his own and not the patrimony of the Dales. At his death the remainder of these purchases had gone. Family arrangements required completion, and Christopher Dale required ready money. The outlying farms flew away, as such new purchases had flown before; but the old patrimony of the Dales remained untouched, as it had ever remained.

It had been a religion among them; and seeing that the worship had been carried on without fail, that the vestal fire had never gone down upon the hearth, I should not have said that the Dales had walked their ways without high principle. To this religion they had all adhered, and the new heir had ever entered in upon his domain without other encumbrances than those with which he himself was then already burdened. And yet there had been no entail. The idea of an entail was not in accordance with the peculiarities of the Dale mind. It was necessary to the Dale religion that each squire should have the power of wasting them. I remember to have dined at a house, the whole glory and fortune of which depended on the safety of a glass goblet. We all know the story. If the luck of Edenhall should be shattered, the doom of the family would be sealed. Nevertheless I was bidden to drink out of the fatal glass, as were all guests in that house. It would not have contented the chivalrous mind of the master to protect his doom by lock and key and padded chest. And so it was with the Dales of Allington. To them an entail would have been a lock and key and a padded chest; but the old chivalry of their house denied to them the use of such protection.

I have spoken something slightingly of the acquirements and doings of the family; and indeed their acquirements had been few and their doings little. At Allington, Dale of Allington had always been known as a king. At Guestwick,

VIP PALATINO

9 point, 1 point leaded

FORMAT	PICAS	LINES	WPL	CPL	WPP	CPP
Royal 8vo	26×43	52	13.9	75	723	3900
Demy 8vo	24×40	48	12.9	69	619	3312
Large Crown 8vo	23×36	43	12.3	66	529	2838
Crown 8vo	21×34	41	11.2	60	459	2460

father to son, and from uncle to nephew, and, in one instance, from second cousin to second cousin, the sceptre had descended in the family of the Dales; and the acres had remained intact, growing in value and not decreasing in number, though guarded by no entail and protected by no wonderful amount of prudence or wisdom. The estate of Dale of Allington had been coterminous with the parish of Allington for some hundreds of years; and though, as I have said, the race of squires had possessed nothing of superhuman discretion and had perhaps been guided in their walks through life by no very distinct principles, still there had been with them so much of adherence to a sacred law, that no acre of the property had ever been parted from the hands of the existing squire. Some futile attempts had been made to increase the territory, as indeed had been done by Kit Dale, the father of Christopher Dale, who will appear as our squire of Allington when the persons of our drama are introduced. Old Kit Dale, who had married money, had bought outlying farms—a bit of ground here and a bit there—talking, as he did so, much of political influence and of the good old Tory cause. But these farms and bits of ground had gone again before our time. To them had been attached no religion. When old Kit had found himself pressed in that matter of the majority of the Nineteenth Dragoons, in which crack regiment his second son made for himself quite a career, he found it easier to sell than to save—seeing that that which he sold was his own and not the patrimony of the Dales. At his death the remainder of these purchases had gone. Family arrangements required completion, and Christopher Dale required ready money. The outlying farms flew away, as such new purchases had flown before; but the old patrimony of the Dales remained untouched, as it had ever remained.

It had been a religion among them; and seeing that the worship had been carried on without fail, that the vestal fire had never gone down upon the hearth, I should not have said that the Dales had walked their ways without high principle. To this religion they had all adhered, and the new heir had ever entered in upon his domain without other encumbrances than those with which he himself was then already burdened. And yet there had been no entail. The idea of an entail was not in accordance with the peculiarities of the Dale mind. It was necessary to the Dale religion that each squire should have the power of wasting them. I remember to have dined at a house, the whole glory and fortune of which depended on the safety of a glass goblet. We all know the story. If the luck of Edenhall should be shattered, the doom of the family would be sealed. Nevertheless I was bidden to drink out of the fatal glass, as were all guests in that house. It would not have contented the chivalrous mind of the master to protect his doom by lock and key and padded chest. And so it was with the Dales of Allington. To them an entail would *have been a lock and key and a padded chest; but the old chivalry of their house denied to them the use of such protection.*

I have spoken something slightingly of the acquirements and doings of the

VIP PALATINO

9 point, 1½ point leaded

FORMAT	PICAS	LINES	WPL	CPL	WPP	CPP
Royal 8vo	26×43	49	13.9	75	681	3675
Demy 8vo	24×40	46	12.9	69	593	3174
Large Crown 8vo	23×36	41	12.3	66	504	2706
Crown 8vo	21×34	39	11.2	60	437	2340

father to son, and from uncle to nephew, and, in one instance, from second cousin to second cousin, the sceptre had descended in the family of the Dales; and the acres had remained intact, growing in value and not decreasing in number, though guarded by no entail and protected by no wonderful amount of prudence or wisdom. The estate of Dale of Allington had been coterminous with the parish of Allington for some hundreds of years; and though, as I have said, the race of squires had possessed nothing of superhuman discretion and had perhaps been guided in their walks through life by no very distinct principles, still there had been with them so much of adherence to a sacred law, that no acre of the property had ever been parted from the hands of the existing squire. Some futile attempts had been made to increase the territory, as indeed had been done by Kit Dale, the father of Christopher Dale, who will appear as our squire of Allington when the persons of our drama are introduced. Old Kit Dale, who had married money, had bought outlying farms—a bit of ground here and a bit there—talking, as he did so, much of political influence and of the good old Tory cause. But these farms and bits of ground had gone again before our time. To them had been attached no religion. When old Kit had found himself pressed in that matter of the majority of the Nineteenth Dragoons, in which crack regiment his second son made for himself quite a career, he found it easier to sell than to save—seeing that that which he sold was his own and not the patrimony of the Dales. At his death the remainder of these purchases had gone. Family arrangements required completion, and Christopher Dale required ready money. The outlying farms flew away, as such new purchases had flown before; but the old patrimony of the Dales remained untouched, as it had ever remained.

It had been a religion among them; and seeing that the worship had been carried on without fail, that the vestal fire had never gone down upon the hearth, I should not have said that the Dales had walked their ways without high principle. To this religion they had all adhered, and the new heir had ever entered in upon his domain without other encumbrances than those with which he himself was then already burdened. And yet there had been no entail. The idea of an entail was not in accordance with the peculiarities of the Dale mind. It was necessary to the Dale religion that each squire should have the power of wasting them. I remember to have dined at a house, the whole glory and fortune of which depended on the safety of a glass goblet. We all know the story. If the luck of Edenhall should be shattered, the doom of the family would be sealed. Nevertheless I was bidden to drink out of the fatal glass, as were all guests in that house. It would not have contented the chivalrous *mind of the master to protect his doom by lock and key and padded chest. And so it was with the Dales of Allington. To them an entail would have been a lock and key and a padded chest; but the old chivalry of their house denied to them the use*

VIP PALATINO

9 point, 2 point leaded

FORMAT	PICAS	LINES	WPL	CPL	WPP	CPP
Royal 8vo	26×43	47	13.9	75	653	3525
Demy 8vo	24×40	44	12.9	69	568	3036
Large Crown 8vo	23×36	39	12.3	66	480	2574
Crown 8vo	21×34	37	11.2	60	414	2220

father to son, and from uncle to nephew, and, in one instance, from second cousin to second cousin, the sceptre had descended in the family of the Dales; and the acres had remained intact, growing in value and not decreasing in number, though guarded by no entail and protected by no wonderful amount of prudence or wisdom. The estate of Dale of Allington had been coterminous with the parish of Allington for some hundreds of years; and though, as I have said, the race of squires had possessed nothing of superhuman discretion and had perhaps been guided in their walks through life by no very distinct principles, still there had been with them so much of adherence to a sacred law, that no acre of the property had ever been parted from the hands of the existing squire. Some futile attempts had been made to increase the territory, as indeed had been done by Kit Dale, the father of Christopher Dale, who will appear as our squire of Allington when the persons of our drama are introduced. Old Kit Dale, who had married money, had bought outlying farms—a bit of ground here and a bit there—talking, as he did so, much of political influence and of the good old Tory cause. But these farms and bits of ground had gone again before our time. To them had been attached no religion. When old Kit had found himself pressed in that matter of the majority of the Nineteenth Dragoons, in which crack regiment his second son made for himself quite a career, he found it easier to sell than to save—seeing that that which he sold was his own and not the patrimony of the Dales. At his death the remainder of these purchases had gone. Family arrangements required completion, and Christopher Dale required ready money. The outlying farms flew away, as such new purchases had flown before; but the old patrimony of the Dales remained untouched, as it had ever remained.

It had been a religion among them; and seeing that the worship had been carried on without fail, that the vestal fire had never gone down upon the hearth, I should not have said that the Dales had walked their ways without high principle. To this religion they had all adhered, and the new heir had ever entered in upon his domain without other encumbrances than those with which he himself was then already burdened. And yet there had been no entail. The idea of an entail was not in accordance with the peculiarities of the Dale mind. It was necessary to the Dale religion that each squire should have the power of wasting them. I remember to have dined at a house, the whole glory and fortune *of which depended on the safety of a glass goblet. We all know the story. If the luck of Edenhall should be shattered, the doom of the family would be sealed. Nevertheless I was bidden to drink out of the fatal glass, as were*

VIP PALATINO

10 point, 1 point leaded

FORMAT	PICAS	LINES	WPL	CPL	WPP	CPP
Royal 8vo	26×43	47	12.0	67	564	3149
Demy 8vo	24×40	44	11.1	62	488	2728
Large Crown 8vo	23×34	39	10.6	59	413	2301
Crown 8vo	21×34	37	9.7	54	359	1998

father to son, and from uncle to nephew, and, in one instance, from second cousin to second cousin, the sceptre had descended in the family of the Dales; and the acres had remained intact, growing in value and not decreasing in number, though guarded by no entail and protected by no wonderful amount of prudence or wisdom. The estate of Dale of Allington had been coterminous with the parish of Allington for some hundreds of years; and though, as I have said, the race of squires had possessed nothing of superhuman discretion and had perhaps been guided in their walks through life by no very distinct principles, still there had been with them so much of adherence to a sacred law, that no acre of the property had ever been parted from the hands of the existing squire. Some futile attempts had been made to increase the territory, as indeed had been done by Kit Dale, the father of Christopher Dale, who will appear as our squire of Allington when the persons of our drama are introduced. Old Kit Dale, who had married money, had bought outlying farms—a bit of ground here and a bit there—talking, as he did so, much of political influence and of the good old Tory cause. But these farms and bits of ground had gone again before our time. To them had been attached no religion. When old Kit had found himself pressed in that matter of the majority of the Nineteenth Dragoons, in which crack regiment his second son made for himself quite a career, he found it easier to sell than to save—seeing that that which he sold was his own and not the patrimony of the Dales. At his death the remainder of these purchases had gone. Family arrangements required completion, and Christopher Dale required ready money. The outlying farms flew away, as such new purchases had flown before; but the old patrimony of the Dales remained untouched, as it had ever remained.

It had been a religion among them; and seeing that the worship had been carried on without fail, that the vestal fire had never gone down upon the hearth, I should not have said that the Dales had walked their ways without high principle. To this religion they had all adhered, and the new heir had ever entered in upon his domain without other encumbrances than those with which he himself was then already burdened. And yet there had been no entail. The idea of an entail was not in accordance with the peculiarities of the Dale mind. It was necessary to the Dale relig*ion that each squire should have the power of wasting them. I remember to have dined at a house, the whole glory and fortune of which depended on the safety of a glass goblet. We all know the story. If the luck of*

VIP PALATINO

10 point, 1½ point leaded

FORMAT	PICAS	LINES	WPL	CPL	WPP	CPP
Royal 8vo	26×43	45	12.0	67	540	3015
Demy 8vo	24×40	42	11.1	62	466	2604
Large Crown 8vo	23×36	38	10.6	59	403	2242
Crown 8vo	21×34	35	9.7	54	340	1890

father to son, and from uncle to nephew, and, in one instance, from second cousin to second cousin, the sceptre had descended in the family of the Dales; and the acres had remained intact, growing in value and not decreasing in number, though guarded by no entail and protected by no wonderful amount of prudence or wisdom. The estate of Dale of Allington had been coterminous with the parish of Allington for some hundreds of years; and though, as I have said, the race of squires had possessed nothing of superhuman discretion and had perhaps been guided in their walks through life by no very distinct principles, still there had been with them so much of adherence to a sacred law, that no acre of the property had ever been parted from the hands of the existing squire. Some futile attempts had been made to increase the territory, as indeed had been done by Kit Dale, the father of Christopher Dale, who will appear as our squire of Allington when the persons of our drama are introduced. Old Kit Dale, who had married money, had bought outlying farms—a bit of ground here and a bit there—talking, as he did so, much of political influence and of the good old Tory cause. But these farms and bits of ground had gone again before our time. To them had been attached no religion. When old Kit had found himself pressed in that matter of the majority of the Nineteenth Dragoons, in which crack regiment his second son made for himself quite a career, he found it easier to sell than to save—seeing that that which he sold was his own and not the patrimony of the Dales. At his death the remainder of these purchases had gone. Family arrangements required completion, and Christopher Dale required ready money. The outlying farms flew away, as such new purchases had flown before; but the old patrimony of the Dales remained untouched, as it had ever remained.

It had been a religion among them; and seeing that the worship had been carried on without fail, that the vestal fire had never gone down upon the hearth, I should not have said that the Dales had walked their ways without high principle. To this religion they had all adhered, and the new heir had ever entered in upon his domain without other encumbrances than those with which he himself was then already burdened. And yet there had been *no entail. The idea of an entail was not in accordance with the peculiarities of the Dale mind. It was necessary to the Dale religion that each squire should have the power of wasting them. I remember to have dined*

VIP PALATINO

10 point, 2 point leaded

FORMAT	PICAS	LINES	WPL	CPL	WPP	CPP
Royal 8vo	26×43	43	12.0	67	516	2881
Demy 8vo	24×40	40	11.1	62	444	2480
Large Crown 8vo	23×36	36	10.6	59	382	2124
Crown 8vo	21×34	34	9.7	54	330	1836

282 *The Small House at Allington*

father to son, and from uncle to nephew, and, in one instance, from second cousin to second cousin, the sceptre had descended in the family of the Dales; and the acres had remained intact, growing in value and not decreasing in number, though guarded by no entail and protected by no wonderful amount of prudence or wisdom. The estate of Dale of Allington had been coterminous with the parish of Allington for some hundreds of years; and though, as I have said, the race of squires had possessed nothing of superhuman discretion and had perhaps been guided in their walks through life by no very distinct principles, still there had been with them so much of adherence to a sacred law, that no acre of the property had ever been parted from the hands of the existing squire. Some futile attempts had been made to increase the territory, as indeed had been done by Kit Dale, the father of Christopher Dale, who will appear as our squire of Allington when the persons of our drama are introduced. Old Kit Dale, who had married money, had bought outlying farms—a bit of ground here and a bit there—talking, as he did so, much of political influence and of the good old Tory cause. But these farms and bits of ground had gone again before our time. To them had been attached no religion. When old Kit had found himself pressed in that matter of the majority of the Nineteenth Dragoons, in which crack regiment his second son made for himself quite a career, he found it easier to sell than to save—seeing that that which he sold was his own and not the patrimony of the Dales. At his death the remainder of these purchases had gone. Family arrangements required completion, and Christopher Dale required ready money. The outlying farms flew away, as such new purchases had flown before; but the old patrimony of the Dales remained untouched, as it had ever remained.

It had been a religion among them; and seeing that the worship had been carried on without fail, that the vestal fire had never gone down upon the hearth, I should not have said that the Dales had walked their ways without high *principle. To this religion they had all adhered, and the new heir had ever entered in upon his domain without other encumbrances than those with which he himself was then already burdened. And*

VIP PALATINO

11 point, 1 point leaded

FORMAT	PICAS	LINES	WPL	CPL	WPP	CPP
Royal 8vo	26×43	43	11.1	61	477	2623
Demy 8vo	24×40	40	10.3	56	412	2240
Large Crown 8vo	23×36	36	9.8	54	353	1944
Crown 8vo	21×34	34	9.0	49	306	1666

father to son, and from uncle to nephew, and, in one instance, from second cousin to second cousin, the sceptre had descended in the family of the Dales; and the acres had remained intact, growing in value and not decreasing in number, though guarded by no entail and protected by no wonderful amount of prudence or wisdom. The estate of Dale of Allington had been coterminous with the parish of Allington for some hundreds of years; and though, as I have said, the race of squires had possessed nothing of superhuman discretion and had perhaps been guided in their walks through life by no very distinct principles, still there had been with them so much of adherence to a sacred law, that no acre of the property had ever been parted from the hands of the existing squire. Some futile attempts had been made to increase the territory, as indeed had been done by Kit Dale, the father of Christopher Dale, who will appear as our squire of Allington when the persons of our drama are introduced. Old Kit Dale, who had married money, had bought outlying farms—a bit of ground here and a bit there—talking, as he did so, much of political influence and of the good old Tory cause. But these farms and bits of ground had gone again before our time. To them had been attached no religion. When old Kit had found himself pressed in that matter of the majority of the Nineteenth Dragoons, in which crack regiment his second son made for himself quite a career, he found it easier to sell than to save—seeing that that which he sold was his own and not the patrimony of the Dales. At his death the remainder of these purchases had gone. Family arrangements required completion, and Christopher Dale required ready money. The outlying farms flew away, as such new purchases had flown before; but the old patrimony of the Dales remained untouched, as it had ever remained.

It had been a religion among them; and seeing that the worship had been carried on without fail, that the vestal fire *had never gone down upon the hearth, I should not have said that the Dales had walked their ways without high principle. To this religion they had all adhered, and the new heir had ever entered in*

VIP PALATINO

11 point, $1\frac{1}{2}$ point leaded

FORMAT	PICAS	LINES	WPL	CPL	WPP	CPP
Royal 8vo	26×43	41	11.1	61	455	2501
Demy 8vo	24×40	38	10.3	56	391	2128
Large Crown 8vo	23×36	35	9.8	54	343	1890
Crown 8vo	21×34	33	9.0	49	297	1617

father to son, and from uncle to nephew, and, in one instance, from second cousin to second cousin, the sceptre had descended in the family of the Dales; and the acres had remained intact, growing in value and not decreasing in number, though guarded by no entail and protected by no wonderful amount of prudence or wisdom. The estate of Dale of Allington had been coterminous with the parish of Allington for some hundreds of years; and though, as I have said, the race of squires had possessed nothing of superhuman discretion and had perhaps been guided in their walks through life by no very distinct principles, still there had been with them so much of adherence to a sacred law, that no acre of the property had ever been parted from the hands of the existing squire. Some futile attempts had been made to increase the territory, as indeed had been done by Kit Dale, the father of Christopher Dale, who will appear as our squire of Allington when the persons of our drama are introduced. Old Kit Dale, who had married money, had bought outlying farms—a bit of ground here and a bit there—talking, as he did so, much of political influence and of the good old Tory cause. But these farms and bits of ground had gone again before our time. To them had been attached no religion. When old Kit had found himself pressed in that matter of the majority of the Nineteenth Dragoons, in which crack regiment his second son made for himself quite a career, he found it easier to sell than to save—seeing that that which he sold was his own and not the patrimony of the Dales. At his death the remainder of these purchases had gone. Family arrangements required completion, and Christopher Dale required ready money. The outlying farms flew away, as such new purchases had flown before; but the old patrimony of the Dales remained untouched, as it had ever remained.

It had been a religion among them; and seeing that the *worship had been carried on without fail, that the vestal fire had never gone down upon the hearth, I should not have said that the Dales had walked their ways without high principle. To this*

VIP PALATINO

11 point, 2 point leaded

FORMAT	PICAS	LINES	WPL	CPL	WPP	CPP
Royal 8vo	26×43	40	11.1	61	444	2440
Demy 8vo	24×40	37	10.3	56	381	2072
Large Crown 8vo	23×36	33	9.8	54	323	1782
Crown 8vo	21×34	31	9.0	49	279	1519

father to son, and from uncle to nephew, and, in one instance, from second cousin to second cousin, the sceptre had descended in the family of the Dales; and the acres had remained intact, growing in value and not decreasing in number, though guarded by no entail and protected by no wonderful amount of prudence or wisdom. The estate of Dale of Allington had been coterminous with the parish of Allington for some hundreds of years; and though, as I have said, the race of squires had possessed nothing of superhuman discretion and had perhaps been guided in their walks through life by no very distinct principles, still there had been with them so much of adherence to a sacred law, that no acre of the property had ever been parted from the hands of the existing squire. Some futile attempts had been made to increase the territory, as indeed had been done by Kit Dale, the father of Christopher Dale, who will appear as our squire of Allington when the persons of our drama are introduced. Old Kit Dale, who had married money, had bought outlying farms—a bit of ground here and a bit there—talking, as he did so, much of political influence and of the good old Tory cause. But these farms and bits of ground had gone again before our time. To them had been attached no religion. When old Kit had found himself pressed in that matter of the majority of the Nineteenth Dragoons, in which crack regiment his second son made for himself quite a career, he found it easier to sell than to save—seeing that that which he sold was his own and not the patrimony of the Dales. At his death the remainder of these purchases had gone. Family arrangements required completion, and *Christopher Dale required ready money. The outlying farms flew away, as such new purchases had flown before; but the old patrimony of the Dales remained untouched, as it had*

VIP PALATINO

12 point, 1½ point leaded

FORMAT	PICAS	LINES	WPL	CPL	WPP	CPP
Royal 8vo	26×43	38	10.8	54	410	2052
Demy 8vo	24×40	36	10.0	50	360	1800
Large Crown 8vo	23×36	32	9.6	48	307	1536
Crown 8vo	21×34	30	8.7	44	261	1320

father to son, and from uncle to nephew, and, in one instance, from second cousin to second cousin, the sceptre had descended in the family of the Dales; and the acres had remained intact, growing in value and not decreasing in number, though guarded by no entail and protected by no wonderful amount of prudence or wisdom. The estate of Dale of Allington had been coterminous with the parish of Allington for some hundreds of years; and though, as I have said, the race of squires had possessed nothing of superhuman discretion and had perhaps been guided in their walks through life by no very distinct principles, still there had been with them so much of adherence to a sacred law, that no acre of the property had ever been parted from the hands of the existing squire. Some futile attempts had been made to increase the territory, as indeed had been done by Kit Dale, the father of Christopher Dale, who will appear as our squire of Allington when the persons of our drama are introduced. Old Kit Dale, who had married money, had bought outlying farms—a bit of ground here and a bit there—talking, as he did so, much of political influence and of the good old Tory cause. But these farms and bits of ground had gone again before our time. To them had been attached no religion. When old Kit had found himself pressed in that matter of the majority of the Nineteenth Dragoons, in which crack regiment his second son made for himself quite a career, he found it easier to sell than to save—seeing that that which he sold was his own and not the patrimony of the Dales. At his death the remainder of these purchases had *gone. Family arrangements required completion, and Christopher Dale required ready money. The outlying farms flew away, as such new purchases had flown before; but the old*

VIP PALATINO

12 point, 2 point leaded

FORMAT	PICAS	LINES	WPL	CPL	WPP	CPP
Royal 8vo	26×43	37	10.9	56	403	2072
Demy 8vo	24×40	34	10.1	52	343	1768
Large Crown 8vo	23×36	31	9.6	50	298	1550
Crown 8vo	21×34	29	8.8	46	255	1334

VIP PLANTIN

Synopsis in 10 point

ABCDEFGHIJKLMNOPQRSTUVWXYZ&ÆŒ

ABCDEFGHIJKLMNOPQRSTUVWXYZ

abcdefghijklmnopqrstuvwxyzæœ

.,:;!?“”-()£ 1234567890 1234567890

ABCDEFGHIJKLMNOPQRSTUVWXYZ&ÆŒ

abcdefghijklmnopqrstuvwxyzæœ

.,:;!?“”-()£ 1234567890 1234567890

Related bold

ABCDEFGHIJKLMNOPQRSTUVWXYZ&ÆŒ

abcdefghijklmnopqrstuvwxyzæœ

.,:;!?“”-()£ 1234567890 1234567890

ABCDEFGHIJKLMNOPQRSTUVWXYZ&ÆŒ

abcdefghijklmnopqrstuvwxyzæœ

.,:;!?“”-()£ 1234567890

All normal European accents available

father to son, and from uncle to nephew, and, in one instance, from second cousin to second cousin, the sceptre had descended in the family of the Dales; and the acres had remained intact, growing in value and not decreasing in number, though guarded by no entail and protected by no wonderful amount of prudence or wisdom. The estate of Dale of Allington had been coterminous with the parish of Allington for some hundreds of years; and though, as I have said, the race of squires had possessed nothing of superhuman discretion and had perhaps been guided in their walks through life by no very distinct principles, still there had been with them so much of adherence to a sacred law, that no acre of the property had ever been parted from the hands of the existing squire. Some futile attempts had been made to increase the territory, as indeed had been done by Kit Dale, the father of Christopher Dale, who will appear as our squire of Allington when the persons of our drama are introduced. Old Kit Dale, who had married money, had bought outlying farms—a bit of ground here and a bit there—talking, as he did so, much of political influence and of the good old Tory cause. But these farms and bits of ground had gone again before our time. To them had been attached no religion. When old Kit had found himself pressed in that matter of the majority of the Nineteenth Dragoons, in which crack regiment his second son made for himself quite a career, he found it easier to sell than to save—seeing that that which he sold was his own and not the patrimony of the Dales. At his death the remainder of these purchases had gone. Family arrangements required completion, and Christopher Dale required ready money. The outlying farms flew away, as such new purchases had flown before; but the old patrimony of the Dales remained untouched, as it had ever remained.

It had been a religion among them; and seeing that the worship had been carried on without fail, that the vestal fire had never gone down upon the hearth, I should not have said that the Dales had walked their ways without high principle. To this religion they had all adhered, and the new heir had ever entered in upon his domain without other encumbrances than those with which he himself was then already burdened. And yet there had been no entail. The idea of an entail was not in accordance with the peculiarities of the Dale mind. It was necessary to the Dale religion that each squire should have the power of wasting them. I remember to have dined at a house, the whole glory and fortune of which depended on the safety of a glass goblet. We all know the story. If the luck of Edenhall should be shattered, the doom of the family would be sealed. Nevertheless I was bidden to drink out of the fatal glass, as were all guests in that house. It would not have contented the chivalrous mind of the master to protect his doom by lock and key and padded chest. And so it was with the Dales of Allington. To them an entail would have been a lock and key and a padded chest; but the old chivalry of their house denied to them the use of such protection.

I have spoken something slightingly of the acquirements and doings of the family; and indeed their acquirements had been few and their doings little. At Allington, Dale of Allington had always been known as a king. At Guestwick, *the neighbouring market town, he was a great man—to be seen frequently on Saturdays, standing in the market-place, and laying down the law as to barley and oxen among men who knew usually more about barley and oxen than he did. At*

VIP PLANTIN

9 point, 1 point leaded

FORMAT	PICAS	LINES	WPL	CPL	WPP	CPP
Royal 8vo	26×43	52	15.2	81	790	4212
Demy 8vo	24×40	48	14.1	75	677	3600
Large Crown 8vo	23×36	43	13.5	72	581	3096
Crown 8vo	21×34	41	11.8	66	484	2706

father to son, and from uncle to nephew, and, in one instance, from second cousin to second cousin, the sceptre had descended in the family of the Dales; and the acres had remained intact, growing in value and not decreasing in number, though guarded by no entail and protected by no wonderful amount of prudence or wisdom. The estate of Dale of Allington had been coterminous with the parish of Allington for some hundreds of years; and though, as I have said, the race of squires had possessed nothing of superhuman discretion and had perhaps been guided in their walks through life by no very distinct principles, still there had been with them so much of adherence to a sacred law, that no acre of the property had ever been parted from the hands of the existing squire. Some futile attempts had been made to increase the territory, as indeed had been done by Kit Dale, the father of Christopher Dale, who will appear as our squire of Allington when the persons of our drama are introduced. Old Kit Dale, who had married money, had bought outlying farms—a bit of ground here and a bit there—talking, as he did so, much of political influence and of the good old Tory cause. But these farms and bits of ground had gone again before our time. To them had been attached no religion. When old Kit had found himself pressed in that matter of the majority of the Nineteenth Dragoons, in which crack regiment his second son made for himself quite a career, he found it easier to sell than to save—seeing that that which he sold was his own and not the patrimony of the Dales. At his death the remainder of these purchases had gone. Family arrangements required completion, and Christopher Dale required ready money. The outlying farms flew away, as such new purchases had flown before; but the old patrimony of the Dales remained untouched, as it had ever remained.

It had been a religion among them; and seeing that the worship had been carried on without fail, that the vestal fire had never gone down upon the hearth, I should not have said that the Dales had walked their ways without high principle. To this religion they had all adhered, and the new heir had ever entered in upon his domain without other encumbrances than those with which he himself was then already burdened. And yet there had been no entail. The idea of an entail was not in accordance with the peculiarities of the Dale mind. It was necessary to the Dale religion that each squire should have the power of wasting them. I remember to have dined at a house, the whole glory and fortune of which depended on the safety of a glass goblet. We all know the story. If the luck of Edenhall should be shattered, the doom of the family would be sealed. Nevertheless I was bidden to drink out of the fatal glass, as were all guests in that house. It would not have contented the chivalrous mind of the master to protect his doom by lock and key and padded chest. And so it was with the Dales of Allington. To them an entail would have been a lock and key and a padded chest; but the old chivalry of their house denied to them the use of such protection.

I have spoken something slightingly of the acquirements and doings of the *family; and indeed their acquirements had been few and their doings little. At Allington, Dale of Allington had always been known as a king. At Guestwick, the neighbouring market town, he was a great man—to be seen frequently on Saturdays,*

VIP PLANTIN

9 point, 1½ point leaded

FORMAT	PICAS	LINES	WPL	CPL	WPP	CPP
Royal 8vo	26×43	49	15.2	81	745	3969
Demy 8vo	24×40	46	14.1	75	649	3450
Large Crown 8vo	23×36	41	13.5	72	554	2952
Crown 8vo	21×34	39	11.8	66	460	2574

father to son, and from uncle to nephew, and, in one instance, from second cousin to second cousin, the sceptre had descended in the family of the Dales; and the acres had remained intact, growing in value and not decreasing in number, though guarded by no entail and protected by no wonderful amount of prudence or wisdom. The estate of Dale of Allington had been coterminous with the parish of Allington for some hundreds of years; and though, as I have said, the race of squires had possessed nothing of superhuman discretion and had perhaps been guided in their walks through life by no very distinct principles, still there had been with them so much of adherence to a sacred law, that no acre of the property had ever been parted from the hands of the existing squire. Some futile attempts had been made to increase the territory, as indeed had been done by Kit Dale, the father of Christopher Dale, who will appear as our squire of Allington when the persons of our drama are introduced. Old Kit Dale, who had married money, had bought outlying farms—a bit of ground here and a bit there—talking, as he did so, much of political influence and of the good old Tory cause. But these farms and bits of ground had gone again before our time. To them had been attached no religion. When old Kit had found himself pressed in that matter of the majority of the Nineteenth Dragoons, in which crack regiment his second son made for himself quite a career, he found it easier to sell than to save—seeing that that which he sold was his own and not the patrimony of the Dales. At his death the remainder of these purchases had gone. Family arrangements required completion, and Christopher Dale required ready money. The outlying farms flew away, as such new purchases had flown before; but the old patrimony of the Dales remained untouched, as it had ever remained.

It had been a religion among them; and seeing that the worship had been carried on without fail, that the vestal fire had never gone down upon the hearth, I should not have said that the Dales had walked their ways without high principle. To this religion they had all adhered, and the new heir had ever entered in upon his domain without other encumbrances than those with which he himself was then already burdened. And yet there had been no entail. The idea of an entail was not in accordance with the peculiarities of the Dale mind. It was necessary to the Dale religion that each squire should have the power of wasting them. I remember to have dined at a house, the whole glory and fortune of which depended on the safety of a glass goblet. We all know the story. If the luck of Edenhall should be shattered, the doom of the family would be sealed. Nevertheless I was bidden to drink out of the fatal glass, as were all guests in that house. It would not have contented the chivalrous mind of the master to protect his doom by lock and key and padded chest. And so it was with the Dales of Allington. To them an entail would have been a lock and key and a padded chest; but the old chivalry of their house *denied to them the use of such protection.*

I have spoken something slightingly of the acquirements and doings of the family; and indeed their acquirements had been few and their doings little. At Allington,

VIP PLANTIN

9 point, 2 point leaded

FORMAT	PICAS	LINES	WPL	CPL	WPP	CPP
Royal 8vo	26×43	47	15.2	81	714	3807
Demy 8vo	24×40	44	14.1	75	620	3300
Large Crown 8vo	23×36	39	13.5	72	527	2808
Crown 8vo	21×34	37	11.8	66	437	2442

father to son, and from uncle to nephew, and, in one instance, from second cousin to second cousin, the sceptre had descended in the family of the Dales; and the acres had remained intact, growing in value and not decreasing in number, though guarded by no entail and protected by no wonderful amount of prudence or wisdom. The estate of Dale of Allington had been coterminous with the parish of Allington for some hundreds of years; and though, as I have said, the race of squires had possessed nothing of superhuman discretion and had perhaps been guided in their walks through life by no very distinct principles, still there had been with them so much of adherence to a sacred law, that no acre of the property had ever been parted from the hands of the existing squire. Some futile attempts had been made to increase the territory, as indeed had been done by Kit Dale, the father of Christopher Dale, who will appear as our squire of Allington when the persons of our drama are introduced. Old Kit Dale, who had married money, had bought outlying farms—a bit of ground here and a bit there—talking, as he did so, much of political influence and of the good old Tory cause. But these farms and bits of ground had gone again before our time. To them had been attached no religion. When old Kit had found himself pressed in that matter of the majority of the Nineteenth Dragoons, in which crack regiment his second son made for himself quite a career, he found it easier to sell than to save—seeing that that which he sold was his own and not the patrimony of the Dales. At his death the remainder of these purchases had gone. Family arrangements required completion, and Christopher Dale required ready money. The outlying farms flew away, as such new purchases had flown before; but the old patrimony of the Dales remained untouched, as it had ever remained.

It had been a religion among them; and seeing that the worship had been carried on without fail, that the vestal fire had never gone down upon the hearth, I should not have said that the Dales had walked their ways without high principle. To this religion they had all adhered, and the new heir had ever entered in upon his domain without other encumbrances than those with which he himself was then already burdened. And yet there had been no entail. The idea of an entail was not in accordance with the peculiarities of the Dale mind. It was necessary to the Dale religion that each squire should have the power of wasting them. I remember to have dined at a house, the whole glory and fortune of which depended on the safety of a glass goblet. We all know the story. If the luck of Edenhall should be shattered, the doom of the family would be sealed. Nevertheless I was *bidden to drink out of the fatal glass, as were all guests in that house. It would not have contented the chivalrous mind of the master to protect his doom by lock and key and padded chest. And so it was with the Dales of*

VIP PLANTIN

10 point, 1 point leaded

FORMAT	PICAS	LINES	WPL	CPL	WPP	CPP
Royal 8vo	26×43	47	13.2	72	620	3384
Demy 8vo	24×40	44	12.2	66	537	2904
Large Crown 8vo	23×36	39	11.7	63	456	2457
Crown 8vo	21×34	37	10.6	58	392	2146

father to son, and from uncle to nephew, and, in one instance, from second cousin to second cousin, the sceptre had descended in the family of the Dales; and the acres had remained intact, growing in value and not decreasing in number, though guarded by no entail and protected by no wonderful amount of prudence or wisdom. The estate of Dale of Allington had been coterminous with the parish of Allington for some hundreds of years; and though, as I have said, the race of squires had possessed nothing of superhuman discretion and had perhaps been guided in their walks through life by no very distinct principles, still there had been with them so much of adherence to a sacred law, that no acre of the property had ever been parted from the hands of the existing squire. Some futile attempts had been made to increase the territory, as indeed had been done by Kit Dale, the father of Christopher Dale, who will appear as our squire of Allington when the persons of our drama are introduced. Old Kit Dale, who had married money, had bought outlying farms—a bit of ground here and a bit there—talking, as he did so, much of political influence and of the good old Tory cause. But these farms and bits of ground had gone again before our time. To them had been attached no religion. When old Kit had found himself pressed in that matter of the majority of the Nineteenth Dragoons, in which crack regiment his second son made for himself quite a career, he found it easier to sell than to save—seeing that that which he sold was his own and not the patrimony of the Dales. At his death the remainder of these purchases had gone. Family arrangements required completion, and Christopher Dale required ready money. The outlying farms flew away, as such new purchases had flown before; but the old patrimony of the Dales remained untouched, as it had ever remained.

It had been a religion among them; and seeing that the worship had been carried on without fail, that the vestal fire had never gone down upon the hearth, I should not have said that the Dales had walked their ways without high principle. To this religion they had all adhered, and the new heir had ever entered in upon his domain without other encumbrances than those with which he himself was then already burdened. And yet there had been no entail. The idea of an entail was not in accordance with the peculiarities of the Dale mind. It was necessary to the Dale religion that each squire should have the power of wasting them. I remember to have dined at a house, the whole glory and fortune of which depended on the safety of a glass *goblet. We all know the story. If the luck of Edenhall should be shattered, the doom of the family would be sealed. Nevertheless I was bidden to drink out of the fatal glass, as were all guests in that house. It would not have*

VIP PLANTIN

10 point, 1½ point leaded

FORMAT	PICAS	LINES	WPL	CPL	WPP	CPP
Royal 8vo	26×43	45	13.2	72	594	3240
Demy 8vo	24×40	42	12.2	66	512	2772
Large Crown 8vo	23×36	38	11.7	63	447	2394
Crown 8vo	21×34	35	10.6	58	371	2030

father to son, and from uncle to nephew, and, in one instance, from second cousin to second cousin, the sceptre had descended in the family of the Dales; and the acres had remained intact, growing in value and not decreasing in number, though guarded by no entail and protected by no wonderful amount of prudence or wisdom. The estate of Dale of Allington had been coterminous with the parish of Allington for some hundreds of years; and though, as I have said, the race of squires had possessed nothing of superhuman discretion and had perhaps been guided in their walks through life by no very distinct principles, still there had been with them so much of adherence to a sacred law, that no acre of the property had ever been parted from the hands of the existing squire. Some futile attempts had been made to increase the territory, as indeed had been done by Kit Dale, the father of Christopher Dale, who will appear as our squire of Allington when the persons of our drama are introduced. Old Kit Dale, who had married money, had bought outlying farms—a bit of ground here and a bit there—talking, as he did so, much of political influence and of the good old Tory cause. But these farms and bits of ground had gone again before our time. To them had been attached no religion. When old Kit had found himself pressed in that matter of the majority of the Nineteenth Dragoons, in which crack regiment his second son made for himself quite a career, he found it easier to sell than to save—seeing that that which he sold was his own and not the patrimony of the Dales. At his death the remainder of these purchases had gone. Family arrangements required completion, and Christopher Dale required ready money. The outlying farms flew away, as such new purchases had flown before; but the old patrimony of the Dales remained untouched, as it had ever remained.

It had been a religion among them; and seeing that the worship had been carried on without fail, that the vestal fire had never gone down upon the hearth, I should not have said that the Dales had walked their ways without high principle. To this religion they had all adhered, and the new heir had ever entered in upon his domain without other encumbrances than those with which he himself was then already burdened. And yet there had been no entail. The idea of an entail was not in accordance with the peculiarities of the Dale mind. It was necessary to the Dale religion that each squire should *have the power of wasting them. I remember to have dined at a house, the whole glory and fortune of which depended on the safety of a glass goblet. We all know the story. If the luck of Edenhall should be shattered, the*

VIP PLANTIN

10 point, 2 point leaded

FORMAT	PICAS	LINES	WPL	CPL	WPP	CPP
Royal 8vo	26×43	43	13.2	72	568	3096
Demy 8vo	24×40	40	12.2	66	488	2640
Large Crown 8vo	23×36	36	11.7	63	422	2268
Crown 8vo	21×34	34	10.6	58	360	1972

father to son, and from uncle to nephew, and, in one instance, from second cousin to second cousin, the sceptre had descended in the family of the Dales; and the acres had remained intact, growing in value and not decreasing in number, though guarded by no entail and protected by no wonderful amount of prudence or wisdom. The estate of Dale of Allington had been coterminous with the parish of Allington for some hundreds of years; and though, as I have said, the race of squires had possessed nothing of superhuman discretion and had perhaps been guided in their walks through life by no very distinct principles, still there had been with them so much of adherence to a sacred law, that no acre of the property had ever been parted from the hands of the existing squire. Some futile attempts had been made to increase the territory, as indeed had been done by Kit Dale, the father of Christopher Dale, who will appear as our squire of Allington when the persons of our drama are introduced. Old Kit Dale, who had married money, had bought outlying farms—a bit of ground here and a bit there—talking, as he did so, much of political influence and of the good old Tory cause. But these farms and bits of ground had gone again before our time. To them had been attached no religion. When old Kit had found himself pressed in that matter of the majority of the Nineteenth Dragoons, in which crack regiment his second son made for himself quite a career, he found it easier to sell than to save—seeing that that which he sold was his own and not the patrimony of the Dales. At his death the remainder of these purchases had gone. Family arrangements required completion, and Christopher Dale required ready money. The outlying farms flew away, as such new purchases had flown before; but the old patrimony of the Dales remained untouched, as it had ever remained.

It had been a religion among them; and seeing that the worship had been carried on without fail, that the vestal fire had never gone down upon the hearth, I should not have said that the Dales had walked their ways without high principle. To this religion they had all adhered, and the new heir had ever entered in upon his domain without other encumbrances than those *with which he himself was then already burdened. And yet there had been no entail. The idea of an entail was not in accordance with the peculiarities of the Dale mind. It was necessary to the Dale religion*

VIP PLANTIN

11 point, 1 point leaded

FORMAT	PICAS	LINES	WPL	CPL	WPP	CPP
Royal 8vo	26×43	43	11.2	65	482	2795
Demy 8vo	24×40	40	10.4	60	416	2400
Large Crown 8vo	23×36	36	9.9	58	356	2088
Crown 8vo	21×34	34	9.0	53	306	1802

father to son, and from uncle to nephew, and, in one instance, from second cousin to second cousin, the sceptre had descended in the family of the Dales; and the acres had remained intact, growing in value and not decreasing in number, though guarded by no entail and protected by no wonderful amount of prudence or wisdom. The estate of Dale of Allington had been coterminous with the parish of Allington for some hundreds of years; and though, as I have said, the race of squires had possessed nothing of superhuman discretion and had perhaps been guided in their walks through life by no very distinct principles, still there had been with them so much of adherence to a sacred law, that no acre of the property had ever been parted from the hands of the existing squire. Some futile attempts had been made to increase the territory, as indeed had been done by Kit Dale, the father of Christopher Dale, who will appear as our squire of Allington when the persons of our drama are introduced. Old Kit Dale, who had married money, had bought outlying farms—a bit of ground here and a bit there—talking, as he did so, much of political influence and of the good old Tory cause. But these farms and bits of ground had gone again before our time. To them had been attached no religion. When old Kit had found himself pressed in that matter of the majority of the Nineteenth Dragoons, in which crack regiment his second son made for himself quite a career, he found it easier to sell than to save—seeing that that which he sold was his own and not the patrimony of the Dales. At his death the remainder of these purchases had gone. Family arrangements required completion, and Christopher Dale required ready money. The outlying farms flew away, as such new purchases had flown before; but the old patrimony of the Dales remained untouched, as it had ever remained.

It had been a religion among them; and seeing that the worship had been carried on without fail, that the vestal fire had never gone down upon the hearth, I should not have said that the Dales had walked their ways without high principle. To this *religion they had all adhered, and the new heir had ever entered in upon his domain without other encumbrances than those with which he himself was then already burdened. And yet there had been no*

father to son, and from uncle to nephew, and, in one instance, from second cousin to second cousin, the sceptre had descended in the family of the Dales; and the acres had remained intact, growing in value and not decreasing in number, though guarded by no entail and protected by no wonderful amount of prudence or wisdom. The estate of Dale of Allington had been coterminous with the parish of Allington for some hundreds of years; and though, as I have said, the race of squires had possessed nothing of superhuman discretion and had perhaps been guided in their walks through life by no very distinct principles, still there had been with them so much of adherence to a sacred law, that no acre of the property had ever been parted from the hands of the existing squire. Some futile attempts had been made to increase the territory, as indeed had been done by Kit Dale, the father of Christopher Dale, who will appear as our squire of Allington when the persons of our drama are introduced. Old Kit Dale, who had married money, had bought outlying farms—a bit of ground here and a bit there—talking, as he did so, much of political influence and of the good old Tory cause. But these farms and bits of ground had gone again before our time. To them had been attached no religion. When old Kit had found himself pressed in that matter of the majority of the Nineteenth Dragoons, in which crack regiment his second son made for himself quite a career, he found it easier to sell than to save—seeing that that which he sold was his own and not the patrimony of the Dales. At his death the remainder of these purchases had gone. Family arrangements required completion, and Christopher Dale required ready money. The outlying farms flew away, as such new purchases had flown before; but the old patrimony of the Dales remained untouched, as it had ever remained.

It had been a religion among them; and seeing that the worship had been carried on without fail, that the vestal fire had never gone down upon the hearth, I should not have said that *the Dales had walked their ways without high principle. To this religion they had all adhered, and the new heir had ever entered in upon his domain without other encumbrances than those with which*

VIP PLANTIN

11 point, 2 point leaded

FORMAT	PICAS	LINES	WPL	CPL	WPP	CPP
Royal 8vo	26×43	40	11.2	65	448	2600
Demy 8vo	24×40	37	10.4	60	385	2220
Large Crown 8vo	23×36	33	9.9	58	327	1914
Crown 8vo	21×34	31	9.0	53	279	1643

VIP SABON

Synopsis in 10 *point*

ABCDEFGHIJKLMNOPQRSTUVWXYZ&ÆŒ

ABCDEFGHIJKLMNOPQRSTUVWXYZ

abcdefghijklmnopqrstuvwxyzæœ

.,:;!?''-()£ 1234567890 1234567890

ABCDEFGHIJKLMNOPQRSTUVWXYZ&ÆŒ

abcdefghijklmnopqrstuvwxyzæœ

.,:;!?''-()£ 1234567890 1234567890

Related bold

ABCDEFGHIJKLMNOPQRSTUVWXYZ&ÆŒ

abcdefghijklmnopqrstuvwxyzæœ

.,:;!?''-()£ 1234567890 1234567890

All normal European accents available

father to son, and from uncle to nephew, and, in one instance, from second cousin to second cousin, the sceptre had descended in the family of the Dales; and the acres had remained intact, growing in value and not decreasing in number, though guarded by no entail and protected by no wonderful amount of prudence or wisdom. The estate of Dale of Allington had been coterminous with the parish of Allington for some hundreds of years; and though, as I have said, the race of squires had possessed nothing of superhuman discretion and had perhaps been guided in their walks through life by no very distinct principles, still there had been with them so much of adherence to a sacred law, that no acre of the property had ever been parted from the hands of the existing squire. Some futile attempts had been made to increase the territory, as indeed had been done by Kit Dale, the father of Christopher Dale, who will appear as our squire of Allington when the persons of our drama are introduced. Old Kit Dale, who had married money, had bought outlying farms—a bit of ground here and a bit there—talking, as he did so, much of political influence and of the good old Tory cause. But these farms and bits of ground had gone again before our time. To them had been attached no religion. When old Kit had found himself pressed in that matter of the majority of the Nineteenth Dragoons, in which crack regiment his second son made for himself quite a career, he found it easier to sell than to save—seeing that that which he sold was his own and not the patrimony of the Dales. At his death the remainder of these purchases had gone. Family arrangements required completion, and Christopher Dale required ready money. The outlying farms flew away, as such new purchases had flown before; but the old patrimony of the Dales remained untouched, as it had ever remained.

It had been a religion among them; and seeing that the worship had been carried on without fail, that the vestal fire had never gone down upon the hearth, I should not have said that the Dales had walked their ways without high principle. To this religion they had all adhered, and the new heir had ever entered in upon his domain without other encumbrances than those with which he himself was then already burdened. And yet there had been no entail. The idea of an entail was not in accordance with the peculiarities of the Dale mind. It was necessary to the Dale religion that each squire should have the power of wasting them. I remember to have dined at a house, the whole glory and fortune of which depended on the safety of a glass goblet. We all know the story. If the luck of Edenhall should be shattered, the doom of the family would be sealed. Nevertheless I was bidden to drink out of the fatal glass, as were all guests in that house. It would not have contented the chivalrous mind of the master to protect his doom by lock and key and padded chest. And so it was with the Dales of Allington. To them an entail would have been a lock and key and a padded chest; but the old chivalry of their house denied to them the use of such protection.

I have spoken something slightingly of the acquirements and doings of the family; and indeed their acquirements had been few and their doings little. *At Allington, Dale of Allington had always been known as a king. At Guestwick, the neighbouring market town, he was a great man—to be seen frequently on Saturdays, standing in the market-place, and laying down the*

VIP SABON

9 point, 1 point leaded

FORMAT	PICAS	LINES	WPL	CPL	WPP	CPP
Royal 8vo	26×43	52	14.9	79	775	4108
Demy 8vo	24×40	48	13.8	73	662	3504
Large Crown 8vo	23×36	43	13.2	70	568	3010
Crown 8vo	21×34	41	12.0	64	492	2624

father to son, and from uncle to nephew, and, in one instance, from second cousin to second cousin, the sceptre had descended in the family of the Dales; and the acres had remained intact, growing in value and not decreasing in number, though guarded by no entail and protected by no wonderful amount of prudence or wisdom. The estate of Dale of Allington had been coterminous with the parish of Allington for some hundreds of years; and though, as I have said, the race of squires had possessed nothing of superhuman discretion and had perhaps been guided in their walks through life by no very distinct principles, still there had been with them so much of adherence to a sacred law, that no acre of the property had ever been parted from the hands of the existing squire. Some futile attempts had been made to increase the territory, as indeed had been done by Kit Dale, the father of Christopher Dale, who will appear as our squire of Allington when the persons of our drama are introduced. Old Kit Dale, who had married money, had bought outlying farms—a bit of ground here and a bit there—talking, as he did so, much of political influence and of the good old Tory cause. But these farms and bits of ground had gone again before our time. To them had been attached no religion. When old Kit had found himself pressed in that matter of the majority of the Nineteenth Dragoons, in which crack regiment his second son made for himself quite a career, he found it easier to sell than to save—seeing that that which he sold was his own and not the patrimony of the Dales. At his death the remainder of these purchases had gone. Family arrangements required completion, and Christopher Dale required ready money. The outlying farms flew away, as such new purchases had flown before; but the old patrimony of the Dales remained untouched, as it had ever remained.

It had been a religion among them; and seeing that the worship had been carried on without fail, that the vestal fire had never gone down upon the hearth, I should not have said that the Dales had walked their ways without high principle. To this religion they had all adhered, and the new heir had ever entered in upon his domain without other encumbrances than those with which he himself was then already burdened. And yet there had been no entail. The idea of an entail was not in accordance with the peculiarities of the Dale mind. It was necessary to the Dale religion that each squire should have the power of wasting them. I remember to have dined at a house, the whole glory and fortune of which depended on the safety of a glass goblet. We all know the story. If the luck of Edenhall should be shattered, the doom of the family would be sealed. Nevertheless I was bidden to drink out of the fatal glass, as were all guests in that house. It would not have contented the chivalrous mind of the master to protect his doom by lock and key and padded chest. And so it was with the Dales of Allington. To them an entail would have been a lock and key and a padded chest; but the old chivalry of their house denied to them the use of such protection.

I have spoken something slightingly of the acquirements and doings of the family; and indeed their acquirements had been few and their doings little. At Allington, Dale of Allington had always been known as a king. At

VIP SABON

9 point, 1½ point leaded

FORMAT	PICAS	LINES	WPL	CPL	WPP	CPP
Royal 8vo	26×43	49	14.9	79	730	3871
Demy 8vo	24×40	46	13.8	73	635	3358
Large Crown 8vo	23×36	41	13.2	70	541	2870
Crown 8vo	21×34	39	12.0	64	468	2496

father to son, and from uncle to nephew, and, in one instance, from second cousin to second cousin, the sceptre had descended in the family of the Dales; and the acres had remained intact, growing in value and not decreasing in number, though guarded by no entail and protected by no wonderful amount of prudence or wisdom. The estate of Dale of Allington had been coterminous with the parish of Allington for some hundreds of years; and though, as I have said, the race of squires had possessed nothing of superhuman discretion and had perhaps been guided in their walks through life by no very distinct principles, still there had been with them so much of adherence to a sacred law, that no acre of the property had ever been parted from the hands of the existing squire. Some futile attempts had been made to increase the territory, as indeed had been done by Kit Dale, the father of Christopher Dale, who will appear as our squire of Allington when the persons of our drama are introduced. Old Kit Dale, who had married money, had bought outlying farms—a bit of ground here and a bit there—talking, as he did so, much of political influence and of the good old Tory cause. But these farms and bits of ground had gone again before our time. To them had been attached no religion. When old Kit had found himself pressed in that matter of the majority of the Nineteenth Dragoons, in which crack regiment his second son made for himself quite a career, he found it easier to sell than to save—seeing that that which he sold was his own and not the patrimony of the Dales. At his death the remainder of these purchases had gone. Family arrangements required completion, and Christopher Dale required ready money. The outlying farms flew away, as such new purchases had flown before; but the old patrimony of the Dales remained untouched, as it had ever remained.

It had been a religion among them; and seeing that the worship had been carried on without fail, that the vestal fire had never gone down upon the hearth, I should not have said that the Dales had walked their ways without high principle. To this religion they had all adhered, and the new heir had ever entered in upon his domain without other encumbrances than those with which he himself was then already burdened. And yet there had been no entail. The idea of an entail was not in accordance with the peculiarities of the Dale mind. It was necessary to the Dale religion that each squire should have the power of wasting them. I remember to have dined at a house, the whole glory and fortune of which depended on the safety of a glass goblet. We all know the story. If the luck of Edenhall should be shattered, the doom of the family would be sealed. Nevertheless I was bidden to drink out of the fatal glass, as were all guests in that house. It would not have contented the chivalrous mind of the master to protect his doom by lock and key and padded chest. And so it was with the Dales of Allington. To them an entail *would have been a lock and key and a padded chest; but the old chivalry of their house denied to them the use of such protection.*

I have spoken something slightingly of the acquirements and doings of the

VIP SABON

9 point, 2 point leaded

FORMAT	PICAS	LINES	WPL	CPL	WPP	CPP
Royal 8vo	26×43	47	14.9	79	700	3713
Demy 8vo	24×40	44	13.8	73	607	3212
Large Crown 8vo	23×36	39	13.2	70	515	2730
Crown 8vo	21×34	37	12.0	64	444	2368

father to son, and from uncle to nephew, and, in one instance, from second cousin to second cousin, the sceptre had descended in the family of the Dales; and the acres had remained intact, growing in value and not decreasing in number, though guarded by no entail and protected by no wonderful amount of prudence or wisdom. The estate of Dale of Allington had been coterminous with the parish of Allington for some hundreds of years; and though, as I have said, the race of squires had possessed nothing of superhuman discretion and had perhaps been guided in their walks through life by no very distinct principles, still there had been with them so much of adherence to a sacred law, that no acre of the property had ever been parted from the hands of the existing squire. Some futile attempts had been made to increase the territory, as indeed had been done by Kit Dale, the father of Christopher Dale, who will appear as our squire of Allington when the persons of our drama are introduced. Old Kit Dale, who had married money, had bought outlying farms—a bit of ground here and a bit there—talking, as he did so, much of political influence and of the good old Tory cause. But these farms and bits of ground had gone again before our time. To them had been attached no religion. When old Kit had found himself pressed in that matter of the majority of the Nineteenth Dragoons, in which crack regiment his second son made for himself quite a career, he found it easier to sell than to save—seeing that that which he sold was his own and not the patrimony of the Dales. At his death the remainder of these purchases had gone. Family arrangements required completion, and Christopher Dale required ready money. The outlying farms flew away, as such new purchases had flown before; but the old patrimony of the Dales remained untouched, as it had ever remained.

It had been a religion among them; and seeing that the worship had been carried on without fail, that the vestal fire had never gone down upon the hearth, I should not have said that the Dales had walked their ways without high principle. To this religion they had all adhered, and the new heir had ever entered in upon his domain without other encumbrances than those with which he himself was then already burdened. And yet there had been no entail. The idea of an entail was not in accordance with the peculiarities of the Dale mind. It was necessary to the Dale religion that each squire should have the power of wasting them. I remember to have dined at a house, the whole glory and fortune of which depended on the safety of a glass goblet. We all know the story. If the luck of Edenhall *should be shattered, the doom of the family would be sealed. Nevertheless I was bidden to drink out of the fatal glass, as were all guests in that house. It would not have contented the chivalrous*

VIP SABON

10 point, 1 point leaded

FORMAT	PICAS	LINES	WPL	CPL	WPP	CPP
Royal 8vo	26×43	47	13.4	70	630	3290
Demy 8vo	24×40	44	12.4	65	546	2860
Large Crown 8vo	23×36	39	11.8	62	460	2418
Crown 8vo	21×34	37	10.8	57	400	2109

father to son, and from uncle to nephew, and, in one instance, from second cousin to second cousin, the sceptre had descended in the family of the Dales; and the acres had remained intact, growing in value and not decreasing in number, though guarded by no entail and protected by no wonderful amount of prudence or wisdom. The estate of Dale of Allington had been coterminous with the parish of Allington for some hundreds of years; and though, as I have said, the race of squires had possessed nothing of superhuman discretion and had perhaps been guided in their walks through life by no very distinct principles, still there had been with them so much of adherence to a sacred law, that no acre of the property had ever been parted from the hands of the existing squire. Some futile attempts had been made to increase the territory, as indeed had been done by Kit Dale, the father of Christopher Dale, who will appear as our squire of Allington when the persons of our drama are introduced. Old Kit Dale, who had married money, had bought outlying farms—a bit of ground here and a bit there—talking, as he did so, much of political influence and of the good old Tory cause. But these farms and bits of ground had gone again before our time. To them had been attached no religion. When old Kit had found himself pressed in that matter of the majority of the Nineteenth Dragoons, in which crack regiment his second son made for himself quite a career, he found it easier to sell than to save—seeing that that which he sold was his own and not the patrimony of the Dales. At his death the remainder of these purchases had gone. Family arrangements required completion, and Christopher Dale required ready money. The outlying farms flew away, as such new purchases had flown before; but the old patrimony of the Dales remained untouched, as it had ever remained.

It had been a religion among them; and seeing that the worship had been carried on without fail, that the vestal fire had never gone down upon the hearth, I should not have said that the Dales had walked their ways without high principle. To this religion they had all adhered, and the new heir had ever entered in upon his domain without other encumbrances than those with which he himself was then already burdened. And yet there had been no entail. The idea of an entail was not in accordance with the peculiarities of the Dale mind. It was necessary to the Dale religion that each squire should have the power of wasting them. I remember to have dined at a *house, the whole glory and fortune of which depended on the safety of a glass goblet. We all know the story. If the luck of Edenhall should be shattered, the doom of the family would be sealed.*

VIP SABON

10 point, 1½ point leaded

FORMAT	PICAS	LINES	WPL	CPL	WPP	CPP
Royal 8vo	26×43	45	13.4	70	603	3150
Demy 8vo	24×40	42	12.4	65	521	2730
Large Crown 8vo	23×36	38	11.8	62	448	2356
Crown 8vo	21×34	35	10.8	57	378	1995

father to son, and from uncle to nephew, and, in one instance, from second cousin to second cousin, the sceptre had descended in the family of the Dales; and the acres had remained intact, growing in value and not decreasing in number, though guarded by no entail and protected by no wonderful amount of prudence or wisdom. The estate of Dale of Allington had been coterminous with the parish of Allington for some hundreds of years; and though, as I have said, the race of squires had possessed nothing of superhuman discretion and had perhaps been guided in their walks through life by no very distinct principles, still there had been with them so much of adherence to a sacred law, that no acre of the property had ever been parted from the hands of the existing squire. Some futile attempts had been made to increase the territory, as indeed had been done by Kit Dale, the father of Christopher Dale, who will appear as our squire of Allington when the persons of our drama are introduced. Old Kit Dale, who had married money, had bought outlying farms—a bit of ground here and a bit there—talking, as he did so, much of political influence and of the good old Tory cause. But these farms and bits of ground had gone again before our time. To them had been attached no religion. When old Kit had found himself pressed in that matter of the majority of the Nineteenth Dragoons, in which crack regiment his second son made for himself quite a career, he found it easier to sell than to save—seeing that that which he sold was his own and not the patrimony of the Dales. At his death the remainder of these purchases had gone. Family arrangements required completion, and Christopher Dale required ready money. The outlying farms flew away, as such new purchases had flown before; but the old patrimony of the Dales remained untouched, as it had ever remained.

It had been a religion among them; and seeing that the worship had been carried on without fail, that the vestal fire had never gone down upon the hearth, I should not have said that the Dales had walked their ways without high principle. To this religion they had all adhered, and the new heir had ever entered in upon his domain without other encumbrances than those with which he himself was then already burdened. And yet there had been no entail. The idea of an entail was not in accordance with the peculiarities of the Dale *mind. It was necessary to the Dale religion that each squire should have the power of wasting them. I remember to have dined at a house, the whole glory and fortune of which depended on the safety*

VIP SABON

10 point, 2 point leaded

FORMAT	PICAS	LINES	WPL	CPL	WPP	CPP
Royal 8vo	26×43	43	13.4	70	576	3010
Demy 8vo	24×40	40	12.4	65	496	2600
Large Crown 8vo	23×36	36	11.8	62	425	2232
Crown 8vo	21×34	34	10.8	57	194	1938

father to son, and from uncle to nephew, and, in one instance, from second cousin to second cousin, the sceptre had descended in the family of the Dales; and the acres had remained intact, growing in value and not decreasing in number, though guarded by no entail and protected by no wonderful amount of prudence or wisdom. The estate of Dale of Allington had been coterminous with the parish of Allington for some hundreds of years; and though, as I have said, the race of squires had possessed nothing of superhuman discretion and had perhaps been guided in their walks through life by no very distinct principles, still there had been with them so much of adherence to a sacred law, that no acre of the property had ever been parted from the hands of the existing squire. Some futile attempts had been made to increase the territory, as indeed had been done by Kit Dale, the father of Christopher Dale, who will appear as our squire of Allington when the persons of our drama are introduced. Old Kit Dale, who had married money, had bought outlying farms—a bit of ground here and a bit there—talking, as he did so, much of political influence and of the good old Tory cause. But these farms and bits of ground had gone again before our time. To them had been attached no religion. When old Kit had found himself pressed in that matter of the majority of the Nineteenth Dragoons, in which crack regiment his second son made for himself quite a career, he found it easier to sell than to save—seeing that that which he sold was his own and not the patrimony of the Dales. At his death the remainder of these purchases had gone. Family arrangements required completion, and Christopher Dale required ready money. The outlying farms flew away, as such new purchases had flown before; but the old patrimony of the Dales remained untouched, as it had ever remained.

It had been a religion among them; and seeing that the worship had been carried on without fail, that the vestal fire had never gone down upon the hearth, I should not have said that the Dales had walked their ways without high principle. To this religion they had all adhered, and the new heir had ever *entered in upon his domain without other encumbrances than those with which he himself was then already burdened. And yet there had been no entail. The idea of an entail was not in*

VIP SABON

11 point, 1 point leaded

FORMAT	PICAS	LINES	WPL	CPL	WPP	CPP
Royal 8vo	26×43	43	11.6	64	499	2752
Demy 8vo	24×40	40	10.7	59	428	2360
Large Crown 8vo	23×36	36	10.2	57	367	2052
Crown 8vo	21×34	34	9.3	52	316	1768

father to son, and from uncle to nephew, and, in one instance, from second cousin to second cousin, the sceptre had descended in the family of the Dales; and the acres had remained intact, growing in value and not decreasing in number, though guarded by no entail and protected by no wonderful amount of prudence or wisdom. The estate of Dale of Allington had been coterminous with the parish of Allington for some hundreds of years; and though, as I have said, the race of squires had possessed nothing of superhuman discretion and had perhaps been guided in their walks through life by no very distinct principles, still there had been with them so much of adherence to a sacred law, that no acre of the property had ever been parted from the hands of the existing squire. Some futile attempts had been made to increase the territory, as indeed had been done by Kit Dale, the father of Christopher Dale, who will appear as our squire of Allington when the persons of our drama are introduced. Old Kit Dale, who had married money, had bought outlying farms—a bit of ground here and a bit there—talking, as he did so, much of political influence and of the good old Tory cause. But these farms and bits of ground had gone again before our time. To them had been attached no religion. When old Kit had found himself pressed in that matter of the majority of the Nineteenth Dragoons, in which crack regiment his second son made for himself quite a career, he found it easier to sell than to save—seeing that that which he sold was his own and not the patrimony of the Dales. At his death the remainder of these purchases had gone. Family arrangements required completion, and Christopher Dale required ready money. The outlying farms flew away, as such new purchases had flown before; but the old patrimony of the Dales remained untouched, as it had ever remained.

It had been a religion among them; and seeing that the worship had been carried on without fail, that the vestal fire had never gone down upon the hearth, I should not have said *that the Dales had walked their ways without high principle. To this religion they had all adhered, and the new heir had ever entered in upon his domain without other encumbrances than*

VIP SABON

11 point, 1½ point leaded

FORMAT	PICAS	LINES	WPL	CPL	WPP	CPP
Royal 8vo	26×43	41	11.6	64	476	2624
Demy 8vo	24×40	38	10.7	59	407	2242
Large Crown 8vo	23×36	35	10.2	57	357	1995
Crown 8vo	21×34	33	9.3	52	307	1716

father to son, and from uncle to nephew, and, in one instance, from second cousin to second cousin, the sceptre had descended in the family of the Dales; and the acres had remained intact, growing in value and not decreasing in number, though guarded by no entail and protected by no wonderful amount of prudence or wisdom. The estate of Dale of Allington had been coterminous with the parish of Allington for some hundreds of years; and though, as I have said, the race of squires had possessed nothing of superhuman discretion and had perhaps been guided in their walks through life by no very distinct principles, still there had been with them so much of adherence to a sacred law, that no acre of the property had ever been parted from the hands of the existing squire. Some futile attempts had been made to increase the territory, as indeed had been done by Kit Dale, the father of Christopher Dale, who will appear as our squire of Allington when the persons of our drama are introduced. Old Kit Dale, who had married money, had bought outlying farms—a bit of ground here and a bit there—talking, as he did so, much of political influence and of the good old Tory cause. But these farms and bits of ground had gone again before our time. To them had been attached no religion. When old Kit had found himself pressed in that matter of the majority of the Nineteenth Dragoons, in which crack regiment his second son made for himself quite a career, he found it easier to sell than to save—seeing that that which he sold was his own and not the patrimony of the Dales. At his death the remainder of these purchases had gone. Family arrangements required completion, and Christopher Dale required ready money. The outlying farms flew away, as such new purchases had flown before; but the old patrimony of the Dales remained untouched, as it had ever remained.

It had been a religion among them; and seeing that the worship had been carried on without fail, that the vestal fire *had never gone down upon the hearth, I should not have said that the Dales had walked their ways without high principle. To this religion they had all adhered, and the new heir had ever*

VIP SABON

11 point, 2 point leaded

FORMAT	PICAS	LINES	WPL	CPL	WPP	CPP
Royal 8vo	26×43	40	11.6	64	464	2560
Demy 8vo	24×40	37	10.7	59	396	2183
Large Crown 8vo	23×36	33	10.2	57	337	1881
Crown 8vo	21×34	31	9.3	52	288	1612

VIP TIMES

Synopsis in 10 point

ABCDEFGHIJKLMNOPQRSTUVWXYZ&ÆŒ

ABCDEFGHIJKLMNOPQRSTUVWXYZ

abcdefghijklmnopqrstuvwxyzæœ

.,:;!?"-()£ 1234567890 1234567890

ABCDEFGHIJKLMNOPQRSTUVWXYZ&ÆŒ

abcdefghijklmnopqrstuvwxyzæœ

.,:;!?"-()£ 1234567890

Related bold

ABCDEFGHIJKLMNOPQRSTUVWXYZ&ÆŒ

abcdefghijklmnopqrstuvwxyzæœ

.,:;!?"-()£ 1234567890

ABCDEFGHIJKLMNOPQRSTUVWXYZ&ÆŒ

abcdefghijklmnopqrstuvwxyzæœ

.,:;!?"-()£ 1234567890

All normal European accents available

father to son, and from uncle to nephew, and, in one instance, from second cousin to second cousin, the sceptre had descended in the family of the Dales; and the acres had remained intact, growing in value and not decreasing in number, though guarded by no entail and protected by no wonderful amount of prudence or wisdom. The estate of Dale of Allington had been coterminous with the parish of Allington for some hundreds of years; and though, as I have said, the race of squires had possessed nothing of superhuman discretion and had perhaps been guided in their walks through life by no very distinct principles, still there had been with them so much of adherence to a sacred law, that no acre of the property had ever been parted from the hands of the existing squire. Some futile attempts had been made to increase the territory, as indeed had been done by Kit Dale, the father of Christopher Dale, who will appear as our squire of Allington when the persons of our drama are introduced. Old Kit Dale, who had married money, had bought outlying farms—a bit of ground here and a bit there—talking, as he did so, much of political influence and of the good old Tory cause. But these farms and bits of ground had gone again before our time. To them had been attached no religion. When old Kit had found himself pressed in that matter of the majority of the Nineteenth Dragoons, in which crack regiment his second son made for himself quite a career, he found it easier to sell than to save—seeing that that which he sold was his own and not the patrimony of the Dales. At his death the remainder of these purchases had gone. Family arrangements required completion, and Christopher Dale required ready money. The outlying farms flew away, as such new purchases had flown before; but the old patrimony of the Dales remained untouched, as it had ever remained.

It had been a religion among them; and seeing that the worship had been carried on without fail, that the vestal fire had never gone down upon the hearth, I should not have said that the Dales had walked their ways without high principle. To this religion they had all adhered, and the new heir had ever entered in upon his domain without other encumbrances than those with which he himself was then already burdened. And yet there had been no entail. The idea of an entail was not in accordance with the peculiarities of the Dale mind. It was necessary to the Dale religion that each squire should have the power of wasting them. I remember to have dined at a house, the whole glory and fortune of which depended on the safety of a glass goblet. We all know the story. If the luck of Edenhall should be shattered, the doom of the family would be sealed. Nevertheless I was bidden to drink out of the fatal glass, as were all guests in that house. It would not have contented the chivalrous mind of the master to protect his doom by lock and key and padded chest. And so it was with the Dales of Allington. To them an entail would have been a lock and key and a padded chest; but the old chivalry of their house denied to them the use of such protection.

I have spoken something slightingly of the acquirements and doings of *the family; and indeed their acquirements had been few and their doings little. At Allington, Dale of Allington had always been known as a king. At Guestwick, the neighbouring market town, he was a great man—to be seen*

VIP TIMES

9 point, 1 point leaded

FORMAT	PICAS	LINES	WPL	CPL	WPP	CPP
Royal 8vo	26×43	52	14.6	78	759	4056
Demy 8vo	24×40	48	13.5	72	648	3456
Large Crown 8vo	23×36	43	12.9	69	555	2967
Crown 8vo	21×34	41	11.8	63	484	2583

father to son, and from uncle to nephew, and, in one instance, from second cousin to second cousin, the sceptre had descended in the family of the Dales; and the acres had remained intact, growing in value and not decreasing in number, though guarded by no entail and protected by no wonderful amount of prudence or wisdom. The estate of Dale of Allington had been coterminous with the parish of Allington for some hundreds of years; and though, as I have said, the race of squires had possessed nothing of superhuman discretion and had perhaps been guided in their walks through life by no very distinct principles, still there had been with them so much of adherence to a sacred law, that no acre of the property had ever been parted from the hands of the existing squire. Some futile attempts had been made to increase the territory, as indeed had been done by Kit Dale, the father of Christopher Dale, who will appear as our squire of Allington when the persons of our drama are introduced. Old Kit Dale, who had married money, had bought outlying farms—a bit of ground here and a bit there—talking, as he did so, much of political influence and of the good old Tory cause. But these farms and bits of ground had gone again before our time. To them had been attached no religion. When old Kit had found himself pressed in that matter of the majority of the Nineteenth Dragoons, in which crack regiment his second son made for himself quite a career, he found it easier to sell than to save—seeing that that which he sold was his own and not the patrimony of the Dales. At his death the remainder of these purchases had gone. Family arrangements required completion, and Christopher Dale required ready money. The outlying farms flew away, as such new purchases had flown before; but the old patrimony of the Dales remained untouched, as it had ever remained.

It had been a religion among them; and seeing that the worship had been carried on without fail, that the vestal fire had never gone down upon the hearth, I should not have said that the Dales had walked their ways without high principle. To this religion they had all adhered, and the new heir had ever entered in upon his domain without other encumbrances than those with which he himself was then already burdened. And yet there had been no entail. The idea of an entail was not in accordance with the peculiarities of the Dale mind. It was necessary to the Dale religion that each squire should have the power of wasting them. I remember to have dined at a house, the whole glory and fortune of which depended on the safety of a glass goblet. We all know the story. If the luck of Edenhall should be shattered, the doom of the family would be sealed. Nevertheless I was bidden to drink out of the fatal glass, as were all guests in that house. It would not have contented the chivalrous mind of the master to protect his doom by lock and key and padded chest. And so it was with the Dales of Allington. To them an entail would have been a lock and key and a padded chest; but the old chivalry of their house denied to them the use of such *protection.*

I have spoken something slightingly of the acquirements and doings of the family; and indeed their acquirements had been few and their doings little. At

VIP TIMES

9 point, 1½ point leaded

FORMAT	PICAS	LINES	WPL	CPL	WPP	CPP
Royal 8vo	26×43	49	14.6	78	715	3822
Demy 8vo	24×40	46	13.5	72	621	3312
Large Crown 8vo	23×36	41	12.9	69	529	2829
Crown 8vo	21×34	39	11.8	63	460	2457

father to son, and from uncle to nephew, and, in one instance, from second cousin to second cousin, the sceptre had descended in the family of the Dales; and the acres had remained intact, growing in value and not decreasing in number, though guarded by no entail and protected by no wonderful amount of prudence or wisdom. The estate of Dale of Allington had been coterminous with the parish of Allington for some hundreds of years; and though, as I have said, the race of squires had possessed nothing of superhuman discretion and had perhaps been guided in their walks through life by no very distinct principles, still there had been with them so much of adherence to a sacred law, that no acre of the property had ever been parted from the hands of the existing squire. Some futile attempts had been made to increase the territory, as indeed had been done by Kit Dale, the father of Christopher Dale, who will appear as our squire of Allington when the persons of our drama are introduced. Old Kit Dale, who had married money, had bought outlying farms—a bit of ground here and a bit there—talking, as he did so, much of political influence and of the good old Tory cause. But these farms and bits of ground had gone again before our time. To them had been attached no religion. When old Kit had found himself pressed in that matter of the majority of the Nineteenth Dragoons, in which crack regiment his second son made for himself quite a career, he found it easier to sell than to save—seeing that that which he sold was his own and not the patrimony of the Dales. At his death the remainder of these purchases had gone. Family arrangements required completion, and Christopher Dale required ready money. The outlying farms flew away, as such new purchases had flown before; but the old patrimony of the Dales remained untouched, as it had ever remained.

It had been a religion among them; and seeing that the worship had been carried on without fail, that the vestal fire had never gone down upon the hearth, I should not have said that the Dales had walked their ways without high principle. To this religion they had all adhered, and the new heir had ever entered in upon his domain without other encumbrances than those with which he himself was then already burdened. And yet there had been no entail. The idea of an entail was not in accordance with the peculiarities of the Dale mind. It was necessary to the Dale religion that each squire should have the power of wasting them. I remember to have dined at a house, the whole glory and fortune of which depended on the safety of a glass goblet. We all know the story. If the luck of Edenhall should be shattered, the doom of the family would be sealed. Nevertheless I was bidden to drink out of the fatal glass, as were all guests in that house. It would not have contented the chivalrous mind of the master to protect his doom by lock and key and padded chest. And so it was with the Dales of *Allington. To them an entail would have been a lock and key and a padded chest; but the old chivalry of their house denied to them the use of such protection.*

VIP TIMES

9 point, 2 point leaded

FORMAT	PICAS	LINES	WPL	CPL	WPP	CPP
Royal 8vo	26×43	47	14.6	78	686	3666
Demy 8vo	24×40	44	13.5	72	594	3168
Large Crown 8vo	23×36	39	12.9	69	503	2691
Crown 8vo	21×34	37	11.8	63	437	2331

father to son, and from uncle to nephew, and, in one instance, from second cousin to second cousin, the sceptre had descended in the family of the Dales; and the acres had remained intact, growing in value and not decreasing in number, though guarded by no entail and protected by no wonderful amount of prudence or wisdom. The estate of Dale of Allington had been coterminous with the parish of Allington for some hundreds of years; and though, as I have said, the race of squires had possessed nothing of superhuman discretion and had perhaps been guided in their walks through life by no very distinct principles, still there had been with them so much of adherence to a sacred law, that no acre of the property had ever been parted from the hands of the existing squire. Some futile attempts had been made to increase the territory, as indeed had been done by Kit Dale, the father of Christopher Dale, who will appear as our squire of Allington when the persons of our drama are introduced. Old Kit Dale, who had married money, had bought outlying farms—a bit of ground here and a bit there—talking, as he did so, much of political influence and of the good old Tory cause. But these farms and bits of ground had gone again before our time. To them had been attached no religion. When old Kit had found himself pressed in that matter of the majority of the Nineteenth Dragoons, in which crack regiment his second son made for himself quite a career, he found it easier to sell than to save—seeing that that which he sold was his own and not the patrimony of the Dales. At his death the remainder of these purchases had gone. Family arrangements required completion, and Christopher Dale required ready money. The outlying farms flew away, as such new purchases had flown before; but the old patrimony of the Dales remained untouched, as it had ever remained.

It had been a religion among them; and seeing that the worship had been carried on without fail, that the vestal fire had never gone down upon the hearth, I should not have said that the Dales had walked their ways without high principle. To this religion they had all adhered, and the new heir had ever entered in upon his domain without other encumbrances than those with which he himself was then already burdened. And yet there had been no entail. The idea of an entail was not in accordance with the peculiarities of the Dale mind. It was necessary to the Dale religion that each squire should have the power of wasting them. I remember to have dined at a house, the whole glory and fortune of which depended on the safety of a glass goblet. We all know the story. If the luck of Edenhall *should be shattered, the doom of the family would be sealed. Nevertheless I was bidden to drink out of the fatal glass, as were all guests in that house. It would not have contented the chivalrous mind*

VIP TIMES

10 point, 1 point leaded

FORMAT	PICAS	LINES	WPL	CPL	WPP	CPP
Royal 8vo	26×43	47	12.8	70	602	3290
Demy 8vo	24×40	44	11.9	65	524	2860
Large Crown 8vo	23×36	39	11.4	62	445	2418
Crown 8vo	21×34	37	10.4	57	385	2109

father to son, and from uncle to nephew, and, in one instance, from second cousin to second cousin, the sceptre had descended in the family of the Dales; and the acres had remained intact, growing in value and not decreasing in number, though guarded by no entail and protected by no wonderful amount of prudence or wisdom. The estate of Dale of Allington had been coterminous with the parish of Allington for some hundreds of years; and though, as I have said, the race of squires had possessed nothing of superhuman discretion and had perhaps been guided in their walks through life by no very distinct principles, still there had been with them so much of adherence to a sacred law, that no acre of the property had ever been parted from the hands of the existing squire. Some futile attempts had been made to increase the territory, as indeed had been done by Kit Dale, the father of Christopher Dale, who will appear as our squire of Allington when the persons of our drama are introduced. Old Kit Dale, who had married money, had bought outlying farms—a bit of ground here and a bit there—talking, as he did so, much of political influence and of the good old Tory cause. But these farms and bits of ground had gone again before our time. To them had been attached no religion. When old Kit had found himself pressed in that matter of the majority of the Nineteenth Dragoons, in which crack regiment his second son made for himself quite a career, he found it easier to sell than to save—seeing that that which he sold was his own and not the patrimony of the Dales. At his death the remainder of these purchases had gone. Family arrangements required completion, and Christopher Dale required ready money. The outlying farms flew away, as such new purchases had flown before; but the old patrimony of the Dales remained untouched, as it had ever remained.

It had been a religion among them; and seeing that the worship had been carried on without fail, that the vestal fire had never gone down upon the hearth, I should not have said that the Dales had walked their ways without high principle. To this religion they had all adhered, and the new heir had ever entered in upon his domain without other encumbrances than those with which he himself was then already burdened. And yet there had been no entail. The idea of an entail was not in accordance with the peculiarities of the Dale mind. It was necessary to the Dale religion that each squire should have the power of wasting them. I remember to have dined at a *house, the whole glory and fortune of which depended on the safety of a glass goblet. We all know the story. If the luck of Edenhall should be shattered, the doom of the family would be sealed. Nevertheless I was*

VIP TIMES

10 point, 1½ point leaded

FORMAT	PICAS	LINES	WPL	CPL	WPP	CPP
Royal 8vo	26×43	45	12.8	70	576	3150
Demy 8vo	24×40	42	11.9	65	500	2730
Large Crown 8vo	23×36	38	11.4	62	433	2356
Crown 8vo	21×33	35	10.4	57	364	1995

father to son, and from uncle to nephew, and, in one instance, from second cousin to second cousin, the sceptre had descended in the family of the Dales; and the acres had remained intact, growing in value and not decreasing in number, though guarded by no entail and protected by no wonderful amount of prudence or wisdom. The estate of Dale of Allington had been coterminous with the parish of Allington for some hundreds of years; and though, as I have said, the race of squires had possessed nothing of superhuman discretion and had perhaps been guided in their walks through life by no very distinct principles, still there had been with them so much of adherence to a sacred law, that no acre of the property had ever been parted from the hands of the existing squire. Some futile attempts had been made to increase the territory, as indeed had been done by Kit Dale, the father of Christopher Dale, who will appear as our squire of Allington when the persons of our drama are introduced. Old Kit Dale, who had married money, had bought outlying farms—a bit of ground here and a bit there—talking, as he did so, much of political influence and of the good old Tory cause. But these farms and bits of ground had gone again before our time. To them had been attached no religion. When old Kit had found himself pressed in that matter of the majority of the Nineteenth Dragoons, in which crack regiment his second son made for himself quite a career, he found it easier to sell than to save—seeing that that which he sold was his own and not the patrimony of the Dales. At his death the remainder of these purchases had gone. Family arrangements required completion, and Christopher Dale required ready money. The outlying farms flew away, as such new purchases had flown before; but the old patrimony of the Dales remained untouched, as it had ever remained.

It had been a religion among them; and seeing that the worship had been carried on without fail, that the vestal fire had never gone down upon the hearth, I should not have said that the Dales had walked their ways without high principle. To this religion they had all adhered, and the new heir had ever entered in upon his domain without other encumbrances than those with which he himself was then already burdened. And yet there had been no entail. The idea of an entail was not in accordance with the peculiarities of the Dale *mind. It was necessary to the Dale religion that each squire should have the power of wasting them. I remember to have dined at a house, the whole glory and fortune of which depended on the safety of a glass*

VIP TIMES

10 point, 2 point leaded

FORMAT	PICAS	LINES	WPL	CPL	WPP	CPP
Royal 8vo	26×43	43	12.8	70	550	3010
Demy 8vo	24×40	40	11.9	65	476	2600
Large Crown 8vo	23×36	36	11.4	62	410	2232
Crown 8vo	21×34	34	10.4	57	354	1938

father to son, and from uncle to nephew, and, in one instance, from second cousin to second cousin, the sceptre had descended in the family of the Dales; and the acres had remained intact, growing in value and not decreasing in number, though guarded by no entail and protected by no wonderful amount of prudence or wisdom. The estate of Dale of Allington had been coterminous with the parish of Allington for some hundreds of years; and though, as I have said, the race of squires had possessed nothing of superhuman discretion and had perhaps been guided in their walks through life by no very distinct principles, still there had been with them so much of adherence to a sacred law, that no acre of the property had ever been parted from the hands of the existing squire. Some futile attempts had been made to increase the territory, as indeed had been done by Kit Dale, the father of Christopher Dale, who will appear as our squire of Allington when the persons of our drama are introduced. Old Kit Dale, who had married money, had bought outlying farms—a bit of ground here and a bit there—talking, as he did so, much of political influence and of the good old Tory cause. But these farms and bits of ground had gone again before our time. To them had been attached no religion. When old Kit had found himself pressed in that matter of the majority of the Nineteenth Dragoons, in which crack regiment his second son made for himself quite a career, he found it easier to sell than to save—seeing that that which he sold was his own and not the patrimony of the Dales. At his death the remainder of these purchases had gone. Family arrangements required completion, and Christopher Dale required ready money. The outlying farms flew away, as such new purchases had flown before; but the old patrimony of the Dales remained untouched, as it had ever remained.

It had been a religion among them; and seeing that the worship had been carried on without fail, that the vestal fire had never gone down upon the hearth, I should not have said that the Dales had walked their ways without high principle. To this religion they had all adhered, and the new heir had *ever entered in upon his domain without other encumbrances than those with which he himself was then already burdened. And yet there had been no entail. The idea of an entail was not*

VIP TIMES

11 point, 1 point leaded

FORMAT	PICAS	LINES	WPL	CPL	WPP	CPP
Royal 8vo	26×43	43	11.4	64	490	2752
Demy 8vo	24×40	40	10.6	59	424	2360
Large Crown 8vo	23×36	36	10.1	57	364	2052
Crown 8vo	21×34	34	9.2	52	313	1768

father to son, and from uncle to nephew, and, in one instance, from second cousin to second cousin, the sceptre had descended in the family of the Dales; and the acres had remained intact, growing in value and not decreasing in number, though guarded by no entail and protected by no wonderful amount of prudence or wisdom. The estate of Dale of Allington had been coterminous with the parish of Allington for some hundreds of years; and though, as I have said, the race of squires had possessed nothing of superhuman discretion and had perhaps been guided in their walks through life by no very distinct principles, still there had been with them so much of adherence to a sacred law, that no acre of the property had ever been parted from the hands of the existing squire. Some futile attempts had been made to increase the territory, as indeed had been done by Kit Dale, the father of Christopher Dale, who will appear as our squire of Allington when the persons of our drama are introduced. Old Kit Dale, who had married money, had bought outlying farms—a bit of ground here and a bit there—talking, as he did so, much of political influence and of the good old Tory cause. But these farms and bits of ground had gone again before our time. To them had been attached no religion. When old Kit had found himself pressed in that matter of the majority of the Nineteenth Dragoons, in which crack regiment his second son made for himself quite a career, he found it easier to sell than to save—seeing that that which he sold was his own and not the patrimony of the Dales. At his death the remainder of these purchases had gone. Family arrangements required completion, and Christopher Dale required ready money. The outlying farms flew away, as such new purchases had flown before; but the old patrimony of the Dales remained untouched, as it had ever remained.

It had been a religion among them; and seeing that the worship had been carried on without fail, that the vestal fire had never gone down upon the hearth, I should not have said *that the Dales had walked their ways without high principle. To this religion they had all adhered, and the new heir had ever entered in upon his domain without other encumbrances than*

FORMAT	PICAS	LINES	WPL	CPL	WPP	CPP
Royal 8vo	26×43	41	11.4	64	467	2624
Demy 8vo	24×40	38	10.6	59	403	2242
Large Crown 8vo	23×36	35	10.1	57	354	1995
Crown 8vo	21×34	33	9.2	52	304	1716

father to son, and from uncle to nephew, and, in one instance, from second cousin to second cousin, the sceptre had descended in the family of the Dales; and the acres had remained intact, growing in value and not decreasing in number, though guarded by no entail and protected by no wonderful amount of prudence or wisdom. The estate of Dale of Allington had been coterminous with the parish of Allington for some hundreds of years; and though, as I have said, the race of squires had possessed nothing of superhuman discretion and had perhaps been guided in their walks through life by no very distinct principles, still there had been with them so much of adherence to a sacred law, that no acre of the property had ever been parted from the hands of the existing squire. Some futile attempts had been made to increase the territory, as indeed had been done by Kit Dale, the father of Christopher Dale, who will appear as our squire of Allington when the persons of our drama are introduced. Old Kit Dale, who had married money, had bought outlying farms—a bit of ground here and a bit there—talking, as he did so, much of political influence and of the good old Tory cause. But these farms and bits of ground had gone again before our time. To them had been attached no religion. When old Kit had found himself pressed in that matter of the majority of the Nineteenth Dragoons, in which crack regiment his second son made for himself quite a career, he found it easier to sell than to save—seeing that that which he sold was his own and not the patrimony of the Dales. At his death the remainder of these purchases had gone. Family arrangements required completion, and Christopher Dale required ready money. The outlying farms flew away, as such new purchases had flown before; but the old patrimony of the Dales remained untouched, as it had ever remained.

It had been a religion among them; and seeing that the worship had been carried on without fail, that the vestal fire *had never gone down upon the hearth, I should not have said that the Dales had walked their ways without high principle. To this religion they had all adhered, and the new heir had ever*

VIP TIMES

11 point, 2 point leaded

FORMAT	PICAS	LINES	WPL	CPL	WPP	CPP
Royal 8vo	26×43	40	11.4	64	456	2560
Demy 8vo	24×40	37	10.6	59	392	2183
Large Crown 8vo	23×36	33	10.1	57	333	1881
Crown 8vo	21×34	31	9.2	52	285	1612

father to son, and from uncle to nephew, and, in one instance, from second cousin to second cousin, the sceptre had descended in the family of the Dales; and the acres had remained intact, growing in value and not decreasing in number, though guarded by no entail and protected by no wonderful amount of prudence or wisdom. The estate of Dale of Allington had been coterminous with the parish of Allington for some hundreds of years; and though, as I have said, the race of squires had possessed nothing of superhuman discretion and had perhaps been guided in their walks through life by no very distinct principles, still there had been with them so much of adherence to a sacred law, that no acre of the property had ever been parted from the hands of the existing squire. Some futile attempts had been made to increase the territory, as indeed had been done by Kit Dale, the father of Christopher Dale, who will appear as our squire of Allington when the persons of our drama are introduced. Old Kit Dale, who had married money, had bought outlying farms—a bit of ground here and a bit there—talking, as he did so, much of political influence and of the good old Tory cause. But these farms and bits of ground had gone again before our time. To them had been attached no religion. When old Kit had found himself pressed in that matter of the majority of the Nineteenth Dragoons, in which crack regiment his second son made for himself quite a career, he found it easier to sell than to save—seeing that that which he sold was his own and not the patrimony of the Dales. At his death the remainder of these purchases had gone. Family arrangements required completion, and Christopher Dale required ready money. The outlying farms flew away, as such new purchases had flown before; but the old patrimony of the Dales remained untouched, as it *had ever remained.*

It had been a religion among them; and seeing that the worship had been carried on without fail, that the vestal

VIP TIMES

12 point, 1 point leaded

FORMAT	PICAS	LINES	WPL	CPL	WPP	CPP
Royal 8vo	26×43	40	10.1	59	404	2360
Demy 8vo	24×40	37	9.4	54	348	1998
Large Crown 8vo	23×36	33	9.0	52	297	1716
Crown 8vo	21×34	31	8.2	47	254	1457

father to son, and from uncle to nephew, and, in one instance, from second cousin to second cousin, the sceptre had descended in the family of the Dales; and the acres had remained intact, growing in value and not decreasing in number, though guarded by no entail and protected by no wonderful amount of prudence or wisdom. The estate of Dale of Allington had been coterminous with the parish of Allington for some hundreds of years; and though, as I have said, the race of squires had possessed nothing of superhuman discretion and had perhaps been guided in their walks through life by no very distinct principles, still there had been with them so much of adherence to a sacred law, that no acre of the property had ever been parted from the hands of the existing squire. Some futile attempts had been made to increase the territory, as indeed had been done by Kit Dale, the father of Christopher Dale, who will appear as our squire of Allington when the persons of our drama are introduced. Old Kit Dale, who had married money, had bought outlying farms—a bit of ground here and a bit there—talking, as he did so, much of political influence and of the good old Tory cause. But these farms and bits of ground had gone again before our time. To them had been attached no religion. When old Kit had found himself pressed in that matter of the majority of the Nineteenth Dragoons, in which crack regiment his second son made for himself quite a career, he found it easier to sell than to save—seeing that that which he sold was his own and not the patrimony of the Dales. At his death the remainder of these purchases had gone. Family arrangements required completion, and Christopher *Dale required ready money. The outlying farms flew away, as such new purchases had flown before; but the old patrimony of the Dales remained untouched, as it had*

VIP TIMES

12 point, 2 point leaded

FORMAT	PICAS	LINES	WPL	CPL	WPP	CPP
Royal 8vo	26×43	37	11.3	60	418	2220
Demy 8vo	24×40	34	10.5	55	357	1870
Large Crown 8vo	23×36	31	10.0	53	310	1643
Crown 8vo	21×34	29	9.1	48	264	1392

5

TWELVE POINT ALPHABETS OF VIP PHOTOSET FACES

Roman Capitals

VIP *Baskerville*	ABCDEFGHIJKLMNOPQRSTUVWXYZ
VIP *Bembo*	ABCDEFGHIJKLMNOPQRSTUVWXYZ
VIP *Century*	ABCDEFGHIJKLMNOPQRSTUVWXYZ
VIP *Garamond*	ABCDEFGHIJKLMNOPQRSTUVWXYZ
VIP *Helvetica*	ABCDEFGHIJKLMNOPQRSTUVWXYZ
VIP *Melior*	ABCDEFGHIJKLMNOPQRSTUVWXYZ
VIP *Optima*	ABCDEFGHIJKLMNOPQRSTUVWXYZ
VIP *Palatino*	ABCDEFGHIJKLMNOPQRSTUVWXYZ
VIP *Plantin*	ABCDEFGHIJKLMNOPQRSTUVWXYZ
VIP *Sabon*	ABCDEFGHIJKLMNOPQRSTUVWXYZ
VIP *Times*	ABCDEFGHIJKLMNOPQRSTUVWXYZ

Italic Capitals

VIP *Baskerville*	*ABCDEFGHIJKLMNOPQRSTUVWXYZ*
VIP *Bembo*	*ABCDEFGHIJKLMNOPQRSTUVWXYZ*
VIP *Century*	*ABCDEFGHIJKLMNOPQRSTUVWXYZ*
VIP *Garamond*	*ABCDEFGHIJKLMNOPQRSTUVWXYZ*
VIP *Helvetica*	*ABCDEFGHIJKLMNOPQRSTUVWXYZ*
VIP *Melior*	*ABCDEFGHIJKLMNOPQRSTUVWXYZ*
VIP *Optima*	*ABCDEFGHIJKLMNOPQRSTUVWXYZ*
VIP *Palatino*	*ABCDEFGHIJKLMNOPQRSTUVWXYZ*
VIP *Plantin*	*ABCDEFGHIJKLMNOPQRSTUVWXYZ*
VIP *Sabon*	*ABCDEFGHIJKLMNOPQRSTUVWXYZ*
VIP *Times*	*ABCDEFGHIJKLMNOPQRSTUVWXYZ*

ROMAN LOWER CASE & FIGURES

VIP *Baskerville*	abcdefghijklmnopqrstuvwxyz	1234567890
VIP *Bembo*	abcdefghijklmnopqrstuvwxyz	1234567890
VIP *Century*	abcdefghijklmnopqrstuvwxyz	1234567890
VIP *Garamond*	abcdefghijklmnopqrstuvwxyz	1234567890
VIP *Helvetica*	abcdefghijklmnopqrstuvwxyz	1234567890
VIP *Melior*	abcdefghijklmnopqrstuvwxyz	1234567890
VIP *Optima*	abcdefghijklmnopqrstuvwxyz	1234567890
VIP *Palatino*	abcdefghijklmnopqrstuvwxyz	1234567890
VIP *Plantin*	abcdefghijklmnopqrstuvwxyz	1234567890
VIP *Sabon*	abcdefghijklmnopqrstuvwxyz	1234567890
VIP *Times*	abcdefghijklmnopqrstuvwxyz	1234567890

ITALIC LOWER CASE & FIGURES

VIP *Baskerville*	*abcdefghijklmnopqrstuvwxyz*	*1234567890*
VIP *Bembo*	*abcdefghijklmnopqrstuvwxyz*	*1234567890*
VIP *Century*	*abcdefghijklmnopqrstuvwxyz*	*1234567890*
VIP *Garamond*	*abcdefghijklmnopqrstuvwxyz*	*1234567890*
VIP *Helvetica*	*abcdefghijklmnopqrstuvwxyz*	*1234567890*
VIP *Melior*	*abcdefghijklmnopqrstuvwxyz*	*1234567890*
VIP *Optima*	*abcdefghijklmnopqrstuvwxyz*	*1234567890*
VIP *Palatino*	*abcdefghijklmnopqrstuvwxyz*	*1234567890*
VIP *Plantin*	*abcdefghijklmnopqrstuvwxyz*	*1234567890*
VIP *Sabon*	*abcdefghijklmnopqrstuvwxyz*	*1234567890*
VIP *Times*	*abcdefghijklmnopqrstuvwxyz*	*1234567890*

12 Point VIP Alphabets

Small Capitals

VIP *Baskerville*	ABCDEKGHIJKLMNOPQRSTUVWXYZ
VIP *Bembo*	ABCDEFGHIJKLMNOPQRSTUVWXYZ
VIP *Garamond*	ABCDEFGHIJKLMNOPQRSTUVWXYZ
VIP *Palatino*	**ABCDEFGHIJKLMNOPQRSTUVWXYZ**
VIP *Plantin*	**ABCDEFGHIJKLMNOPQRSTUVWXYZ**
VIP *Sabon*	ABCDEFGHIJKLMNOPQRSTUVWXYZ
VIP *Times*	ABCDEFGHIJKLMNOPQRSTUVWXYZ

Bold Roman Capitals

VIP *Baskerville*	**ABCDEFGHIJKLMNOPQRSTUVWXYZ**
VIP *Bembo*	**ABCDEFGHIJKLMNOPQRSTUVWXYZ**
VIP *Century*	**ABCDEFGHIJKLMNOPQRSTUVWXYZ**
VIP *Garamond*	**ABCDEFGHIJKLMNOPQRSTUVWXYZ**
VIP *Helvetica*	**ABCDEFGHIJKLMNOPQRSTUVWXYZ**
VIP *Melior*	**ABCDEFGHIJKLMNOPQRSTUVWXYZ**
VIP *Optima*	**ABCDEFGHIJKLMNOPQRSTUVWXYZ**
VIP *Palatino*	**ABCDEFGHIJKLMNOPQRSTUVWXYZ**
VIP *Plantin*	**ABCDEFGHIJKLMNOPQRSTUVWXYZ**
VIP *Sabon*	**ABCDEFGHIJKLMNOPQRSTUVWXYZ**
VIP *Times*	**ABCDEFGHIJKLMNOPQRSTUVWXYZ**

Bold Italic Capitals

VIP *Baskerville*	***ABCDEFGHIJKLMNOPQRSTUVWXYZ***
VIP *Bembo*	***ABCDEFGHIJKLMNOPQRSTUVWXYZ***
VIP *Garamond*	***ABCDEFGHIJKLMNOPQRSTUVWXYZ***
VIP *Helvetica*	***ABCDEFGHIJKLMNOPQRSTUVWXYZ***
VIP *Palatino*	***ABCDEFGHIJKLMNOPQRSTUVWXYZ***
VIP *Plantin*	***ABCDEFGHIJKLMNOPQRSTUVWXYZ***
VIP *Times*	***ABCDEFGHIJKLMNOPQRSTUVWXYZ***

Bold Roman Lower Case & Figures

VIP *Baskerville*	**abcdefghijklmnopqrstuvwxyz**	**1234567890**
VIP *Bembo*	**abcdefghijklmnopqrstuvwxyz**	**1234567890**
VIP *Century*	**abcdefghijklmnopqrstuvwxyz**	**1234567890**
VIP *Garamond*	abcdefghijklmnopqrstuvwxyz	1234567890
VIP *Helvetica*	**abcdefghijklmnopqrstuvwxyz**	**1234567890**
VIP *Melior*	**abcdefghijklmnopqrstuvwxyz**	**1234567890**
VIP *Optima*	**abcdefghijklmnopqrstuvwxyz**	**1234567890**
VIP *Palatino*	**abcdefghijklmnopqrstuvwxyz**	**1234567890**
VIP *Plantin*	**abcdefghijklmnopqrstuvwxyz**	**1234567890**
VIP *Sabon*	abcdefghijklmnopqrstuvwxyz	1234567890
VIP *Times*	**abcdefghijklmnopqrstuvwxyz**	**1234567890**

Bold Italic Lower Case & Figures

VIP *Baskerville*	***abcdefghijklmnopqrstuvwxyz***	***1234567890***
VIP *Bembo*	***abcdefghijklmnopqrstuvwxyz***	***1234567890***
VIP *Garamond*	*abcdefghijklmnopqrstuvwxyz*	*1234567890*
VIP *Helvetica*	***abcdefghijklmnopqrstuvwxyz***	***1234567890***
VIP *Palatino*	***abcdefghijklmnopqrstuvwxyz***	***1234567890***
VIP *Plantin*	***abcdefghijklmnopqrstuvwxyz***	***1234567890***
VIP *Times*	***abcdefghijklmnopqrstuvwxyz***	***1234567890***

6

COMPLETE LIST OF TYPE FACES AVAILABLE AT WESTERN PRINTING SERVICES

Series numbers shown in bold figures · Composition sizes in italic figures
★ Indicates large & small face

Albertus Titling **324**	18 24
Albertus **481**	18
Arrighi (Centaur) Italic **252**	14 16 18 24 30 36
Baskerville **169**	*6 8 9 10 11 12* 14 18 24 30 36
Baskerville Italic **169**	*6 8 9 10 11 12* 14 18 24 30 36
Baskerville Bold **312**	*6 8 9 10 11 12*
Baskerville Semi-Bold **313**	*8 9 10 11 12*
Bell **341**	*8 10 11 12 14* 18 24 30 36
Bell Italic **341**	*8 10 11 12 14* 18 24
Bembo **270**	*6 8 9 10 11 12 13* 14 *16* 18 24 30 36
Bembo Italic **270**	*6 8 9 10 11 12 13* 14 *16* 18 24 30 36
Bembo Bold **428**	*6 8 9 10 11 12*
Bembo Titling **370**	24 30 36 42
Blado Italic **119**	*10 11 12 13 16* 24
Bodoni No. 3 **135**	*8 10 11★ 12* 14 18 24
Bodoni Italic No. 3 **135**	*8 10 11★ 12* 14 18 24
Bodoni Bold **195**	*12*
Bodoni Bold No. 2 **260**	*8 10 12* 14 18 24
Bodoni Bold No. 2 Italic **260**	*8 10 12* 14 18 24
Bodoni Bold Condensed **529**	14 18 24
Caslon Old Face **128**	*9 10 11 12 14* 18 24 30 36 48
Caslon Old Face Italic **128**	*9 10 11 12 14* 18 24 30 36
Centaur **252**	14 *16* 18 24 30 36 42 48
Clarendon **12**	*5 6 8 10 11*
Clear Face Bold **157**	*8 10 12*
Cochin Italic **165**	18
Colonna **225**	18 24
Cushing **17**	*8 10*
Cushing Italic **17**	*8 10*
Ehrhardt **453**	*8 9 10 11 12* 18 24
Ehrhardt Italic **453**	*8 9 10 11 12*
Ehrhardt Initial Teaching Alphabet **453**	*12* 18
Ehrhardt Semi-Bold **573**	*8 9 10 11 12*
Ehrhardt Semi-Bold Italic **573**	*11*
Falstaff **323**	8D 10D
Fournier **185**	*8 9 10 11 12* 14 18 24 30 36
Fournier Italic **185**	*8 9 10 11 12* 14 18
Garamond **156**	*8 9 10 11 12 14 18* 24 30 36 42 48 60 72
Garamond Italic **156**	*8 9 10 11 12* 14 18 24 30 36 48
Garamond Bold **201**	*8 9 10 11 12* 14 18 24
Garamond Bold Italic **201**	14 18 24
Gill Sans Light **362**	*6 8 10 12* 14 18 24

Gill Sans Light Italic **362**	*6 8 10 12* 14 18 24
Gill Sans **262**	*6 8 10 12 14* 18 24 30 36 42 48
Gill Sans Italic **262**	*6 8 10 12* 14 18 24 30 36
Gill Sans Bold **275**	*6 8 10 12 14* 18 24 30 36 42 48
Gill Sans Bold Italic **275**	*6 8 12* 14 18 24
Gill Sans Bold Condensed **343**	*8 10 12* 14 18 24 30 36 48
Gill Sans Extra Bold **321**	*8 12* 14 18 24
Gill Sans Condensed **485**	14 18 24
Gloucester Bold Italic **160**	*6 8 12*
Gloucester Bold Condensed **198**	*6 8 10 12*
Gloucester Bold Extended **243**	8 10 12
Goudy Old Style **291**	*8 10 12*
Goudy Old Style Italic **291**	*8 10 12*
Goudy Bold **269**	*8 10 12*
Goudy Bold Italic **269**	6 8 10 12
Goudy Extra Bold **214**	10 12
Goudy Modern **249**	10 12
Goudy Modern Italic **249**	10 12
Grotesque Bold Extended **150**	8 10 12 14 18 24
Grotesque Condensed **33**	14 18 24 30 36 42 48
Grotesque No. 2 **51**	*6 8 10*
Grotesque Bold Condensed No. 2 **15**	*6 8 10 12*
Grotesque Condensed **318**	10 12 14 18 24 30 36 48
Headline Bold **595**	18 24
Horley Old Style **199**	*8 10 12*
Horley Old Style Italic **199**	*8 10 12*
Imprint **101**	*7 8 9 10 11 12 14 18* 24 30 36
Imprint Italic **101**	*7 8 9 10 11 12 14* 18 24 30 36
Imprint Bold **310**	*8 9 10 11 12*
Imprint Shadow **190**	14 18 24
Imprint Shadow Italic **190**	14 18 24
Klang **593**	14 18 24
Latin Antique **9**	*8 10 11 12*
Modern Extended No. 1 **7**	*5 6 7 8 9 10 11 12* 14
Modern Italic **7**	*6 7 8 9 10 11 12* 14
Modern Bold **570**	7
Old English Text **456, 356**	8 10 12
Old Style No. 2 **2**	*6 8 9 10 11 12*
Old Style No. 2 Italic **2**	*6 8 9 10 11 12*
Old Style Bold No. 1 **53**	*6 8 9 10 11 12* 14 18 24
Old Style Bold Italic No. 1 **53**	*8 10 12*
Old Style Bold No. 5 **544**	*6 8 9 10 11 12*
Othello **246**	10 12
Perpetua **239**	*8 10 11 12 13 14* 18 24 30 36 42 48
Perpetua Italic **239**	*8 10 11 12 13 14* 18 24 30 36 42 48
Perpetua Bold **461**	*8 10 11 12* 14 18 24
Perpetua Titling **258**	10 12 14 18 24 30 36 42 48
Perpetua Light Titling **480**	18 24 36

Plantin **110**	*6 8 9 10 11 12* 14 18 24
Plantin Italic **110**	*6 8 9 10 11 12* 14 18 24
Plantin Bold **194**	*6 8 9 10 11 12* 14 18 24
Plantin Bold Italic **194**	*8 10 12*
Plantin Bold Condensed **236**	6 8 10 12
Poliphilus **170**	*10 11 12 13 16*
Poliphilus Titling **230**	18 24
Rockwell Light **390**	*8 10 12*
Rockwell **371**	*8 10 12* 14 18 24 36
Rockwell Italic **371**	*6 8 10 12*
Rockwell Bold **391**	*8 10 12* 14 18 24 36
Scotch Roman No. 1 **46**	*9 10 11 12*
Scotch Roman No. 1 Italic **46**	*9 10 11 12*
Spartan Condensed **143**	*6*(1 2 3 4) *12*(1 2 3 4)
Spartan Light **139**	*6*(1 2 3 4) *12*(1 2 3 4) 18(3 4 5) 24(1 2 3 4 5)
Spartan **140E**	*6*(1 2 3 4) *12*(1 2 3 4) 18(3 4 5) 24(1 2 3 4 5)
Spartan Bold **141**	*6*(1 2 3 4) *12*(1 2 3 4) 18(3 4 5) 24(1 2 3 4 5)
Spectrum **556**	*8/9 10/11 12/13*
Spectrum Italic **556**	*8/9 10/11 12/13*
Times **327**	*6 7 8 9 10 11 12* 14 18 24 30 36 48
Times Italic **327**	*6 7 8 9 10 11 12* 14 18 24
Times Bold **334**	*6 7 8 9 10 11 12* 14 18 30 36 42 48
Times Bold Italic **334**	*8 9 10 11*
Times Titling **339**	8 10 12
Typewriter No. 2 **100**	*12*
Typewriter No. 4 **127**	*10*
Typewriter No. 5 **235**	*12*
Walbaum **374**	*8/9 9/10 10/11 11/12 12/13* 14–16/18 20/24
Walbaum Italic **374**	*8/9 9/10 10/11 11/12 12/13* 14–16/18 20/24
Walbaum Medium **375**	18 24

Linotype & Intertype

Intertype Baskerville	*8 9 10 11 12*
Intertype Baskerville Italic	*8 9 10 11 12*
Linotype Caledonia	*8 10 11 12*
Linotype Caledonia Italic	*8 10 11 12*
Linotype Granjon	*9 10 11 12*
Linotype Granjon Italic	*9 10 11 12*
Linotype Juliana	*8 10 11*
Linotype Juliana Italic	*8 10 11*
Linotype Times	*8 10 11*
Linotype Times Italic	*8 10 11*

VIP Faces for Photosetting

All faces are available in the following point sizes
6 7 8 9 10 11 12 14 16 18 20 24 30 36 42 48 54 60 72

Baskerville
Baskerville Italic
Baskerville Bold
Baskerville Bold Italic

Bembo
Bembo Italic
Bembo Bold
Bembo Bold Italic

Century Schoolbook
Century Schoolbook Italic
Century Schoolbook Bold

Garamond
Garamond Italic
Garamond Bold
Garamond Bold Italic

Helvetica
Helvetica Italic
Helvetica Bold
Helvetica Bold Italic

Melior
Melior Italic
Melior Bold

Optima
Optima Italic
Optima Bold

Palatino
Palatino Italic
Palatino Bold
Palatino Bold Italic

Plantin
Plantin Italic
Plantin Bold
Plantin Bold Italic

Sabon
Sabon Italic
Sabon Bold

Times
Times Italic
Times Bold
Times Bold Italic